The Information Seekers

An International Study
of Consumer Information
and Advertising Image

Hans B. Thorelli
Helmut Becker
Jack Engledow

Published in cooperation with
Consumer Research Institute, Inc.

D1745333

Ballinger Publishing Co. ● Cambridge, Mass.
A Subsidiary of J.B. Lippincott Company

International Standard Book Number: 0-88410-265-3

Library of Congress Catalog Card Number: 74-9635

Printed in the United States of America

Library of Congress Cataloging in Publication Data

Thorelli, Hans Birger, 1921–
    The information seekers.

    "Published in cooperation with Consumer Research Institute."
    Bibliography: p.
    1. Consumers–United States. 2. Consumers–Germany (Federal Republic, 1949-   ) 3. Consumer education–United States. 4. Consumer education–Germany (Federal Republic, 1949-   ) 5. Advertising.
I. Becker, Helmut, 1937-   joint author. II. Engledow, Jack, joint author. III. Title.
HC110.C6T47   658.8'34   74-9635
ISBN 0-88410-265-3

Contents

v

Chapter Nine
Consumer Information and Advertising Image

List of Figures

List of Tables

Preface

The Information Seekers is a study of German and American consumers in action, focused on the impact of independent consumer information on different categories of consumers and on their reactions to advertising. The prime exponents of independent consumer information (CI) programs are the German journals *test* and *DM* (*Deutsche Mark*) and the American magazine *Consumer Reports*.

In the book we present the results of the first comparative study to deal with consumer awareness, perceived usage and opinion of such programs. Although we make no similar claim with regard to our examination of the image of advertising, that part of the research is equally germane; for better or worse, advertising is the most important source of product information available to consumers in industrial societies with open market economies. In addition, we are able to draw significant inferences about the interrelationships between consumer attitudes and their use of these two major categories of non-personal product information.

At an early stage of our research we first encountered the *Information Seeker*; we found some consumers who are much more concerned with information than others. We have been particularly interested in identifying the Information Seekers as a group and establishing the characteristics which distinguish them from other consumers. Finally, we wanted to find out whether the Information Seekers represent a fairly homogeneous cross-cultural segment of the population in industrially advanced countries. Both our research and ancillary findings in other studies affirmed that this is the case.

Students, makers, and administrators of consumer policy in government, consumer organizations, business and academia are the readers to whom this work is primarily directed. It will also be of interest to students of consumer behavior and of decision-making processes and information theory. Because we are making a bit of a thrust into the area of comparative study, we hope the book will attract the attention of cross-cultural researchers. Finally, we think it will be of interest to marketing and international business executives. To facilitate rapid assimilation by managers and other hurried people, the book begins with an Executive Summary.

This is the second of three volumes planned as the principal result of a five-year research project, the International Consumer Information Survey (ICIS). Both of the other volumes deal with CI programs themselves, rather than with consumer reactions to them. Although they are companions, each book is written to stand alone. The first, *Consumer Information Handbook: Europe and North America*, published in 1974, is a detailed survey of compara-tive testing, informative labeling and quality certifying organizations in the North Atlantic community of nations. It provides an indispensable background for a reader of the present volume interested in the *Stiftung Warentest, Deutsche Mark* and the Consumers Union, the three bodies publishing the comparative testing journals of key concern here. He will find that although these organiza-tions are dramatically different in sponsorship and outlook, their information-seeking clienteles—with few, though interesting exceptions—are amazingly alike.

The forthcoming companion volume, *Consumer Information Systems*, is an in-depth analysis of the experience, problems and prospects of independent CI programs, focusing on clusters of subject matter rather than on organizations and countries. Applying a systems approach, the book opens with a discussion of consumer sovereignty, consumer manipulation and consumer information gap in post-industrial societies, and proceeds to inventory the area of consumer policy from the viewpoint of consumer rights and responsibilities. It examines the philosophical and practical rationales of CI programs and views the problems and prospects of such programs from an environmental perspective, thus permitting a reasoned discussion of the international trans-ferability of local experience and of the inferences of relevance to less developed countries.

Although the authors have no urge to purvey their personal beliefs and have throughout this book attempted to quench the influence of bias, overtones of personal preference or disdain are difficult to avoid in the social sciences; and the authors provide a declaration of their personal viewpoint at the end of the introductory chapter.

The planning and direction of this project have been a joint effort in the best sense of the word, under the general guidance of Hans B. Thorelli, the Project Leader. The authors accept joint intellectual responsibility for the entire book, and every chapter has been both planned and reviewed at least twice by the team. There has, nevertheless, been a fairly clear-cut division of labor in drafting the chapters: Engledow wrote chapters 2, 4 and 6; Becker wrote chapters 5, 8 and 9; Thorelli assisted by Engledow wrote chapter 7; Engledow assisted by Thorelli wrote chapter 1; and Becker assisted by Thorelli wrote chapter 3. Thorelli wrote the Executive Summary, and thus has prime responsibility for any perversion attending that drastic condensation of our research results; he also wrote chapter 10. The execution of the American field survey was independently managed by Jack Engledow, and that of the German field survey by Helmut Becker, in both cases as doctoral thesis projects. Finally we wish to express our appreciation to Dr. Sarah V. Thorelli whose contribution at the critical planning and final editorial stages was invaluable.

A field survey involving major samples on both sides of the Atlantic is an expensive undertaking. The requisite economic resources were placed at the disposal of the ICIS by the International Business Research Institute at Indiana University. This indispensable support is hereby gratefully acknowledged. The Consumer Research Institute (CRI) has made a special grant towards the publication of this volume, as it did in the case of the companion volume, *Consumer Information Handbook*. We are gratified by the willingness of the CRI to promote the dissemination of basic social science research in the consumer policy area. This act exemplifies its stated aim of "providing the facts to help government, business and consumers develop policies which serve the best interests of all concerned."

In concluding this part of the project we wish to express our sincere gratitude to the three organizations which made these surveys possible: Consumers Union, *Stiftung Warentest* and *DM*. Organizations act through people, and there were many who helped. To some of them we owe a special allegiance: Dr. Colston E. Warne, President; Walker Sandbach, then Executive Director; and Laurence F. Downes, Subscription Director of CU; Dr. Roland Hüttenrauch, Director; and Diplom-Volkswirtin Christin Carsten, Information Officer of *Warentest*; and Erich Bärmeier, Co-Publisher and Editor-in-Chief and Horst Wolf, then Editor-in-Chief of *DM*. We are forever grateful to Walker Research of Indianapolis and *DIVO-Institut* of Frankfurt for oustanding cooperation in the field survey phase. The Project Leader expresses personal thanks to Mrs. Inger Louise Valle, the then Bureau Chief of the Norwegian Consumer Council, and Mr. Sverre Hove, Bureau Chief of the Central Bureau of Statistics of Norway, for agreeing to let ICIS co-sponsor a consumer information survey in part summarized in chapter 7. He is also grateful to Mr. Robert Bez, the then Associate Director of *Institut National de la Consommation* of France, for making available survey reports also in part summarized in that chapter. We appreciate the cooperation of W. Peter Michna and Gerald D. Sentell for participation in computer work.

Finally, our most heartfelt thanks are reserved for our wives, Sarah V. Thorelli, Nancy Engledow and Margit Becker. They have contributed ideas, participated in data preparation and provided the kind of spiritual renewal on which men are so dependent.

Hans B. Thorelli
Helmut Becker
Jack Engledow

May, 1974.

Executive Summary

INFORMATION SEEKERS AND AVERAGE CONSUMERS—GENERALIZATIONS

1. The Information Seekers—a Cosmopolitan Set.

On the basis of comparative field surveys in Germany and the United States, this study identifies the Information Seekers as a cosmopolitan set of consumer sophisticates which may be found in significant numbers in industrially advanced countries. Although constituting a relatively small group in most cultures, the Information Seekers apparently exercise a vital influence in the marketplace as opinion leaders, critics and proxy purchasing agents for other consumers. The significance of this audience to business in general and the multinational corporation in particular would seem obvious; naturally its importance extends to makers of public policy and administrators of consumer information, education and protection programs both private and public.

2. Sampling Information Seekers (IS) and Average Consumers (AC).

Subscribers to comparative testing magazines, while not comprising all of the Information Seeker species, constitute the most readily specifiable embodiment of this group. The study contrasted subscribers to *Consumer Reports* in the United States and to *DM* and *test* in Germany with average consumers. Generalizations about IS in items 1-19 of this summary are based on comparisons of nationwide samples of subscribers. Items contrasting IS and AC are based on comparisons of metropolitan samples taken separately on subscribers and average consumers in the two countries and in some related studies by us and others. Items 20-30 are based mainly on the metropolitan samples, these samples being combined by country in direct cross-cultural comparisons.

3. Information Seeker Demographics.

IS have significantly *much* higher income, education and occupational status than average consumers. A typical IS is a professional person at the upper middle income level with at least a four-year college degree. IS also possess a significantly larger assortment of consumer durables than AC.

4. Self-perception of IS.

He designates himself as an opinion leader, who tends to be more planful in his activities than the AC. While he is not generally an early adopter of new products, his advice is sought by others. IS much more often than AC think that they are better at getting value for money than average persons.

5. IS Views of Business, Government and Consumerism.

Generally liberal in outlook, the typical IS nonetheless will often take a conservative stand on individual issues. He is, however, strongly in favor of governmental action in the consumer policy area. In the United States he is more critical of advertising than the AC, while in Germany the reverse is true.

6. Media Usage.

To maintain that IS are readers, AC are listeners is a gross generalization of differences in media habits.

7. Buying Criteria.

By and large, there is a striking similarity in the rankings of stated buying criteria for autos and consumer durables between IS and AC, durability and performance generally being given top ranking among 13 alternative criteria. IS uniformly ranked the availability of information as a relatively more important criterion than did AC. Beyond these generalizations considerable inter-cultural and inter-product variation were found.

8. Information Sources in Buying.

There is much inter-cultural variation in the relative use of personal, commercial and independent information sources. As would be expected, independent information from testing journals ranks relatively higher (and in most cases absolutely higher) among IS than AC. However, independent information from other consumer magazines and from the German consumer advice centers (*Verbraucherzentrale*) enjoys no such distinction. Personal observation ranks as the single most important information source for both IS and AC across commodities. Interestingly, general testing journals are consistently ranked higher in significance in durable goods than in auto purchases.

INFORMATION SEEKERS—
INTER-CULTURAL DIFFERENCES

9. Government Control of Business.

German IS were more favorable toward increased government control of business than AC, but American IS were less favorable than their AC counterparts. If the four groups were arrayed, the German IS would be most favorable to increased government control, followed by the average German, then the average American, and finally the American IS. Possible explanation: American IS had a more favorable view of the honesty of businessmen than German.

10. Welfare State Effects.

German IS had a less favorable opinion of the effect of welfare measures on recipients than did AC, but German IS still had a more positive opinion in this regard than American. Possible explanation: the German heritage of welfare state thinking since the Bismarck era a hundred years ago.

11. Media Usage.

American IS perceive themselves as making more use of *all* media in a quantitative sense than German. Possible explanation: American culture is generally more media-intensive than German. German media usage may also be qualitatively more intense than American.

12. American IS the More Experienced Consumer.

Though both IS groups are far more experienced in terms of prior ownership of autos and consumer durables than AC groups in their own countries, the American IS is also a more experienced consumer than the German. One likely explanation: the era of affluence arrived later in Germany.

13. Buying Criteria.

American IS feel that brand reputation is a more important shopping criterion than AC, but were less interested in product availability, economy of operation and credit. Surprisingly, German IS are more likely to cite styling as a shopping criterion than AC. Economy of operation was much more important to the German IS than to the American. Possible explanation: higher German energy costs. Brand and dealer reputation were more important to the American IS than to the German. Possible explanation: reputation may be linked to service, a source of increasing frustration in the United States. Price—contrary to expectation—ranked higher among American IS than German. Possible explanation: bargaining on autos and durables more prevalent in the United States. Credit was unimportant to the American IS but even less important to the German. Possible explanation: traditional stigma of credit in Germany.

14. Information Sources.

American IS see themselves as users of commercial information sources more than Germans. German IS see other magazines and newspapers as a more valuable supplement to test reports as an information source than American, especially in auto buying. Possible explanation: *DM* and *test* carried much fewer reports on autos than *Consumer Reports*.

15. Satisfaction with Product and Shopping Process.

German IS were generally more satisfied with products, information available and their own shopping activity than AC, while American IS were generally less satisfied. This is only clear-cut opposite trend between German and American IS. Possible explanation: the advanced stage of consumerism in the United States. Note that American IS who also perceived themselves as having *used* comparative test results in their shopping were better satisfied on all dimensions than fellow IS who had not used the ratings.

IMPACT, USE AND IMAGE OF COMPARATIVE TEST REPORTS

16. Aggregate Impact.

The study was more concerned with impact at the individual than at the aggregate level. At the aggregate level, the rate of subscription varies substantially between cultures, from 2–3 percent of householders in Germany and the United States to 15–18 percent in Norway. However, test reports are also sold on newsstands and heavily borrowed between families. They are also saved much longer than other journals and newspapers. No less than 22 percent of our American non-subscriber sample reported reading *Consumer Reports* more than once per year. In Germany the results of *Stiftung Warentest's* activities are also freely reported in the press and often by radio, sometimes TV.

It is known that test reports also have an impact on manufacturers and distributors, although the present project attempted no research in this area.

17. Impact and Use at Individual Subscriber Level.

About two-thirds of American and over one-half of German subscribers said they were aware of the brand recommended by testing magazines for their last purchase of a major durable. Awareness of recommendation was only about one-half among American and one-fourth among Germans in the case of autos. One-half of the subscribers in both countries said the recommendation was important in their durable goods purchase (much less in autos). Over 40 percent said they purchased a highly recommended brand. Some 90 percent of subscribers in this group said that they agreed with the brand recommendations for durable goods after user experience with the products. (Note that some upward bias in respondent perceptions of awareness and usage is likely.)

Some 85 percent of subscribers on both sides of the Atlantic keep their copies of test magazines "for a year or two" or even "indefinitely." About two-thirds of them lend copies to others.

18. General Image and Satisfaction.

Although the three journals have radically different types of sponsorship, 80 percent of the subscribers to each journal correctly classified its sponsor. In the United States, subscribers mostly prefer testing by consumer groups alone, with a joint sponsorship by consumers and government as second alternative; in Germany these preferences were reversed. In neither country do subscribers wish to see testing by government alone or business alone.

No less than 85 percent of American and 72 percent of German subscribers like to see the magazines recommend particular brands (as opposed to merely giving facts about each brand).

The general level of satisfaction among subscribers with their testing journals is very high.

19. Credibility, Relevance, Readability.

The credibility of all three journals among their subscribers is high, although there is a distinct différence between high-ranking *Consumer Reports* and low-ranking *DM* (*DM* is commercially sponsored). The situation is a great deal more split on various dimensions of the relevance and timeliness of the reports. Heavy emphasis on safety gets only mildly positive response.

Readability rates surprisingly high marks. Not unexpectedly, subscribers to *DM* consider it a bit brighter and more stimulating than subscribers to the other two journals find them to be.

ADVERTISING IMAGE AND CONSUMER INFORMATION

20. Background.

American advertisers, responsible for two-thirds of the world's advertising in 1968, outspent their German counterparts by a margin of four to one. However, Germany was the second-ranking nation in advertising, and advertising's share of the GNP was higher in Germany than in the United States. It may also be noted that aggregate advertising expenditures are increasing at a fairly rapid rate in Germany. In the United States, advertising's share of the GNP has been stationary or on the decline of late. As for media usage, the most dramatic difference between the two countries occurs in broadcast media, which are used very much less in Germany.

21. Overall Image of Advertising.

While a majority of metropolitan American and German consumers had an overall favorable attitude towards advertising, the Americans were more positively disposed than the Germans. (In the national samples of IS the overall disposition was also favorable, although the Germans here were more positive than the Americans.) This overall attitude was reflected in more positive opinions among American metropolitan consumers than German on each of eight specific questions concerning economic and social effects. Americans make a more clear-cut distinction between economic and social aspects than Germans.

22. Specific Advertising Attitudes: Economic Aspects.

American metropolitan consumers believe more strongly than German that advertising is essential. Americans tend to believe that advertising results in better products, while Germans are only mildly positive in this regard. Americans also feel that advertising helps raise the standard of living, but Germans tend to disagree. Neither group believes that advertising results in lower prices.

23. Specific Advertising Attitudes: Social Aspects.

American metropolitan consumers feel that advertising standards were higher "now" (1970) than ten years ago; German feelings are mildly in the same direction. Americans average out as about neutral in considering whether advertising "insults the intelligence" and "presents a true picture," while Germans are disbelievers on both scores. Both groups believe that advertising "often persuades people to buy things they shouldn't buy."

24. Psychographics and Advertising.

No really strong relationships were found. Metropolitan women tended to have a more favorable view of advertising overall—and of its ability to generate better products—than men. Highly educated consumers tended to be less favorably disposed toward advertising than others. German businessmen were distinctly more favorable to advertising than German workers; in America no clear-cut occupational differences were evident.

25. IS and Advertising.

American metropolitan IS showed a slightly less favorable attitude to advertising than AC. Surprisingly, German metropolitan IS gave slightly more positive overall ratings than AC. In neither country was the difference statistically significant. Interestingly, the results again imply a substantial cross-cultural homogeneity among Information Seekers.

On specific advertising issues, nevertheless, American IS still tend to be a bit more positive than German, notably about all economic aspects, except that neither group believes advertising helps to lower prices. With regard to social effects, both groups have ambiguous feelings relative to the truthfulness of advertising; and they believe—American IS even more strongly than German—that advertising persuades people to buy things they do not need.

26. Advertising Usage and Image.

As would be expected, there seemed to be a strong positive correlation among metropolitan consumers in both countries between favorable general attitude toward advertising, heavy perceived use of advertising in purchasing, and satisfaction with advertising as source of information in specific purchases.

The exception was the American IS, with whom no significant connection was discovered between attitude toward advertising and use of advertising in purchase situations.

27. Comparative Image of Product Testing and Advertising.

American and German metropolitan consumers give product testing a definitely higher overall rating than advertising as an information source. This applies particularly to the dimensions of trustworthiness, aid to brand comparisons, informativeness and, perhaps surprisingly, cost. Preference for test reports is less clear cut with regard to timeliness, and ambiguous feelings are voiced concerning both the time and effort required to take in the information and the understandability of the data. American consumers discriminate more in their views of different dimensions than Germans do. It appears to the researchers that product testing's surprisingly high ratings on some dimensions were (at least in part) reflections of its current social commendability and, paradoxically, of some lack of acquaintance with its characteristics on the part of AC. When in doubt AC consistently seemed to favor product testing over advertising.

28. Testing and Advertising as Seen by IS and AC.

American metropolitan IS rate product testing higher on all dimensions than metropolitan AC, and German metropolitan IS rate test reports higher on seven of eight dimensions than metropolitan AC. In Germany both groups equally give the timeliness of test reports a small preference to advertising. The only preferences for advertising are expressed by American metropolitan AC on the dimensions of time and effort required for comprehension and understandability of test data. While American IS were more favorable to test reports relative to advertising than German, the reverse was true of German and American AC.

To some extent the general attitudes toward advertising discussed in items 21–26 colored respondents' relative evaluation of test reports and advertising. It may be that a generally unfavorable view of advertising strongly affected the relative evaluation of testing and advertising in favor of testing among those AC whose actual knowledge of testing is quite limited.

29. Image and Usage of Test Reports and Advertising.

One might expect that respondents who had designated test reports or advertising as an important source of information in a recent major purchase would have a generally more favorable impression of the information source designated. Reasonably strong in Germany, this relationship was only mildly evident in America.

30. Misleading Advertising a Key Consumerist Concern.

On both sides of the Atlantic, among IS as well as average consumers, the prevention of misleading advertising emerged as a key consumerist concern.

Part One

Background and Concepts

Chapter One

Introduction

THE PURPOSE OF THIS BOOK

Information may well be the most important single "product" of an affluent economy based upon open markets. Without sources of information that are both available and accurate, there is little hope that the buyer will find his way through the maze of proffered products and services toward purchases which best serve his wants and needs. As markets grow more complex, information accumulation, transmission and usage become increasingly critical determinants of marketing efficiency.

If only two products are available in the market to serve a particular need, the buyer must gather information on each and compare the two; but if six products are available in a more highly developed market to fill the same need, the buyer must not only gather three times the information, he must also make 15 separate paired comparisons instead of one in order to do a complete job of shopping. In all likelihood the six products will be more complicated and specialized than the two, making information gathering and comparison more complex, errors more costly.

In the highly industrialized countries around the North Atlantic the consumer faces a myriad of potential sources of product and market information, which he must somehow sort, selectively absorb, blend and utilize in making buying decisions. Regardless of the merit of products available, the buyer is likely to make poor decisions if he has poor information or utilizes it poorly. It is not surprising, then, that the adequacy of current market information has become a topic of widespread interest and debate in both the United States and other nations with advanced consumer economies.[1] In such economies, information is at the same time the guide through the maze and the glue that holds the system together.

It is customary to distinguish among three sources of of product information: personal, commercial and independent. Of these, we have defined independent consumer information (CI) as data about products and services emanating from organizations which themselves have no economic interest in the sale of these offerings. The distinctions among information, education and protection as three mainstreams of contemporary consumer policy are elaborated elsewhere in *Consumer Information Systems.*

Although this book is concerned with all three sources of product information, it is focused on the most important variants of CI and commercial information: comparative testing (as reported in product test journals) and advertising. Advertising and CI have figured prominently in the debate on the efficacy of present market information, since they frequently have been characterized by critics as occupying these two poles: *advertising*, in the context of a biased output of the seller whose primary purpose is to persuade, is often seen as part of "the problem;"[2] and *product test reports*, as the output of "neutral" sources whose primary purpose is to inform, are often seen as part of "the solution."[3]

A common argument contends that consumers are (or should be) growing wary of the emotional persuasive terms of most advertising, and are (or should be) turning toward more factual, rational information sources such as product test reports. Indeed, it is obvious that advertising is under intense pressure in such countries as the United States and Sweden and, to a lesser extent in Germany.[4] As documented in *Consumer Information Handbook*, it is also obvious that product testing agencies are growing in number, size and importance all around the North Atlantic, as a result of both government activity and private support. Although product testing agencies are frequently mentioned in "consumer behavior" literature, such citations are often based on logical suppositions rather than on empirical data.[5]

In view of the heated debate about advertising and its possible complements or antidotes, it is amazing that relatively little organized effort has been made to gauge the attitudes and perceptions of the consumer himself in this area, particularly with regard to product testing. Generalizations have been common; empirical studies few.

The prime purpose of this book is to present the results of a study of representative consumers in Germany and the United States. The five basic objectives of the study were:

1. To explore the degree to which and the manner in which product test reports are used, and to record and analyze attitudes toward the reports on the part of subscribers and average consumers.
2. To query the same subscribers and average consumers about their attitudes toward current advertising in several dimensions.
3. To examine linkages we assumed to exist between use of and attitudes to CI and attitudes to advertising.

4. To cast our research in a comparative mold in order to establish whether information-minded consumers tend to have similar characteristics across cultures or, in other words, whether there is a cosmopolitan group of Information Seekers. We also wanted to quantify to what extent the attitudes of various categories of consumers in industrially advanced countries seem to be culture-specific rather than cosmopolitan.
5. To relate our own research to similar studies.

It should be stressed that our purpose was not to trace in a definitive way the complex and interactive effects of different information sources on ultimate purchases. Such a task would have required longitudinal and behavioral research of a complexity beyond the current state of the art and in excess of reasonable resource constraints. We emphasize rather the attitudes and perceptions of the consumer himself toward product test reports, both in a general context and in regard to certain specific purchase situations. We also begin an attempt to trace the impact of test reports and theorize about it where little theory and research experience currently exist. The question of advertising effectiveness is somewhat related and has received considerable attention of late;[6] but it is beyond the purview of this study. Our interest in advertising is confined essentially to its "image" and to the interrelations of attitudes toward advertising and those toward CI.

Throughout our research we have made an effort to build on, supplement and to extend what has gone before; too much social research is being done in an effort to stand apart, to be unique solely for the sake of uniqueness. We do not feel that an endless series of isolated studies will provide the bricks with which a solid edifice will be built; a more likely result is a huge pile of bricks. We do not deny the value of brilliant departures from the beaten track; we do, however, maintain that the need for synergy, for cumulative, coordinated thrusts, is just as great in research as in business, government or other areas of human endeavor and that in the behavioral sciences this need has been neglected to an appalling degree. Cooperation, like charity, begins at home. We have conscientiously tried to integrate the various facets of the International Consumer Information Survey (ICIS). Likewise, the research on CI programs covered in the *Handbook* [7] logically called for the present study of the impact of such programs on their clientele; conversely, the present study is rich in implications for the administrators of such programs as well as for business, government and consumer group executives concerned with the formulation and implementation of consumer policy. Policy implications of the entire ICIS project are discussed in *Consumer Information Systems*.[8] Although the three volumes are written to be read independently, they are all directed to the overall purpose of better understanding CI agencies and their outputs. Cross references will be made when it is felt that one of the companion volumes contains material germane to portions of the present book.

It will be seen that we have related to other studies made in various industrialized countries both of the impact of and attitudes to CI programs and of the image of advertising. Two observations should be added here. We promoted synergistic effects in both areas by in effect co-sponsoring with the government of Norway a survey of Norwegian consumer attitudes. Our work in the advertising image area is a direct extension of the pioneering research by Professors Raymond A. Bauer and Stephen A. Greyser of Harvard.[9]

THE RATIONALE FOR AN INTERNATIONAL STUDY

Data gathering, analysis and interpretation in this book are *immensely* complicated by its international character. The reasoning governing an international study of CI organizations as described in the *Handbook* is straightforward; no single nation has enough diversity in its agencies to provide much insight into the many possible forms of organizations and outputs or their advantages and disadvantages. The focus of the present work is more upon comparing users of product test reports with "average" consumers, and reasons suggested previously for moving across national boundaries may bear spelling out. The following considerations were critical in the decision to make comparisons international:

1. Product testing and reporting originated in the United States, but recently has developed rapidly and diversely in Europe. Experience thus covers a longer time span in the United States, but may in a sense be more intense and varied in Europe at present.
2. With increasing affluence, better communication, widespread travel and greater product similarities between countries, there is reason to believe that consumer behavior is becoming less culture-specific. Location of cross-cultural commonalities (as well as distinctions) in needs, attitudes and behavior seems a desirable end for breadth of understanding in the consumer information area.
3. We have already cited the value of cross-cultural research to public and private consumer policy makers. In addition, the increasing number of multinational corporations has caused higher value to be placed upon all types of cross-cultural comparisons of consumer behavior. Isolation of similarities and differences among countries makes possible greater efficiency in the marketing efforts of such firms.

For these reasons, a comparative framework was chosen for this study. This format allows comparisons not only between subscribers to product-testing magazines and non-subscribers within countries—or between Information Seekers and other consumers—but also between Germans and Americans in both categories. Chapter 3 outlines details of sample compositions for the study.

ORGANIZATION OF THE BOOK

This book is arranged into three main sections:

Part One is devoted to a discussion of the purpose of the book, the form of the
investigation, and the theoretical background—including the general question
of consumer decision-making and the specific role of product test results
as an information source. A simple information-use model is developed in
chapter 2 as background for the empirical work and for the discussion of the
"impact" of CI and its measurement in the same chapter.

Part Two is concerned with unfolding the results of the survey. Chapter 3 is a
detailed discussion of the research design; chapters 4 and 5 present subscribers and "average" consumers in the United States and Germany respectively,
and chapter 6 goes on to make direct cross-cultural comparisons between
the two countries. It should be noted that chapters 4, 5 and 6 all follow
the same basic format to facilitate cross-references and comparisons. Chapter
7 is a precis of closely related studies, many of which are from other
countries.

Part Three draws upon theory, the present study, and other investigations to
draw together material on the measurement of impact of CI, the "image" of
advertising, and the relationship between advertising and CI. Chapter 8 surveys advertising image in this and other studies; and chapter 9 examines
the interrelationships between advertising image and CI in the two countries,
also incorporating material from the study in Norway co-sponsored by ICIS.
Chapter 10 is an epilog drawing some of the threads of the book together.

THE AUTHORS' VIEWPOINT

The discussion in the following chapters will be specifically concerned with the
published outputs of three separate CI agencies and with the consumers who subscribe to them and use them. The agencies—two in Germany and one in the
United States—provide a particularly apt cross section, in that each represents a
different sponsorship orientation:

1. The United States agency (Consumers Union) is a member-sponsored con-
    sumer organization and has no official ties to either government or business.
    It has rigorously maintained its independence by refusing advertising and
    continuing to buy at retail all products used in testing.
2. One German organization (*Stiftung Warentest*) is organized and financially
    sponsored by the government. This foundation was largely free from minis-
    terial influence in 1970 (its independence is even greater in 1974).
3. The second German organization (*DM*) is a privately owned publishing

venture. *DM* has been notably more free-wheeling than the Consumers Union in that advertising is routinely solicited from business.

This trichotomy is typical of the division in philosophy among CI agencies which have developed around the North Atlantic. Some are rigorously independent, others struggle to maintain an independent stance while relying upon government or business for partial resources and support, while still others are wholly government or business sponsored.[10] We were curious to see whether there appeared to be any systematic differences in the images of the three agencies among consumers.

The authors' intent is to report the findings of this research into consumer information and advertising image with scientific detachment. In fairness to the reader, however, they must confess to a primary, rather basic faith in what might be called "alternativism"—the belief that the market is best served if free choice of information sources as well of products is equally available. Independent CI agencies—private or governmentally supported—are thus seen to be legitimate responses to the insufficiency of objective product information from other sources, and to offer increasingly important information alternatives and supplements to commercially-dominated promotion.[11]

SUMMARY

Adequate sources of market information are critical to the functioning of a complex consumer economy. The purpose of this book is to discuss the findings of a study of one such source which seems to be of growing importance—product test reports, and to examine attitudinal interrelationships with a second important source—advertising. This study and the International Consumer Information Survey of which it is a part are seen as first steps toward an organized body of knowledge about CI agencies and their patrons not previously available.

The next chapter will conclude Part One by discussing some of the basic consumer behavior principles which form the theoretical framework of the study. A simple model of buyer behavior will be developed as a background against which the methodology of the study will be explained in Part Two.

NOTES TO CHAPTER ONE

1. A typical set of American opinions on the adequacy of market information is found in *Freedom of Information in the Marketplace* (Columbia, Mo.: Freedom of Information Center, 1967). John Galbraith's comments on the power of sellers to use information to manipulate consumers are discussed in the companion volume by Hans B. Thorelli and Sarah V. Thorelli, *Consumer Information Systems* (forthcoming). Two representative German works are Christa von Braunschweig, *Der Konsument und Seine Vertretung* (Heidelberg:

Quelle & Meyer, 1965) and Peter Meyer-Dohm, *Sozialökonomische Aspekte der Konsumfreiheit* (Freiburg: Rombach, 1965). For further references—also from other countries—see bibliography in *Consumer Information Systems*.

2. See, for instance, Colston E. Warne, "Advertising–A Critic's View," *Journal of Marketing* (October 1962): 10–14 and Herbert Gross, "Der 'gemachte Markt' in der technischen Gesellschaft," *Gewerkschaftliche Monatshefte* 8 (July 1957): 75 ff.

3. As in John R. Hicks, "Economic Theory and Evaluation of Consumer Wants," *Journal of Business* 35 (July 1962): 256–63. Hicks cites Consumers Union type organizations or government agencies as possible supplements to commercial information sources to minimize what he calls "inefficiency in consumption." For a German work in the same vein see Dieter Meiners, *Ordnungspolitische Probleme des Warentests* (Berlin: Duncker & Humblot, 1968).

4. In the United States recent demands for detailed substantiation of advertising claims and for corrective ads to point out possible misinformation in previous ads are cases in point.

5. James F. Engel, David T. Kollat and Roger D. Blackwell, *Consumer Behavior* (New York: Holt, Rinehart and Winston, 1968) as an example state that organizations such as Consumers Union ". . . appear to influence the behavior of a significant percentage of consumers" (p. 389), citing a 14 year old article whose conclusions were based upon a survey of businessmen and marketing managers plus numbers extrapolated from one question in the *Consumer Reports* annual questionnaire. John A. Howard and Jagdish N. Sheth, *The Theory of Buyer Behavior* (New York: John Wiley and Sons, 1969) use *Consumer Reports* as an example of a "high effort" information source (p. 294) and a "neutral" source with implied primary choice criteria of price and technical performance. They offer no empirical support for these quite logical assumptions.

6. A collection of articles on the subject may be found in John J. Wheatley, ed., *Measuring Advertising Effectiveness*, American Marketing Association reprint series (Homewood, Ill.: Richard D. Irwin, 1969).

7. Hans B. Thorelli and Sarah V. Thorelli, *Consumer Information Handbook: Europe and North America* (New York: Praeger, 1974). This book is hereinafter cited as the *Handbook*.

8. See note 1. above.

9. Raymond A. Bauer and Stephen A. Greyser, *Advertising in America: The Consumer View* (Boston: Harvard University, Division of Research, Graduate School of Business Administration, 1968). We are grateful to Professor Greyser for the opportunity for personal consultation.

10. As it happens, *DM* currently is the only straight business venture in the comparative testing field known to the authors. Even so, *DM* in recent years has relied more heavily on *Warentest* for data.

11. For a fuller development of these notions see chapters 1 and 2 of *Consumer Information Systems*.

Chapter Two

Consumer Decision-Making and the Impact of Consumer Information

Twenty-five years ago, when Consumers Union and Consumers' Research Inc. were fledgling organizations sending test reports to a few thousand zealous subscribers in the United States, they were an interesting phenomenon; but their total influence on the economy was probably negligible. Now that these two have been joined by dozens of similar but diverse organizations reaching millions of consumers nearly throughout the world, it would be difficult to argue that the marketplace is not changed by the resultant outpouring of information. Consumer information agencies are increasing rapidly in both number and size, and the scattered research available suggests that the information they transmit influences the buying behavior of those it reaches. Some economic transactions in affluent, consumer-conscious nations, particularly in America and Europe, have been changed radically by the extensive circulation of product test information. This chapter will discuss the role played by product tests in the consumer decision process and examine methods for evaluating their effects.

PRODUCT TEST INFORMATION AND THE CONSUMER DECISION PROCESS

The Importance of Individual Transactions

The essence of economics and marketing is contained in the instant when the consumer exchanges a quantity of his resources for a quantity of product. The subtle forces which influence a buyer to purchase Brand A rather than purchasing Brand B or not purchasing at all are the determinants of satisfaction or dissatisfaction for buyers, success or failure for individual firms and prosperity or depression for nations. Although an individual sale or purchase is essentially a two person transaction between a specific buyer and a specific seller, it is not surprising that each such transaction has broader implications:

11

1. To the buyer, the transaction is one of a series of purchases (or non-purchases) by which he seeks to maximize his own utility within his income constraint. He seeks the "best" combination of products or services to fit his personal needs.
2. To the successful seller, the transaction is the ultimate reward for his marketing efforts. He normally seeks to maximize the number of successful transactions involving his own product, and also searches for the causes of successful transactions for purposes of future policy-making.
3. To the unsuccessful competitor, the transaction represents the failure of his own marketing efforts. He seeks to minimize the number of such failures and searches for the causes of failure as a guide to future policy-making.
4. The government is interested in the transaction first of all because although the degree and form of encouragement is controversial, there is support for the idea that government should encourage activities which lead to "better" purchases by individual consumers; and there is a substantial amount of government activity currently directed to that end. In addition, transactions, considered in the aggregate, determine the economic well-being of a nation for any given period; and their number, value and nature both in total and in various sub-sets of that total are of critical importance.
5. Professionals and organizations in the field of market information (including advertising media, advertising agencies, CI agencies and others) are concerned with the influence upon transactions of their own efforts, since this influence is their ultimate "product." Their broadest goal is to maximize their influence upon a given transaction at a given level of effort or expenditure. In this sense they are also concerned with the influence of "competitive" or complementary sources on the transaction.
6. Professionals, particularly academicians, in economics and marketing are interested in how and why transactions are made, in the interest of building better theories to serve the array of specialized concerns listed above.

Each of these organizations and individuals requires substantially different information about transactions, and various viewpoints and levels of aggregation have been used in the attempt to formulate useful theory.[1] It seems clear, however, that the interests of all will best be served by better overall understanding of transactions, leading to more reliable information to all concerned. This suggests the development of a common framework or theory which is understood and used by all interested groups and which makes findings cumulative.

The Transaction as Part of a Decision Process

At the present time, the most widely accepted and promising approach seems to be a view of the transaction not as an instantaneous event with an absolute outcome, but rather as a part of a complex decision process by the individual consumer over time. Accordingly the actual transaction or purchase may be preceded by an involved series of related psychological and physiological activities which influence its nature and may be followed by other psychological and physiological activities which may influence similar transactions in the future.

This model of purchase as a decision process was pioneered by Lazarsfeld and Katona,[2] and has probably been most extensively developed to date by Nicosia,[3] who builds a model for advertising influence, and by Howard and Sheth,[4] who propose a more generalized model of buying behavior. These broad efforts have served as springboards to more specialized research which is currently seeking to add detail and improve the original models.[5]

A Simple Purchase Decision Model

The research described in this book accepts the principle of purchase as a decision process. The methodology presupposes the existence of a series of semi-discrete steps which take place over time for the buyers and purchases examined. Figure 2-1 illustrates a simple decision model of the type assumed in the study. It suggests that the following events may take place in a "typical" purchase decision.[6]

1. *Predispositions (Before Purchase).* The prospective buyer possesses a certain "stock" of cognitive content, including his own personality or self-concept, attitudes and opinions both in general and on specific products, and stored information and past experience. This stock has been formed as a result of his interaction with his environment over time, and it will help determine the environment in which he places himself in the future as well as influence his perception of that environment.
2. *Product Need.* As a result of either cognitive activity or some environmental stimulus, the buyer perceives a need which is capable of being satisfied by a product or service.
3. *External Search.* The perceived need for a product suggests activity designed to identify and evaluate available product alternatives. This stage represents all search of the external environment for alternative solutions as well as for information helpful in evaluating these alternatives. It is obvious that a possible corollary activity at this stage is the "internal" search for information from previous experience which might be relevant to the present purchase situation. The extent and nature of external search for information likely in any given purchase has been the subject of a great deal of research. Since the main concern of this book is with particular information sources, a more extensive discussion of this stage will follow below.
4. *Evaluation of Alternatives.* This stage consists of the physical and cognitive activities involved in comparing alternatives on the basis of information gathered from "external search" above.

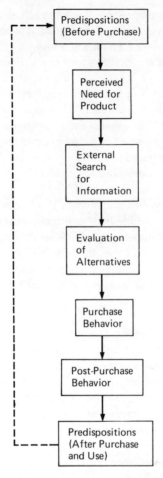

Figure 2-1.   A Simple Purchase Decision Model.

5. *Purchase Activity.* Involves the actual final decision and physical activities involved in making (or not making) the purchase. This stage includes the actual transaction as discussed at the beginning of this chapter.
6. *Post-Purchase Behavior.* This step is concerned primarily with the buyer's use of the product purchased. As consumer behavior researchers have come to view purchase as a process over time rather than as an instantaneous event, more attention has been focused upon the post-purchase stage. Alderson long ago suggested that both marketers and economists should concentrate more of their research on this area.[7] It is clear that unless returned merchandise is a factor, post-purchase behavior can have no impact upon the purchase under consideration. It is equally clear, however, that satisfactions and dis-

satisfactions created by product performance will be important determinants of attitudes and information stored as inputs to future purchase decisions.

7. *Predispositons (After Purchase and Use)*. This stage suggests that following the purchase process, the buyer (or non-buyer) is left with cognitive content which may be quite different from that which was present at the beginning of the process. The time and events which have transpired may have left the buyer with changed attitudes, information and experience. All of these may serve to change substantially the nature of the decision process for future purchases of the same type.

This model is oversimplified and makes no attempt to capture the details and subtleties suggested in the more comprehensive models listed above. [8] It is intended to establish allegiance to the general principle of the consumer decision process and show gross linkages to the general model. Considering the early stage of development in theory for buyer behavior and the almost complete lack of previous empirical data on CI as a buyer information source, this simplified approach seems most functional. It will be left for future investigators to hypothesize and study more intricate models and linkages.

Information and its Use

Entry Points for Product Information.   Information about products may enter into the purchase process at a number of different points:

1. From *Predisposition* (Before Purchase), in the form of information and attitudes stored as a result of past experience or exposure.
2. From *External Search,* as the result of conscious search for information as a part of a particular purchase process.
3. From what might be termed accidental exposure at any stage during the purchase process, as the result of casual encounters with information from advertising, in conversation and from similar sources routinely encountered by the individual.

Information obtained by the first method is both difficult to trace and already "given" in any purchase situation, while that obtained by the third is, by definition, essentially acquired at random. Only the second, information obtained by External Search, is generally the result of a conscious, rational, physically traceable, and sometimes predictable activity. It is not surprising that this phase of information entry has received the most attention from investigators into the purchase decision process. Because CI is, almost by definition, a lengthy and complex type of information to absorb, CI is most likely to enter any given transaction as a result of conscious activity by the buyer. For these reasons, this study concentrates upon External Search as the most common and important entry point for CI, even though it can also enter the decision process at other points or by other means.

Determinants of Information Search. In a variety of different studies, it has been found that the amount and intensity of search for product information is a function of the interplay between the cost and value of that information to the prospective user.[9]

Acquiring information from external sources almost invariably involves some type of cost to the buyer, though not always money cost.[10] The most common costs are:

1. Direct cash outlays—as in a subscription to a consumer magazine or admission to a trade show.
2. Indirect cash outlays—as in paying a premium price for known brand names, or using higher-priced stores as assurance of a certain quality level.
3. Opportunity costs—most commonly in the time used in information search. Stigler has pointed out that the cost of a given amount of search may vary widely among individuals because of varying opportunity costs for the same amount of time.[11]
4. Psychological costs—an ambiguous and difficult cost to measure, but no less real. Self-consciousness in facing haughty clerks in a prestige store or frustration with assimilating a glut of available information might be examples.

The consumer's perception of the magnitude of these costs is one determinant of the quantity and type of information sought and "purchased" by him in any given purchase situation.

The other major determinant of search is the perceived value of information, both the general value placed on information by the individual consumer and the value to him of a specific information source in a given purchase situation. It would be expected that the greater the quantity and the greater the credibility of stored experience and information (Predispositions before Purchase), the less the value of additional information search;[12] the consumer who has an adequate "stock" of information already on hand is unlikely to place a high value on adding to that stock. This observation, however, says little about how the consumer decides when his information stock is adequate.

An extensive body of research suggests that any consumer's valuation of information may be tightly linked to his perception of the *risk* involved in a given purchase situation; broadly speaking, the greater the risk, the greater the likelihood that a search for information will be instituted. The theory of *perceived risk* may briefly be summarized as follows:[13]

1. Perceived risk in any given purchase decision is a function of two perceptions: the importance to the consumer of the *consequences* of that decision and

the *uncertainty* about its outcome. If a consumer thinks a purchase is extremely important and his existing information stock leaves him highly uncertain as to how to evaluate alternatives or as to what the consequences of purchase may be, he is said to have high perceived risk.

2. The evaluation of consequences is seen to have two dimensions: performance – the actual physical workings of the product or service in question; and psycho-social – involving personal evaluation of status, prestige, social acceptance or the like associated with the purchase.

3. Individuals tend to reduce perceived risk to some acceptable level in any given purchase situation.

4. Perceived risk may be lowered either by reducing uncertainty (obtaining additional information) or by reducing the value of the outcome.

5. Consequently, the amount and type of information search carried out by the consumer is closely tied to the amount and type of perceived risk in the situation. If a housewife were highly uncertain about the suitability of a certain dress for a neighborhood coffee (psycho-social risk), she would be likely to turn to a fashionable friend for information. If she were concerned about the durability and wrinkle resistance of the fabric for the same dress (performance risk) she would be more likely to consult a consumer magazine or a trusted sales clerk.

Perceived risk offers a convenient general theory for evaluating the likelihood, extent and type of external search for information in a given purchase situation. More specifically, a study by Katona and Mueller [14] indicates that search is more likely (and external information presumably given higher valuation) when the consumer: (1) is in a middle class rather than higher or lower class category; (2) has a college education; (3) is under 35 years old; and (4) has a white collar occupation.

This brief summary of findings and theory not only gives some insight into the variables determining information search, but also makes it obvious that the interplay between information cost and information value is likely to be complex, individualistic and difficult to trace or predict.

Sources of Information. Product information is available to the consumer from a myriad of different sources; various authors have suggested that they may be divided into three broad categories: [15]

1. *Buyer sources*—including interpersonal sources, such as word of mouth, advice from friends, observation of persons from a reference group, or seeking of knowledge from an opinion leader among the most common examples. A great deal of study has been done in this area, mostly under the broad title of 'diffusion of innovations.' [16]

2. *Commercial sources*—including all the information sources controlled by the

seller: advertising, personal selling, displays, packaging, and all other sales promotion media and techniques.
3. *Neutral sources* – an "all others" category which implies that their content is outside the control of either buyer or seller. Most CI fits neatly into this category, and product testing magazines such as *Consumer Reports* are most often cited as the best examples of this type of source. Product-related articles in newspapers and general magazines could also be included here.

Any given product decision involving information search is likely to be based upon some artful mix of the above sources types, the actual sources used and their relative importance being dependent upon the nature of the product, the characteristics of the purchaser, and the type of risk perceived in the overall purchase. In the study of diffusion of innovations, it has been found that commercial sources are most helpful in providing awareness and general knowledge of the product, but that buyers are more likely to seek out personal sources when they reach the evaluation and comparison stage.[17]

In evaluating the use of these three major types of information source, Cox concludes that:[18]

1. *Buyer sources* – a relatively expensive source, but with high credibility and high value, particularly in the area of psycho-social risk – are more likely to be used: (a) when performance risks and/or psycho-social risks are high enough to merit the use of these relatively expensive sources, or (b) when the buyer is particularly interested in avoiding mistakes, and hence actively seeks negative or unfavorable information if it is available;
2. *Commercial sources* – usually low in cost, but also low in credibility and not particularly helpful in giving psycho-social information – most likely to be used: (a) when perceived risk is low, (b) when perceived risk is moderate and the result of performance uncertainty, or (c) when the higher cost of using alternative sources is not justified;
3. *Neutral sources* – excellent sources of performance information with high credibility, but little help in the psycho-social area. (Howard and Sheth concur with this general opinion, with the further observation that neutral sources tend to be the most expensive of all, usually requiring a degree of intellectual skill for proper use.)[19]

PRODUCT TESTING MAGAZINES AS AN INFORMATION SOURCE

At the present time, product test reports demonstrate the following basic characteristics:

1. They are directed toward the retail consumer;

2. They usually deal with medium- and higher-priced durable products but also, with considerable variation from agency to agency, cover automobiles, inexpensive durables, convenience goods and foods;
3. They provide comparative data about selected brands for specific buying criteria;
4. They frequently rate or rank order brands upon some evaluation of performance of the selected criteria and/or price;
5. They usually include generalized buying advice about the product itself along with the evaluation of particular brands.
6. They are most frequently distributed in print in the form of magazines, bulletins or guides, though some agencies have made use of radio and television presentations;[20]
7. They often charge the consumer for the use of the information through a subscription fee, membership fee, or price of an individual copy of the periodical in which the reports are published.[21]

Combining these characteristics of product test information with general theory on information usage immediately suggests that test reports are a rather specialized source whose influence is likely to be limited because of:

1. *Communications skills required for usage.* The comparatively lengthy and technical nature of test reports demands intellectual skills not normally found among low-income, low-education consumers.
2. *Limited scope of tests.* Only a limited number of products are tested in any given time period, involving only a limited number of brands within that product category. The scope of testing varies with the purpose and resources of the testing agency, but in every case test information is available for only a small subset of possible product purchases.
3. *"Expensive" nature of information.* The cost of purchasing publications, and particularly the time and effort required to read them, make them a rather expensive information source. It is likely that they are used only for more important purchases or by those who place a high value on information.[22] Absorption by accidental or casual contact is less probable than for some other sources.
4. *Rational quality of evaluation criteria.* Most product test reports presuppose the use of "rational," performance-related choice criteria by consumers and are of little use to the buyer seeking psycho-social reinforcement.

It is not surprising to find that all existing data concerning subscribers and users show them to be of a higher income and education level than the average consumer.[23] We might also expect that test reports are more likely to be used in making major durable purchases than in making convenience purchases, partly because of the greater importance and risk and partly because more

test information is available. It would also be expected that the more information conscious and planful the consumer, the more likely he would be to use
test reports.

Since one of the purposes of this study is to learn more about the
way in which CI is used in the purchase process, these generalizations are not
made as a final judgement nor to limit exploration. They are meant, rather, to
summarize current "conventional wisdom" and to explain the reasoning behind
the framework for the empirical study. This framework is outlined broadly in
the section just following and in detail in chapter 3.

THE IMPACT OF PRODUCT TEST INFORMATION ON CONSUMERS

It was contended at the beginning of this chapter that product test information
may change the nature of transactions in economies where it is distributed; and
the sections just above speculated on ways in which such information may enter
into the purchase decisions of individual consumers. Although such contentions
and speculations are interesting, concrete measurement of the influences of test
information would certainly be more useful. The following sections will discuss
possible ways of empirically measuring effects and influences and outline the
general scheme used in this study.

Definitions and Background

It is possible to measure the influence of Consumer Information
organizations on a number of separate dimensions. Three of these dimensions
will be discussed, defined here in order of increasing specificity:

1. *Impact* is an all-inclusive term referring to any change whatever in the market
   caused by Consumer Information agencies. Total impact, if measurable,
   would be the difference between market behavior and performance with CI
   organizations and behavior and performance without them.
2. *Effectiveness* refers to the degree to which an organization is successful in
   accomplishing its stated purpose. Thus, while impact refers to any effect—
   good, bad, deliberate or unintentional; effectiveness is restricted to the
   effects of an organization's activities in comparison with its overt objectives.
3. *Efficiency* is the amount of effective output per unit of resources expended.
   Efficiency measures the amount of effect consistent with the organization's
   purpose resulting from a given expenditure.

Over time, scholars and practitioners should work toward theoretically correct
and workable measurement techniques on all three dimensions for activities of

CI agencies. Such measurements would be of practical value to the organizations themselves, to businesses whose products are affected, and to government policy makers concerned with market information.

The following discussion will be a great deal less ambitious: given the dearth both of experience and of published material in this whole area, no attempt will be made to offer any definitive scheme for measuring the impact, effectiveness or efficiency of CI agencies. A number of practical measurements of impact, however, will be proposed and discussed and will be related to the agencies and experiences covered by this study. Some brief discussion will be offered of the areas of effectiveness and efficiency and the problems related to their measurement.

The discussion will be further limited by giving primary attention to the area of product testing. This emphasis is not intended to minimize the importance of the many other activities of various CI agencies (lobbying, consumer education, etc.) or their interaction with product testing; it is simply a reflection of the fact that this study focuses on the testing and reporting area. Briefly, the balance of this chapter offers an exploratory discussion of the problems involved in measuring the effect of selected outputs of CI organizations. It is hoped that this beginning will lead to more sophisticated and useful measures as experience and theory accumulate.

Impact on Consumers

The most obvious and most important impact of product test reports upon consumers occurs in influencing purchase decisions for various products. All three magazines covered in this study have as their expressed purpose providing unbiased information to aid consumers; which implies that their information will lead to different, presumably "better" purchases. To measure and evaluate the nature of changes induced by product test information, however, is a challenge.

Figure 2-2 illustrates two separate approaches for evaluating the influence of an information source on product sales in a given time. In the aggregate approach, total flows of information from a source or group of sources are thought of as moving into the total market, and the reaction of the market to these flows is a distribution of purchases among available brands during the period. It is possible to specify the number of salesmen or pages of advertising or dollars of sales promotion in a given time and to identify total sales or market shares for the same period. Such information is comparatively easy to accumulate, and can be used in regression or other multivariate analyses with some exploratory capability. The great complexity of the information-influence process, however, generally supplies quantitative tools with little power, and confines the major applications of the aggregate approach to drawing broad, qualitative conclusions about the nature of influence. In any case, this approach begs the question of the actual causation or motivation behind any influence.

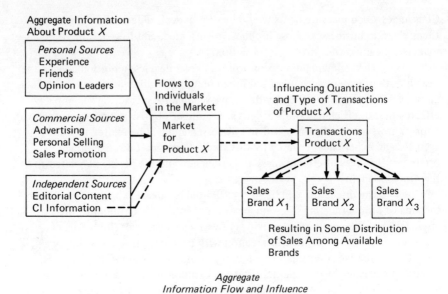

Aggregate Information
About Product *X*

Personal Sources	
Experience	
Friends	
Opinion Leaders	

Flows to
Individuals
in the Market

Influencing Quantities
and Type of Transactions
of Product *X*

| Commercial Sources |
| Advertising |
| Personal Selling |
| Sales Promotion |

Market
for
Product *X*

Transactions
Product *X*

| Independent Sources |
| Editorial Content |
| CI Information |

| Sales | Sales | Sales |
| Brand X_1 | Brand X_2 | Brand X_3 |

Resulting in Some Distribution
of Sales Among Available
Brands

Aggregate
Information Flow and Influence

Consumer$_1$ + Consumer$_2$ + . . . + Consumer$_n$ = Total Market for Product *X*

| Predispositions (Before Purchase) | Predispositions (Before Purchase) | Predispositions (Before Purchase) |

Information
Flows to
Individuals in
the Decision
Process

| Search for Information | + | Search for Information | + . . . + | Search for Information |

Aggregate
Information
= Input
About *X*

Influencing
Individual
Purchase
Decisions

| Purchase Behavior | + | Purchase Behavior | + . . . + | Purchase Behavior |

Sales of
= Product *X*
All Brands

Resulting in Some Distribution
of Sales Among Available
Brands

Individual
Information Flow and Influence

Figure 2-2. Two Views of Information Influence on Sales of Product *X*.

Some proposed aggregate measures of the extent of product test information in the market include:[24]

1. *Number of subscribers* serves as a gross measure of the extent of circulation of product test reports, and perhaps affords some clues as to their geographic or demographic dispersion.
2. *Number and nature of tests performed and published* should serve to place some practical boundaries on the types of purchase decisions likely to be directly affected in a given period of time.
3. *Growth of product test agencies* is perhaps a crude measure of proportionate influence and success in an economy when compared with growth of other competing information sources (advertising, etc.).
4. *Sales or income* is in most cases closely related to the number of subscribers or members, but it is another general measure of an agency's success and an indication of its potential influence in the aggregate marketplace.[25]

The lower half of figure 2-2 illustrates a second approach to tracing influence by adding together the purchase decisions of individual buyers. This method is to monitor the decision process of a representative group of buyers in the hope of attaining greater understanding of information-influence processes in individuals which may then be generalized into larger aggregates of buyers. This behavioral approach offers far greater promise for explaining the subtleties of information impact but involves complexities in measurement and aggregation that are at best difficult to handle. Possible measures of impact using this methodology are:

1. *Awareness and exposure*—identifying the buyers who are cognizant of the information and hence have the potential of using it in buying decisions;
2. *Users*—identify perceived or actual users by demographic characteristics, geography, attitudes and other measures as indication of total number of purchase decisions affected and their value and distribution;
3. *Attitudes*—attitudes toward CI agencies (credibility, accuracy) are indications of their ability to influence buying behavior. Attitude change toward brands and products may be a direct (or indirect) measure of influence on buying. General attitudes, helping to characterize personality and life style of users, may be useful in predicting future behavior or explaining past behavior;
4. *Usage*—the nature of perceived and actual usage addresses directly the question of impact on purchases. Importance of various shopping criteria, interaction with other information sources, types of products where use was made, experience and

planfulness of users and other considerations all give dimensions to the picture of the size and nature of the impact of product test information on actual purchases;

5. *Satisfaction* – is a measure of past success in using test reports and a crude gauge of future potential impact. Users satisfied with the quality and form of information provided are likely to be future users as are buyers satisfied with products purchased with the aid of test information.

Both the aggregate and behavioral approaches can make contributions toward understanding the nature of the impact of product tests in consumers' purchase decisions. Given the current state of knowledge, however, it is doubtful that either separately or combined they can quantitatively indicate the nature of this impact in any clear-cut way.

This study will offer several different interpretations of the impact of product test information dispensed by the three agencies studied. It will particularly emphasize an exploratory attempt to trace influence by monitoring buyers' perceptions of a large number of individual purchase decisions in the manner suggested in the lower half of figure 2-2.

The actual methodology, explained in detail in chapter 3, involved administering an extensive questionnaire to several population samples in Germany and the United States. Some of the samples consisted entirely of subscribers to CI magazines and others were random samples of some segment of the population as a whole. Each sample was quizzed in a number of general areas, including demographic characteristics and attitudes toward advertising, CI agencies, and several consumerist issues. The respondents were then asked to recall the details of three specific purchase decisions, including both attitudinal and behavioral questions.

The nature of the samples and the content of the interviews thereby makes it possible to compare demographic characteristics, attitudes and behavior between the "average" consumer and the "average" subscriber to CI magazines, and among various other sample combinations. In essence, the study methodology comprises a "quasi-experiment"[26] in which subscription to a product testing magazine is the manipulated variable.

Figure 2-3 is a reiteration of the original purchase decision model modified to illustrate the basic comparisons between samples made in the study. In reference to the model, the interviews in the study were conducted after the purchase was completed. Questions were asked pertaining to the respondents' demographic characteristics and attitudes at that time together with retrospective questions about purchase behavior concerning the selected series of purchases.

Although some subscribers are clearly non-users, and some users are not subscribers, this method offers a convenient way for isolating differences

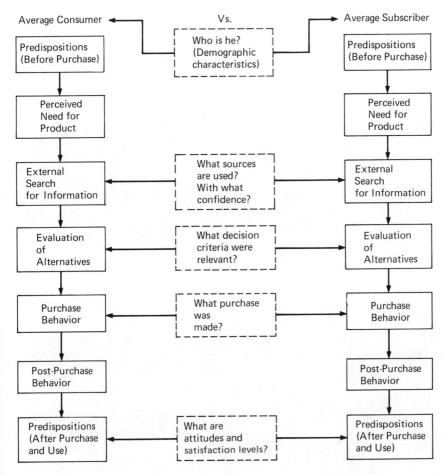

Figure 2-3. Comparing Two Samples in a Purchase Decision.

between groups with high potential for impact on decision-making by product tests and an "average" group of consumers with much lower potential for such impact. The bulk of chapters 4, 5 and 6 will be devoted to revealing the results of these comparisons and the clues which they provide toward measuring the impact of the three agencies and of the information they dispense.

A Look at Effectiveness

Effectiveness was defined above as the special case where impact is compared to the stated purpose of an organization. CI organizations are seldom explicit enough in stating their purpose to make this measure meaningful.[27] The three organizations in this study all profess the general goal of helping the

consumer by providing unbiased product information, and the mastheads of
each of their three publications carry a statement to this effect. All CI agencies,
however, implicitly promise "better" purchase decisions when their information is used over time.

It has been argued that the theoretical goal of all CI programs should
be to reduce "mistakes in purchase," to bring the consumer closer to the purchase which he would have made had he possessed perfect information.[28] No
true measure of this goal is possible, since no consumer is ever likely to possess
perfect information either before or after a purchase; his knowledge, however,
should be much greater after experience using the product than it was prior
to purchase. Hence, *satisfaction*—a comparison between expectations and perceived performance—is available as a beginning measure of mistake-reduction
through the use of an information source. If satisfaction is clearly higher for
purchases where a given information source is utilized than for those made without that information source, there is presumptive evidence of reduced mistakes
in purchase resulting from that source.

Although there is little prior experience or theory in evaluating the
effectiveness of CI programs, there are decades of attempts to isolate the
effectiveness of advertising, obviously a closely related exercise. In both cases
an attempt is made to trace the influence of a particular information source on
the ultimate outcome of a particular purchase process. Those interested in
measuring the effectiveness of CI can profit by utilizing variations of a battery
of models and techniques developed particularly for advertising, hopefully
avoiding some of the pitfalls and frustrations which have been encountered in
attempting advertising measurement.[29]

Despite the obvious parallels, however, measurement of product test
effectiveness differs from that of advertising in several substantive ways, and it
may be helpful to note these differences. In both cases a process similar to the
one shown in figure 2-4 is assumed in any given purchase situation. In each case
exposure to the information source may lead to some degree of attitude change
and in turn to some actual influence in the final decision to buy (or not buy) a
particular product and brand. In using the product, the buyer evaluates its
performance in accordance with his needs and expectations and experiences
satisfactions or dissatisfactions which may be guides to future actions.

The basic process is the same whether the information input is an
advertisement or a product test. But in evaluating *effectiveness*, the focus
changes. Advertising's main goal is increasing sales of a particular product or
brand, and Step 3 is the ideal measure of its effectiveness. Product testing's
goal is reducing mistakes in purchase, so the outcome of Step 4 is the ideal
measure of its effectiveness.

Actually there are innumerable practical barriers to measuring
influence on sales or on "better" purchases, so that proxies are most often used
to estimate the degree of influence. Advertising effectiveness has always been

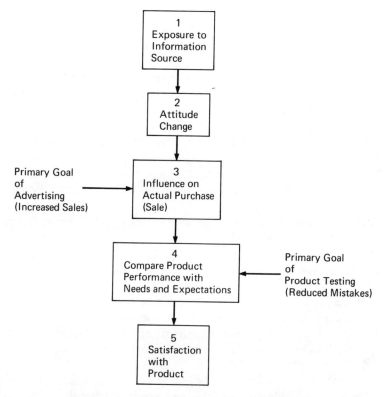

Figure 2-4. Basic Information Influence Model.

measured by such indirect means as subscription exposure, recall of copy, and more recently by attitude change and brand preference which presumably lead to changed purchase probability.[30] Little attention has been given to post-purchase activities in connection with advertising measures.

The best available proxy for estimating the reduction of mistakes in purchase is probably satisfaction with products and purchase procedures. Even though satisfaction itself has some serious flaws as an absolute measuring stick, [31] it is the effectiveness measure used in this study. Readings were taken on the purchaser's satisfaction with his own shopping activity, with available information, with the quality of product test information and with the product itself.

Even though attempts to measure the effectiveness of advertising precisely have mostly been disappointing because of the great complexity of the influence process, there is reason to be more optimistic about measuring product test effectiveness. The following advantages, at least, are present in an attempt to trace product test influence:

1. Product test publications and articles have as their direct purpose the distribution of product information, while advertising is regarded by readers as a tangential (and sometimes resented) sidelight to publications in which it appears. Thus subscribing to or reading a test magazine implies a search for product information. Reading a magazine or newspaper containing advertisements carries no such implication. It seems likely that readers of test magazines are looking for CI ratings whereas readers of other magazines are not necessarily looking for the information to be found in the advertisements. In addition, readers of test magazines are likely to be sympathetic to the magazines' points of view.

2. Product test readers receive a relatively straightforward and unambiguous reading on the performance ranks of various brands of a product. Reading a magazine or newspaper may expose the consumer to a whole battery of advertising recommendations for the same product, each biased and all quite contradictory to one another.

3. As noted above, (see p. 18) various authors have assumed or concluded that product test magazines are a more credible information source than advertising and hence should be more influential.

4. In the case of perceived use, reading product test reports is more likely to be a purposeful, calculated activity than noting an advertisement incidentally in reading for some other purpose. Thus, recall of use and influence may be more accurate in the case of a test rating than an advertisement.

All of these points carry the probability that the impact of consumer reports is more direct, less diffuse, and more easily traced than that of advertising, and the corresponding hope that it may eventually be measured in a more straightforward manner.

SUMMARY

Two basic approaches are potentially helpful in measuring consumer impact: an aggregate, macro method; and a behavioral, micro approach. Some possible measurements using each are:

Aggregate:
Growth and survival of organizations
Sales or income of organizations
Numbers of subscribers or buyers
Number of tests performed and published

Individual:
Exposure to reports
Identity of users
Attitudes of users
Nature of usage
Satisfaction with purchases and purchase processes

Until more data and better theory are available, all of these measurements are potentially helpful in specifying the nature of the impact of product test reports. A section was devoted to discussing the effectiveness of test reports, and satisfaction measurements were proposed as the best available indicators of success in improving the users' purchases. Strong parallels exist between advertising influence and product test influence in the market, but several characteristics of test reports promise that measurement of their impact will eventually be more direct and accurate than is currently possible for advertising.

Product test reports are written expressly for consumers, and their most important effect undoubtedly takes the form of changes in buying behavior among those consumers. Yet the information dispensed certainly has the potential of influencing the success of manufacturers and distributors of products; and in some countries, test agencies' activity has been closely intertwined with government policy and activity. Few data exist which might help evaluate the impact of test reporting on businesses, government and other organizations; but logic suggests that some influence must exist and that such influence may be growing apace with testing activities. These matters are discussed in *Consumer Information Systems*.

NOTES TO CHAPTER 2

1. Lazarsfeld has characterized three basic approaches to studying action: a *distributive* approach, focused primarily upon outcomes; a *morphological* approach, describing various action paths; and an *analytical* approach which seeks causal implications. Current emphasis seems to be shifting to the analytical approach. Paul Lazarsfeld, "Sociological Reflections in Business," in Robert Alan Dahl, ed., *Social Science Research in Business* (New York: Columbia University Press, 1959).
2. Lazarsfeld's earliest work appeared in A.W. Kornhauser and P.F. Lazarsfeld, "The Techniques of Market Research from the Standpoint of a Psychologist," The Institute of Management Series, *Institute of Management* 16 (1935): 3-15 and 19-21. Katona's earlier work is summarized in George Katona, *The Powerful Consumer* (New York: McGraw-Hill, 1960). Actual formulation of buyer behavior schemes by Katona began as early as 1940.
3. Francesco Nicosia, *Consumer Decision Processes* (Englewood Cliffs, N.J.: Prentice Hall, 1966).
4. John A. Howard and Jagdish N. Sheth, *The Theory of Buyer Behavior* (New York: John Wiley and Sons, 1969).
5. See for instance: John U. Farley & L. Winston Ring, "An Empirical Test of the Howard-Sheth Model of Buyer Behavior," *Journal of Marketing Research* 7 (November 1970): 427-38.
6. Though much more simplified, this model owes some allegiance to the model developed in James F. Engel, David T. Kollat and Roger D. Blackwell, *Consumer Behavior* (New York: Holt, Rinehart and Winston, 1968). The reader who is unfamiliar with such models may wish to refer to the detailed exposition in that source.

7. Wroe Alderson, *Marketing Behavior and Executive Action* (Homewood, Ill.: Richard D. Irwin, 1965): 285.
8. A detailed comparison of several of the most fully developed models of buyer behavior is contained in Harold H. Kassarjran and Thomas S. Robertson, *Perspectives in Consumer Behavior* (Glenview, Ill.: Scott-Foresman, 1968), part V.
9. A discussion and bibliography of this notion is contained in Engel, Kollat and Blackwell: 380–8.
10. The concept of cost of information has been explored in George Stigler, "The Economics of Information," *Journal of Political Economy* 69 (June 1961): 213–25 and in Anthony Downs, "A Theory of Consumer Efficiency," *Journal of Retailing* (Spring 1961): 6–12.
11. Stigler: 213.
12. Engel, Kollat and Blackwell: 382–3.
13. A broad array of findings in the perceived risk area is contained in Donald M. Cox, ed., *Risk Taking and Information Handling in Consumer Behavior* (Boston: Harvard University, Division of Research, Graduate School of Business Administration, 1967). The theory of perceived risk is summarized in the Introduction (1–19) and in section IV (603–39).
14. George Katona and Eva Meuller, "A Study of Purchasing Decisions," in Lincoln Clark, ed., *Consumer Behavior, the Dynamics of Consumer Reaction* (New York: New York University Press, 1955): 30–87. See also Hans B. Thorelli, "Concentration of Information Power Among Consumers," *Journal of Marketing Research* 8 (November 1971): 427–32.
15. The categories used here are those proposed by Howard and Sheth: 294–321, but they are quite analagous to Marketer Dominated, Consumer Dominated, and Neutral as used in Cox: 605.
16. A thorough summary of work in this field is contained in Everett M. Rogers and F.F. Shoemaker, *Communication of Innovations: A Cross-Cultural Approach,* 2nd ed. (New York: Free Press, 1971).
17. Rogers and Shoemaker: 255.
18. Cox: 605–8.
19. Howard and Sheth: 321.
20. Test reports have been given on radio and TV in a half dozen European countries. Consumers Union has a syndicated radio program in the United States, but has confined itself to generalized buying advice and given no brand ratings.
21. There are some exceptions: the test information of *Stiftung Warrentest* in Germany is available free of charge to any other publication that wishes to publish it (many do); and most test magazines are available and widely used in public libraries.
22. Green separates consumers into those who are "information sensitive" and those who are not in Paul E. Green, "Consumer Use of Information," in Joseph Newman, ed., *On Knowing the Consumer* (New York: John Wiley and Sons, 1966). Wilding and Bauer identified "problem

solvers" who use "rational" criteria as opposed to "psycho-social" shoppers, in J. Wilding and R.A. Bauer, "Consumer Goals and Reaction to a Communications Source," *Journal of Marketing Research* 5 (February 1968): 73–77.

23. The annual subscriber questionnaire of *Consumer Reports* and studies by various other agencies have consistently confirmed this characteristic. See also Hugh Sargent, "The Influence of Consumer Product-Testing and Reporting Services on Consumer Buying Behavior," (Ph.D. diss., University of Illinois, 1958).

24. For a discussion of an ecological view of the way CI agencies adapt to their economic and social environment and a listing of CI outputs, see Hans B. Thorelli, "Consumer Information Programmes," *International Consumer* (Autumn 1972): 15–21.

25. The most complete set of statistics available on these and other characteristics of CI agencies is contained in Hans B. and Sarah V. Thorelli, *Consumer Information Handbook: Europe and North America* (New York: Praeger, 1974). A more theoretical look at the nature of CI outputs and impacts is contained in Thorelli and Thorelli, *Consumer Information Systems* (in process).

26. Donald G. Campbell and Julian C. Stanley, *Experimental and Quasi-Experimental Designs for Research* (Chicago: Rand-McNally, 1966). A quasi-experiment is defined as data collecting in which the "when" and "to whom" of measurement may be controlled, but not the "when" and "to whom" or exposure nor the ability to randomize exposure: 34.

27. A sizable controversy is now going on within the board of Consumers Union concerning their precise purpose as a consumer organization; the board seems to be split between those stressing "information giving" and those stressing the overall advocacy of consumer interest on a broad scale.

28. This argument is fully presented in Jack Engledow, "The Impact of *Consumer Reports* Ratings on Product Purchase and Post-Purchase Product Satisfaction," (DBA diss., Indiana University, 1971), chapter 3.

29. Some good discussion of current techniques may be found in Patrick J. Robinson, ed., *Advertising Measurement and Decision-Making* (Boston: Allyn & Bacon, 1968) and in John J. Wheatly, ed., *Measuring Advertising Effectiveness,* American Marketing Association reprint series, (Homewood, Ill.: Richard D. Irwin, 1969).

30. A dissenting view is contained in Kristian Palda, "The Hypothesis of a Hierarchy of Effects: A Partial Evaluation," *Journal of Marketing Research* 3 (February 1966): 13–24.

31. Some drawbacks are enumerated in Engledow, and in John A. Miller, "Satisfaction and Modes of Response to Dissatisfaction for Supermarket Customer Segments," (DBA diss., Indiana University, 1972).

Part Two

The Consumer Information Study and its Results

Chapter Three

Consumer Views of Consumer Information in Germany and the United States: Research Design

This study is based on survey data collected simultaneously and in near-identical ways in Germany and the United States during the early months of 1970. The phenomena included for country-by-country analysis as well as international comparison revolve around product information search, usage and evaluation as perceived by various population segments. This chapter will account for the research methodology of the investigation, including a brief discussion of the nature and philosophy of comparison as viewed by the authors, the rationale for choosing Germany and the United States as the primary countries for comparison, the framework for analysis and comparison used, the parallel, coordinated survey and questionnaire designs applied in both countries, and some illustrative propositions indicating expectations of findings and hoped-for accomplishments of this research. The results, analysis of results, and comparison of sample subgroups are presented in separate country studies of the American and German surveys in chapters 4 and 5 respectively. The cross-cultural comparison between the two countries is deferred to chapter 6.

COMPARATIVE METHOD AND ANALYSIS

Comparative method and analysis, one of the oldest forms of scientific inquiry, is utilized in such diverse fields as religion, philosophy, literature and the traditional social sciences; but its use in the comparative study of market institutions and processes is more novel. Interest in comparative studies of marketing phenomena, however, has been confined largely to abstract theorizing, to multiple-regression studies of macro-marketing systems and to the compilation of country case studies on a given topic (wholesaling, say) but without a common approach. Various marketing scholars have suggested theoretical frameworks for the systematic comparison of events, functions and systems across national boundaries; but rarely in the past have these models been operationalized and implemented in empirical research, because of such varied reasons as lack of financial support or the unavailability of qualified research talent simultaneously in more than one place. As a consequence, there exists only a handful of empirical marketing studies that could truly be termed "comparative" in the sense of a coordinated, synchronized research design, execution and analysis.

An additional, perhaps more fundamental explanation for the relative absence of such comparative studies of market phenomena can be found in the complexities of the set of societal institutions on which marketing is based. Paradoxically, it is a great deal easier to make studies at the macro level of the "comparative economic systems" type than it is to do comparative research at the micro level of the functioning of the marketing system in different countries. Also, there is still a frustrating lack of standardization in census concepts (e.g., in the education area) and yardsticks (e.g., in the income area) used by different national statistical bureaus. The definitional problems of marketing as a discipline are also very much in evidence, and the practical realities behind such concepts as "advertising" or "drug store" are very different in different cultures. When a way around these complexities cannot be found, comparisons may at best be imprecise and at worst misleading. An attempt has been made in this study to reduce some of the difficulties of comparability through careful coordination and synchronization of the survey design, data collection and analysis. Before detailing these phases of the project, it may be helpful to outline briefly the philosophy of comparative research underlying this work.

Philosophy of Comparison

It is generally agreed that valid comparisons can be made only among comparable phenomena but that at some level of generalization, certain identifiable similarities between distinct phenomena are presumed to exist. (E.g., "To make intelligent purchases, consumers need product information.") Reavis Cox applied the concept of "universals" to this level of generalization.[1] At a lower level, such universal concepts and similarities are likely to disappear and to be replaced by varying degrees of dissimilarity, from the subtle differentiation to the obvious contrast. (E.g., "In getting product information, Germans and Americans tend to use different sources.") The task of comparative analysis, then, involves "the systematic detection, identification, classification, measurement, and interpretation of similarities and differences among phenomena [whereby] the focus of comparison can be temporal (historical), spatial (geographical), or sectoral (subcultural)."[2]

The nature of comparisons in the present study is both sectoral and spatial. The sectoral concept of comparison applies to the separate country studies of the United States and Germany in the next two chapters. The primary objective of these country analyses is to compare and contrast differential perceptions of consumer information variables among and between several segments (sectors) of the American and German populations, respectively. This part of the investigation, then, is intended to stay within the national and cultural boundaries of each country.

Chapter 6, in contrast, deals with phenomena occurring in two different countries. The analysis is in the class of spatial or geographical comparisons. Geographical comparisons are often used synonymously with "cross-cultural" comparisons because they typically cut across political, national and cultural boundaries as well as geographical ones. The latter interpretation obviously applies also to the present investigation.

It is apparent that the comparisons in the present study are not historical because the data were gathered through cross-sectional surveys in two different countries. A longitudinal, panel type study (one asking the same people the same questions at specified intervals of time), for example, would have the advantage of making temporal comparisons possible. Although a longitudinal design could have added a desirable dimension—the measurement of attitude change over time—it was not a feasible extension of the research due to the additional logistical, financial and timing complexities it would have entailed. And, of course, panel designs have their own well-known methodological weaknesses.

While students of marketing, consumer and business phenomena are indeed late-comers to the field of cross-cultural research, various writers have addressed themselves to what we consider a key challenge in the field: the manner in which environmental variables are handled in the analysis. For example, Bartels suggests that "comparative study is not simply a description of either marketing or environmental differences, but rather a comparison of 'relationships between marketing and its environment' in two or more countries."[3] Boddewyn proposes a conceptual framework of the "aspects which should be studied comparatively" among marketing systems, in which the concepts of actors, process, structure and function are interrelated with environmental factors.[4] Thorelli applies the concept of "ecology" in developing organizational theory. While his basic approach could be termed environmentalist, its focus is organization-environment "interaction."[5] Indeed, "interaction" could be said to be the mark which distinguishes the concept of ecology from that of the environment. The ecological approach to comparative analysis is applied in the companion volume of this project, *Consumer Information Systems.*

Where the study of market phenomena is confined to one country, the environment is often assumed to be a given quantity—the big "uncontrollable" considered incidental to the task of marketing management. In such cases the environment tends to be treated as a constant or at best as a slowly, predictably changing, variable on which the firm (or the consumer, etc.) has little, if any, influence but to which it must continuously react and adapt through flexibility and continual adjustments to its marketing mix. In cases involving two or more countries, the assumption of environmental constancy becomes invalid. On the contrary, the environment typically would be purposely included in the analysis in cross-cultural comparisons. The environment in such a context is seen as the fountainhead of the explanatory variables of research propositions. The emphasis has thus shifted toward the explicit inclusion of environmental elements in cross-cultural analysis. These elements are seen as interacting, constraining and stimulating forces which influence the uniqueness of solutions to common problems in different cultural localities.

This point is illustrated in figure 3-1. It is assumed here that the market problems that arise in two high-level economies tend to be quite similar, if not the same. That is, the specific needs and wants of individuals and households must be satisfied from the random assortment of goods and services available. The institutional overlay which bridges the gap between the *random* assortment of goods and the *specific* needs of households is commonly called the marketing channel. The smooth functioning of the marketing system not only requires an efficient channel structure, but also depends on the effective flow of communication among consumers, marketers and producers. This study concerns aspects of marketing communications dealing with consumer information and advertising.

Problems of consumer information (CI) appear to exist in all affluent societies. As was shown in the companion *Handbook* volume, however, different countries have met similar CI problems with individual solutions. Some of them are widely divergent, as might be expected in view of divergent environmental circumstances. A major objective of this research project is to detect and describe similarities and dissimilarities in attitudinal and perceptual response patterns with respect to product information in the United States and Germany, and,

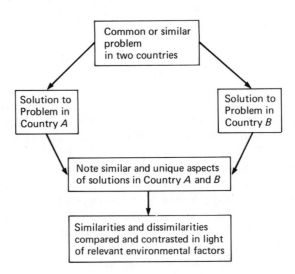

Figure 3-1. Making Cross-Cultural Comparisons.

when possible, to compare and contrast these patterns in light of their inter-action with relevant environmental factors in the two countries. Admittedly, however, the treatment of environmental variables in this study is impression-istic rather than systematic. The effort and resources required to research con-sumer attitudes and responses to CI and advertising precluded environmental analysis of desirable depth.

The What, How and Why of Comparison

The primary purpose of the investigation is to compare consumer views of market (mostly product) information in the United States and Germany. Of special interest are:

1. The relative importance of information as a shopping criterion as perceived by German and American consumers;
2. The media through which market information is typically obtained;
3. The relative importance of information derived from personal, commercial and independent sources;
4. The post-purchase evaluation of the product and the shopping process by the consumer.

Also compared are several attitudinal variables which may influence the uses and views of consumer information and some environmental factors that help shape these attitudes. These variables are explained in some detail in the section on the framework of analysis.

The comparative analysis takes the form of a systematic examination of similarities and dissimilarities of survey results in Germany and the United States (see figure 3-2). This examination of results is interwoven with environ-mental peculiarities of the German and American ecosystems, as perceived by these writers and other commentators. On one hand, these peculiarities may serve as explanations of resemblance and difference in German and American views toward consumer information; on the other, the findings may help in the formulation of policy by governments as well as consumer and business organiza-tions in both the domestic and international spheres. The findings should also broaden the base of the intense and important discussion concerning the cross-cultural transferability of institutions and policies.

There is a variety of additional reasons to compare phenomena in two or more countries. Perhaps the most important of these is the possibility that one might learn from the other. While examining a problem in another country, one might gain a better understanding of one's own problems. We are also looking for cross-cultural universals, e.g., whether there is a cosmopolitan elite of information-seeking consumers (analogous to the cosmopolitan jet-set or the hippie cultures). Somewhat differently, the issue may be formulated thus: are the differences between subscribers to test reports and average consumers in each country greater than the cross-cultural differences between subscribers (or average consumers) in the two countries?

WHY GERMANY AND THE UNITED STATES?

Although several other countries are introduced from time to time in the analysis, Germany and the United States were singled out as the primary countries for comparison. An important practical reason for this selection was that a member of the research team had a corresponding bicultural background. Of greater principal significance, Germany and the United States were considered to be sufficiently similar in several respects to make the comparison feasible. Both countries have a Western cultural orientation founded on the Judeo-Christian ethic and tradition. They have similar political and economic systems and subscribe to similar open-market philosophies. The standards of living in the two countries as measured by per capita gross national product are reasonably similar. Indeed, even among the countries of the enlarged European Community there is none resembling the United States so much as Germany. In sum, there are enough similarities between the United States and Germany to make them "comparable" countries in many respects.

Even so, Germany and the United States exhibit so many dissimilarities as to render comparisons between the two countries both challenging and interesting. Besides obvious differences in size, population and population density, there are others perhaps more subtle. For example, according to one survey, Americans seem to differ from Germans in their views of education, attitudes toward innovation and feelings of security.[6] Despite similarities in affluence and living standard, American and German styles of life appear to be rather distinctly different from each other. The difference is reflected, among other ways, in such mundane factors as the savings rate and automobile ownership; while Germans tend to save a greater proportion of their disposable income than Americans, Americans own more cars per capita than Germans.

Some idiosyncrasies of the two countries are discussed in chapter 6. In addition, the reader is advised to turn to appendix D for selected national statistical data. These data are presented to give a picture, however incomplete, of the relative proportions of Germany and the United States.

THE COUNTRY STUDIES—ANALYTICAL FRAMEWORK

Product Test Subscribers and Average Consumers
The framework for the analysis of the parallel American and German country studies is depicted in figure 3-2. The major thrust of the analysis lies in the comparison of the test-report subscriber sample with the average consumer (non-subscriber) sample within each country. These samples are analyzed in terms

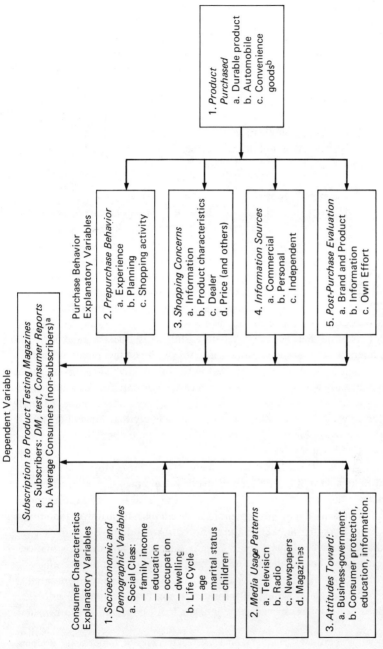

Consumer Characteristics
Explanatory Variables

1. *Socioeconomic and Demographic Variables*
   a. Social Class:
      — family income
      — education
      — occupation
      — dwelling
   b. Life Cycle
      — age
      — marital status
      — children

2. *Media Usage Patterns*
   a. Television
   b. Radio
   c. Newspapers
   d. Magazines

3. *Attitudes Toward:*
   a. Business-government
   b. Consumer protection, education, information.

Dependent Variable

Subscription to Product Testing Magazines
   a. Subscribers: *DM, test, Consumer Reports*
   b. Average Consumers (non-subscribers)[a]

Purchase Behavior
Explanatory Variables

1. *Product Purchased*
   a. Durable product
   b. Automobile
   c. Convenience goods[b]

2. *Prepurchase Behavior*
   a. Experience
   b. Planning
   c. Shopping activity

3. *Shopping Concerns*
   a. Information
   b. Product characteristics
   c. Dealer
   d. Price (and others)

4. *Information Sources*
   a. Commercial
   b. Personal
   c. Independent

5. *Post-Purchase Evaluation*
   a. Brand and Product
   b. Information
   c. Own Effort

[a] Additionally in the United States a special sample of non-subscribers matching subscribers in several respects.
[b] The convenience goods category is only included in limited sections of the analysis.

Figure 3-2. Framework for Analysis for the German and American Country Studies.

of two sets of explanatory variables derived respectively from consumer characteristics and from purchasing behavior. A respondent "profile" is developed in which subscribers are compared and contrasted with average consumers in terms of their socioeconomic and demographic makeup, media usage patterns and consumer policy attitudes. Data from respondents' shopping behavior in making their latest purchases of durable goods, an automobile and convenience goods are then analyzed and the samples compared and contrasted as before.

The focus of the investigation is the dependent variable of "subscribership to product testing publications." The key question is, To what extent can personal characteristics and purchasing behavior "explain" whether or not a consumer is a subscriber to such test reports?

Illustrative Propositions

One proposition illustrating expected findings in the consumer profile area holds that subscribers belong to higher social strata than average consumers; that is: subscribers, compared to average consumers, tend to have higher family incomes, more education, and a greater proportion of more prestigious types of occupation. As members of higher social strata, subscribers should also exhibit different media usage patterns from non-subscribers; that is: subscribers would probably read more while average consumers would pay greater attention to the broadcast media.

Despite their upper class membership, subscribers were expected to be more liberal than average consumers and to have a less favorable attitude toward business and advertising. One reason for this relative liberalism might be a finding that subscribers tend to be younger than non-subscribers. Another reason might be that subscribers feel strongly about consumerist issues generally in addition to wanting test reports. It also seemed likely that subscribers are considerably more in favor of government intervention on behalf of the consumer than are the non-subscribers.

As regards consumer buying behavior patterns, subscribers are expected to be all-around more "rationalistic" buyers than non-subscribers, irrespective of the type of product involved.[a] Compared to average consumers (AC), subscribers are expected to plan their purchases more carefully and to shop more often in a greater number of stores. Subscribers should also be more concerned than average consumers about certain aspects of the purchase situation, such as quality of the product and economy of operation, but in particular about the availability of information prior to purchase. Similarly, subscribers should tend to consult a greater variety of information sources than non-subscribers. This supposition applies especially to "independent" information sources such

---

[a]We are using the term "rationalistic" in the sense of "prone to use decision-making procedures typically associated with rational behavior." It must be understood that such behavior need not invariably result in better decisions than less systematic, intuitively based processes.

as product test reports, but may also be valid for personal sources. On the other hand, it seems quite probable that AC value sources such as advertising more than subscribers. In Engledow's phrase, subscribers should make fewer purchase "mistakes" than average consumers,[7] and in the post-purchase evaluation phase should be more satisfied, *ceteris paribus*, with the outcome of their decisions than average consumers. Assuming that subscriber aspiration levels as regards their own shopping behavior are not out of proportion relative to those of average consumers, it could also be expected that subscribers, in retrospect, would be more pleased with their own information search and shopping effort. In short, subscribers more than others might be viewed as "professional consumers."

The picture of a typical subscriber that seems to emerge from these propositions is one of a prosperous, intelligent, information-minded consumer who tends to be more satisfied with his own shopping efforts and buying decisions than most. An important question must, however, be raised: Are subscribers alike in these respects, regardless of country and cultural background? The cross-cultural comparative phase of the project is addressed to this and similar questions.

Nature of the Product Testing Agencies

The agencies that publish the product testing magazines from whose subscriber lists the samples were selected cover a whole spectrum of organizational forms. These organizations are discussed in detail in the companion *Handbook*.[8] For present purposes, a brief description is sufficient. Consumers Union in the United States, publisher of *Consumer Reports*, is a private, subscriber-sponsored and managed, independent, non-profit organization. "Independent" in this case implies independence from any government, industry or labor group, and from any power structure other than consumers themselves. It also connotes objectivity in the product and brand selection, testing and reporting procedures employed by this agency.

The two agencies sampled in Germany occupy, in a sense, polar extremes of organizations in the business of CI dissemination. The *Stiftung Warentest*, which publishes *test*, is a "private" foundation funded by public means. It is thus a hybrid organization, sponsored and financed by the German federal government although its independence of operation is at least formally guaranteed by the law governing private, non-profit foundations.

The *DM-Verlag*, in contrast, is a subsidiary of a publishing company. At least one of its objectives is profitability. It is therefore neither a government-sponsored agency (like the *Stiftung Warentest*) nor an independent consumer organization (like Consumers Union). The *DM-Verlag* is, rather, a private firm; and *DM* magazine both accepts and publishes advertisements for the purpose of generating revenue—in stark contrast to both *test* and *Consumer Reports*.

It is interesting that we should find such different CI organizations side by side in the modern market economy. Their commonality, of course, as far as this study is concerned, lies in their publication of comparative product test reports although their varying organizational character has important policy implications, as discussed in the *Handbook*. In the meantime, the present study will report on consumer perceptions of the reliability and objectivity of the three test journals.

THE CROSS-CULTURAL STUDY— COMPARATIVE FRAMEWORK

The reader may have wondered why the plan of analysis and research propositions of the foregoing section did not distinguish between the German and American country studies. In fact it was presumed that subscribers to product test publications have certain characteristics, attitudes and behavioral patterns in common so that one can generalize across the boundaries of these two national cultures. A likely outcome from these speculations would be findings of important similarities as well as discrepancies between subscriber groups in the two countries. Such findings would imply that cross-cultural similarities of American and German subscribers obliterate national differences, and that we have in fact identified a group of cosmopolitan Information Seekers. If this is the case, certain generalizations may be made regarding CI policies in both Germany and the United States; and certain conclusions can be drawn concerning the transferability of CI systems and techniques from one country to the other.

It was hoped that the comparative analysis of the German and American data would provide some answers to these kinds of issues. The cross-cultural comparisons were based on the principles developed earlier. The model for comparison is illustrated in figure 3-3. The diagram suggests certain relationships between consumer types, characteristics and buying behavior, and the environment of the country in which they were observed. For example, the level of education predominant in key market segments is a determinant of the media and the degree of sophistication most effective in the dissemination of CI. Economic conditions are largely responsible for such factors as real income and leisure time which are vital ingredients in the formation of buying behavior patterns. As the affluence of a people rises, discretionary spending tends to increase, and so does the complexity of the marketplace. Not only is there a greater number of items to choose from, but there are also more consumption decisions of greater variety required by a majority of individuals. This, in turn, implies the requirement for greater amounts and variety of consumer information.

A major part of the cross-cultural analysis will focus on direct comparison of nationwide samples in the two countries (chapter 6) using the format for analysis that was indicated earlier for the country studies. A set of metropolitan samples will be used in the cross-cultural comparison of advertising image (chapters 8 and 9). As suggested by the illustrations above and by figure

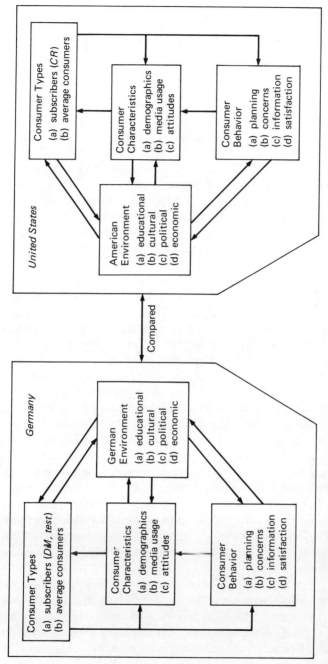

Figure 3-3. Model for Cross-Cultural Comparison Between Germany and the United States.

3-3 itself, it is also imperative to take into consideration as much as possible the interaction between the consumer variables and the broader educational, cultural and economic environment in Germany and the United States. Thus, what are presumably relevant environmental elements will be introduced into the comparative analysis in an attempt to explain differential characteristics of consumer groups in the two countries.

Many of the environmental variables intended to serve as the explanatory basis of differential perceptions and attitudes in Germany and the United States, however, are measurable only in qualitative terms. Some demographic and socioeconomic factors, moreover, do not lend themselves to easy comparison between the two countries. For example, occupational descriptions and categories in Germany are not identical with those in America. Income distribution in America varies over a wider range than in Germany, and comparison is further distorted by the fact that the fringe benefits of German employees, while not the highest in the Common Market, far exceed those of most Americans. Finally, the educational systems in the two countries are far apart, and completion of various specific educational programs comes at different points in time. Comparative analysis is further complicated by differences in the quality and intensity of instruction in Germany and America. Based on the research by Denison and others, and in the absence of a more valid yardstick, a number of years of formal education has been adopted as the basis for comparison.[9]

Even after all the explanatory variables in the two countries have been matched as carefully as possible, one additional barrier to comparative survey research must be conquered: that is the matter of translation from the language of one country to that of the other. For example, the German word for business is *Industrie* and for government is *Regierung*; but such abstract terms may carry slightly different connotations in the two languages. In translating the questions into German, special attention was given to keeping the essence and meaning of the statements intact in terms of German culture and peculiarities. For example the statement, "I enjoy planning work carefully before carrying it out," was translated, *"Es macht mir Spass, meine Arbeit sorgfältig voraus zu planen."* Preserving the essence of a question was very deliberately given priority over verisimilitude in wording.[10] Nevertheless, when comparing German and American responses, one must be cognizant of the fact that perceptions of questions and of predetermined answers may sometimes not be identical in the two countries.

Further comments of caution apply to the sampling and questionnaire designs employed in both Germany and the United States. Although intensive efforts were made to approximate the research methodologies in the two countries as closely as possible, it does not absolutely follow that the surveys were exactly alike. Considerations and problems of the survey design are the subject of the next section.

SURVEY METHODOLOGY

To fulfill the purposes of the study several methodological prerequisites had to be met:

1. The consumers to be reached in the survey were to include two types: those who were exposed to and therefore were at least potential users of the information provided by the respective product testing agencies in each country, and those who were not so exposed;
2. The data collected had to be suitable for statistical comparisons of certain attitudes, purchase behavior and demographic characteristics between product test information users and non-users, both within countries and between countries;
3. The method of data collection itself had to be capable of standardization between countries and feasible within given budget constraints.

Some of the complications encountered in the course of research stemmed from the following sources:

1. Low concentration of product test subscribers in the general population; these concentrations were believed to be under 3 percent of American households and less than 1 percent of German households. (Although the number of non-subscribing readers might well be three to five times as many, no easy way of identifying such readers presented itself. Nor could it be taken for granted that the average secondary reader had as strong an interest in CI as the average subscriber);
2. Multiple levels of analysis:
   a) "Within country, subscriber" comparisons between questions such as effectiveness of publications, reasons for subscribing, and usage-of versus satisfaction-with product information. In these comparisons one is, in effect, looking for consistencies (or lack thereof) in attitudes and/or behavior. Another type of "within country, subscriber" comparison is between *DM* and *test* subscribers in Germany;
   b) "Subscriber–average consumer" comparisons, to identify differential characteristics in regard to key attitudes, demographics and purchase behavior;
   c) "Between countries, subscriber" comparisons, seeking to identify those subscriber characteristics which are country specific and those which might be universal and gaining insights into comparative strengths and weaknesses of agencies as perceived by subscribers in each country.
3. The international nature of the study:
   a) Language and semantic differences as well as other cultural subtleties pose powerful obstacles to the creation of a multi-country, cross-cultural survey instrument;

b) Problems of physical coordination in time and distance must be solved to synchronize data collection;

c) Differences between countries in interviewing agencies and practices, mail service, geographical and legal boundaries of metropolitan areas and other relevant factors must be resolved.

Despite these limiting factors, the survey methodology was adapted to the requirements of the project objectives. The data were collected through personal interviews and mail questionnaires within a relatively complex sampling structure to be explained in the following paragraphs.

Metropolitan and National Samples

In view of the foregoing, the sampling structure had to meet two distinct criteria: it had to permit comparisons between subscribers and average consumers, and it had to enable researchers to make valid inter-national comparisons, at least between subscriber groups, in the two countries. The reader will recall that we were interested in whether there exists in affluent nations a cosmopolitan set of Information Seekers with similar demographic, attitudinal and shopping characteristics. We were willing to postulate that if such a group of consumer information sophisticates does indeed exist, it will include among its core membership the subscribers to product test reports.

The low concentration of subscribers in the general population in these countries[b] made it clear from the outset that separate samples for subscribers and average consumers would have to be used.

Presupposing an hour long questionnaire, we frankly doubted that adequate cooperation could be obtained from average consumers if they were surveyed by mail. They would, therefore, have to be interviewed; but fiscal and administrative constraints made two national interview samples in each country an impossibility. Thus was born the idea of interview samples of subscribers and average consumers in a representative metropolitan area in each country. It was decided that for average consumers a sample size of 200 was required, while the presumed greater homogeneity of the subscriber group would make a sample size of about 100 sufficient. Research results seem to bear out these estimates.

The problem of accommodating the international comparison requirement remained. A "representative" metropolitan area would presumably be typical of metropolitan areas in the country in question rather than of the nation itself. On the other hand, cost concerns at this stage indicated the use of a mail survey. On the basis of the project leader's belief that consumers conscious

[b]Contrast Norway with a subscriber rate of 14–18 percent of all households. In that country a study of consumer issues comprising a single sample of 1,817 households contained a sufficient number of subscribers to permit statistically significant comparisons between subscribers and average consumers on most questions. For further details see chapter 7.

enough about the value of information to subscribe to test reports would also themselves be willing sources of information, it was decided to incorporate national mail samples of 1000 subscribers in each country for inter-national comparison purposes. Response rates of over 60 percent in the mail surveys in each country clearly justified this decision.

The two-tier sampling presented an opportunity to compare response rates and nature of response between a lengthy mail questionnaire and a nearly identical questionnaire administered by personal interview. Somewhat to our surprise, the refusal rate was lower for the mail questionnaire than for personal interviews. Cooperation was generally excellent among average consumers personally interviewed.

In comparing overall results between mail and interview samples within countries, few significant differences appeared beyond those which were inevitable due to occasional differences in questionnaire design (primarily in sections where unaided recall was used in order to take advantage of the greater flexibility of the personal interview). Appendix A contains a summary of statistical differences found between samples and a discussion of the importance of such differences to the study.[c]

The two metropolitan areas chosen for interview purposes were Frankfurt, Germany and Indianapolis, United States. Their selection was based on similarity in size and centrality of location as well as on accessibility to the researchers. To add a note on the subject of the local representativeness of Indianapolis and Frankfurt: Indianapolis is often mentioned as the archetypical Middle American city. For this reason it is a well-known center of test marketing for national brands. Within an hour's drive is Muncie, the "Middletown" of pioneer sociology. That Middle America may be a shade more conservative than the Eastern or Western seaboards does not of itself make Indianapolis less representative of American metropolitan areas in general, for it is the tenth largest metropolitan area in the United States. Frankfurt, in comparison, is the sixth largest West German city. This seems only reasonable, in view of the fact that there are a greater number of big cities in the United States than in Germany.

It might be objected that Frankfurt is a more cosmopolitan city than Indianapolis. We have no doubt that it is, but so is nearly *every* European city in the size class of half a million inhabitants or more, if nothing else by virtue of the fact that most places in Europe tend to be within an hour or two's traveling distance of two or three national borders. The authors do not feel that Frankfurt is remarkably more cosmopolitan than other large German cities, and we do not

[c]It would have been interesting to establish unequivocally that the differences between the metropolitan and national subscriber samples within each country were indeed smaller than the differences between the American and German national subscriber samples. This type of comparison does not directly lend itself to any standard statistical test that we are aware of. On the basis of our own examination of the data, however, we have personally no doubt that this is the case.

believe that this is a factor which might unduly bias comparison. In line with Kish's statement that "if a research project must be confined to a single city . . . I would rather use my own judgment to choose a 'typical' city than select one at random,"[11] it was reasoned that Frankfurt and Indianapolis would be as "representative" as any two cities selected by other methods.

The metropolitan subscriber samples were randomly selected from subscriber addresses included within the city limits of Frankfurt and Indianapolis. Analogous procedures were followed to draw the nationwide German and American mail subscriber samples. We gratefully acknowledge the cooperation of *Stiftung Warentest* (for *test* subscribers), *DM-Verlag (DM)* and Consumers Union (*Consumer Reports*) in arranging access to their subscriber files.

Finally, a third metropolitan sample was drawn in Indianapolis, essentially for its methodological interest. This so-called "matched" sample was based on the notion that age, income and educational differences between subscribers and average consumers in the general population were potentially capable of causing substantial attitudinal and behavioral differences, quite aside from any subscriber-average consumer differences. The "matched" sample was an attempt to hold these major demographic variables constant. It was obtained by using a residence close to a subscriber as a proxy variable for socioeconomic similarity between the "matched" and subscriber samples. The results from the "matched" sample are discussed in detail in Engledow's "Impact of *Consumer Reports*." In the present volume illustrations from these results are used sparingly in the American study and only when they seemed particularly pungent.

The nature of the various samples, their size, and major purposes are summarized in table 3-1. All samples were selected at random with specific attention given to obtaining the closest possible comparability of sampling methodology in each country and location. A detailed description of techniques and selection procedures utilized in all samples can be found in appendix B.

Use of Metropolitan and National Survey Samples

The overall scheme for the use of the two-tier sample structure is probably now apparent. Subscribers and average consumers within each nation are analyzed and compared separately using the metropolitan interview samples. The results are detailed in the country studies accounted for in chapters 4 and 5. The nationwide mail subscriber samples are used for the cross-cultural comparison in chapter 6.

As noted above, the bridge between the two tiers is placed in appendix A where similarities and differences between the results obtained from the metropolitan and national subscriber samples in the two cultures are noted. On the whole, the similarities are striking, which reenforces our faith in the two-tier sample structure.

Although it would often be unjustified to make direct inferences from the metropolitan samples to the national populations, we feel entitled to

Table 3-1. Summary of All Samples: International Consumer Information Survey

Name of Sample	Country	Sample Size	Nature of Sample	Purpose of Sample
Nationwide Mail Subscriber Sample	United States	630	Systematic random sample of subscribers to *Consumer Reports*.	Intercountry comparisons on subscriber characteristics, behavior, attitudes, and perceptions of agencies and information. Intracountry analysis of satisfaction in purchases using agencies' information *vs.* those not using, etc. (Good inference to subscriber population as a whole.)
	Germany	610	Systematic random sample of subscribers to *DM and test*.	
Metropolitan Interview Random Sample	United States	200	Stratified random sample of Indianapolis residents.	Intracountry comparisons with interview subscribers. Analysis of non-subscriber use of CI. Analysis of information use and needs of average consumer. (Good inference to local population, but questionable inference to national population.)
	Germany	198	Stratified random sample of Frankfurt residents.	
Metropolitan Interview Subscriber Sample	United States	101	Systematic random sample of Indianapolis subscribers to *Consumer Reports*.	Intracountry comparisons with interview random and matched. More comprehensive and accurate recording of behavior, attitudes, perceptions and demographic characteristics than by mail survey. (Good inference to local subscriber population but questionable to national subscriber population.)
	Germany	97	Systematic random sample of Frankfurt subscribers to *DM and test*.	
Interview Matched	United States only	101	Close residential neighbors of subscribers matched one-to-one with interview subscribers in Indianapolis.	Intracountry comparisons with interview subscribers (United States only) with better control over key demographic characteristics than at random.

make such inferences about the *metropolitan* populations of the two countries from the Frankfurt and Indianapolis samples. In chapters 8 and 9 images and use of advertising between German and American metropolitan populations are compared using the samples from these two cities.

Questionnaire Design

The design of the instrument was determined by both the purposes and the international character of the investigation. The construction of a "master questionnaire" including content, sequence and formulation of questions proved to be one of the most difficult tasks of the project. The difficulty was amplified by two factors: first, the master questionnaire was to be utilized in both countries with the least possible variation for maximum comparability, creating the linguistic and semantic problems noted earlier; second, the instrument was to serve as the data collection vehicle in both the mail and interview situations for maximum intra-country comparability among the various samples outlined in the last section.

Because of the several areas of interest covered by the research, it soon became evident that the questionnaire would evolve into a lengthy instrument. The German version was 16 pages long, and the American, 24; the difference in page numbers arising from the different printing process used in each country. The physical length of a questionnaire tends to be less critical in an interviewing situation if the interview can be kept shorter than an hour. One hour is often considered a physiological and psychological limitation in terms of the attention span of average respondents, after which their interest and hence the reliability of their information can decline rapidly. For mail surveys the response rate tends to decrease markedly with increasing length of the questionnaire.

The length problem was solved in part by adopting a closely structured survey instrument. Through the structuring process it was possible to effect standardization of response sets, both by using predetermined, identical wording and sequencing of questions, and by providing structured alternative answers to these questions. At the same time, of course, certain advantages of open-ended questions had to be given up. Open-ended questions undoubtedly would have added richness and spontaneity to the data, but it was felt that the problems of increased length, lack of standardization, and absence of cross-cultural comparability were of overriding importance in this case.

The bulk of the instrument consisted of multiple response questions, primarily Likert-type statements, and similar ratings and ranking scales. Likert-type statements are commonly used for attitude and opinion measurement. Several statements are rated by the respondents, typically on a five-point scale, from "strongly agree" to "strongly disagree," with a neutral midpoint. Such scales normally reflect ordinal rankings and offer no metric or interval measure between the polar extremes of agreement and disagreement. Likert-type data do, however, lend themselves to a variety of non-parametric statistical significance tests, such as the Mann-Whitney U test widely employed in this volume.[12]

To minimize biases that can be introduced in structuring the instrument itself, two techniques were employed. Whenever possible, alternate positively and negatively phrased questions were used in a balanced mix in any given section of the questionnaire. In addition the so-called "split-sample" technique was used for the Likert statements. In effect, each sample was split into two groups. The respondents of each group were given questionnaire versions in which the positively and negatively formulated Likert statements had been, when feasible, reversed. At the same time, the five-point scales were reversed from "strongly disagree" to "strongly agree." In this way all respondents could be combined regardless of which questionnaire version was answered by any one individual.[13]

There was also some evidence that the sequencing of questions within the instrument might evoke perceptual bias on part of the respondents regarding their usage of certain types of product information.[14] To illustrate, the "rationality" implied by reading such publications as *Consumer Reports* may have socially acceptable implications and lead to biased answers under direct questioning. It was therefore considered important that respondents be asked all important questions on general attitudes, purchase behavior and media usage *before* they became aware that the study was directly concerned with the evaluation of product test publications.

The overall structure of the instrument and its question sequencing, then, followed the so-called "funnel design." The questionnaire began with general attitudes towards self and about business and government, and gravitated toward more specific attitudes on advertising. Readership questions, as well as evaluation of and attitudes toward the product testing publications themselves were saved for the latter part of the questionnaire, as were the sometimes antagonizing demographic questions.

The American version of the questionnaire is reproduced in appendix G. The major topical areas are summarized in figure 3-4.

Fieldwork

Both the national mail and the metropolitan interview surveys were carried out during the first three months of 1970. This included two follow-up letters to the mail questionnaires spaced at two-week intervals. The mail survey had a gratifying response rate—in excess of 60 percent in both countries.

As will be remembered from the last section, the interview structure was practically identical with the mail questionnaire—the only difference being the omission of the "convenience goods" section from the mail survey. Nevertheless, the response rate of some of the metropolitan interview samples fell below expectations. The primary response rate of the general populations ("aver-

1	General Attitudes:	Planning Propensity
		Liberal-Conservative Attitude
		Business
		Government
		Opinion Leader
2	Durable Product:	Inventory of Durable Products Owned
		Specific Purchase Recall:
		Shopping Concerns
		Information Sources
		Experience with Product
		Planning for Purchase
		Role in Purchase Decision
		Post-Purchase Evaluation:
		Product
		Information
		Shopping Activity
		Shopping Effort
		Advertising
3	Automobile:	Inventory of Automobiles Owned
		Specific Purchase Recall:
		Shopping Concerns
		Information Sources
		Experience with Product
		Planning for Purchase
		Role in Purchase Decision
		Post-Purchase Evaluation:
		Product
		Information
		Shopping Activity
		Shopping Effort
		Advertising
4	Convenience Product:	Inventory of Convenience Products
		Regularly Purchased
	(This section not	Specific Brand Experience
	included in the mail	Post-Purchase Evaluation:
	questionnaires.)	Product
		Information
		Shopping Activity
		Shopping Effort
		Advertising
5	Media Usage:	Television
		Radio
		Newspapers
		Magazines
		Specific Advertising Attitudes
6	CI and Consumer	Consumer Policy Issues
	Policy Issues:	Sources of Product Testing Information
		Attitudes toward Product Tests and Agencies
		Product Testing versus Advertising
		Perceived Usage of Test Information
7	Demographic and	Sex of Respondent
	Socioeconomic Data:	Respondent's Age
		Marital Status
		Number of Children and Persons in Household
		Housing
		Years of Formal Education
		Occupation of Chief Wage Earner
		Family Income

Figure 3–4. Outline of Questionnaire Topics.

age consumers") of both Frankfurt and Indianapolis, of almost 70 percent, was satisfactory. But the 45 percent (approximate) response rate of subscribers to *Consumer Reports, DM* and *test* in metropolitan Indianapolis and Frankfurt respectively was disappointing.

The most important reason for the relatively low interview completion rate among subscribers can be found in the "not-at-home" category. The difficulty in reaching these respondents lay in the fact that only subscribers of record could be interviewed. The subscriber was in most instances also the breadwinner of the family, and it proved difficult to find him (her) at home for the interview, despite two call-backs at different times and the use of prior appointments whenever possible. Also disturbing, particularly in the Frankfurt survey, was a relatively high rate of outright refusal to cooperate by the subscribers (20 percent) and the fact that some respondents broke off the interview in the middle (6 percent). We were led to conclude that subscribers lead a busier life than average consumers, and that many were frustrated by the prospect of an hour-long interview. On the other hand, the response rate in the mail survey demonstrates that they were glad to cooperate given the change to schedule the job of filling in the questionnaire at their own convenience.

To obtain an adequate data base in the interview surveys, additional respondents from a reserve pool were used. In accordance with orthodox procedures, the addresses in the reserve pool had been randomly selected along with the primary respondents in anticipation of a possible shortfall. The possibility of a residual self-selection bias had to be taken into account, but the authors did not discover any consistent differences between the shortfall and the cooperating respondents. Our general assumption that the subscriber respondents represented a homogeneous group was supported by considerable evidence in the course of this project.

STATISTICAL TESTS AND DATA PRESENTATION

This book is written for policy makers, business executives, consumer sophisticates and the general reader. The fact that it is not limited to a scholarly audience does not mean that we have compromised orthodox standards of rigor in research and analysis—at least not knowingly. The standard statistical analysis used whenever applicable is the Mann-Whitney U test for determining whether the ranks given by one given group are consistently higher than those given by another. Otherwise the Chi Square (χ^2) test for any difference in distribution between groups is used. Thorough discussions of these well-known tests may be found in Siegel's *Nonparametric Statistics*. The outcome of the tests and the significance levels are everywhere given in the tables of chapters 4–6, and in a way unobtrusive enough to avoid confusion with the actual data. Since we are working with more than two samples in chapters 8–9, the resulting proliferation of tests precluded recording them in the tables. The size of the sample (or number of respondents) is given at the head of each table (or column, when required). The lay reader may be assured that whenever we use the word "significant" in the text, the finding in question is indeed "statistically significant" at at least the 0.05 significance level. Roughly, this means that chances are not more than 5 in 100 that the findings were due to chance.

To collapse the five-point attitude scales (ranging from "strongly agree" to "strongly disagree" with given questionnaire statements) for presentation in capsule yet meaningful form we frequently make use of a simple index (the first appears in table 4-2). The index is calculated by adding, for a given attitude question, the percentage of respondents who agreed or strongly agreed and subtracting from the total the percentage of respondents who disagreed or strongly disagreed. A positive index indicates a preponderance of agreement, a negative index means disagreement.[d] Katona and associates in a recent comparative study used a similar index.[15] It may be added that in several instances we found graphic presentations of rankings of index numbers and differences in index numbers particularly instructive (see tables 4-7 and 4-9).

The reader is cautioned that since the Mann-Whitney U and other statistical tests shown in our tables are based upon data utilizing the full five-part Likert scales, the test results may occasionally seem inconsistent with the simplified index numbers. We felt that this occasional confusion was a price worth paying for the simplification and clarity otherwise provided by the indexes.

SUMMARY

In this chapter the background for comparative study in marketing and consumer policy was discussed, including some of the problems, shortcomings and difficulties which frequently are encountered. A framework for analysis of individual country studies of consumer information in Germany and the United States was developed as well as a framework for cross-cultural comparison between the two countries. Sample and questionnaire design and other aspects of research methodology were discussed in some detail. The presentation of results and analysis follows. The American and German country studies are presented in chapters 4 and 5, respectively, and the comparison between the two is reserved for chapter 6.

NOTES TO CHAPTER 3

1. See Reavis Cox, "The Search for Universals in Comparative Studies of Domestic Marketing Systems," in Peter D. Bennett, ed., *Marketing and*

[d]The percentage of respondents who neither agreed nor disagreed does not enter the calculation of the index. Thus, a small index in some definitely extreme case might be due to a majority of respondents who neither agreed nor disagreed.

Economic Development: Proceedings of the 1965 Fall Conference of the American Marketing Association (Chicago: American Marketing Association, 1965): 147.

2. Jean Boddewyn, "The Comparative Approach to the Study of Business Administration," *The Academy of Management Journal* 8 (December 1965): 261.
3. Robert Bartels, "Are Domestic and International Marketing Dissimilar?" *Journal of Marketing* 32 (July 1968): 56–61.
4. Jean Boddewyn, "A Construct for Comparative Marketing Research," *Journal of Marketing Research* 3 (May 1966): 149–53.
5. See Hans B. Thorelli, "Organizational Theory: An Ecological View," *The Academy of Management Journal* 10 (December 1967): 68–83, and Thorelli, ed., *International Marketing Strategy* (London: Penguin Management Series, 1973): reading 1.
6. See George Katona, Burkhard Strumpel and Ernest Zahn, *Aspirations and Affluence—Comparative Studies in the United States and Western Europe* (New York: McGraw-Hill, 1971).
7. For a fuller development of the notion that mistake reduction may be a more suitable rationale of CI programs than hard-to-measure optimization of satisfaction, see Jack Engledow, "The Impact of *Consumer Reports* Ratings on Product Purchase and Post-Purchase Product Satisfaction," (DBA diss., Indiana University, 1971), chapter 3.
8. See also the first sections of chapters 4 and 5.
9. See Edward F. Denison, *Why Growth Rates Differ: Postwar Experience in Nine Western Countries* (Washington, D.C.: The Brookings Institution, 1967).
10. That this is preferable procedure is now broadly recognized. See Erwin K. Scheuch, "The Cross-cultural Use of Sample Surveys: Problems of Comparability," in Stein Rokkan, ed., *Comparative Research Across Cultures and Nations* (Paris: Mouton, 1968): 176–209.
11. Leslie Kish, *Survey Sampling* (New York: John Wiley & Sons, 1965): 20.
12. See A.N. Oppenheim, *Questionnaire Design and Attitude Measurement* (New York: Basic Books, Inc., 1966): 133.
13. A similar split sample technique was utilized by Bauer and Greyser in their 1966 study of the image of advertising in the United States, a study with which this project had some elements in common. See Raymond A. Bauer and Stephen A. Greyser, *Advertising in America: The Consumer View* (Boston, Mass.: Harvard University, Division of Research, Graduate School of Business Administration, 1968).
14. See Engledow: 120f, and also chapter 6.
15. Katona et al.: chapter 4.

Chapter Four

Product Test Reports and Their Users: The United States Study

Consumer Reports is a unique magazine. Although it has characteristics in common with the two German magazines covered in this study and with other CI publications, its character and philosophy are distinctly its own. It is suspected that the same may be true of readers and subscribers of *Consumer Reports*. It has already been conclusively demonstrated that these subscribers are different from the general population in several obvious socioeconomic characteristics.[a] It is probably true also that subscribers to *Consumer Reports* (*CR*) are different from average consumers in other more subtle, but equally interesting ways. This chapter will examine the how and why of some differences discovered in the study.

The purpose of chapters 4, 5 and 6 will be to explore the similarities and differences among the three product test reporting magazines in the study, and the similarities and differences among the subscribers to these magazines and their "average consumer" counterparts in each country. Chapters 4 and 5 will primarily be concerned with characterizing the Information Seeker in the United States and Germany respectively by contrasting him with the average consumer. Chapter 6 will then include the major findings of both these chapters and additional cross-cultural comparisons to examine the concept of "universals"– characteristics which may be common to the Information Seeker in whatever affluent economy he is found.

Cultural and environmental variances dictate that Germans differ substantially from Americans. An important question here, however, is whether the affluent market place and the culture of affluence contain enough international similarities to generate parallels in description, attitudes and behavior between German and American Information Seekers. This possibility will be one of the principal concerns of the next three chapters.

[a]The annual questionnaires to *Consumer Reports* subscribers have consistently indicated that subscribers are much higher than the general populace in income and education.

CONSUMER REPORTS AND CONSUMERS UNION—
A BRIEF CHARACTER SKETCH

Consumers Union is the largest, the second-oldest, and perhaps the most influential product testing and reporting agency in the world.[1] Its current annual budget of over $16 million probably equals the combined total budgetary resources of all similar agencies currently active in the world.[2] Circulation of *Consumer Reports* moved above two million in 1971, and is growing rapidly.

Although Consumers Union engages in a variety of consumer-related activities, including publishing books and pamphlets of consumer interest, consumer education, testifying at government hearings and modest lobbying, the main thrust of its work has always been product testing and reporting. Most of the product tests are conducted in Consumers Union's own laboratories and test facilities by their own personnel, though consultants are used for some specialized products. Between 75 and 100 products are tested annually, including most automobile makes and types, a wide range of small and large appliances and other durables, and a scattering of convenience goods, foodstuffs and services.

Tests and their results are reported in monthly issues of *Consumer Reports*, along with other articles of general buying advice and items of consumer interest. The December issue is the annual *Buying Guide*, a compendium of product tests and buying information, mostly condensed from regular issues of *Consumer Reports*. For most products, brands are rated Acceptable or Not Acceptable; the Acceptable brands are ranked based upon various price and quality criteria.

The primary distinguishing characteristic of Consumers Union from its beginning in 1937 to the present is its assiduous avoidance of any contact with business that might tarnish its reputation for impartiality. As an official of Consumers Union remarked jokingly but quite truthfully, "Here at Consumers Union credibility is our most important product." Consumers Union accepts no advertising, gifts or grants from commercial sources; products for testing are purchased at retail; and commercial use of any test results is not only strictly forbidden but fought spiritedly in the courts when it occurs. *Consumer Reports* is often chastized by businessmen for what they perceive as too-small samples, use of irrelevant evaluation criteria or omission of particular brands from consideration; but in general Consumers Union seems to have maintained its cherished reputation for unbiased reporting.[3] An excerpt from a recent court decision reads:

> Throughout the years it [CU] has been scrupulous in avoiding even the slightest affiliation with any commercial interest. Its most important asset is its good name for independence and accuracy; its reputation as an impartial and untainted adviser is the foundation upon which the public's confidence rests.[4]

Consumers Union is large, powerful, somewhat conservative, aloof from commercial interests, and a major spokesman for product testing and consumer causes nation- and world-wide. It seems to have gained a position of pre-eminent respectability in the growing field of consumer information.

THE *CONSUMER REPORTS* SUBSCRIBER AND THE AVERAGE METROPOLITAN CONSUMER: GENERAL CHARACTERISTICS

The average subscriber differs from the average consumer in that he "purchases" the information available in *Consumer Reports* on a continuing basis. It is a reasonable presumption, however, that subscription may be accompanied by, or may even influence, other attitudes and other behavior which distinguish the subscriber from the general populace in ways that have meaning to consumer and marketing policy-makers. The following sections will attempt to isolate such differences and comment on them in some detail.

It should be remembered that the interviewers asked the subjects each to walk through a series of actual purchase decisions, giving information on their behavior and attitudes during the purchase process. The results below compare the answers to those questions by the 101 subscribers in Indianapolis to those of the 200 randomly chosen consumers.[b]

Demographic and Socioeconomic Characteristics

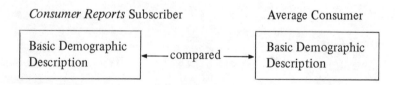

All empirical work has indicated that subscribers to and users of product test reports are an education and income "elite" group when compared to the general population. Table 4-1 lists several important demographic and socioeconomic variables. It is apparent that our subscriber conforms to the well established pattern of high income, education and social class. He is also more likely to be married, but not significantly different in age from the average consumer. He is substantially more likely to own each of a selected list of common durable goods.

In addition to these overall trends, some interesting differences stand out within individual characteristics:

[b]At the beginning of most sections in chapters 4 and 5, a diagram like the one just below will alert the reader as to what samples are being analyzed or compared, and what stage of the purchase decision model developed in chapter 2 is under consideration.

Table 4-1. Comparison of Subscribers and Average Consumers on Demographic and Socioeconomic Characteristics (Indianapolis Samples)

	Subscriber (Base = 101)	Average Consumer (Base = 200)	Significance[b] Test
Family Annual Income[a]			
$25,000 and over	5.9%	4.0%	
15,000–24,999	35.6	14.1	
10,000–14,999	31.7	24.6	MWU
5,000– 9,999	18.8	26.7	Subscriber Higher
Under $5,000	4.0	17.0	$p < .002$
No Answer	4.0	13.6	
	100.0%	100.0%	
Education of Head of Household[a]			
More than 16 years	21.8%	10.0%	
16 years	21.8	11.0	
13–15 years	18.8	19.0	MWU
12 years	27.7	33.5	Subscriber Higher
9–11 years	7.9	10.0	$p < .000$
Less than 9 years	2.0	16.5	
	100.0%	100.0%	
Occupation of Head of Household[a]			
Professional, Technical	33.6%	16.5%	
Manager, Proprietor	18.8	11.0	
Clerical, Sales	14.8	13.0	Chi Square
Craftsman, Foreman	13.9	17.5	$p < .01$
Operative, Laborer or Service Worker	11.0	23.5	
Retired and Unclassified	7.9	18.5	
	100.0%	100.0%	
Social Class[c]			
Duncan Scale			MWU
Mean Class Index	59.9	43.9	Subscriber Higher
			$p < .000$
Age of Respondent[a]			
Under 25	3.0%	15.0%	
25–34	25.7	21.0	
35–44	19.8	14.0	MWU
45–54	25.7	18.5	Subscriber Higher
55–64	15.8	16.5	(Older)
65 and over	10.0	15.0	$p < .29$
	100.0%	100.0%	
Marital Status of Respondent[a]			
Married	93.0%	79.0%	Chi Square
Single	3.0	8.0	$p < .01$
Widowed or Divorced	4.0	13.0	
	100.0%	100.0%	
Sex of Respondent[a]			
Male	91%	33%	Chi Square
Female	9	67	$p < .001$
	100%	100%	

Table 4-1 continued

Ownership of Selected Durable Goods[d] (Ranked by Percent of Subscriber Ownership)	Subscriber (Base = 101)		Average Consumer (Base = 200)	
Kitchen Range	91.0%		80.0%	
Refrigerator	90.0		82.0	
Black and White TV	89.0		80.0	
Automatic Washer	81.0		65.0	
Sewing Machine	81.0		70.0	
Clothes Dryer	78.0	Average	59.0	Average
Typewriter	74.0	Number	54.0	Number
Rotary Lawn Mower	71.0	Owned	59.0	Owned
Color TV	57.0	9.2	46.0	7.3
Stereo Receiver	57.0		42.0	
Room Air Conditioner	42.0		26.0	
Dishwasher	38.0		15.0	
Movie Camera	33.0		22.0	
Home Freezer	32.0		27.0	
Outboard Motor	16.0		10.0	
Autos				
At least one	100.0	Average	87.0	Average
At least two	59.0	Number	39.0	Number
At least three	10.0	Owned	7.0	Owned
At least four	0.0	1.7	2.0	1.3

[a]Data based upon questions in section 7 of questionnaire, reproduced in appendix G.

[b]Where applicable, The Mann-Whitney U test for determining higher groups is used. Otherwise the Chi square (χ^2) test for any difference in distribution is used. Thorough discussions of these tests may be found in Sidney Siegel, *Nonparametric Statistics for the Behavioral Sciences* (New York: McGraw-Hill, 1956).

[c]The Duncan Scale Index is an index of social class based solely upon occupational prestige. (Ratings range roughly from 0–100) For a complete listing and rating of occupations, see A.N. Oppenheim, *Questionnaire Design and Attitude Measurement* (New York: Free Press, 1961), appendix A.

[d]Data based on durable goods list in section 2 and automobile list in section 3 of the questionnaire.

1. In *Income*, though the subscribers outweigh the average consumer in all of the higher income categories, the most noticeable difference is not in the highest income group (over $25,000), but rather in the $15,000–24,999 category, where the percentage proportion of subscribers is two and one half times that of the average group. This tendency for subscribership to concentrate in the upper middle income groups will be explored further in later sections.

2. In *Education*, proportions of college graduate and post-graduate subscribers are more than double that of the average consumer, and only 2 percent have a grammar school education, as opposed to over 16 percent of average consumers. Unlike *Income*, differences here are clear throughout, with greatest differences at the "poles."

3. In *Occupation*, the subscriber is twice as likely to be a professional and half

as likely to be a laborer as the average consumer. Although proportions of managers are not as extreme, it is apparent from examination of individual job status rankings (not shown in the table) that the subscriber-manager interviewed in the study held a much more prestigious or responsible position in the firm than the average consumer-manager. (The mean Class Index of the subscriber-manager was 77 as contrasted with 59 for the average consumer-manager.)[5]

The characteristics of the consumer indicated in table 4-1 present a consistent picture of a subscriber who is far above average in both social and economic status. He owns more goods than the average consumer and has the income with which to buy more in the future. There is nothing in this picture to refute the current conventional wisdom about the subscriber.

Basic Attitudes of Interest

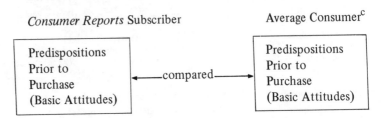

Consumer Reports Subscriber   Average Consumer[c]

Attitudes are generally assumed to be closely related to purchase behavior.[6] It seems helpful, then, to search for distinctive patterns of attitudes in purchase and information-related areas which may characterize the Information Seeker. Accordingly, respondents were asked to answer a series of introductory questions designed to measure attitudes toward general planfulness; liberalism (both from standpoint of confidence in the individual and attitude toward government and social action measures); new product adoption; opinion leadership; business; and advertising. Past speculation and a smattering of empirical work would have suggested that the subscriber should be more planful and more likely to be an opinion leader,[7] less favorable to business and advertising, and more liberal and sympathetic to social action by the government.[d]

The results of the attitude question comparisons are summarized in table 4-2.[8] In the opinion leader and planfulness sections, the subscriber fits

[c]The data in this section came from the general attitude questions which comprise section 1 of the questionnaire, reproduced in appendix G. The advertising attitude is based upon the single question: "On the whole, would you say that your attitude about advertising was favorable or unfavorable?" found in section 5. A much more complete look at attitudes toward advertising is contained in chapter 8.
[d]From the general editorial stance of *Consumer Reports* which is decidedly critical of business and advertising, and closely monitors (and generally favors) consumer-related legislation and regulation.

Table 4-2. General Attitude Comparisons[a] (Indianapolis Samples) (By Index Numbers)[b]

	Comparisons		
Attitude Questions	*Subscriber (Base = 101)*	*Average Consumer (Base = 200)*	*Higher Group and Significance[c]*
Planfulness			
Enjoy planning work	70	65	Sub
Better at getting value for money	18	-10	Sub**
Liberal-Conservative			
You can change human nature	11	-14	Sub*
Government should control business more	-42	-27	AC*
Students should have more power	-43	-32	AC**
Welfare does not cause less work	-50	-35	AC
Opinion Leadership			
Likely to influence group opinion	31	0	Sub**
Likely to be asked advice	6	-8	Sub
Early Adopter			
Usually tries brands before others	-19	-8	AC
Usually one of first to buy new product	-34	-24	AC
Business			
Businessmen as honest as others	55	41	Sub**
Business performs job rather well	27	14	Sub**
Advertising			
Overall attitude is favorable	48	66	AC**

[a]All data based upon questions taken from section 1 of questionnaire, reproduced in appendix G, except advertising attitude which is from section 5, question 6.

[b]Index = (% sample agree or strongly agree minus % sample disagree or strongly disagree). Positive index indicates general agreement, negative index means disagreement.

[c]Statistical significance by Mann-Whitney U Test· * $p < .05$; ** $p < .01$. See table 4-1, note b.

well with expectations. He is not, however, in the first wave of buyers for a new product, even though he feels he has strong influence on others' decisions once he enters the market. He envisions himself as a planner who gets more for his money than others.

In the liberal-conservative and business attitude dimensions the subscriber does not fit so comfortably into conventional molds. He is comparatively liberal as gauged by the strong screening question "You can change human nature," but is relatively cool toward government and social action measures generally associated with liberalism. (Later in the chapter, however, it will be found that the subscriber gives substantial backing to increased government activity in areas of direct consumer interest.) In addition, he is comparatively favorable toward business both as regards its general effectiveness and the honesty of individual businessmen. This was true even when the subscriber was compared to the high-income "average neighbor" sample (not shown in the table)—a surprising development given the decidedly critical editorial stance of *Consumer Reports*. Despite his generally favorable disposition toward business, however, the subscriber has a less favorable opinion of advertising. Though this reading is based upon a single question in the study, (see note c above) it is highly consistent with more detailed measurements that will be discussed in chapter 9.

When the attitude comparisons of this section are combined with the demographic data from the last, a generalized comparative picture of the *Consumer Reports* subscriber begins to emerge:[e]

> He forms an education-income elite group—somewhat cautious in economic matters—which is relatively critical of advertising as currently practiced, but maintains confidence in the general integrity of the individual businessman and efficiency of the business system. He is somewhat skeptical of government and social action schemes not involving consumer problems, but possesses the traditional liberal virtue of faith in the individual. Though not innovative in adopting new products, he plans purchases carefully and others turn to him for advice and influence once he has entered the market.

This picture has several interesting differences from the conventional image of the subscriber and is certainly far removed from the usual flaming-liberal, business-disdaining stereotype of the consumer activist which some are inclined to equate with subscribership. It is this cautious-influential, liberal-conservative, friend-critic of business whose behavior during the purchase process will now be compared to that of the average consumer.

Media Habits and Usage

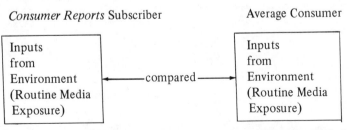

Consumer Reports Subscriber   Average Consumer

| Inputs from Environment (Routine Media Exposure) | compared | Inputs from Environment (Routine Media Exposure) |

[e]This is the first of a series of capsule summaries which will present the findings of each section in condensed, simplified form. The purpose is to sketch a cumulative picture of the Information Seeker as the results are presented.

What an individual buys in a given time period is a function of what he is (personality, social roles) and what he has (current product holdings, disposable income). But what he buys is also highly dependent upon what he *knows*. Product information is critical to locating and evaluating viable product alternatives.

Information about products flows into the purchase process experience based upon past exposure to products and information, as well as from casual screening of the environment in routine reading, observation and personal contacts. In a more purposeful way, information about a specific product decision may be generated by what in chapter 2 was called "external search." It was suggested there that external search varies dramatically from individual to individual and from purchase to purchase, probably depending upon the perceived cost and value of the information available and the perceived risk in the purchase situation. Product test reports were seen as a specialized information source entering the purchase process as a result of external search.

In the sections just above, it has been established that those most likely to be exposed to product test reports (the subscribers) constitute a rather unique group of consumers. Because of the decided differences in income and education alone between this group and the average consumer, it would be expected that the information-seeking habits and routine media exposure of the two groups are quite different.

In any given purchase decision, then, we would expect that a subscriber will come armed with a bundle of information that substantially differs from an average consumer's, and has more similarities to a fellow-subscriber's than only a high probability of exposure to *Consumer Reports*. This section will be devoted to discussing some differences in these information bundles as estimated by media exposure perceptions in the study.[f] A secondary purpose is to comment upon the extent to which *CR* routinely finds its way into the information mix of the average consumer. More detailed perceptions of actual information sources used in purchases will be treated in the following section.

Income-education differences suggest that the subscriber should be exposed to more media overall; that he should spend proportionately more time with printed than broadcast media; that he should be less interested in advertising in any media; and that he should subscribe to and read more decidedly "high-brow" magazines. A summary of some of the media exposure data is contained in table 4-3. As in the demographic data, there is little here to dispute the predicted results. The subscriber basically reads more and listens less than the average consumer. He reads more newspapers per day and both subscribes to and regularly reads more magazines than the average consumer, even after *Consumer Reports* is removed from the data.

[f]Here, as in other areas of the study, *perceptions* of respondents are used rather than actual behavior. The potential inaccuracy of perceptions in documenting behavior is acknowledged, but no practical means currently exists for measuring actual behavior in most areas covered.

**Table 4-3.   Comparison of Perceived Exposure to Various Media[a]
(Indianapolis Samples) (In percent)**

	Subscriber (Base = 101)	Average Consumer (Base = 200)	Significance Tests[b]
Television			
No viewing	0%	3%	
1-6 hours per week	31	21	MWU
7-18 hours per week	37	31	AC Higher
19 or more hours per week	32	45	$p < .02$
Radio			
No listening	2%	11%	
1-6 hours per week	54	32	MWU
7-18 hours per week	27	18	AC Higher
19 or more hours per week	17	39	$p < .05$
Newspapers			
None read	2%	8%	
1 per day	54	64	MWU
2 per day	37	27	Sub. Higher
3 or more per day	7	1	$p < .01$

	Number of Magazines per Respondent	
	Subscriber	Average Consumer
Magazines		
Subscribe to:		
Including *Consumer Reports*	2.2	.9
Excluding *Consumer Reports*	1.2	.7
Read regularly:		
Including *Consumer Reports*	2.3	1.1
Excluding *Consumer Reports*	1.4	1.0

[a]Data taken from section 5 of the questionnaire, reproduced in appendix G.
[b]See table 4-1, note b.

There are also few surprises in the magazine readership data shown in table 4-4. The subscribers are comparatively more inclined to read the "highbrow" *New Yorker, Atlantic Monthly* and *Playboy* (if this be "high-brow") and are less likely to read "lower-brow" magazines such as *Woman's Day, TV Guide* and *Modern Romances*. As a sidelight, however, it is interesting to note that when subscribers were compared to the matched "neighbor of a subscriber" sample, two striking differences emerged:

1. A tendency of subscribers toward *higher* readership of and/or subscription to consumer-oriented magazines such as *Good Housekeeping*—long noted for its

Table 4-4. American Magazines—Ranked by Percentage Reading Regularly or Occasionally[a] (Indianapolis Samples) (*Consumer Reports* Excluded from Ranking)

Subscriber (Base = 101)		*Average Consumer (Base = 200)*	
1. Reader's Digest	78%	1. Reader's Digest	71%
2. Life	57	2. Life	54
3. Playboy	43	3. Good Housekeeping	44
4. Good Housekeeping	41	4. TV Guide	38
5. Mechanics Illustrated	31	5. Woman's Day	36
6. Family Circle	30	6. Family Circle	35
7. Woman's Day	26	7. Playboy	25
8. New Yorker	19	8. Mechanics Illustrated	21
9. TV Guide	19	9. Modern Romances	10
10. Atlantic Monthly	11	10. New Yorker	10
11. Modern Romances	3	11. Atlantic Monthly	3

(Consumer Reports ranked 1st–perceived readership: 100%.)

(Consumer Reports ranked 7th–perceived readership: 28%.)

[a]This is the first of several similar tables in chapters 4, 5 and 6 which display relative ranks on some characteristic of interest. A word of explanation may be helpful. For both subscribers and average consumers the items are listed in rank order of decreasing importance, along with the applicable percentage. (*Reader's Digest* is read most by subscribers–78%, followed by *Life*–57%, etc.) Like items are then connected with a line which accentuates their relative rank in the two groups. A horizontal line represents identical ranking, with more acute angles indicating greater difference in relative rank. The connecting lines add nothing to the data, but are a quick and convenient way of calling attention to and keeping track of interesting differences and similarities.

Seal of Approval; and *Mechanics Illustrated*—which is strongly committed to discussions of new products and automotive innovations.

2. Much *less* readership of *TV Guide*, following the general trend of lack of interest in television and its advertising by subscribers.

Exposure to *Consumer Reports* of the Average Consumer

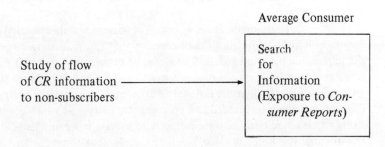

Since only a small percentage of the households in the country at a given time (about 3 percent for *Consumer Reports* at this writing) are likely to subscribe to product testing magazines, efficient research design dictated that this study concentrate on tracing the input of this information chiefly through subscribers, who are assumed to be the most intense users. It is obvious, however, that product test reports reach readers other than subscribers (by way of news-stand sales, borrowed copies and other means) and that information about the reports is transmitted by personal contact. Various attempts have been made to trace such non-subscriber inputs, but most have been made using highly tenuous assumptions and/or data.[9] With this in mind, the average consumer was given several chances in the questionnaire to mention *Consumer Reports* as a source of product information.

Early in the interview, while reconstructing purchase behavior on a recent durable goods and automobile purchase, he was asked to cite (by unaided recall in the American study) any important sources of information used in purchase. Later, respondents were asked if they knew any sources for information from comparative product tests (which was defined for them). Finally, after all purchase and attitude data had been gathered, they were asked a series of direct questions concerning their knowledge of and perceived exposure to *Consumer Reports*. The results of these various lines of questioning are presented in table 4-5, in the order mentioned above.

Although it is difficult to evaluate the quantitative worth of these questions, it is obvious that there is considerable general knowledge of *CR* on the part of the population as a whole. Twenty percent of all respondents named *Consumer Reports* spontaneously as a source of test reports; under direct questioning 22 percent claimed to be either subscribers or to know a great deal about the magazine, and 29 percent said that the magazine is read or consulted in their households once a year or more. The claim by non-subscribers that borrowing is the most frequent method of exposure is substantiated by responses of subscribers, 60 percent of whom "keep copies indefinitely" with a similar percentage sometimes lending copies or passing them along altogether. It seems that once information is published in *CR*, it remains available for comparatively long periods of time and is shared by subscribers with another 20 percent of the population who are aware of its existence and who think highly enough of it to read or consult it on occasion.

Even though there is a consistent pattern in data collected under varying conditions throughout the interviews that approximately 20 percent of the population has good general knowledge of *Consumer Reports*, it seems prudent always to view such results conservatively. There is evidence from this and previous studies that the rational decision-making associated with use of *Consumer Reports* is regarded as a prestigious activity, one which consumers are likely either consciously or unconsciously to overstate in response to direct questioning. It is noted in table 4-5, for example, that 18 respondents (9 percent) of the average consumer sample identified themselves as subscribers, a fact

Table 4-5.   Knowledge and Use of *Consumer Reports*[a] (Indianapolis Average Consumer Sample)

A. *Mention of* Consumer Reports *by Unaided Recall*
Mentioned *CR* as important information source in specific purchase:

Durable Goods Purchase	(Base = 152)	3%
Automobile Purchase	(Base = 171)	2%
Mentioned *CR* as source of information on comparative product tests	(Base = 200)	20%

B. *Direct Questioning on* Consumer Reports

How much do you know about *CR*?	(Base = 200)	
I am a subscriber		9%
I know a great deal about it		13
I have glanced through it or talked about it with friends		28
I have heard the name–nothing more		23
I have never heard of it		28
		100%

Non-Subscribers Only (Base = 182)

	Almost Every Month	More Than Once Per Year, Not Each Month	Maybe Once Per Year
Do you ever buy *CR* at a newsstand?	1%	3%	3%
Do you ever look at or borrow *CR* at a library?	1	5	4
Do you ever borrow *CR* from friends or relatives	1	12	6
In all, how often would you say *CR* is read in your household?	2	20	7

[a]Data in A based upon "information source" question 5 in sections 2 and 3 plus question 3 in section 6. Data in B based upon questions 8–12 in section 6. Questionnaire reproduced in appendix G.

which at first had alarming implications for the accuracy of the sampling techniques used, since it was three times the expected percentage of subscribers in a truly random sample. A check with subscriber lists of *Consumer Reports*, however, identified only 5 of the 18 as actual subscribers shortly after the interviews; and although some small discrepancies due to lapsed subscriptions might have been expected, it is clear that a remarkably broad definition of subscription must have been used by some respondents. In an earlier experience with pre-test questions in Indianapolis, 97 percent of a sample of husbands from relatively high-income families professed to read *CR* "some," another figure which seems exaggerated given the limited circulation of the magazine.[10] This result led to a questionnaire design which carefully avoided any direct or indirect reference to *CR* until all buying behavior and attitude data had been collected.

THE *CONSUMER REPORTS* SUBSCRIBER AND
THE AVERAGE METROPOLITAN CONSUMER:
BUYING BEHAVIOR AND INFORMATION USE

The above sections dealing with demographic characteristics, attitudes and media usage, all derived from sections of the interview where the same general questions were asked of all the respondents. In the sections which follow, the emphasis shifts to recall of specific *personal* purchase situations by the individual. It will be recalled from chapter 3 that individuals were asked if they had made recent purchases of a durable good (from a selected list), an auto, and a convenience good (from a selected list). Then in each case where they had made a purchase, they were asked to trace their *latest* purchase through the buying process by answering a series of detailed questions. Specific questions involved identification of important shopping criteria and important information sources, various satisfaction measures, information on previous experience, amount of planning, personal role in purchase and other relevant purchase data including the nature of the product finally bought. In the sections below, therefore, all data are based upon the individuals' perceptions of their actual attitudes and behavior in *specific* buying situations. Since it seems important to set the stage by identifying the number and nature of purchases included, this section will start out of sequence by taking a look at actual purchases—the culmination of the process. Subsequent sections will then move back to the previously established format of examining the buying process in sequence by looking at aspects of Evaluation of Alternatives and Revised Predispositions.

Products Purchased

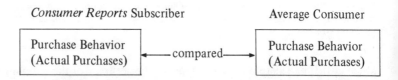

Consumer Reports Subscriber   Average Consumer

Purchase Behavior (Actual Purchases) ◄— compared —► Purchase Behavior (Actual Purchases)

A few of the respondents in each sample were eliminated from the questioning because they had made no recent purchase during the time specified in the interview, so that in this section most questions were answered by less than the full samples. In most instances percentages in tables will be based upon actual number of purchasers as follows:

	Total Sample	Purchased Durable Good	Purchased Auto	Purchased Convenience Good
Subscribers	101	83	99	99
Average Consumers	200	152	171	195

Some attempt was made in the United States study to estimate the impact of *CR* ratings on sales by comparing all purchases in both samples with brands recommended in the ratings. The number of brands and models rated coupled with other complexities and comparatively small sample sizes made analysis unfeasible for autos and inconclusive for durable goods. In convenience goods, however, subscribers did tend to prefer the brands recommended by *Consumer Reports* (see table 4-6). Of 15 convenience goods included, subscribers preferred the brands more highly rated by *Consumer Reports* on 12, with 6 of the 12 at statistically significant levels. Given the fact that convenience goods are generally considered low risk items with consequent low information search activity by buyers, the strength of this relationship was not expected. Results of this limited test indicate that subscribers may follow the recommendations of *Consumer Reports* to a measurable extent even for such common purchases as dish detergent and floor wax.[11] A larger-scale test designed to gauge the proportionate impact of *Consumer Reports* ratings and recommendations on durable goods and auto sales would seem worthwhile, given the growth of *CR* circulation and this hint of its importance in brand selection. The failure of this study to isolate significant relationships may be more a function of sample size than of lack of actual impact.

It is also interesting to note the relative importance in "buying

Table 4-6. Preference for Brands Recommended by *Consumer Reports*: Selected Convenience Goods[a] Subscribers and Average Consumers Compared (Indianapolis Samples)

Product	Low Group With Significance[b]
Dish Detergent	Subscriber **
Insect Repellent	Subscriber **
Floor Wax	Subscriber *
Tennis Balls	Subscriber *
Bourbon	Subscriber *
Hair Spray	Subscriber *
Hand Lotion	Subscriber
Beer	Subscriber
Suntan Lotion	Subscriber
Shampoo	Subscriber
Fabric Softener	Subscriber
Furniture Polish	Subscriber
Paper Towels	Average Consumer
Auto Polish	Average Consumer
Frozen Fruit Pies	Average Consumer

[a]Data based upon convenience goods preference list at beginning of section 4. Questionnaire reproduced in appendix G.

[b]Low group indicates sample with greater tendency to follow ratings of *Consumer Reports*. Significance levels based upon Mann-Whitney U Test: * $p < .05$; ** $p < .01$.

power" of the subscriber group suggested by the study. As might be expected because of their higher income, the subscribers have a substantially higher inventory of durable goods than the AC. Of the 15 selected durable goods in the study as shown in table 4-1 above, subscribers own an average of 9.2, while the AC owns 7.3. As was noted in discussion of demographic characteristics, percentage ownership of each of the selected items is higher in the subscriber sample, with the largest proportionate differences in products which are fairly new and/ or have reached only limited concentration in the population as a whole (clothes dryers, dishwashers). Interestingly, subscribers were also higher than their "average neighbor" (comparisons not shown in chart) in percentage ownership of every item in the list but one (rotary mowers) although differences were much smaller. This higher ownership pattern also carries into autos, where subscribers own a mean of 1.7 cars, while the average consumer owns 1.3. Subscribers' autos are a year newer overall.

There is a further suggestion in this section, then, that although information from *Consumer Reports* reaches but a limited percentage of consumers directly, it may substantially affect the behavior of those whom it reaches and that they are well above average in the number and dollar importance of purchases made.

Having made these general observations on the number and nature of actual purchases made by respondents in the study, the commentary will now take a step backward to examine in some detail the way in which the purchases in question were made, particularly regarding shopping criteria and product information sources used.

Shopping Criteria

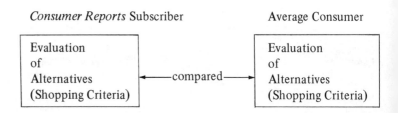

The product ultimately selected by a consumer is a function of many variables, but certainly among the most important are the *choice criteria* (durability, price, etc.) upon which he elects to evaluate various alternatives and the information which he accumulates regarding the fit of various alternatives to those selected criteria. It might logically be expected that information sources are selected at least partially in accordance with choice criteria the consumer sees as important. It was noted in chapter 2 that perceived risk theory suggests that information is sought out in accordance with the nature of the risk seen by the buyer in a given purchase situation, and that *CR* information is more attuned to evaluating performance than psycho-social style buying criteria.[12] It might be expected that those who routinely turn to *Consumer Reports* for advice are more likely to be "rational" shoppers who prefer technical and economic criteria, and less likely to be "emotional" shoppers who are more concerned with the psycho-social aspects of products.

In both the durable goods and autos section of the questionnaire respondents were asked about their perceptions of the importance of a series of common shopping criteria. These included the usual performance and economic based concerns, as well as ones more concerned with convenience and style, plus a criterion of our own—availability of information about product (make). The 13 criteria listed in figure 4-1 where they are divided into categories along with the authors' preconceptions as to how subscribers might be expected to differ from average consumers. As the figure indicates, it was expected that the subscribers would be particularly concerned with specific performance and economic related criteria, less interested in styling and shopping convenience and more information sensitive than the average consumer. Since subscribers have higher income and more credit options available, and the credit decision is "detachable" from the product decision, it was expected to be less important to the subscriber. It has been frequently postulated that brand and dealer reputation are relied upon as proxies of quality and performance by those who lack the skill or inclination to

Figure 4-1. Shopping Criteria Used in Study.

General Category and Specific Criteria	*Expected Relative Importance to Subscriber*
Performance, Economic and Service	
1. Performance of Product (Make)	
2. Durability	
3. Service after Purchase	High
4. Warranty	
5. Price and/or Trade-in Allowance	
6. Economy of Operation	
General	
1. Brand's General Reputation	Low
2. Reputation of Dealer	
Styling and Shopping Convenience	
1. Styling of Product (Make)	
2. Availability (in stock for immediate delivery)	Low
3. Location of Dealer	
Credit	
1. Credit Terms Available	Low
Information Sensitivity	
1. Availability of Information about Product	High

use more detailed individual criteria (low income groups in particular). It was thus expected that the high-income subscribers with high propensity to seek out and use product information would find such generalized criteria much less useful.

Tables 4-7 and 4-8 summarize the findings regarding shopping criteria. A word of explanation on the tables themselves may be helpful. Once again, index numbers are used. Part A of each table shows the perceived relative importance of each criterion *within* each group. Table 4-7A for instance, indi-

**Table 4-7. Shopping Criteria–Durable Goods Purchase[a]
(Indianapolis Samples)**

Subscribers (Base = 83)				Average Consumers (Base = 152)		
Rank	*Criterion*	*Index*		*Rank*	*Criterion*	*Index*
A. Ranked by Index Numbers[b]						
1.	Durability	94		1.	Durability	89
2.	Performance	93		2.	Performance	85
3.	Brand Reputation	87		3.	Service	76
4.	Service	78		4.	Warranty	76
5.	Information Availability	78		5.	Dealer Reputation	73
6.	Warranty	72		6.	Brand Reputation	64
7.	Dealer Reputation	71		7.	Price	58
8.	Price	49		8.	Availability of Product	57
9.	Availability of Product	35		9.	Information Availability	52
10.	Style	22		10.	Style	43
11.	Economy	16		11.	Economy	41
12.	Location of Dealer	-2		12.	Location of Dealer	18
13.	Credit	-51		13.	Credit	-7

	Subscribers compared to Average Consumers				
	40	20	0	20	40
B. Ranked by Differences in Index Number[b]					
Information Availability			(26)		Criteria
Brand Reputation			(23)		more
Performance			(8)		important
Durability			(5)		to
Service			(2)		Subscribers
Dealer Reputation			(2)		
Warranty	Criteria		(4)		
Price	more		(9)		
Location of Dealer	important		(20)		
Style	to		(21)		
Availability of Product	Average		(22)		
Economy	Consumers		(25)		
Credit			(44)		

[a]Data based on question 4 in section 2 of questionnaire, reproduced in appendix G.

[b]Index = (% of sample rating important or very important minus % unimportant or very unimportant). Positive Index indicates important criterion, negative unimportant.

cates that both subscribers and AC perceived durability as the *most* important single criterion and credit availability as *least* important (though degree of importance differed). As before, sloped lines represent differences in rank between groups. In Part B of each table, differences in relative importance *between* groups are emphasized, so that interesting patterns in these differences may be identified and evaluated. In table 4-7B, information availability had an "importance index" of 78 to subscribers, but only 52 to AC. It shows the great-

Table 4-8. Shopping Criteria–Auto Purchase[a] (Indianapolis Samples)

Subscribers (Base = 99)			Average Consumers (Base = 171)		
Rank	*Criterion*	*Index*	*Rank*	*Criterion*	*Index*
A. Ranked by Index Numbers[b]					
1.	Performance	97	1.	Performance	92
2.	Brand Reputation	92	2.	Durability	86
3.	Durability	91	3.	Brand Reputation	84
4.	Price	88	4.	Price	84
5.	Service	68	5.	Service	77
6.	Information Availability	66	6.	Economy	73
7.	Style	63	7.	Warranty	68
8.	Warranty	62	8.	Dealer Reputation	65
9.	Economy	56	9.	Style	62
10.	Dealer Reputation	52	10.	Information Availability	62
11.	Availability of Product	31	11.	Availability of Product	46
12.	Location of Dealer	13	12.	Credit	20
13.	Credit	-47	13.	Location of Dealer	13

	Subscribers compared to Average Consumers				
	20	10	0	10	20
B. Ranked by Differences in Index Numbers[b]					
Brand Reputation			(8)		Criteria
Performance			(5)		more
Durability			(5)		important
Price			(4)		to
Information Availability			(4)		Subscribers
Style			(1)		
Location of Dealer			(0)	(0)	
Warranty	Criteria		(6)		
Service	more		(9)		
Dealer Reputation	important		(13)		
Availability of Product	to		(15)		
Economy	Average		(17)		
Credit	Consumer		(67)		67

[a]Data based on question 4, section 3 of questionnaire, reproduced in appendix G.
[b]Index = (% sample rating important or very important minus % sample unimportant or very unimportant).

est difference (26) of the five criteria rated more important by subscribers. Credit had an importance index of –51 for subscribers and –7 for AC. The difference of 44 is the greatest among the eight characteristics relatively more important to the average consumer. This general format will be used for several tables in this and later sections.

An overview of the shopping criteria used for both the auto and durable goods purchases suggests the following:

1. In the "absolute" sense, *the two groups have more similarities than differences* in their approach to decision criteria. Performance and durability are perceived as the most important characteristics and availability of products, location of dealer and credit the least important for both products and both groups. Performance, economic and service criteria tend overall to be most important, with styling and convenience less important;

2. Overall, *subscribers* are consistently more interested than other consumers in the *performance–economic–service* criteria and less interested in style–convenience considerations, as expected, though importance of individual criteria varies between the durables and auto purchases;

3. *Price* is a far greater concern, both absolutely and proportionately, in autos than in durable goods;[g]

4. *Information availability* is a strong concern of the subscriber, but in both an absolute and a comparative sense, it is a much more important factor in durable goods purchases than in auto purchases;

5. The *generalized reputation criteria*-brand and dealer-are among the most "volatile," (showing differences between samples) with brand reputation consistently regarded by subscribers as a comparatively important criterion, and with dealer reputation less important;

6. *Economy of operation* was generally lightly regarded by both groups as a shopping criterion, but unlike the case in most of the other performance-economic criteria, subscribers were even less concerned than other consumers;

7. *Credit* was, as noted, the least important criterion to both groups, but it also showed the greatest percentage difference between groups for both purchases. Subscribers are obviously very little worried about credit as a shopping criterion;

8. Overall, there would seem to be a tendency of subscribers to favor shopping criteria which are functional and longer term, while average consumers are relatively more interested in shorter-term and psycho-socially oriented qualities.

[g]There may be some ambiguity involved in evaluating price as a shopping criterion. Price alone may be less important to the sophisticated shopper than price/quality = value. There is also some possible confusion over whether price as a criterion means shopping for a low-priced model group, or shopping for the lowest price *within* any given model group.

In brief, then we might sketch some further detail into our cumulative picture of the *Consumer Reports* subscriber as follows:

He has the basic features of the traditional economic man: he tends to shop using "rational" shopping criteria, concerned with price, performance and service rather than with those catering to convenience and style. He is sensitive to information availability, particularly in the durable goods area, where purchases are less frequent and his available stock of experience is less likely to be adequate and timely. The economic man picture is, however, not completely consistent, since, perhaps because of his affluence or his valuation of time, he eschews economy of operation as a primary criterion, and (quite unlike *CR* itself) perceives himself as placing heavy reliance on brand reputation.

Armed with this overview of the standards by which subscribers and consumers perceive that they judged their products in the study, along with some notion from previous sections on their routine exposure to common media, the discussion will now turn to the information sources actually sought out and used in the purchases.

Perceived Information Sources

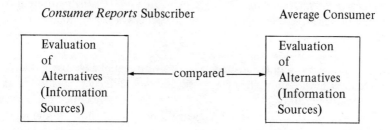

Since product information and its use are the major concerns of this book, there has been extensive discussion of the "mix" of information which is used by a given consumer in making a given purchase. In chapter 2, there was a discussion of risk and cost-value considerations as determinants of information sought, and some speculation about the suitability of general types of information sources to certain types of shopping criteria. In the media habits sections results were presented which gave clues as to routine exposure to various common media by subscribers and average consumers. The data presented in this section reflect the consumers' best judgements as to what sources they used and considered important in some actual purchase situations. Answers were given by unaided recall (no list was used); respondents were allowed to give as many answers as they wished; and interviewers coded responses into the following categories:

Personal Sources
1. Past Experience (Use)
2. Personal Observation and Examination
3. Friend, Relative or Acquaintance

Commercial Sources
1. Advertising
2. Salesman

Independent Sources
1. *Consumer Reports*
2. Other Magazine or Newspaper Articles
3. Other Consumer Magazines.

It was expected that subscribers would show far more use of independent sources and less use of commercial sources. The high educational level and social status of subscribers and the general confidence in controlling personal outcomes and high personal experience with products which usually accompanies these levels also suggested that personal sources might be of more relative importance.

As is apparent from tables 4-9 and 4-10, results were not entirely consistent with these expectations. As anticipated in this highly biased sample, the largest single difference between the groups was in perceived usage of *Consumer Reports*. Other within-group rankings are not strikingly different for either purchase. In considering overall differences *between* groups, however, two interesting patterns emerge:

1. Although subscribers are decidedly more critical of advertising than all other groups in the study, they are consistently more likely to mention it as an important source of information. This trend was even more pronounced in comparing subscribers to "average neighbors" (not shown in the tables);
2. Despite the high educational and social standings of subscribers, they perceive themselves as substantially *less* reliant upon personal judgement (experience, observation) than other consumers; this trend was also more pronounced when subscribers were compared to their equally-high-income, high-status "average neighbors."

These observations add another dimension to the characterization of the subscriber:

He sees himself as using the information available from *Consumer Reports* (a point which will be documented in more detail in the next section) and other independent sources. Despite a less favorable general attitude toward advertising, he uses it more, suggesting that he puts it to a more critical and selective use than the average consumer. Whether from some lack of general self-confidence or a better

Table 4-9. Information Sources–Durable Goods Purchase[a] (Indianapolis Samples)

Subscribers (Base = 83)			Average Consumers (Base = 152)		
Rank	Source	Index	Rank	Source	Index
A. Ranked by Index Number– Unaided Recall[b]					
1.	Consumer Reports	33	1.	Personal Observation	51
2.	Personal Observation	31	2.	Past Experience	25
3.	Friend, Relative, etc.	24	3.	Friend, Relative, etc.	18
4.	Advertising	20	4.	Salesman	16
5.	Past Experience	18	5.	Advertising	13
6.	Salesman	16	6.	Other Mags. or Newsp.	3
7.	Other Mags. or Newsp.	6	7.	Consumer Reports	3
8.	Other Consumer Mags.	1	8.	Other Consumer Mags.	0
	(Other Sources	25)		(Other Sources	13)

	Subscribers compared to Average Consumers				
	40	20	0	20	40
B. Ranked by Differences in Index Numbers[b]					
Consumer Reports			(30)	Sources more important to Subscribers	
Advertising			(7)		
Friend, Relative, etc.			(6)		
Other Magazines			(3)		
Other Consumer Mags.			(1)		
Salesman			(0) (0)		
Past Experience	Sources more important to AC		(7)		
Personal Observation			(20)		

[a]Data based upon question 5, section 2 of questionnaire, reproduced in appendix G.

[b]Index = (% sample ranking important or very important minus % sample unimportant or very unimportant).

recognition of the complexity of product evaluation, he places less reliance on personal experience and observation in the decision process.

Consumer Reports as an Information Source

Consumer Reports Subscriber

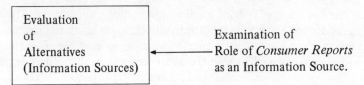

Evaluation of Alternatives (Information Sources)	←	Examination of Role of *Consumer Reports* as an Information Source.

Table 4-10.   Information Sources–Auto Purchase[a] (Indianapolis Samples)

Subscribers (Base = 99)			Average Consumers (Base = 171)		
Rank	Source	Index	Rank	Source	Index
A. Ranked by Index Number–Unaided Recall[b]					
1.	Past Experience	39	1.	Personal Observation	41
2.	Personal Observation	33	2.	Past Experience	39
3.	Friend, Relative, etc.	26	3.	Friend, Relative, etc.	30
4.	*Consumer Reports*	13	4.	Advertising	11
5.	Advertising	13	5.	Salesman	13
6.	Salesman	7	6.	Other Mags. or Newsp.	5
7.	Other Mags. or Newsp.	-2	7.	*Consumer Reports*	2
8.	Other Consumer Mags.	1	8.	Other Consumer Mags.	0
	(Other Sources	15)		(Other Sources	12)

Subscribers compared to Average Consumers

	20	10	0	10	20
B. Ranked by Differences in Index Number[b]				Sources	
Consumer Reports			(11)	more important	
Advertising			(2)	to	
Other Consumer Mags.			(1)	Subscribers	
Past Experience			(0) (0)		
Friend, Relative, etc.		Sources	(4)		
Salesman		more important	(6)		
Other Mags. or Newsp.		to AC	(7)		
Personal Observation			(8)		

[a]Data from question 5, section 3 of questionnaire, reproduced in appendix G.
[b]Index = (% sample rating important or very important minus % unimportant or very unimportant).

After all of the purchase and attitude questions in the study had been asked, each individual who had made a purchase was presented with a series of direct questions on his knowledge and use of *Consumer Reports* ratings in his particular purchases. The results of this questioning are summarized in table 4-11.

Naturally enough, the subscriber perceived awareness and use are far higher than those of the average consumer. More interestingly, use in durable goods purchases is significantly higher than in autos, confirming the trend shown in the discussion of unaided recall of information sources above. This was true for all United States samples. Apparently the complexity and psycho-social aspects of the auto purchase coupled with greater available experience (personal and shared) make reliance on *Consumer Reports* less likely, despite the obvious

Table 4-11. Awareness and Use of *Consumer Reports* Recommendations[a] (Indianapolis Samples) (By Percent of Actual Purchasers in Each Group)

	Durable		Auto		Convenience	
	Aware of Recommendations	Used in Purchase	Aware of Recommendations	Used in Purchase	Aware of Recommendations	Used in Purchase
Subscriber	53	41	41	28	16	7
Average Consumer	12	10	8	5	4	1

[a]Data taken from questions 38 and 39 in section 6 of questionnaire, reproduced in appendix G.

financial importance of an auto purchase.[h] In the low price, usually low risk convenience goods, both awareness and use are least, even though this study earlier detected a significant trend to purchase recommended brands in some convenience goods tested by *CR*.

Using these questions on awareness and perceived use of the ratings, after excluding those who made no purchase, it was possible to divide subscribers into two groups for each purchase situation:

1. *Perceived Users*—those who knew the recommendation of *Consumer Reports* for the product under consideration, and thought that the recommendation was important in the final decision;
2. *Perceived Non-users*—those who either did not know of the *CR* recommendation or considered it unimportant.

Such a division allows some insights into situations in which *CR* information is actually put into use. Comparison of non-users with users for the purchases in the study suggested the following conclusions: [13]

1. The more important the product to the purchaser, the more likely that *CR* recommendations will be considered;
2. The greater the amount of planning carried out for the purchase, the more likely that *CR* will be used;
3. The relation between past buying experience with the product and use of

[h]Given the stress placed upon auto test reporting in *CR* and the high price of autos relative to other durables, this finding was somewhat unexpected. The annual auto issue of *CR* is consistently the largest selling single issue of the year, with very heavy newsstand sales.

ratings is not clear cut, but there is some suggestion that greater purchase experience implies *more* use of *CR* ratings;

4. Subscribers with more favorable attitude toward *Consumer Reports* are more likely to use the ratings in any given purchase;
5. There is high overlap of use. Those who use the ratings to make a durables purchase are more likely to also use them for convenience and autos purchases as well, etc.;
6. Once again, subscriber-users in any given purchase situation tend to be of higher income and educational levels than subscriber non-users.

The only one of these findings contrary to past findings is the experience–use relation. It is normally assumed that information search and use is in part a substitute for buying experience and that those who have more experience will seek out less "new" information. The findings here leave some suggestion that at least for this information-sensitive subscriber group, experience may serve to whet the appetite for more detailed information in future purchases.

The subscriber's use of recommendations does not seem to be random or universal but selective in a way that might be broadly characterized as follows:

> He tends to use the ratings most for durable purchases, some for autos, and occasionally for convenience goods. He is more likely to use the ratings the more important the product, the more favorable his general attitude toward *Consumer Reports*, the higher his income and educational level, and perhaps the greater his previous purchase experience with the product.

Satisfaction and the Use of *Consumer Reports*

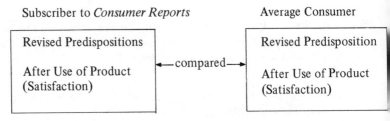

It is generally assumed that greater shopping activity and use of "better" product information should lead to more satisfaction with purchases finally made. Because information from *Consumer Reports* is regarded as something of a model of factual, rational information, and because it requires a comparatively great amount of effort to assimilate, the use of such information should presumably lead to more satisfied consumers. To check this proposition, several measures of satisfaction were included in the purchase sections of the questionnaire. Specific questions dealt with: satisfaction with the product itself; satisfaction with available information; and satisfaction with personal shopping activities in connection with the purchase.

Since subscription to *CR* seems to be accompanied by use of its ratings, a possible hypothesis is that subscribers would therefore be better satisfied on all dimensions than non-subscribers. Table 4–12A suggests that just the opposite is true. The majority of the measures of satisfaction made for all items purchased show the subscribers to be *less* satisfied than the average consumer. If this table were interpreted to mean that greater use of *CR* information leads to less satisfaction with products purchased, it would deal a major blow to those who propose product test reports as a partial answer to the product information problem. But a slightly different set of comparisons helps to throw a much different light on the same set of questions:

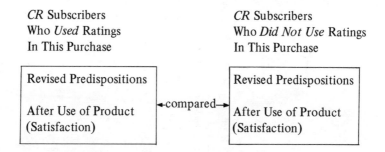

The results, shown in table 4–12B, summarize comparisons between perceived users of the *CR* recommendations and perceived non-users within the subscribers sample only. The pattern of results here is dramatically different from that in table 4–12A, consistently suggesting that users are *better* satisfied with products and purchase procedures than those who do not use the ratings. Similar comparisons made within the average consumer and matched neighbor samples showed the same strong patterns, but the number of perceived users was too small to justify their inclusion here.

These results, when combined, suggest two important conclusions:

1. Subscribers are harder to satisfy than the average consumer. Satisfaction is based upon two highly subjective and volatile cognitive constructs: the individual's aspiration level and his evaluation of outcomes. The fact that subscribers are generally less satisfied than their neighbors and fellow consumers suggests that they must have higher expectations for products, or more stringent performance criteria, or both;
2. Satisfaction is increased when the subscriber perceives himself as having used the recommendations of *Consumer Reports*. In the limited sample included

Table 4-12.   Selected Satisfaction Measures[a] (Indianapolis Samples) (By Index Numbers)[b]

	Durable Goods Purchase			Auto Purchase		
	Subscribers	Average Consumers	Higher Group[c]	Subscribers	Average Consumers	Higher Group[c]
A. Subscribers vs. Average Consumers	(Base = 83)	(Base = 152)		(Base = 99)	(Base = 171)	
Product						
Turned out to be all I expected	73	78	AC	68	57	Sub.
I would recommend to a friend	73	75	AC	66	77	AC
Information Availability						
Little trouble finding how brands differ	19	18	Sub.	35	60	AC
Plenty of information available	52	49	Sub.	49	58	AC
Personal Shopping Activity						
Even with more information–no better brand	70	64	Sub.	42	58	AC
Shopped enough to get lowest price	42	41	Sub.	32	45	AC
Safety						
This brand is safe to use	93	91	Sub.	60	91	AC
Advertising						
Advertising was accurate and helpful	40	41	AC	-10	7	AC

B. Perceived Users vs. Non-Users	Durable Goods Purchase			Auto Purchase		
	User	Non-User	Higher Group	User	Non-User	Higher Group
	(Base = 40)	(Base = 59)		(Base = 44)	(Base = 39)	
Product						
Turned out to be all I expected	80	66	U	78	62	U
Would recommend to a friend	80	66	U	85	53	U*
Information Availability						
Little trouble finding how brands differ	23	15	U	43	31	U
Plenty of information available	55	49	U	63	41	U
Personal Shopping Activity						
Even with more information, no better brand	80	59	U*	43	43	Tie
Shopped enough to get lowest price	59	23	U*	35	31	U
Safety						
This brand is safe to use	89	97	N	78	85	N
Advertising						
Advertising was accurate and helpful	39	49	N	0	-17	U

[a] Data based on questions 8-17 in sections 2 and 3 and questions 4-13 in section 4 of the questionnaire reproduced in Appendix G.

[b] Index = (% sample rating agree or strongly agree minus % disagree or strongly disagree).

[c] Statistical significance based upon Mann-Whitney U Test.

* $p < .05$; ** $p < .01$. Note absence of significant results in part A.

here this increase applied to satisfaction with thoroughness of personal shopping activity as well as with the product itself.

So to the growing picture of the subscriber, the following might be added:

He is a picky consumer, hard to satisfy in the marketplace, but he finds *CR* recommendations helpful in increasing his satisfaction in any given purchase.

THE *CONSUMER REPORTS* SUBSCRIBER AND THE AVERAGE CONSUMER: ATTITUDES TOWARD CONSUMER POLICY ISSUES

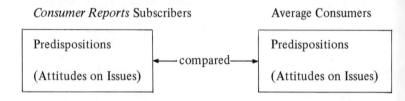

The consumer movement has stirred much discussion about what should be done about the "dilemma of the consumer" in a complex and affluent economy. There has been an outpouring of proposals on means of aiding the consumer by both public and private organizations. As was mentioned at the beginning of this chapter, Consumers Union has always been a major spokesman for consumerist causes; except for direct lobbying, CU has been perhaps *the* major spokesman in the United States over time. Steady readers are given a continuous commentary upon the status of various consumer problems and proposed solutions along with more specific information on product testing.

It might be expected, then, that subscribers are among the better informed individuals on consumer policy issues; and, because of their professional and social standing, should also have the potential to be highly influential in this area. It has already been established that subscribers seem to be far from the business-baiting, flaming liberal school of consumerists. It should be interesting to discover some attitudes toward key consumerist issues of this well-informed, potentially influential group with reasonably strong pro-private enterprise feelings, but likewise strong interest in consumer concerns.

Respondents were asked to examine a list of seven frequently-proposed ways of helping the consumer. They were then asked to mention those which they would "like to see more of," ranking those mentioned in order of importance. Finally, they were asked for their opinion on government involvement in each of the seven areas. The results as shown in tables 4-13 and 4-14 suggest the following conclusions:

1. Subscribers are greater consumer "activists" than average consumers. They want more general activity than average consumers on four of the seven measures listed, and desire greater *government* activity on all but one;
2. Subscribers tend to be relatively more interested in having available "self activated" information such as labeling, product testing, quality certification and minimum quality standards—all of which fall under the CI definition established in chapter 1. Average consumers show more concern with "action" measures where someone else is responsible for preventing or right-

Table 4-13. Need for Increase Overall Activity in Selected Consumer Policy Areas[a] (Indianapolis Samples)

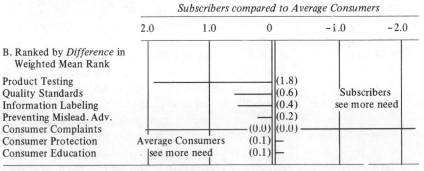

Subscriber	Weighted Mean Rank[b]	Average Consumer	Weighted Mean Rank[b]
A. Listed by Weighted Mean Rank			
1. Product Testing	4.8	1. Preventing Mislead. Adv.	3.7
2. Preventing Mislead. Adv.	3.9	2. Product Testing	3.0
3. Information Labeling	3.3	3. Consumer Production	3.0
4. Consumer Production	2.9	4. Information Labeling	2.9
5. Quality Standards	2.9	5. Consumer Complaints	2.7
6. Consumer Complaints	2.7	6. Consumer Education	2.4
7. Consumer Education	2.3	7. Quality Standards	2.3

Subscribers compared to Average Consumers

	2.0	1.0	0	-1.0	-2.0
B. Ranked by *Difference* in Weighted Mean Rank					
Product Testing			(1.8)		
Quality Standards			(0.6)	Subscribers	
Information Labeling			(0.4)	see more need	
Preventing Mislead. Adv.			(0.2)		
Consumer Complaints			(0.0) (0.0)		
Consumer Protection	Average Consumers	(0.1)			
Consumer Education	see more need	(0.1)			

[a]Data taken from question 1, section 6 of questionnaire, reproduced in appendix G.
[b]Ranks adjusted so that highest ranking given highest number. Highest rank attainable = 7, Lowest rank = 1. Weighted Mean = Proportion of sample mentioning multiplied by the mean rank given. Example: 81% of subscriber sample mentioned Product Testing and gave it a mean rank of 5.9. (.81 X 5.9 = 4.8 Weighted Mean Rank.)

Table 4-14. Need for Government Activity in Selected Consumer Policy Areas[a] (Indianapolis Samples)

Consumer Reports *Subscribers*			*Average Consumers*		
Rank Activity		*Index*	*Rank Activity*		*Index*
A. Ranked by Index Numbers[b]					
1.	Product Testing	69	1.	Misleading Advertising	47
2.	Misleading Advertising	66	2.	Consumer Complaints	45
3.	Min. Quality Standards	53	3.	Min. Quality Standards	42
4.	Information Labeling	47	4.	Product Testing	40
5.	Consumer Complaints	40	5.	Information Labeling	32
6.	Consumer Protection	32	6.	Consumer Protection	28
7.	Consumer Education	28	7.	Consumer Education	23

Subscribers compared to Average Consumers

	40	20	0	20	40
B. Ranked by Differences in Index Numbers[b]					
Product Testing				(29)	More need seen by Subscribers
Misleading Advertising				(19)	
Information Labeling				(15)	
Min. Quality Standards				(11)	
Consumer Education				(5)	
Consumer Protection				(4)	
Consumer Complaints		AC see more need	(5)		

[a]Data taken from question 2, section 6 of questionnaire, reproduced in appendix G.
[b]Index = (% sample answering *too little* government activity minus % *too much*).

ing consumer grievances (helping with complaints, consumer protection, etc.). This same emphasis holds for the government involvement section as well;

3. Subscribers are loyal to product testing as a desirable consumer-help activity. Differences between subscribers and average consumers are highest here, and subscribers are more interested in increased government activity in this area than in any other. Paradoxically, in response to another question, subscribers showed no confidence whatever in product tests conducted by the government alone. They professed greatest confidence in tests performed by a consumer group alone (53 percent) and next most to a consumer group *aided* by the government (25 percent) or business (10 percent). The general skepticism earlier shown toward government activities which control business seems to hold to some extent when specifics are considered even though the subscriber does opt for increased government involvement overall;

4. Consumer education in the schools generates the least enthusiasm of any of the proposed measures. It ranks lowest in percentage mentioned for both

samples, last in desire for increased government activity, and highest in percentage of "don't know" or "no opinion." Despite the contention of some consumer experts that this may be one of the best long-range consumer policy measures, it seems to have comparatively little popular support.[i]

The consumerist stance of the subscriber as shown in this part of the study might be briefly characterized as follows:

> He is something of a consumer activist, showing interest in increased activity over a broad range of consumer help measures, both by government and private initiative. In keeping with his information sensitive nature, he has the greatest enthusiasm for measures which would bring him additional information (testing, labeling, product quality standards) or more truthful information (preventing misleading advertising) and least enthusiasm for measures which would bring him help from outside sources (protection, help with complaints, etc.). He has particular confidence in product testing, presumably based upon his experience with *CR*.

SUMMARY AND CONCLUSION: THE COMPLEAT AMERICAN INFORMATION SEEKER

In this chapter an attempt has been made to summarize a substantial number of comparisons between a selected group of subscribers to *Consumer Reports* in the Indianapolis area and a random sample of consumers in the same area. The intent was to isolate interesting differences between the two groups in demographic characteristics, attitudes and behavior, with the goal of sketching a basic portrait of a subscriber. It is expected, however, that the finished portrait may have significance beyond a simple characterization of the readers of a particular magazine. In a broader sense, the affluent, critical consumer identified here may well be the first wave of a sizable new breed of consumers spawned by affluence, more education, and increasing general interest in consumer problems. We call them the Information Seekers.

Having gradually revealed a large number of comparisons and comments in a rather long chapter, we think it worthwhile to pull the various threads together. Broadly, the results of this chapter seem to characterize the *CR* subscriber (whom we think we may call the American Information Seeker) as follows:

1. *He forms an education and income elite.* He has higher income and education

[i]This may be tied up with the fact that consumer education is an ill-defined area, perhaps most often envisioned as some offshoot of classroom home economics. It is obvious that consumer education can (and probably should) be defined much more broadly and imaginatively than this if it is to be a major weapon in improving the lot of the consumer.

than his neighbors in the matched sample, *much* higher than the populace
as a whole. The higher his income and education, the more likely he is to use
CR information. He also tends to have higher social status than his immediate
neighbors and is slightly older and more likely to be married;

2. *He is information-sensitive in general and product and consumer information
sensitive in particular.* He reads more newspapers, subscribes to and reads
more magazines, and is generally more sensitive to the problem of information
availability and more critical of advertising than average consumers. He is,
however, somewhat less likely to expose himself to radio and TV; he is
particularly attracted to media with content directed to consumer and product activities and information, and has great interest in increased product
testing and labeling;

3. *He is a curious blend of liberal–conservative.* In a general way, he expresses
belief in the integrity of the individual and honesty and efficiency of business. Yet in a more specific context he is less amenable to such government
activities as welfare and government "control" over business, but more
favorable toward government involvement in almost all consumer related
activities—obviously to some extent at the expense of business;

4. *He is a "rational" buyer in the traditional sense.* He plans more and is cautious
at accepting new products (though envisioning himself as rather influential
over others in this regard). He uses more utilitarian, performance-related
choice criteria in shopping, and finds price particularly important in buying
the more expensive autos, despite his clear edge in income. He has less
interest in criteria more generally involved with esthetics, status and convenience. He sets great stock in outside, "rational" information sources
(particularly *Consumer Reports*) and is less likely to rely upon his own
judgment as formulated either from past experience or personal observation;

5. *He is committed to* Consumer Reports. He reads it far more regularly than
any other magazine to which he subscribes; he sees himself as using it quite
frequently and buying the brands it recommends (most often in the purchase
of durable goods, least in convenience). He expresses satisfaction with its
performance on all counts and would like to see more activity in the product
testing area overall;

6. *He has high standards as a buyer.* He is more critical in all types of buying
situations, not only with regard to products themselves and availability of
information about them, but also about his own efforts at shopping;

7. *He reduces his mistakes in purchase as a result of using* Consumer Reports
ratings. When he uses the ratings, he is better satisfied with the products he
purchases. He is also better satisfied with information available in the purchase situation when *Consumer Reports* is involved, and better satisfied
with his own shopping efforts;

8. *He is a consumer "activist."* He supports increases in a broad range of consumer policy activities, giving the most confidence to product testing and

least to consumer education. He is generally favorable to government involvement in these areas, particularly in product testing and information labeling, but expresses no confidence in tests run solely by the government. After Consumers Union style consumer organizations, he would favor government–consumer combines then government–business combines for testing activities.

Sketched in the broadest possible strokes, this is the picture of the subscriber–user–Information Seeker drawn from this array of results. A similar picture of the German subscriber–Information Seeker will be drawn in the next chapter. Building on the country studies, chapter 6 will then compare the national mail subscriber samples and speculate upon the extent to which results warrant the assumption that the Information Seeker is in ascendancy: an international intercultural product of the affluent, educated, consumer goods society.

NOTES TO CHAPTER 4

1. A more detailed and analytical examination of Consumers Union and other CI agencies is contained in Hans B. and Sarah V. Thorelli, *Consumer Information Handbook: Europe and North America* (New York: Praeger, 1974).
2. *Handbook*: 420–48.
3. See Eugene Beem and John Ewing, "Business Appraises Consumer Testing Agencies," *Harvard Business Review* 32 (March-April 1954): 113–26, and "Consumer Reports: Read, Respected, and Feared," *The National Observer* (February 26, 1968).
4. Judge Robert C. Zampano, United States District Court. *Consumers Union of the United States, Inc. vs Theodore Hamm Brewing Co.*, 314 F. Supp. 697 (1970): 700.
5. These index numbers are Duncan Scale Indexes, in which any given occupation is rated (from 0 to 100) in social prestige. See table 4–1, note c.
6. An interesting discussion of the soundness of empirical justification for this assumption is contained in Kristian Palda, "The Hypothesis of a Hierarchy of Effects: A Partial Evaluation," *Journal of Marketing Research* 3 (February 1966): 13–24.
7. See Reuben Hill, "Judgement and Consumership in the Management of Family Resources," *Sociology and Social Research* 47 (July 1963): 451.
8. For an explanation of the index numbers, see chapter 3, p. 56.
9. For a discussion of some attempts to evaluate exposure to *CR*, see Jack Engledow, "The Impact of *Consumer Reports* Ratings on Product Purchase and Post-Purchase Product Satisfaction," (DBA diss., Indiana University, 1971), chapter 1.
10. From test questions administered in September 1968 as part of Family Behavior Project, an 11-month longitudinal study of buying behavior in Indianapolis; supervised by Ronald P. Willett, Donald G. Granbois

and Ronald A. Stephenson of the Graduate School of Business, Indiana University.

11. For a discussion of some possible competing explanations, see Engledow: 208.

12. David M. Cox, ed., *Risk Taking and Information Handling in Consumer Behavior* (Boston: Harvard University, Division of Research, Graduate School of Business Administration, 1967): 604, 607–8.

13. Substantiating data are not shown here, but may be found in Engledow: 186–99.

Chapter Five

Product Test Reports and Their Users: The German Study

The German phase of the project was complicated by the fact that, unlike in the United States phase, it included two consumer organizations and their publications—*DM* and *test*. Of the two, *DM* is the more colorful magazine and *test* the more conservative, but both are fairly similar in consumer information content. The inclusion of the two magazines—rather than only one—presented a challenge in research design. It also offered a unique opportunity to enrich the study by examining subscribers to magazines whose content is similar, but whose sponsoring organizations are quite dissimilar.

The first section of this chapter contains a brief description of the agencies which publish *DM* and *test*. The remainder then compares subscribers to these magazines with average consumers on the basis of demographic characteristics, attitudes, purchase behavior and information use. The presentation and analysis follow, whenever possible, the precedents set in the American country study in chapter 4, so that the reader can easily compare the two.

TWO GERMAN CONSUMER INFORMATION MAGAZINES

DM and *test* are not vastly dissimilar from *Consumer Reports*, but they are unique magazines in Germany. Both assert their independence from industry or specific manufacturers of goods or dispensers of services, from governments and interest groups other than consumers. The avowed objective of both organizations is to serve both consumers and the public interest, primarily by disseminating various forms of consumer information. Comparative product test reports are regularly featured in both magazines and indeed comprise a major ingredient of their repertoires.

DM

DM is the older, and in 1970 it was certainly the better known, of the two magazines in Germany. Founded in 1961, *DM* quickly rose to success, increasing its monthly circulation to 700,000 within three years. Its fortunes faded with equal rapidity, however, and declining sales and increasing operating losses forced the company to file for bankruptcy in 1966. A Frankfurt publisher picked up the pieces later that year; and, although the magazine has been unable to regain its former popularity, *DM* circulation seems to have stabilized at 150,000. Most copies are sold through newsstands, but subscription sales accounted for over 24,000 copies at the time of the survey in Spring, 1970; and that figure was expected to grow in the years ahead.

Compared to other consumer information and product test reporting publications, *DM* is unique in at least two respects. First, *DM* is published by a privately owned and operated company; as such, one of the firm's presumed long-term objectives is to earn a profit on its consumer information venture. Although this goal had not been met at the time of this study, a breakeven level of operations was reportedly reached in 1972.

On a modest circulation base like that of *DM*, the profitability of almost any publication would seem to be suspect if sales revenues were not supplemented by advertising revenues. In fact, the inclusion of advertising side by side with other types of product information is the second unique feature of *DM*. In 1969 advertising comprised 30–35 percent of *DM*'s content and contributed 50 percent of its operating revenues. Charges of "partiality" are countered by *DM* management with the assertion that advertising neither interferes with nor influences its product test reports and other consumer information; and, apparently, *DM* does not shy from publishing reports on its own advertisers—both favorable and unfavorable. The advertisers in turn have management's blanket permission to incorporate product test results and other information in their advertisements.

test

In contrast to *DM*, *test* is published by a non-commercial, non-profit, government-sponsored organization in Berlin called the *Stiftung Warentest*. The *Stiftung* began operations in 1965 and since then has grown into a respected agency. Its consumer magazine, *test*, has gained a reputation for objectivity, accuracy and fairness in reporting, and has become remarkably influential among other consumer organizations in and outside Germany   at the time of the survey *test* was mailed to some 34,000 subscribers—the number growing at a monthly rate of 5 percent. More recently, this magazine has also been made available for sale on newsstands.

The emphasis of *test* is clearly on comparative product testing, with over 60 reports annually; but many other topics, features and information of general and specific consumer interest occupy a substantial proportion of its content. The *Stiftung*, largely financed by public means, views itself as a public interest agency and, as such, excludes advertisements from all its publications as a matter of policy. In addition to distributing *test*, the *Stiftung* disseminates consumer information through other media, including radio, TV and the daily press. Other magazines may obtain the *Stiftung*'s permission to reprint product test reports either in full or in condensed versions. The information which originates from this organization thus reaches many more segments of the consuming public than is reflected in the *test* circulation figures alone.[1]

Aside from the presence of advertisements in *DM*, the content and purpose of *DM* and *test* do not appear to differ too much from each other. *Test*, not unlike *Consumer Reports*, allows for more prominent and extensive coverage of comparative product test reports relative to other consumer information. Since 1967 *DM* has commissioned few comparative product tests on its own, mainly because of the increasingly high costs of the testing procedures; but along with its own test reports *DM* regularly features three to five condensed versions and summaries of product test results from *test* in every issue. *DM* and *test* have achieved leadership in the consumer information field in Germany by competing with and complementing each other's efforts.

We hypothesized from the outset that "subscribers to product testing information" would represent, at least demographically, a relatively homogeneous subgroup of the consumer population, irrespective of the particular magazine involved. This hypothesis was consistently confirmed in subsequent analysis of *DM* and *test* subscribers, and the interested reader may wish to turn to the "no difference" test between the two in appendix E for details. For the purpose of this chapter, the subscribers of *DM* and *test*, in combination, comprise our population of German Information Seekers to be compared and contrasted to the general population of average consumers.

THE SUBSCRIBER AND THE AVERAGE
METROPOLITAN CONSUMER:
GENERAL CHARACTERISTICS

The basic and most obvious difference between average consumers and subscribers is the fact that the latter continuously buy and (presumably) use specific types of consumer information—information not so readily available to the former. This difference was defined and then built into the research design by randomly selecting a subscriber sample, from the Frankfurt subscription lists provided by the *DM* and *test* organizations respectively, and an average consumer sample from the general population residing within the Frankfurt city limits. The remainder of this chapter is concerned with comparisons between this subscriber and the average metropolitan consumer in the German cultural and economic setting. Differences between *DM* and *test* respondents will be pointed out where this seems of interest.[2]

Demographic and Socioeconomic Characteristics

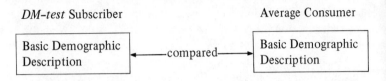

DM–test Subscriber   Average Consumer

As measured by conventional socioeconomic criteria, it was expected that subscribers would exhibit higher social status than AC. As the data in table 5-1 show, the subscribers did in fact have a greater income and more education and were situated in higher level occupational positions. The two groups were not much different from each other in household size and the number of children in the family.

In addition to these broad differences, a few subtle ones can be deduced from the data.

1. *Income.* The income differences between subscribers and AC were particularly evident at the extremes of the income distribution. AC respondents were concentrated in the lower income brackets. In the upper income categories subscribers exceeded AC proportionately by a two-to-one margin. Both groups were equally represented in the middle segments. Clearly, the income distribution of subscribers was skewed toward the higher side and that of the AC toward the lower end of the scale. However, the higher overall personal income in metropolitan areas in Germany compared to national averages was reflected in both Frankfurt samples.[3] The relatively large proportion of "no answers" to the income question on the part of all respondents is indicative of the reluctance to divulge so secretive a matter as one's personal income—a reaction typical of German culture.
2. *Education. DM* and *test* subscribers also form an educational elite. None of the subscriber respondents had less than nine years of formal education, compared to 26 percent of the AC. On the other extreme, the proportion of subscribers having completed 16 or more years of formal education was 2.5 times that of AC. Respondents in the study reflected a close correlation between income and education; the differences between the two groups attained their sharpest focus at the polar extremes of the distribution.
3. *Occupation.* The higher income and education on the part of subscriber respondents were mirrored again by the fact that more than half of the subscriber sample was included in the managerial and professional occupations, compared to a third of the AC sample; average consumers were represented by a larger proportion of craftsmen, service workers and retired individuals.

Table 5-1.   Comparison of Subscribers and Average Consumers on Demographic and Socioeconomic Characteristics (Frankfurt Samples)

	Subscriber (Base = 97)	Average Consumer (Base = 198)	Significance Test [b]
Family Net Income Per Month[a]			
2500 D-Marks and more	18%	9%	
2000–2499 D-Marks	15	8	MWU
1500–1999 D-Marks	18	16	Subscribers higher
1000–1499 D-Marks	21	24	$p < .00$
Under 1000 D-Marks	2	20	
No answer	26	23	
	100%	100%	
Education of Head of Household[a]			
16 years and more	30%	12%	
13–15 years	19	14	MWU
12 years	7	7	Subscribers higher
9–11 years	44	41	$p < .00$
Under 9 years	0	26	
	100%	100%	
Occupation of Head of Household[a]			
Professional, technical	28%	26%	
Proprietor, manager, official	24	9	
Clerical, sales	22	14	Chi Square
Craftsman, foreman, service	4	14	$p < .01$
Operative, laborer	10	9	
Retired, others	4	10	
No answer, not classified	8	18	
	100%	100%	
Age of Respondent[a]			
Under 25 years of age	4%	15%	
25–34	28	31	MWU
35–44	32	21	Subscribers older
45–54	17	17	$p < .04$
55–64	14	11	
65 years and over	5	5	
	100%	100%	
Marital Status of Respondent[a]			
Married	87%	69%	
Single	10	23	Chi Square
Widowed, divorced	3	8	$p < .01$
	100%	100%	
Sex of Respondent[a]			
Male	75%	48%	Chi Square
Female	25	52	$p < .01$
	100%	100%	

(continued)

Table 5-1 continued

	Subscriber (Base = 97)		Average Consumer (Base = 198)	
Ownership of Selected Durable Goods[c] (Ranked by Percent of Subscriber Ownership)				
Refrigerator	98%		89%	
Vacuum Cleaner	91		81	
Kitchen Range	88		81	
Typewriter	72		50	
Black and White TV	70		76	
Automatic Washer	65	Average	64	Average
Sewing Machine	58	Number	55	Number
Tape recorder	49	Owned	33	Owned
Stereo receiver	34	7.5	19	6.3
Movie camera	33		16	
Color TV	16		7	
Power mower	13		12	
Freezer	12		15	
Ironing Machine	11		11	
Dishwasher	11		9	
Autos				
At least one	72%	Average	55%	Average
At least two	10	Number	5	Number
At least three	2	Owned	0	Owned
At least four	0	.9	0	.6

[a]Data based on questions in section 7 of questionnaire, reproduced in appendix G.
[b]Where applicable, the Mann-Whitney U test (MWU) for determining the higher group is used. Otherwise, the Chi Square test (χ^2) for any difference in distribution is used.
[c]Data based on durable goods list in section 2 and automobile list in section 3 of questionnaire.

The mean class index used in the American study does not apply to the occupational distribution in Germany because of the cross-cultural limitations of the Duncan scale.[4] Even without it, the evidence from the data clearly points out the fact that subscribers to both *DM* and *test* are entrenched in higher level and more prestigious positions than AC.

Compared to the average consumer, the picture of the subscriber we get from the Frankfurt sample thus far is fairly consistent with the conventional impressions one gains from readership surveys of *test* and *DM* subscribers.[5] The subscriber is an individual who has above average income and education and has a commensurate position in life. He is somewhat older than the average consumer and more likely to be married; he more often owns costly items from a selective list of durable consumer goods. There is no difference, however, in the size of his household and in the number of children in his family.

Basic Attitudes of Interest

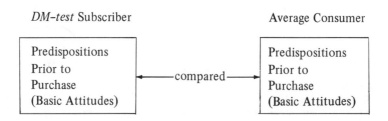

Some individuals, unlike others, seem naturally inclined to explore things, to investigate opportunities, to compare alternatives. This tendency may be reflected in a propensity to systematically search for and gather information prior to the purchase of a product—a process modified by environmental factors and by personal characteristics such as experience, perceptions and attitudes. Based on the very fact of their subscription, the German Information Seekers were expected to represent a segment of the consuming public that seeks and uses information as a matter of inclination. To the extent that the purchase activities of individuals are linked to and influenced by certain basic attitudes, it follows that subscribers differ from average consumers in the attitudinal patterns relevant to information search and use.

The German respondents were asked to answer the same attitudinal questions as their American counterparts on planfulness, liberalism, new product adoption, opinion leadership, business, and advertising.[6]

The data, presented in table 5-2, fit well into the established mold of the Information Seeker in several ways but not so well in others. For example, the German subscriber, as anticipated, perceives himself as a better planner; and he believes he is getting better value for his money. He also views himself as an opinion leader, although he is not necessarily more adventurous in seeking out new products. Although he may not be the first one to try new products, the subscriber generally feels that his advice is sought by others when it comes to product purchases.

The subscriber also tends to be selectively conservative or liberal, depending on the issue involved. For instance, the conservative, pro-business and advertising attitude exhibited by the metropolitan subscribers may be characteristic of their professional and managerial occupations; but their liberal attitude toward government control of business and industry stands in sharp contrast to this. While approving greater student power, they agree that welfare reduces work output. However, as measured by the screening statement, "You can change human nature," both AC and subscribers project a conservative image

Table 5-2.   General Attitude Comparisons[a] (Frankfurt Samples) (By Index Numbers)[b]

Attitude Questions	Subscribers (Base = 97)	Average Consumers (Base = 198)	Higher Group and Significance[c]
Planfulness			
Enjoy planning work	54	51	Sub.
Better at getting value for money	29	-24	Sub. **
Liberal–Conservative			
You can change human nature	-17	-33	Sub.
Government should control business more	46	21	Sub. **
Students should have more power	28	31	AC
Welfare does not cause less work	-19	23	AC **
Opinion Leadership			
Likely to influence group opinion	15	-5	Sub. **
Likely to be asked advice	34	9	Sub. **
Early Adopter			
Usually tries brands before others	-1	14	AC
Usually one of first to buy new product	-21	-33	Sub.
Business			
Businessmen are as honest as others	23	17	Sub.
Business performs its job well	14	-4	Sub. *
Advertising			
Overall attitude is favorable	41	38	Sub.

[a]Data based on questions from section 1 of questionnaire, except advertising attitude, which is from section 5, question 6.

[b]Index = (% sample agree or strongly agree minus % sample disagree or strongly disagree). Positive index indicates general agreement, negative index general disagreement, with the statement.

[c]Statistical significance based on Mann-Whitney U test. $* p < .05; ** p < .01$. See table 5-1, note b.

perhaps typical of Germans in general. It may be noted here that average consumers were slightly more conservative in this respect.

At this point, the following comparative image of the German subscriber can be sketched:

> He is an individual of relatively high social standing with above average income and education who cannot easily be stereotyped as a conservative or liberal. On the contrary, he shows the ability to dis-

criminate between issues and thus may take a contradictory stance in his attitudes. He may seem to have confidence in the integrity and performance of business and the merits of advertising in general, but he also envisions the necessity for increased government control of the industrial sector. Although he does not set himself apart from the average consumer in his degree of innovativeness, the subscriber carefully plans his purchases, is asked for purchase advice, and perceives himself as an opinion leader.

This picture of the subscriber may only partly agree with one's preconceived notions about the Information Seeker as a person subscribing to either *DM* or *test*. For instance, it is interesting to note that respondents were positively inclined toward advertising, even though both publications tend to be editorially critical of it. This finding may hint at the intellectual independence of the subscriber who, as an educated individual, makes up his own mind about the pros and cons of an issue or problem. An independence in thinking is also reflected in the individualistic attitudes toward social responsibility, student power and business and government relationships, which swing freely between conservative and liberal. The attitudes of average consumers tend to be more consistently conservative or liberal. As an aside it may be mentioned that the *DM–test* subscriber differences on most attitudes were minor (not shown in table) and in any case were far less than the attitudinal differences between AC and average subscribers.

Media Habits and Usage

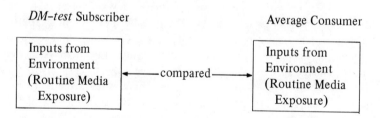

DM–test Subscriber   Average Consumer

Inputs from Environment (Routine Media Exposure) ←— compared —→ Inputs from Environment (Routine Media Exposure)

Individual market segments are likely to be exposed to varying types of information of different content and intensity. Although media usage per se cannot be equated with the utilization of information in consumer decision making, media habits can give realistic clues as to *perceived* information usage in terms of the nature, relevance and timeliness of the sources from which it was derived.

Inasmuch as the German subscriber was not like the AC in several socioeconomic characteristics, one would expect him to reflect certain media usage patterns typical of higher education-income consumer segments. In general, this means that subscribers should read more while average consumers should listen to the radio more often and watch more television.

The average consumer in the sample did indeed indicate that he spends a greater number of hours per week in front of his television set. (See table 5-3). For example, 20 percent of the AC said they watched 19 or more hours of television per week, compared to 10 percent of the subscribers. The data from the survey thus confirm what one would hypothesize on the basis of other findings on leisure time activities in Germany. But considering the fact of television's market penetration to over 80 percent of German households, it is surprising that 13 percent of the subscriber respondents claimed that they never watch any television—proportionately twice the number of average consumers. Contrary to expectations, AC listen little more to the radio than do subscribers. But the Frankfurt data clearly bear out the fact that metropolitan consumers in general spend more time watching television than listening to radios.

The Information Seeker as a member of the education-income elite acquires much information through reading. As expected, the German subscriber expressed a greater avocation for reading than the average consumer. Subscribers indicated more frequent regular reading of a greater number of daily newspapers and of various magazines. In fact, the Information Seeker reads 2.1 magazines on the average and subscribes to 1.7 of them, including *DM* and *test*. Even excluding *DM* and *test* from the tabulation, his rate of subscription is double and his readership 1.5 times that of the AC.

The differences in reading patterns shows neither the depth, nor the extent or type of reading involved within the respective newspapers or magazines —what may be called the quality of media use. However, inasmuch as subscribers exceed average consumers in reading quantity, they are at least exposed to much information which can aid in the purchase decision process in a variety of ways. Such information may include items of general consumer and economic interest, shopping tips and advice, legal developments and company news, as well as advertisements, all of which often go far beyond the more specialized content normally included in consumer magazines. There were, incidentally, no differences between *DM* and *test* subscribers with regard to overall use of either broadcast or printed media.

A clue about the type of information to which respondents were exposed may be obtained through an analysis of the nature of the magazines included in the list in the questionnaire (see table 5-4). Among subscribers it is self-evident that *DM* subscribers would read *DM* more often and *test* subscribers would read *test* more often, but neither seemed to read the other product testing magazine any more frequently than the AC. Both *Der Spiegel* and *Stern* were given favorable receptions by all respondents. *Der Spiegel* is a weekly newsmagazine patterned after *Time*, and *Stern* mildly resembles the now defunct *Life* with a more sensational build-up. *Capital*, a specialized, high-brow financial and investment monthly, seems to find its target market in the higher income segments typical of the subscriber respondents. All in all, seven of the ten magazines,

Table 5-3. Comparison of Perceived Exposure to Various Media[a]
(Frankfurt Samples) (In Percent)

	Subscriber (Base = 97)	Average Consumer (Base = 198)	Significance Tests[b]
Television			
No viewing	13%	7%	MWU
1–6 hours per week	31	30	AC higher
7–18 hours per week	46	43	$p < .02$
19 or more hours per week	10	20	
Radio			
No listening	18%	10%	MWU
1–6 hours per week	40	50	AC higher
7–18 hours per week	28	26	$p < .20$
19 or more hours per week	14	14	(not significant)
Newspapers			
None read	7%	14%	MWU
1 per day	68	75	Sub. higher
2 per day	21	9	$p < .001$
3 or more per day	4	2	

	Number of Magazines per Respondent	
	Subscriber	Average Consumer
Magazines		
Subscribe to:		
Including *DM* and *test*	1.7	.3
Excluding *DM* and *test*	.7	.3
Read regularly:		
Including *DM* and *test*	2.1	.9
Excluding *DM* and *test*	1.2	.8

[a]Data based on section 5 of questionnaire, reproduced in appendix G.
[b]See table 5-1, note b.

not counting *DM* and *test*, were ranked higher in reading frequency by subscribers than by AC.

AC on the other hand, tended to favor popular magazines. Of these, *Hoer Zu, Brigitte* and *Neue Revue* showed higher scores for average consumers. *Hoer Zu* is a richly illustrated television and radio program magazine, *Brigitte* a woman's magazine, and *Neue Revue* an illustrated news and human interest magazine which tends to cater to blue-collar and lower-middle class social strata. This finding is consistent with the preference for broadcast media on the part of AC, the larger proportion of female respondents in that sample, and the socio-economic characteristics discussed above.

Table 5-4.   German Magazines—Ranked by Percentage Reading Regularly or Occasionally[a] (Frankfurt Samples)

Subscriber (Base = 97)		*Average Consumer (Base = 198)*	
1. Spiegel	77%	1. Stern	56%
2. DM	67	2. Spiegel	52
3. Stern	59	3. Hoer Zu!	41
4. test	56	4. Bunte Illustrierte	31
5. Capital	40	5. Brigitte/Constanze	30
6. Das Beste	40	6. DM	29
7. Bunte Illustrierte	39	7. Neue Revue	26
8. Die Zeit	36	8. Das Beste	25
9. Auto–Motor–Sport	34	9. Die Zeit	23
10. Hoer Zu!	32	10. Auto–Motor–Sport	21
11. Brigitte/Constanze	26	11. test	19
12. Neue Revue	19	12. Capital	16

Perceived Readership and Rank

DM Subscribers	(Base = 63)
1. DM	100%
9. test	33

test Subscribers	(Base = 34)
1. test	100%
12. DM	12

[a]Data based on questions in section 5 of questionnaire, reproduced in appendix G. For explanation of chart see table 4-4, note a.

In summary then, AC seem to pay greater attention to broadcast media, particularly television; and subscribers seem to read more, including newspapers and periodicals. Not only the quantitative, but also the qualitative differences in media habits seem to support and complement the socioeconomic characteristics found to describe subscribers of *DM* and *test* in comparison to AC.

Exposure of the Average Consumer to *DM* and *test*

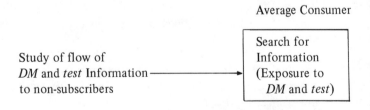

The Information Seeker was operationally defined for purposes of this study as a subscriber to product test information. We recognized this as only a workable approximation, since some information-intensive consumers might not utilize test reports, and others might use them though not subscribe to them. One concern, therefore, is to learn the extent of the German average consumer's knowledge and use of product test reports from *DM* and *test*.

The line of questioning and the interviewing procedure in the German survey were identical to the American.[7] One exception, however, was the use of aided rather than unaided recall in asking the importance of alternate information sources in the purchase decision for durable goods and an automobile. The results are summarized in table 5-5.

The data clearly reflect the average consumer's greater awareness and perceived knowledge of *DM* compared to *test*. Seventy-five percent of the respondents spontaneously mentioned *DM* as a source of product test reports and only 45 percent *test*, while 44 percent listed both magazines. Thirty percent, on the other hand, said they had never heard of *test* but only 11 percent never of *DM*. The greater public cognizance of *DM* could be a result of the historical evolution and age of the two magazines. At the time of the study, *DM* was nine years old (with interruptions as previously noted) and *test* three. Also, in the Spring of 1970, *test* was as yet available only through subscription while *DM* was widely sold over the counter in addition to its subscription sales. Newsstand display alone would have a positive effect on public awareness of *DM*, and the more popular nature of that magazine would also serve to increase knowledge of it.

Perceived exposure to the two consumer magazines was relatively low among the AC respondents, *DM* again scoring higher; one-third of the respondents said they read *DM* at least once a year, almost twice the number of *test* readers. If and when non-subscribing consumers read the magazines, they are likely to borrow them from friends or relatives but to make little use of library copies. This reaction corresponds to the practice of over one-half of the subscriber sample of keeping their *DM* or *test* issues indefinitely or for at least a year or two, and of willingly lending them to others for reading. Even so, *DM* and *test* articles or reports showed some importance as an informational decision input only in a minority (under 10 percent) of all the durable goods and automobile purchases.

A few respondents purported to buy *DM* and/or *test* on the newsstand occasionally or even regularly. This is believable enough for *DM*, but *test* was not sold in this manner at the time of the study. This would seem to reflect lack of familiarity rather than acquaintance with the magazine. Among the average consumer respondents there were 13 subscribers (eight *DM* and five *test*). Although this number far exceeds the national percentage distribution, *DM* and *test* subscribers tend to concentrate more in metropolitan areas. Since *DM* is headquartered in Frankfurt, a little local patriotism may also be involved. *DM* and *test* being fairly prominent consumer magazines, it is possible that the images they project in the consumer's mind are associated with "rational" and hence socially acceptable consumer behavior and that reported awareness of, exposure to, and acquaintance with them may be somewhat exaggerated.

Table 5–5. Knowledge and Use of *DM* and *Test*[a] (Frankfurt Average Consumer Sample)

	DM	test	*Both*
A. *Mention of* DM *or* test *or Both*			
Mentioned *DM* or *test* or both as important information source in specific purchase			
Durable Goods Purchase (Base = 154)	9%	7%	5%
Automobile Purchase (Base = 108)	6%	5%	4%
Mentioned *DM* or *test* or both as source of information comparative product test			
(unaided recall) (Base = 198)	75%	45%	44%
B. *Direct Questioning on* DM *and* test			
(Base = 198)			
How much do you know about *DM/test*			
I am a subscriber	4%	2%	
I know a great deal about it	22%	10%	
I have glanced through it or talked about it with friends	36%	19%	
I have neard the name, nothing more	28%	39%	
I have never heard of it	11%	30%	

	Almost Every Month		More Than Once Per Year Not Each Month		Maybe Once Per Year	
	DM	*test*	*DM*	*test*	*DM*	*test*
Non-subscribers only (Base = 185)						
Do you ever buy *DM/test* at a newsstand?	1%	1%	17%	6%	11%	6%
Do you ever look at or borrow *DM/test* at a library?	1	1	8	5	2	1
Do you ever borrow *DM/test* from friends or relatives?	2	0	23	12	12	8
In all, how often would you say *DM/test* is read in your household?	4	2	31	16	14	11

[a]Data in A based on question 5 in sections 2 and 3 plus question 3 in section 6. Data in B based on questions 8–12 in section 6. See questionnaire in appendix G.

THE SUBSCRIBER AND THE AVERAGE CONSUMER: BUYING BEHAVIOR AND INFORMATION USE

Our attention now shifts to the recollection of various aspects of buying behavior in specific purchase situations. As in the American study, German respondents were asked in a series of detailed questions to trace their last purchase decision in three product categories, the buying process which led up to each, and the post-purchase evaluation and perceived satisfaction which followed them.

Products Purchased

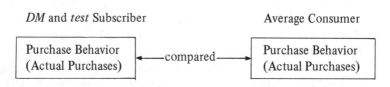

DM and *test* Subscriber   Average Consumer

The study design included three product categories—a major durable product, an automobile and a frequently purchased convenience item. The individual product items in each category listed on the questionnaire were chosen by their extent of market penetration, and all had recently been tested by *DM* or *test*. Although an attempt was made to use identical product lists in both the German and the American versions of the questionnaire, it was not always possible in those cases where a product had relatively low market penetration, was relatively unknown in one or the other country, or had not been the subject of recent comparative product tests. Thus, the clothes dryer on the American list of durable products was replaced by the ironing machine, the room air conditioner by the tape recorder, and the outboard motor by the vacuum cleaner. Similar substitutions were required in the list of convenience goods as can be seen by comparing the items in table 5-6 with those in table 4-6.

Of the German respondents, only those who had made a purchase during the time specified in the interview were included in the analysis. Thus, the remaining samples comprise only the purchasers in each of the three product categories.

	Total Sample	Durable Product		Auto-mobile		Convenience Goods	
DM Subscriber	63	54	86%	48	76%	63	100%
test Subscribers	34	29	85%	22	65%	34	100%
All Subscribers	97	83	86%	70	72%	97	100%
Average Consumers	198	154	78%	108	55%	189	96%

As was anticipated, subscribers not only had bought a proportionately greater number of durable products and automobiles within the two years preceding the interview; they also *owned* a larger inventory of durable products and automobiles (see table 5-1). Subscribers in the sample possessed on the average 7.5 durable product items from the list and .9 cars, while the consumers averaged 6.3 durables and .6 cars. There was also a greater proportion of two-car families among subscribers.

Such possessions and purchase patterns add further evidence to the finding that the German Information Seeker belongs to a higher than average socioeconomic stratum. As an example of the qualitative difference between the two respondent groups, subscribers owned twice as many and had recently bought five times as many color television sets as average consumers. The price of color sets at the time of the survey was from six to eight times that of black and white sets; obviously color television sets still carry a great deal of prestige in Germany.

The comparison of convenience goods brand preference to test report recommendations was not made in Germany as it was in the United States (table 4-6). Instead, subscribers were compared to average consumers in their frequency of purchase for a similar list of convenience goods. According to the sample, subscribers buy (and presumably drink) whisky twice as often as average consumers—and whisky is a relatively expensive and prestigious alcoholic beverage in Germany (see table 5-6). Subscribers also use more after-shave lotion, while average consumers buy more nylon stockings and pantyhose; but these differences are probably due to the differences in the sex distribution between the two respondent groups. Otherwise, no significant dissimilarities between subscribers and average consumers in the number and type of frequently purchased convenience goods were evident.

Shopping Criteria

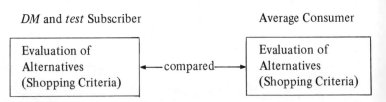

What kinds of factors are important to German consumers in evaluating product alternatives and in making purchase choices? Given the nature of the Information Seeker and the continuous, editorial admonition of *DM* and *test* for "rational" consumption, it was expected that subscribers would endeavor to obtain "value for money" as the single most important criterion in shopping. In pursuit of this objective, they would seek performance, durability, service and economy of operation. The price factor would be relevant to the extent that these criteria could be achieved at a lower price. But the brand name itself, styling, the dealer's location and availability of credit would be of secondary importance. To carry out his objective the subscriber would consider the availability of information as a critical requirement.[8]

Table 5-6. List of Convenience Goods Frequently Purchased[a] (Frankfurt Sample) (Ranked by Percent of Sample Mentioned)

		Subscriber (Base = 97)		Average Consumer (Base = 198)		
		% of sample			*% of sample*	
Rank	*Item*	*mention*	*last purchase*	*Rank* *Item*	*mention*	*last purchase*
1.	Detergent	89%	26%	1. Detergent	84%	28%
2.	Dish Detergent	83	18	2. Dish Detergent	81	12
3.	Skin Cream	74	6	3. Nylons and Pantyhose	77	9
4.	Deodorant	61	3	4. Skin Cream	69	5
5.	After Shave	57	3	5. Hair Shampoo	68	5
6.	Hair Shampoo	55	3	6. Deodorant	57	4
7.	Cigarettes	52	20	7. Hairspray	57	2
8.	Frozen Food	49	4	8. Cigarettes	47	21
9.	Nylons and Pantyhose	45	4	9. After Shave	41	3
10.	Whiskey	40	5	10. Frozen Food	40	1
11.	Hairspray	35	4	11. Make-up	30	1
12.	Auto Polish	33	1	12. Furniture Polish	25	0
13.	Furniture Polish	28	0	13. Whiskey	24	3
14.	Make-up	25	2	14. Auto Polish	15	0
15.	Floor Wax	18	0	15. Floor Wax	14	1

Average Number of Convenience Goods mentioned 7.3   Average Number of Convenience Goods mentioned 7.3

[a]Data based on list of frequently purchased convenience goods at beginning of section 4 of the German questionnaire, and appearing at the end of the questionnaire in appendix G.

In all, 13 shopping criteria or concerns of possible consumer interest, before, during and after the buying process were listed in the questionnaire. The respondents were asked to indicate the importance of each of the shopping criteria associated with the most recent durable product and automobile purchase. The answers were ranked on a five-point scale from "very important" to "very unimportant" with a neutral midpoint. The results and comparisons of subscriber and average consumer responses appear in tables 5–7 and 5–8.

Subscribers, on the whole, distinguished themselves relatively little from AC in the criteria they consider important in a shopping situation. Performance and quality of the product appear to be the most significant to German consumers in general. Styling, convenience and dealer variables seem to be less important, and credit considerations unimportant. Several other similarities and differences between consumer and product categories were noted.

1. *Performance, economic and service criteria* emerged as the most important shopping concerns for the German consumers in both major product buying situations. Subscribers and average consumers almost unanimously agreed that performance and durability in a product and an automobile are very important features to be taken into account. Economy of operation is also a critical factor, but more so for automobiles than for durable goods—not surprising if one considers the high cost of operating motor vehicles in Germany.[9] Warranty and service, on the other hand, appeared to be more significant for durables than for cars. This may be so because buyers in the sample tended to rely more on the reputation of the make of their cars than on the brand name of their durables.

2. *Price* was of greater importance in the automobile purchase than in the durable goods purchase, but its relative salience in comparison to other shopping concerns remains almost unchanged across product categories. Price was a more relevant factor to subscribers than to average consumers, but neither included it among the *most* important criteria. It is possible that price considerations are really more important to consumers than this relative indifference seems to suggest. In a culture where bargaining is not usually practiced, price may well become so fixed in the consumer's mind that this perceived inability individually to influence it relegates it to relative obscurity compared with other considerations of value and quality.

3. The *general reputation* criteria were the least consistent of any in their importance rankings. *Brand* reputation was unimportant as a factor in buying the durable product, but became critical in the automobile purchase. *Dealer* reputation comparatively was one of the least concerns in either situation, but the differential ranking by the two respondent groups was one of the most pronounced of any criterion, reversing direction from one purchase to the next. Thus, AC considered the dealer's reputation to be more important in the durable buying situation. In purchasing the automobile,

Table 5-7. Shopping Criteria–Durable Goods Purchase[a]
(Frankfurt Samples)

Subscriber (Base = 83)			Average Consumer (Base = 154)		
Rank	Criterion	Index	Rank	Criterion	Index
A. Ranked by Index Numbers[b]					
1.	Performance	96	1.	Performance	95
2.	Durability	92	2.	Durability	91
3.	Warranty	87	3.	Warranty	84
4.	Service	81	4.	Service	69
5.	Information Availability	72	5.	Brand Reputation	58
6.	Economy	62	6.	Economy	52
7.	Brand Reputation	58	7.	Product Availability	50
8.	Styling	53	8.	Information Availability	44
9.	Product Availability	44	9.	Styling	35
10.	Price	14	10.	Dealer Reputation	18
11.	Dealer Location	-2	11.	Dealer Location	4
12.	Dealer Reputation	-3	12.	Price	-2
13.	Credit	-69	13.	Credit	-65

Subscribers compared to Average Consumers

	30	20	10	0	10	20
B. Ranked by Differences in Index Numbers[b]						
1. Information Availability				(28)	Criteria more	
2. Styling				(18)	important to	
3. Price				(16)	Subscribers	
4. Service				(12)		
5. Economy				(10)		
6. Warranty				(3)		
7. Performance				(1)		
8. Durability				(1)		
9. Brand Reputation				(0) (0)		
10. Credit		Criteria more		(4)		
11. Product Availability		important to		(6)		
12. Dealer Location		Average		(6)		
13. Dealer Reputation		Consumers		(21)		

[a]Data based on section 2 of questionnaire, reproduced in appendix G.
[b]Index = (% of sample rating criterion important or very important minus % of sample rating unimportant or very unimportant).

Table 5-8.   Shopping Criteria–Auto Purchase[a] (Frankfurt Samples)

Subscriber (Base = 70)			*Average Consumer (Base = 108)*		
Rank *Criterion*		*Index*	*Rank* *Criterion*		*Index*

A. Ranked by Index Numbers[b]

Rank	Criterion	Index		Rank	Criterion	Index
1.	Durability	97		1.	Performance	97
2.	Performance	96		2.	Durability	92
3.	Brand Reputation	89		3.	Brand Reputation	84
4.	Economy	89		4.	Economy	82
5.	Information Availability	82		5.	Service	69
6.	Service	81		6.	Warranty	59
7.	Warranty	62		7.	Information Availability	52
8.	Styling	60		8.	Styling	45
9.	Price	39		9.	Product Availability	37
10.	Dealer Reputation	36		10.	Price	34
11.	Product Availability	31		11.	Dealer Reputation	14
12.	Dealer Location	17		12.	Dealer Location	8
13.	Credit	−50		13.	Credit	−52

Subscribers compared to Average Consumers

		30	20	10	0	10	20

B. Ranked by Differences in Index Numbers[b]

Rank	Criterion	Difference	
1.	Information Availability	(30)	
2.	Dealer Reputation	(22)	Criteria more
3.	Styling	(15)	important to
4.	Service	(12)	Subscribers
5.	Dealer Location	(9)	
6.	Economy	(7)	
7.	Durability	(5)	
8.	Brand Reputation	(5)	
9.	Price	(5)	
10.	Warranty	(3)	
11.	Credit	(2)	
12.	Performance	Criteria more important to AC	(1)
13.	Product Availability		(6)

[a]Data based on section 3 of questionnaire, reproduced in appendix G.

[b]Index = (% of sample rating criterion very important or important minus % of sample rating unimportant or very unimportant).

however, subscribers attributed greater concern to this factor. *DM* and *test* carried little information on car buying, which perhaps forced subscribers toward greater reliance on dealer reputation. Also, service and warranty fulfillment are more important in autos and so consequently are their dealers.

Neither subscribers nor average consumers considered *styling and shopping convenience* as highly important criteria. In the absence of any real significance in these purchase situations, little inter-product differences between durables and autos occurred with respect to dealer location and product availability.

4. *Credit availability* was unanimously ranked as the criterion of least concern in both purchases. This attitude seems to reflect the German tradition of buying for cash only. A 1969 survey, for example, showed that only 6 percent of German households were making monthly car payments, and 86 percent of households had no monthly obligations of any kind except for their homes.[10]

5. Among all the shopping criteria, *information availability* emerged as the factor with the largest subscriber-average consumer difference in relative ranking for both purchases. The data thus supported our expectations. Information availability appeared as a strong shopping concern on the part of subscribers in the durable goods and stronger still in the automobile buying situation.

In summary, we may identify and add several more pieces to the picture puzzle of the German Information Seeker.

In evaluating buying alternatives, he exhibits certain characteristics reminiscent of the classical "economic man." He is concerned with normative "value and quality" criteria, including performance, durability and economy of operation. He also worries a great deal about product usage after the purchase and hence considers warranty and service to be important buying factors. The order of these normative criteria is not transitive from one buying situation to another, but may depend on the individual circumstances in each case. Thus, the reputation of the make of car is an important informational input where other sources—including *DM* and *test*—are insufficient. Price is of relatively little concern, as are styling and convenience, as long as the important quality demands are met. Finally, he is information-minded although he may worry a little less about the availability of information per se than about value and quality of the product.

According to all measurements in the study so far, the subscriber is a highly information-intensive consumer. He is exposed to far more print media, and specifically to those which are inclined to carry product and buying information. He attributes much more importance to information availability in the purchase situations studied. We now turn to a more specific look at his perceived use of particular information sources in those situations.

Perceived Information Sources

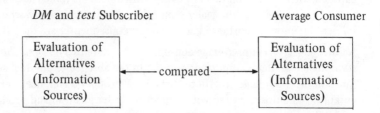

The mix of information sources used by a consumer can provide revealing insights into the purchase decision process. The *type* of sources, on which he relies in evaluating alternatives, may be linked to consumer "rationality" identified with the Information Seeker, or to the "emotionalism" of the average consumer. The *number* of sources thought to be important in a purchase may also be indicative of the amount and duration of information seeking and deliberation which has taken place as a risk reduction process. The results for the durable goods and automobile purchase situations are tabulated in tables 5-9 and 5-10 respectively.

On the whole, subscribers discerned more information sources to be of greater importance than average consumers. In the automobile buying decision, *all* information sources were more important to subscribers. In the durable goods purchase, the independent sources were more useful to subscribers; personal and commercial sources more important to AC. In particular, several distinctions between respondents and between product categories can be made.

> The most pronounced *difference* between subscribers and average consumers in their perceived importance rating of information sources had to do with *DM* and *test*. Of course, considering the nature of the sample, this finding should come as no surprise. Other *independent sources* were also favored by subscribers. An exception to the rule were the consumer centers, even though these typically provide information on most consumer products.
>
> *Personal information sources* are valued highly by all respondents, no matter what the product involved. This is particularly true for personal observation which ranked most important among all respondents for both the durable goods and automobile buying decisions. Past experience, another integral part of an individual's personal information repertoire, is also a vital input into the decision system— especially in the automobile acquisition where *DM* and *test* would have been of relatively little help in 1969. As a well educated, high status individual, the subscriber could be expected to use these personal sources with confidence. It is apparent, however, from section B of tables 5-9 and 5-10 that these sources are considered

Table 5-9. Information Sources–Durable Goods Purchase[a]
(Frankfurt Samples)

	Subscriber (Base = 83)			*Average Consumer (Base = 154)*	
Rank	*Source*	*Index*	*Rank*	*Source*	*Index*
A. Ranked by Index Number– Aided Recall[b]					
1.	Personal Observation	74	1.	Personal Observation	75
2.	*DM*	38	2.	Past Experience	32
3.	*test*	32	3.	Friend, Relative, etc.	24
4.	Past Experience	22	4.	Advertising	−12
5.	Friend, Relative, etc.	12	5.	*DM*	−26
6.	Other Mags. or Newsp.	4	6.	Other Mags. or Newsp.	−26
7.	Consumer Centers	−14	7.	Salesman	−26
8.	Advertising	−23	8.	Consumer Centers	−31
9.	Salesman	−49	9.	*test*[c]	−32

	DM Subscriber alone (Base = 54)	
2.	*DM*	59
3.	*test*	36

	test Subscriber alone (Base = 29)	
2.	*test*	48
6.	*DM*	3

Subscribers compared to Average Consumers

	60	40	20	0	20
B. Ranked by Differences in Index Numbers[b]					
DM				(64)	Sources more
test				(64)	important
Other Mags. or Newsp.				(30)	to
Consumer Centers				(17)	Subscribers
Personal Observation				(1)	
Past Experience		Source more		(10)	
Advertising		important to		(11)	
Friend, Relative, etc.		Average		(12)	
Salesman		Consumers		(23)	

[a]Data based on section 2 of questionnaire, reproduced in appendix G.

[b]Index = (% sample rating important or very important minus % sample unimportant or very unimportant).

[c]In considering the low ranking of *test* among average consumers it should be borne in mind that the journal was only three years old at the time of the study and was not then available at newsstands.

Table 5-10.   Information Sources–Auto Purchase[a] (Frankfurt Samples)

Subscriber (Base = 70)			Average Consumer (Base = 108)		
Rank	*Source*	*Index*	*Rank*	*Source*	*Index*
A. Ranked by Index Numbers[b] –Aided Recall					
1.	Personal Observation	84	1.	Personal Observation	83
2.	Past Experience	67	2.	Past Experience	51
3.	Other Mags. or Newsp.	50	3.	Friend, Relative, etc.	23
4.	Friend, Relative, etc.	42	4.	Other Mags. or Newsp.	-13
5.	*DM*	31	5.	Advertising	-28
6.	*test*	16	6.	Salesman	-35
7.	Advertising	-17	7.	*DM*	-39
8.	Salesman	-25	8.	*test*	-39
9.	Consumer Center	-40	9.	Consumer Center	-45

DM Subscriber alone (Base = 48)		
3.	*DM*	50
6.	*test*	21

test Subscriber alone (Base = 22)		
5.	*test*	5
6.	*DM*	-9

Subscribers compared to Average Consumers

	60	40	20	0	20
B. Ranked by Differences in Index Numbers[b]					
DM				(70)	
Other Mags. or Newsp.				(63)	*All*
test				(55)	sources
Friend, Relative, etc.				(19)	more
Past Experience				(16)	important
Advertising				(11)	to
Salesman				(10)	Subscribers
Consumer Center				(5)	
Personal Observation				(1)	

[a]Data based on section 3 of questionnaire, reproduced in appendix G.

[b]Index = (% sample rating important or very important minus % sample unimportant or very unimportant).

relatively *less* important by subscribers. While personal sources are literally the *only* important sources for average consumers, they become only one of many important sources to subscribers in both purchase situations.

An indication of the subscriber's information-mindedness is the positive index rating of six of the nine information sources in each of the two purchase decisions. Average consumers assigned a positive index to only three of the nine sources. The perception of importance and mix of information sources thus adds another dimension to the characterization of *DM* and *test* subscribers.

The subscriber not only uses "rational" shopping criteria, but he also perceives many information sources as important contributions to his capability o f evaluating alternatives. He thinks highly of independent sources of information—much more so than other consumers. He uses personal sources extensively, but they are relatively less important to him than to the average consumer. These personal sources are more important in auto purchases, where information in both *test* and *DM* is spotty (though *Stern* and other magazines offer better coverage). The subscriber is, in short, a self-reliant Information Seeker who searches for objective sources of information, independent of business, and supplements them with his own experience and examination. Commercial information is perceived as relatively unimportant.

DM and *test* as Information Sources

DM and *test* Subscriber

One of the questions to be answered by this study is the extent of both awareness and use of product test information directly pertaining to a given product purchase. Without belaboring the obvious, the results in table 5-11 clearly indicate the significantly greater direct awareness and use of product tests on the part of *DM* and *test* subscribers. Moreover, *test* subscribers utilized predominantly *test*, and *DM* prevailed among *DM* subscribers; in fact, the proportion of subscriber-users of the alternative magazine was hardly different from that of AC. The magazines found their greatest application in the durable goods purchase and, to a more limited degree, in the low-risk convenience product situation. Auto purchase involved relatively little use of tests—primarily because such tests were not one of the strong features of *DM* and *test*.

On the basis of a specific line of questioning on the awareness and perceived use of *DM* and *test* recommendations in their purchase decisions, subscribers were separated into two subgroups:

1. *Perceived users*—those who were aware of *DM* and/or *test* recommendations

Table 5-11. Awareness and Use of *DM/Test* Recommendations[a] (Frankfurt Samples) (By Percent of Actual Purchasers in Each Group)

	Durable		Auto		Convenience	
	Aware of Recommendations	*Used in Purchase*	*Aware of Recommendations*	*Used in Purchase*	*Aware of Recommendations*	*Used in Purchase*
DM						
DM subscribers	48	44	33	12	35	27
test subscribers	3	3	4	4	0	0
All subscribers	36	34	24	19	26	21
Average Consumers	8	6	6	6	3	0
test						
DM subscribers	7	7	4	4	5	5
test subscribers	38	35	14	14	29	26
All subscribers	17	15	7	7	11	10
Average Consumers	3	3	0	0	2	2

[a]Data taken from questions 38 and 39 in section 6 of questionnaire, reproduced in appendix G.

for the product purchased and who thought that the recommendation was an important decision input; and

2. *Perceived non-users*—those who were either unaware of any *DM* and/or *test* recommendation, or regarded it as unimportant.

This dichotomy permitted several conclusions:

1. Subscriber-users of *DM/test* tended to plan even more than non-users.
2. Users had slightly more experience.
3. Users had significantly higher regard for *DM* and *test* articles as important information sources in their product purchases.
4. No difference in the amount of comparative shopping appeared between users and non-users.
5. Users tended to be slightly more educated, have somewhat more income.

Although the perceived awareness and usage of specific *DM* and/or *test* recommendations among subscribers is not overwhelming, some definite patterns of import are detectable.

The subscriber who is aware of and makes use of *DM/test* recommendations tends to be slightly better educated and at the higher end of the income scale. He makes greater use of *DM/test* despite his greater experience—or because of it. He tends to plan his purchases more carefully and in general believes *DM/test* to be an important information source. His use increases with the importance of the product considered for purchase—that is, recommendations are utilized much more frequently for the purchase of a durable product than of convenience goods. When it comes to automobile acquisitions, however, *DM/test* take a backseat to personal and commercial sources, primarily because of the lack of auto-specific test information.

Satisfaction and the Use of *DM* and *test*

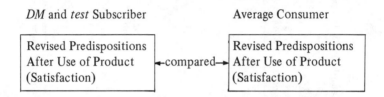

We have seen that the German Information Seeker has several features characteristic of "economic man." He is planful, greatly concerned about the performance and value of the product (rather than its styling), and he is highly information-minded and experienced. Armed with quantities of high-quality information, he should be able to detect and select that product which he prefers most among the alternatives in any given purchase situation. And one might expect him to be more satisfied with the results of his acquisitions than the average consumer.

To test these propositions, a line of questioning was included in the questionnaire designed to measure various dimensions of post-purchase evaluation. These included satisfaction with the product and brand itself, the information available for deliberation, personal shopping effort, safety of the product, and advertising. Comparisons of the data are tabulated in table 5-12.

The data suggest that subscribers are in fact happier and more satisfied consumers than average citizens. This satisfaction seems to be the more pronounced the more significant the product purchased. Thus, subscribers—as did average consumers—scored the highest satisfaction in the automobile and durable product purchases and somewhat less for the convenience goods.[11] At the same time, the difference in perceived satisfaction between the two respondent groups was greatest for the automobile, an important, high-risk item, next in durable products and least in the convenience goods category. It is interesting

Table 5-12. Selected Satisfaction Measures[a] (Frankfurt Samples) (By Index Numbers)[b]

	Durable Goods Purchase			Auto Purchase		
	Subscribers	Average Consumers	Higher[c] Group	Subscribers	Average Consumers	Higher[c] Group
	(Base = 83)	(Base = 154)		(Base = 70)	(Base = 108)	
Product						
Turned out to be all I expected	83	79	Sub.	79	81	Sub. **
I would recommend to a friend	83	84	Sub. *	92	79	Sub. **
Information Availability						
Little trouble finding how brands differ	26	48	AC	66	53	Sub. *
Plenty of information available	58	54	Sub.	88	61	Sub. **
Personal Shopping Activity						
Even with more information, no better brand	70	67	Sub.	76	69	Sub. *
Shopped enough to get lowest price	71	58	Sub. **	59	53	Sub. *
Safety						
This brand is safe to use	68	70	Sub.	87	86	Sub. **
Advertising						
Advertising was accurate and helpful	51	47	Sub.	42	43	Sub.

[a]Data based on questions 8–17 in sections 2 and 3 and questions 4–13 in section 4 of questionnaire, reproduced in appendix G.

[b]Index = (% of sample rating agree or strongly agree minus % of sample disagree or strongly disagree).

[c]Higher group indicates greater satisfaction. Statistical significance by Mann-Whitney U Test.

$*p < .05; **p < .01$.

to note that the criterion of information availability created the least satisfaction for subscribers and also the least distinction between them and average consumers. On the other hand, subscribers are more satisfied than AC, even with the advertising of the product.

In summary, it may be concluded that:

1. German subscribers are more satisfied than average consumers with the outcome of their purchases;
2. The satisfaction on the part of subscribers, both in absolute terms and relative to average consumers, is greatest where the effort, planning and information search is also at its best and most extensive. Satisfaction ranked first with the automobile purchase, second with the durable product, and last with convenience goods;
3. The safety of the product—a satisfaction dimension so strongly stressed by *DM* and *test* that it becomes a standard for minimal product acceptance—was not a predominant satisfaction criterion among subscribers; but average consumers were even less satisfied with this aspect of the product;
4. The differences between subscribers and average consumers—although frequently statistically significant in favor of subscribers—are largely a matter of degree. The evidence from this study suggests that the average consumer is reasonably satisfied with product, information, personal shopping effort and product safety, even though he does not express his satisfaction as convincingly as the subscriber.

These conclusions add another piece to the characterization of the German Information Seeker as personified by the *DM* and *test* subscriber.

He puts much effort and planning into his purchase decisions which tend to be motivated by performance, value and thorough information. He does use recommendations and other consumer information from his magazine subscriptions. As a result of his activities, he is rather successful in gaining purchase satisfaction.

THE SUBSCRIBER AND THE AVERAGE CONSUMER: ATTITUDES TOWARD CONSUMER POLICY ISSUES

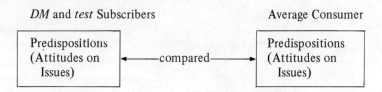

DM and *test* Subscribers   Average Consumer

| Predispositions (Attitudes on Issues) | ←——compared——→ | Predispositions (Attitudes on Issues) |

It can be expected that along with his rational, economic, planful, information-minded approach to buying decisions, the *DM* and *test* subscriber is strongly consumer-oriented in his beliefs and values. In particular, the consumerist stance editorially assumed by the two magazines should be reflected in subscriber knowledge of and attitudes toward consumer problems, pending consumer legislation, public policy, and other kinds of consumerist issues. Of special interest here are attitudes on the government's role in these issues, which has been a controversial topic since the founding of the *Stiftung Warentest* in 1965. [12] Respondents were first asked to assign rating numbers to each of seven consumerist issues, assessing their perceived importance as activities "which you would like to see more of." They were then requested to indicate whether, in their opinion, government was doing "the right amount," "too much," or "too little" in each of these areas. These data are summarized in tables 5-13 and 5-14, allowing several observations and conclusions.

1. Average subscribers are not necessarily much more avid activists than average consumers in most areas of consumerist concern. In fact, little difference was discernible between the two groups of respondents in either the order of ranking or the strength of conviction on selected consumerist actions and possible remedies for consumer problems. But subscribers vigorously support increased government involvement in each, consistently and considerably more so than AC.

2. *Consumer protection* is rated as an important consumerist activity by subscribers and non-subscribers alike. Apparently they feel relatively insecure and therefore in need of protection as consumers vis-à-vis the seller. It may be that this need for protection reflects a more general insecurity in economic matters and market affairs on the part of German consumers.[13]

3. *Consumer education* and provisions for *helping consumers with complaints* were considered the two least important consumerist concerns by respondents in general. In a sense, these types of activity would minimize the necessity for consumer protection. German consumers, however, opted for protection to a considerably greater degree than for education or help with complaints. The feeling seems widespread, however, that government is not sufficiently involved in consumer education and the handling of complaints, a feeling which is particularly strong among subscribers. In addition, all respondents favored stronger government action to prevent misleading advertising. But government is only moderately welcomed as a source of consumer protection per se.

4. *Product testing* in general is not one of the greatest concerns among German respondents, not even among subscribers; and it has only limited appeal as an area for increased government activity. *Test* is, of course, government sponsored and in part government financed; hence the attitude that "government is doing the *right* amount" in the area of concern can be easier understood.

Table 5-13. Need for Increased Overall Activity in Selected Consumer Policy Areas[a] (Frankfurt Samples)

Subscriber	Weighted Mean Rank[b]	Average Consumer	Weighted Mean Rank[b]
A. Listed by Weighted Mean Rank			
1. Consumer Protection	5.3	1. Information Labeling	4.8
2. Information Labeling	5.2	2. Consumer Protection	4.6
3. Product Testing	4.7	3. Product Testing	4.4
4. Preventing Misleading Adv.	4.5	4. Preventing Misleading Adv.	4.3
5. Quality Standards	4.0	5. Quality Standards	4.1
6. Consumer Complaints	4.0	6. Consumer Complaints	3.9
7. Consumer Education	3.7	7. Consumer Education	3.5

Subscribers compared to Average Consumers

	1.0	0.5	0	−0.5	−1.0

B. Ranked by *Difference* in Weighted Rank

Consumer Protection	(0.7)
Information Labeling	(0.5)
Product Testing	(0.3)
Consumer Education	(0.2)
Preventing Misleading Adv.	(0.2)
Consumer Complaints	(0.1)
Quality Standards	(0.1)

Subscribers see more need

AC see more need

[a]Data taken from question 1, section 6 of questionnaire, reproduced in appendix G.
[b]Ranks adjusted so that highest ranking given highest number. Highest rank attainable = 7, Lowest rank = 1. Weighted Mean Rank = Proportion of sample mentioning multiplied by the mean rank given.

5. Interestingly, *DM* subscribers rather strongly advocated *more* government product testing and reporting, while *test* subscribers were relatively satisfied with this amount of government activity.

6. *Informative product labeling*—a CI function related to product testing—was in general ranked as highly desirable; but again, comparatively little increase in government involvement was sought by the respondents. Instead, consumers, particularly subscribers, seem to recommend a stronger government stand on the establishment and enforcement of minimum quality standards.

These results may be summarized and thus adding one further piece to the description of the Information Seeker:

On the whole, the subscriber is not a great consumer activist himself, but he wants government to do more in this area. Of the two groups

Table 5-14. Need for Government Activity in Selected Consumer Policy Areas[a] (Frankfurt Samples)

Subscriber (Base = 97)			Average Consumer (Base = 198)		
Rank	Activity	Index	Rank	Activity	Index
A. Ranked by Index Numbers[b]					
1.	Misleading Advertising	72	1.	Misleading Advertising	60
2.	Consumer Education	65	2.	Consumer Education	44
3.	Min. Quality Standards	61	3.	Consumer Complaints	44
4.	Consumer Complaints	58	4.	Min. Quality Standards	43
5.	Consumer Protection	55	5.	Information Labeling	43
6.	Information Labeling	44	6.	Consumer Protection	41
7.	Product Testing	44	7.	Product Testing	37
	(*DM* Subscribers alone	49)			
	(*test* Subscribers alone	39)			

	Subscribers compared to Average Consumers				
	20	10	0	10	20
B. Ranked by *Differences* in Index Numbers[b]					
Consumer Education			(21)		
Min. Quality Standards			(18)		Subscribers
Consumer Protection			(14)		see more
Consumer Complaints			(14)		need in *all*
Misleading Advertising			(12)		activities.
Product Testing			(7)		
(*DM* Subscribers alone)			(12)		
(*test* Subscribers alone)			(2)		
Information Labeling			(1)		

[a]Data based on question 2 in section 6 of questionnaire, reproduced in appendix G.
[b]Index = (% sample answering *too little* government activity minus % sample *too much*). Higher Index indicates greater perceived need for government activity.

of subscribers, *test* subscribers are somewhat closer to the consumer activism one might expect from the Information Seeker. Comparatively, *DM* subscribers somewhat more resembled average consumers in this respect. But both *DM* and *test* subscribers strongly advocate greater government involvement in consumerist matters, particularly in the areas of truth in advertising, consumer education and complaints handling.

SUMMARY AND CONCLUSIONS: THE GERMAN INFORMATION SEEKER

This chapter presented summary findings and comparisons from the survey of *DM* and *test* subscribers and average consumers, randomly selected from the metropolitan area of Frankfurt. The purpose was to identify certain differences between the metropolitan subscriber and the average metropolitan consumer with respect to demographic and socioeconomic characteristics, media usage patterns, attitudes and buying behavior. Little by little, a picture of the German subscriber emerged, revealing him as an affluent, educated, information-minded, "rational" consumer. He is planful, experienced, critical and deliberate; he is aware of and interested in consumer problems, and, on many scores, in favor of government intervention on behalf of the consuming public.

It is these *DM* and *test* subscribers to whom we have given the name of "German Information Seekers." Highlighting the major characteristics of this Information Seeker, the substance of the survey results is briefly recapitulated in the following paragraphs.

1. *He is a member of the high-income-education elite.* The typical subscriber earns considerably more than the average consumer. His higher earnings are the result of a more prestigious, better paying type of occupation, concentrating in the managerial or professional areas. He is well equipped for this with far more than average education. He is not older than the average consumer, but he is more likely to be married, has a larger family, and occupies a roomier house or apartment.

2. *Deep down he may be a typical German conservative, but with respect to various issues, he is a mixture of a conservative-liberal, moderate consumer activist.* The subscriber is conservative in his attitude toward welfare and liberal toward student power. Despite his pro-business stance, he is not at all against greater government control of business, and he favors increased government involvement in consumerist affairs.

3. *He is a planner and an opinion leader, but not an innovator.* He is planful in general and also in specific purchase situations. He perceives himself as one who is asked for purchase advice, whose opinion is respected by others, and whose influence contributes materially to group decisions. On the other hand, he does not believe that he is among the first to try out a new product.

4. *He reads more but attends to the broadcast media less frequently.* The subscriber regularly reads two or more daily newspapers and two magazines. These quite naturally include *DM* and/or *test* on a regular basis, other consumer magazines, and also so-called "high-brow" publications such as *Capital*. His television watching and radio listening tend to be restricted to less than ten hours per week.

5. *He owns a greater number of items from a list of durable products and automobiles.* The proportionately large incidence of automobile and durable products ownership underscores the high-income status of subscribers. Their buying power is exemplified by such high-priced items as color television sets.

6. *He plans his purchases more carefully.* Planning, comparative shopping and

information search are important ingredients in his prepurchase behavior—in spite of his somewhat greater experience, or perhaps because of it.

7. *True to the ideal of the "economic man," his most important shopping criteria are economic, concentrating on performance, durability and value for money.* Price per se is relatively unimportant, perhaps because of the absence of bargaining practices in the German culture. Much less important to the subscriber are convenience and styling criteria, but credit availability bears by far the least importance of any shopping concern—a typically German character trait. The availability of information is a vital criterion before he makes up his mind about a product.

8. *He is information-minded and finds several alternate information sources of great importance in the decision making process.* He values independent information sources highly, particularly *DM* and *test*, but this does not diminish his reliance on personal observation and experience—both his own and those of friends. Commercial sources are considered by him as least important except in cases where other information is not readily available.

9. *He reads* DM *and* test *faithfully and follows their recommendations. DM and test* reports play a key role in the information repertoire of the subscriber. He follows their recommendations if he can—primarily when he buys expensive items for the household. Use of *DM* and *test* is curtailed when he buys cars, perhaps because of their restrictive coverage of this area.

10. *He has high buying standards and his shopping effort is rewarded.* He tends to be well satisfied with brand and product purchases, pertinent information, and his own shopping efforts. The data suggest that through his effort and information search, his purchase mistakes are greatly reduced. It seems that within the subscriber's mind, *DM* and *test* contribute substantially to reducing mistakes and increasing satisfaction in the buying process.

11. *He is a moderate consumer activist who favors greater government contribution toward the solution of consumer problems.* His advocacy of increased government involvement is strongest in such passive areas as the prevention of misleading advertising and the establishment of minimum product quality standards. Consumer education, which is considered only mildly important per se, also should receive substantially more government attention in his opinion.

NOTES TO CHAPTER 5

1. For a more detailed description and analytical examination of the *DM* and *test* organizations and their operations, see Hans B. Thorelli and Sarah V. Thorelli, *Consumer Information Handbook: Europe and North America* (New York: Praeger, 1974).

2. For a comparison of *DM* and *test* subscribers on the national level, see chapter 6.

3. See appendixes C and D for selected Frankfurt metropolitan and German national demographic statistics.
4. See chapter 4, table 4–1, for explanation of and reference to the Duncan scale.
5. Other studies on consumer information in both Germany and other countries are reviewed in chapter 7.
6. See chapter 4, p. 64–66.
7. See chapter 4, p. 69–71.
8. Cf. also table 4–7.
9. At the time of the study, for example, gasoline prices in Germany were roughly double those in the United States.
10. See *Der Deutsche Markt in Zahlen* (Frankfurt: DIVO-INMAR GmbH., 1970), p. 120. Partly as a result of pent-up demand following World War II, 25 percent of German households were involved in consumer credit purchases in 1953. The number declined to 17 percent in 1958 and 11 percent in 1964. See Dieter Claessens, Arno Kloenne and Armin Tschoeppe, *Sozialkunde der Bundesrepublik Deutschland* (Duessel-dorf: Eugen Diederich, 1964): 274.
11. To maintain consistency in table format, convenience goods data are not included here. Detailed data are summarized in Helmut Becker, "Consumer Information and the Image of Advertising in Germany with Significant Comparisons to America," (DBA diss., Indiana University, 1971):217–18, table 9–2.
12. See Christa von Braunschweig, *Der Konsument und seine Vertretung* (Heidelburg: Quelle und Meyer, 1965).
13. See Becker, chapter 5.

Chapter Six

American and German Information Seekers—A Comparison

GENERAL CHARACTERISTICS OF INFORMATION SEEKERS

Is there *really* a universal Information Seeker—an information-sensitive consumer whose identifiable characteristics and behavior are distinctive enough to transcend national and cultural boundaries? Chapters 4 and 5 presented some strong preliminary evidence that Information Seekers in Germany and the United States have in common certain demographic characteristics, attitudes and patterns of purchase behavior that are distinctly different from those of average consumers.[a] Though no direct comparisons were made between countries, there were also indications of some substantive differences between German and American Information Seekers. The purpose of this chapter is to explore the nature of these similarities and differences in more detail.

It is easy to generalize about substantive differences by specifying the stereotypes for each country:

> The American is affluent, gregarious, free-spending, trustful, ambitious, independent, acquisitive. He lives in a country which is rich, rapidly changing, and oriented toward growth, profit and consumption.
> The German is serious, well-organized, disciplined, wary, thrifty, conservative. His nation is proud, productive, efficient, technically magnificent, burgeoning.

It might be convincingly argued, however, that the two nations are more similar than different. They share a religious heritage which places strong emphasis on personal and national ambition and accomplishment; both are noted for technical

---

[a]There is also indication that the same is true in other countries. See chapter 7.

131

creativity which has in part been responsible for their present affluent, consumer-based economies.

These generalizations are interesting and probably contain some truth. Yet as in the case of the man with his head in the freezer and his feet on the stove, the "average" may not give a helpful insight into the condition of separate parts of the whole. Our concern here is with a far from average group selected from each country. Each group has been characterized as above average in income, education, social standing, and interest in product information and related concerns. Our task is to compare these two atypical groups.

We will specifically compare the nation-wide samples of over 600 subscribers in each country,[b] and will conjoin these comparisons with the intra-country comparisons of previous chapters in an attempt to isolate meaningful patterns. The structure of this chapter will be less formal than the previous two, but the same basic sequence and outline will be followed.

To summarize the results of the comparisons within countries from chapters 4 and 5, the most significant findings have been accumulated in figure 6-1. This chart is a matrix showing how subscribers compared to AC in both countries on variables where differences were statistically significant. For example, subscribers' income was significantly higher than AC's in the United States, putting that outcome in the left column; subscribers' income in Germany was significantly higher than AC's, putting that result into the top row; therefore "income" appears in the upper left cell of the matrix.

The chart serves to isolate the following types of characteristics of the Information Seeker:

1. *Universals.* Characteristics in which subscribers in each country varied significantly (in the same direction) from average consumers. Examples: income was higher in both countries; television viewing was lower. These appear in boxes A and I of figure 6-1.
2. *Culture Specifics.* Characteristics in which subscribers in one country varied significantly from AC, but there were no significant differences in the other country. Example: American subscribers found Brand Reputation more important, but German subscribers were not significantly different from AC. These are in boxes B, D, F and H.
3. *Opposites.* Characteristics where there were significant differences in each country between subscribers and AC, but in *opposite* directions. Example: satisfaction of subscribers with products and purchase procedures was higher than AC in Germany, but lower in the United States. These are in boxes C and G.

[b]Chapter 3 presents a description of these samples, the means of selecting respondents, and our rationale for choosing which samples to use for specific parts of the analysis. A note on similarities between the metropolitan and national subscriber samples is contained in appendix A.

	American Comparisons — Subscribers vs. Average Consumers		
German Comparisons — Subscribers vs. Average Consumers	Subscribers High	Neutral[a]	Subscribers Low

Subscribers High	A. Universal "Highs"
	Demographics:
	  Income
	  Education
	  Social Class
	Attitudes:
	  Planfulness
	  Business
	  Opinion Leader
	Newspaper and Magazine:
	  Readership
	Shopping Concern:
	  Available Information
	Information Source:
	  Product Testing
	Consumer Activity
	  by Government
	Ownership of Selected
	  Durables
		B. German High–American Neutral
		Demographic:
		  Age
		Information Source:
		  Other newspaper
		  or magazine
		Shopping Concern:
		  Styling
			C. German High–American Low
			Attitude:
			  Increased Government
			  Control of Business
			Satisfaction Measures:
			  All, including satisfaction
			  with product and shopping
			  activity and available information

Neutral[a]	D. American High–German Neutral
	Attitude:
	  General Liberalism
	Shopping Concern:
	  Brand Reputation
	  Increased Consumerist
	  Activities
		E. No Significant Difference From Average Consumer
		Most other variables were not
		listed elsewhere fell into
		this category.
			F. American Low–German Neutral
			Attitudes:
			  Advertising
			  Student Power
			Shopping Concerns:
			  Product Availability
			  Economy of Operation
			  Credit
			Information Source:
			  Personal Observation

Subscribers Low	G. American High–German Low None	H. German Low–American Neutral Attitude: Welfare	I. Universal "Lows" Television Viewing Radio Listening

aNo significant difference between Subscribers and Average Consumers

Figure 6–1. Summary of Comparisons Within Countries (From chapters 4 and 5).

Cell E, the middle of the matrix, contains all variables in which no significant differences were noted, but since these are not interesting here, they are not listed. This comparison matrix will be cited specifically on occasion in this chapter. More important, it will be the source for brief capsule summaries at the beginning of each section where findings were significant and interesting. These summaries will in turn serve as springboards to the comparisons between countries.

Demographic and Socioeconomic Characteristics

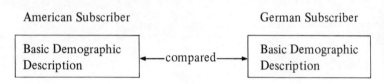

American Subscriber   German Subscriber

Basic Demographic Description ←—compared—→ Basic Demographic Description

Summary of Within-Country Comparisons
    Universals: Subscribers were higher in income, education and social class than AC.
    Culture Specifics: German subscribers were older than AC.

The subscriber demographic data examined in chapters 4 and 5 were taken from samples of approximately 100 each in Indianapolis and Frankfurt. The mail subscriber samples to be examined in this chapter are not only national in scope, but consist of over 600 respondents per country, relatively sizable statistical samples given the limited subscriber populations in the two countries. Since national demographic data are available for both countries, it is possible to subject the universals suggested above to a more rigorous test using these larger samples.

Table 6–1 shows comparisons in the major demographic characteristics between the national samples of subscribers and census data or other official statistics. It is clear that the conclusions suggested by the metropolitan samples are strongly supported by the national data. In the United States, subscribers are under-represented in the under 25 and over 65 age groups relative to the general population, and are heavily concentrated between 25 and 54, particularly between 25 and 34. Subscribers are four times as likely to have a college education, but only one-tenth as likely to have so little as a grade school education. Subscribers are heavily concentrated in the professional and managerial areas, with proportionately few clerical and service workers and laborers. Eighty percent of subscribers have incomes over $10,000, but less than 50 percent of average Americans enjoy the same level. The German findings are quite similar, including heavy concentration in the 25–34 year old and professional-managerial groups, extremely high levels of education and income, and a higher proportion married.

In the five important demographic characteristics shown here, there is a striking pattern of similarity between the two subscriber groups. Although no true statistical tests are valid because of differences in measuring units in most variables it is apparent that while the two subscriber groups are quite unlike average consumers in their own countries, they are very much like each other. In the area of demographic characteristics, there is good evidence that the Universal Information Seeker exists and that he makes up an income-education-occupation aristocracy.

Basic Attitudes of Interest

American Subscriber   German Subscriber

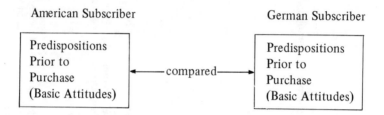

Summary of Within-Country Comparisons

Universals: Subscribers in both countries were more planful and likely to be opinion leaders than AC and had a more favorable attitude toward business and businessmen.

Culture Specifics: In the liberal-conservative dimension, American subscribers were more liberal than AC on the general screening question, "You can't change human nature," but much less favorable toward more student power; German subscribers were less favorable toward welfare. American subscribers were significantly less favorable toward advertising.

Opposites: German subscribers were more favorable toward increased government control of business than average consumers, but American subscribers were less favorable than their AC counterparts.

The attitude patterns shown in table 6-2 are strikingly similar except in areas where obvious cultural differences exist between the two countries. In both countries, subscribers seem to be self-designated opinion leaders, do not see themselves as early adopters of new products, and are strongly oriented toward

Table 6-1. Comparison of Subscribers to Census Data on Important Demographic and Socioeconomic Characteristics (National Mail Subscriber Samples)

	United States			Germany	
	Subscribers[a]	*Census[b]*		*Subscribers[a]*	*Census[c]*
Income					
Over $15,000	47%	22%	Over DM 18,000	56%	15%
10,000–14,999	33	27	12,000–17,999	29	25
5,000–9,999	18	32	7,200–11,999	13	39
Under 5,000	2	19	Under 7,200	2	21
	100%	100%		100%	100%
Education					
College Graduate (16 yrs.+)	40%	11%	Abitur/University (13 yrs.+)	46%	5%
Some College (13–15)	20	10	Middle School (11–12)	22	17
High School Graduate (12)	20	34	Primary-D Apprenticeship (9–10)	26	43
Some High School (9–11)	7	17	Primary with No Apprenticeship (8–)	6	32
Grade School or Less (8–)	3	28			
	100%	100%		100%	100%
Occupation					
Professional and Technical	37%	15%	Professional and Technical	35%	NA[d]
Managers and Proprietors	24	11	Managers, Officials and Proprietors	24	24%
Clerical	4	18	Minor Officials and Salaried Employees	12	21
Sales	6	7	Craftsmen and Foremen	10	26
Craftsmen and Foremen	11	14	Operatives, Service Laborers and Farm	13	20
Operatives, Service and Laborers	10	35	Miscellaneous	6	9
Miscellaneous	8	0			
	100%	100%		100%	100%

Age[e]

	American		German	
	Survey	Census	Survey	Census
Under 25	5%	18%	8%	12%
25–34	31	19	42	21
35–44	23	17	16	18
45–54	22	17	17	15
55–64	14	14	11	16
65 and Over	5	15	6	18
	100%	100%	100%	100%

Marital Status[f]

	American		German	
	Male	Female	Male	Female
Married	87%	69%	82%	63%
Single	10	19	13	15
Widowed or Divorced	3	12	5	22
	100%	100%	100%	100%

[a] Data from section 7 of questionnaire, reproduced in appendix G.

[b] American statistics from 1970 Census, Bureau of Census, various reports.

[c] German statistics from Divo-Institut, *Der Westdeutsche Markt in Zahlen*, Frankfurt, 1969.

[d] German census data do not include this category. Self-employed professionals included under Managers, Officials and Proprietors. Percentages are of total *employed* population.

[e] Census age data have been standardized (to remove under 18 years old) to make comparable to survey data.

[f] Census data refer to population over 14 years of age.

Table 6-2.   General Attitude Comparisons[a] (National Mail Samples) (By Index Numbers)[b]

Attitude Questions	Favorable Attitude		Unfavorable Attitude		High Group Difference G = Germany
	100	50	−50	−100	
Planfulness					
Enjoy planning work					G +3[c]
Better at getting value for money					U.S. +19
Liberal–Conservative					
Can change human nature					G +4
More government control of business					G +44
More power to students					G +73
Welfare doesn't mean less work					G +76
Opinion Leadership					
Influence opinion in a group					U.S. +18
Asked by others about products					Tie
Early Adopter					
Wait for others to try new brands					G +17
First to use new product					U.S. +5
Business					
Businessman honest as others					U.S. +30
Business does job well					U.S. +11
Advertising					
Favorable attitude					G +24

[a]Data based upon section 1, page 1 of questionnaire, reproduced in appendix G.

[b]Index = (% of sample strongly agree or agree minus % sample disagree or strongly disagree).

[c]Read G +3, German subscribers more favorable by 3 index points.

——————— = American Mail Subscribers (Base = 630)

— — — — — = German Mail Subscribers (Base = 610)

careful planning. Slightly favorable attitudes are present toward advertising and the general liberalism question, "You can't change human nature."[c]

Sharp contrasts exist in attitudes on several areas where obvious or previously-documented cultural differences exist. Almond and Verba and others have demonstrated that Germans are much less trustful and more suspicious of others than Americans.[1] This quality is apparent in the "businessmen are honest" question, where American subscribers agreed very strongly but German subscribers were nearly neutral. Neither group was convinced that business does its job well, both showing slightly negative attitudes on this question. The contrast between favorable attitudes toward advertising and unfavorable attitudes toward business is striking, particularly in Germany. The discussion will return to this point later.

While the tendency toward liberalism as judged by the general screening question was consistent between countries, strong differences existed in the "action" liberal–conservative areas, that is, those relating to specific activities with liberal connotations. All of the differences are obviously related to the cultural and political histories of the two countries. Germans favor more power for students (who have had virtually none) while Americans gave unfavorable answers to this question (asked in the midst of the student turmoil of 1970). German subscribers are convinced that welfare does not damage overall work output, but American subscribers are even more certain that it does. Katona has noted that Americans favor individual action, but Europeans more broadly accept the concept of the welfare state. "(T)he poor, the unemployed have a claim against the state."[2] The same split exists on the question of more government control of business, where American subscribers are decidedly unfavorable, Germans quite favorable. It is interesting to note that this is one of the two areas in the study where truly opposite trends were noted in the within-country comparisons. German subscribers were more favorable toward increased government control than their average countrymen, while American subscribers were much less so. When the four groups are arrayed, the German subscriber is most favorable to increased government control of business, followed by the average German, then the average American, and finally the American subscriber, who is decidedly negative toward the idea. Other sections of the study will add substance and complexity to subscribers' opinions in the interesting area of government-business relationships.

An overview of the attitude study further supports the concept of a Universal Information Seeker. In the attitudes linked unambiguously to purchase processes and economic relationships, he perceives himself as a carefully planning buyer who influences others but is reluctant to be a true innovator. He is slightly

[c]This question is seen as a powerful screening tool for identifying the quantity of general liberalism in the individual. See Herbert McClosky, "Conservatism and Personality," *American Political Science Review* 52 (March 1958): 27–45.

liberal, with neutral to mildly favorable overall attitudes toward business in general and advertising in particular.

Despite the cross-cultural consistency in these purchase-related attitudes, it is apparent that the Information Seeker is still a product of his own country with regard to broader and more deeply ingrained issues. The German is still very much the guarded German and the American the trustful American when it comes time to evaluate the honesty of a businessman, or (presumably) anyone else. It is obvious that even if the Universal Information Seeker exists, he still bears a strong imprint of his own nation's culture.

Media Habits and Usage

American Subscriber   German Subscriber

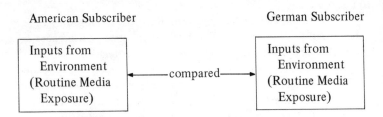

Summary of Within-Country Comparisons

Universals: Subscribers read more newspapers and magazines than average consumers, but spent less time watching television or listening to radio.

The country studies suggested that the Information Seeker is not a uniformly higher "consumer" of information media but that he perceives himself as more oriented toward print media. The summary above notes that he actually spends less time than the average consumer with the broadcast media. However, a comparison of Information Seekers in the two countries shows that the American subscribers spend more time with all types of media. Table 6–3 indicates that American subscribers watch more TV, listen to more radio, read more newspapers and subscribe to and read more magazines than their German counterparts.

This finding could be in part due to the higher educational level of the American group, but more probably is linked to the media-intensive nature of American culture. Particularly in radio and television there are simply more stations on the air and more receiving equipment to pick them up. Many households have more than one TV set, including a portable model, not to mention the abundance of radios, ranging from elaborate stereophonic rigs to miniature portables. Thus exposure to broadcast media is both routine and frequent, often as a background to other activities. In Germany, by contrast, television broadcasting by the two networks is limited to an average of seven hours a day, and unlike commercial American TV, content is oriented more toward culture and

Table 6-3. Comparison of Perceived Exposure to Various Media[a] (National Mail Samples) (In Percent)

	American Subscriber (Base = 630)	German Subscriber (Base = 610)	Significance Tests[b]
Television			
No Viewing	0%	8%	MWU
1–6 hours per week	27	30	U.S. Higher
7–18 hours per week	47	46	$p < .000$
19 or more hours per week	26	16	
	100%	100%	
Radio			
No listening	6%	5%	MWU
1–6 hours per week	43	51	U.S. Higher
7–18 hours per week	34	30	$p < .01$
19 or more hours per week	17	14	
	100%	100%	
Newspapers			
None Read	4%	9%	MWU
1 per day	50	63	U.S. Higher
2 per day	39	24	$p < .000$
3 or more per day	7	4	
	100%	100%	

	Number of Magazines per Respondent	
	Subscriber	Average Consumer
Magazines		
Subscribed to:		
Including *CR* or *DM/test*	2.6	1.5
Excluding *CR* or *DM/test*	1.6	.5
Read Regularly:		
Including *CR* or *DM/test*	2.3	2.0
Excluding *CR* or *DM/test*	1.3	1.1

[a]Data based upon section 5 of questionnaire, reproduced in appendix G.
[b]Mann-Whitney U Test (MWU) was used for determining higher group. See table 4-1, (note b), for source.

education. It is probably also true that a greater variety of special-interest magazines and newspapers is available in the United States, generally at less cost than in Germany.

The study cannot estimate the qualitative aspects of media exposure that might offset the quantitative edge shown by American subscribers: both radio and television are so pervasive in the United States that they often become casual background to other activities, while Germans tend to devote full attention to listening or watching. Observers of both nations have also suggested that while Americans may scan quantities of newspapers and magazines, Germans tend to read such materials more thoroughly and may also read more books. Although American subscribers certainly receive more routine exposure to most media, Germans probably absorb their more limited exposure with a greater intensity.

BUYING BEHAVIOR AND INFORMATION USE
OF THE INFORMATION SEEKERS

This section begins the presentation of the results of a unique exercise: directly comparing perceptions of buying behavior of some of the most expert consumers in two of the most advanced consumer economies in the world. Chapters 4 and 5 established the subscribers in each country as a high-income, high education, socially elite group with high interest in market information and information media. The groups have also been demonstrated to be quite similar on most demographic and some attitudinal dimensions, though certain cultural attributes provide exceptions to their overall homogeneity. These two samples of Information Seekers will now be "walked through" a pair of purchases (one of durable goods and one of an auto) as in previous chapters, giving direct comparisons of perceptions of purchase behavior and purchase-related attitudes.

Products Purchased

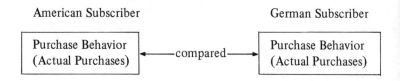

Table 6-4 first illustrates a point which will prove to be of great importance in this section: though both groups of subscribers are far more experienced and affluent than average for their own countries, American Information Seekers are more experienced consumers than German Information Seekers. For nearly all durables where direct comparisons were made, concentration was greater in the American group, with differences the greatest in more recently introduced products such as color TV sets and dishwashers. Ownership is far greater in the United States both for the list of durable products and for autos. Table 6-4 may understate the real experience and ownership differential between countries. Note the implication of notes c and d of that table. Data on previous ownership and purchase of durables and autos in table 6-5 also clearly indicates the greater experience of the American subscribers. The United States is more involved in the game of consumption than any other nation in the world; even these highly select samples reflect this fact.

Summary of Within-Country Comparisons

Universals: Both American and German subscribers are more concerned with availability of product information than average consumers.

Culture Specifics: American subscribers feel that brand reputation is important as a shopping criterion more than average consumers, but are less interested in product availability, economy and credit. German subscribers are more apt than average consumers to cite styling as a shopping criterion.

In response to the question, "How important were the following items as you shopped?" the two samples perceived the importance of various shopping concerns as shown in tables 6-6 and 6-7. As in previous chapters, the first part of each table compares the rankings of the various shopping criteria within each subscriber group, and the second part of the table illustrates differences in the index numbers *between* samples for all criteria. There was a tendency for the American subscribers to be more positive about lower-ranked criteria than Germans, or, put another way, Germans discriminated more distinctly between high and low ranked criteria. For this reason the differences in rank shown in part A of tables 6-6 and 6-7 may be more interesting than the absolute comparisons of indexes shown in part B.

Some distinctive patterns are noticeable when the rankings are surveyed in the two tables:

1. *Economy of Operation* is much more important to the German Information Seeker than to the American, for both durables and autos. With the cost of gasoline and electricity substantially higher in Europe, this would be a logical expectation. This price differential has probably narrowed sharply since the survey was completed.

2. *Brand and Dealer Reputation*, shopping criteria which are normally assumed to be proxies for individual product quality and substitutes for personal product evaluation, are ranked higher in the United States. This is contrary to the conventional wisdom that more experienced shoppers place less reliance upon these generalized criteria, but quite consistent with the within-country findings, where the American Information Seeker considered brand reputation more important than the average consumer. There has been a tendency to regard reliance upon brand reputation as a rather sloppy and inferior tactic in selecting individual products. It is quite thought-provoking to discover that this presumably sophisticated group of consumers from the world's most consuming-conscious nation places high reliance on these criteria. Brand and dealer reputation may also quite logically help establish expectations about *service* on products, a source of increasing frustration and importance in the United States.

Table 6-6. Shopping Criteria-Durable Goods Purchase[a] (National Mail Samples)

Consumer Reports *Subscribers* (Base = 530)			DM–test *Subscribers (Base = 549)*		
Rank	Criterion	Index	Rank	Criterion	Index

A. Ranked by Index Numbers[b]

	Consumer Reports *Subscribers*			DM–test *Subscribers*	
1.	Performance	91	1.	Performance	92
2.	Durability	84	2.	Durability	83
3.	Brand Reputation	84	3.	Service	72
4.	Service	73	4.	Warranty	69
5.	Warranty	68	5.	Information Availability	64
6.	Information Availability	67	6.	Brand Reputation	55
7.	Reputation of Dealer	61	7.	Economy of Operation	50
8.	Price	48	8.	Styling	36
9.	Availability of Product	45	9.	Price	26
10.	Styling	32	10.	Availability of Product	23
11.	Location of Dealer	17	11.	Reputation of Dealer	21
12.	Economy of Operation	15	12.	Location of Dealer	-13
13.	Credit	-49	13.	Credit	-76

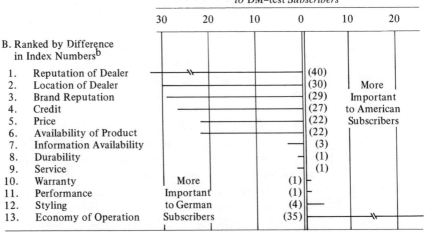

Consumer Reports *Subscribers compared to* DM–test *Subscribers*

30   20   10   0   10   20

B. Ranked by Difference in Index Numbers[b]

1.	Reputation of Dealer	(40)	More
2.	Location of Dealer	(30)	Important
3.	Brand Reputation	(29)	to American
4.	Credit	(27)	Subscribers
5.	Price	(22)	
6.	Availability of Product	(22)	
7.	Information Availability	(3)	
8.	Durability	(1)	
9.	Service	(1)	
10.	Warranty	(1)	More
11.	Performance	(1)	Important
12.	Styling	(4)	to German
13.	Economy of Operation	(35)	Subscribers

[a]Data based upon section 2 of questionnaire, reproduced in appendix G.

[b]Index = (% of sample rating criterion very important or important minus % of sample rating unimportant or very unimportant).

Table 6-7. Shopping Criteria-Auto Purchase[a] (National Mail Samples)

Consumer Reports *Subscriber (Base = 597)*			DM-test *Subscriber (Base = 470)*		
Rank	*Criterion*	*Index*	*Rank*	*Criterion*	*Index*
A. Ranked by Index Numbers[b]					
1.	Performance	91	1.	Performance	91
2.	Brand Reputation	88	2.	Durability	87
3.	Durability	85	3.	Economy of Oper.	81
4.	Price	74	4.	Brand Reputation	80
5.	Service	70	5.	Service	75
6.	Styling	63	6.	Information Avail.	51
7.	Information Avail.	60	7.	Warranty	47
8.	Warranty	60	8.	Styling	44
9.	Reputation of Dealer	57	9.	Price	42
10.	Economy of Oper.	56	10.	Reputation of Dealer	27
11.	Location of Dealer	33	11.	Location of Dealer	12
12.	Availability	23	12.	Availability	10
13.	Credit	-33	13.	Credit	-69

Consumer Reports *Subscribers compared to* DM-test *Subscribers*

			40	20	0	20	40
B. Ranked by Difference in Index Numbers[b]							
1.	Credit				(36)	More important to American Subscribers	
2.	Price				(32)		
3.	Reputation of Dealer				(30)		
4.	Location of Dealer				(21)		
5.	Styling				(19)		
6.	Availability				(13)		
7.	Warranty				(13)		
8.	Information Avail.				(9)		
9.	Brand Reputation				(8)		
10.	Performance		More important to German Subscribers	(0)	(0)		
11.	Durability			(2)			
12.	Service			(5)			
13.	Economy of Oper.			(25)			

[a]Data based upon section 3 of questionnaire, reproduced in appendix G.
[b]Index = (% of sample rating criterion very important or important minus % sample rating unimportant or very unimportant).

3. *Price* is consistently rated higher both in rank and index in the United States. This is somewhat surprising, but bargaining is more prevalent in durable goods shopping in the United States, making price shopping a more artful and challenging procedure there; and perhaps accounting in part for its greater perceived importance.

4. *Credit*, while low-rated for both countries and both purchases, is perceived as much less important (or perhaps much more unimportant is better phrasing) in Germany. Given the well-documented German stigma attendant upon credit purchases, this is a logical finding.

Perceived Information Sources

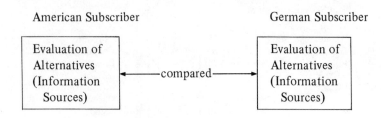

American Subscriber   German Subscriber

Summary of Within-Country Comparisons

Universals: Both American and German subscribers use the magazines to which they subscribe more as a source than average consumers.

Culture Specifics: German subscribers use other magazines and newspapers more than average consumers; American subscribers use personal observation less than average consumers.

Information sources appear in advance to be one of the most likely areas for substantial difference in buying behavior between countries. The two countries have different languages and different communications systems in addition to the cultural differences noted above, but data in this area revealed some striking parallels in perception of important sources accompanying expected variations:

1. *Personal Sources*, including observation, experience and consultation with friends and relatives, were perceived as highly important by both groups for both products. The indexes are remarkably consistent across countries, with no significant difference in any of the three categories for either product.
2. *Commercial Sources*, including advertising and salesmen, were uniformly perceived as more important in the United States. It will be found in later sections that the American Information Seeker is critical of many facets of advertising in some areas; much more so than the German; but the data in tables 6–8 and 6–9 give the first of several indications that the American still is more likely than the German to perceive value in commercial sources and to find them useful. It must also be realized that these results are based upon buyers' *perceptions* rather than actual use and that the current wave of criticism makes commercial sources (particularly advertising) unpopular.

**Table 6-8. Information Sources–Durable Goods Purchase[a]
(National Mail Samples)**

Consumer Reports *Subscriber* (Base = 530)			DM–test *Subscriber (Base = 549)*		
Rank	*Source*	*Index*	*Rank*	*Source*	*Index*
A. Ranked by Index Numbers[b]					
1.	Personal Observation	68	1.	Personal observation	67
2.	*Consumer Reports*	55	2.	*test*	40[c]
3.	Past Experience	25	3.	*DM*	32[c]
4.	Friend, Relative, etc.	8	4.	Past Experience	25
5.	Advertising	−9	5.	Friend Relative, etc.	3
6.	Salesman	−27	6.	Counseling Services	−9
7.	Other Mags. or Newsp.	−32	7.	Other Mags. or Newsp.	−13
8.	Other Consumer Mags.	−34	8.	Salesman	−34
			9.	Advertising	−36

Consumer Reports *Subscribers compared*
to DM–test *Subscribers*

	40	20	0	20	40
B. Ranked by Differences in Index Numbers[b]					
1. Advertising			(27)	Sources more	
2. Salesman			(7)	important to	
3. Friend, Relative, etc.			(5)	American	
4. Personal Observation			(1)	Subscribers	
5. Past Experience	Source more	(0)	(0)		
6. Other Mags. or Newsp.	important to	(19)			
(Others Not Comparable)	German Subscribers				

[a]Data based on section 2 of questionnaire reproduced in appendix G.

[b]Index = (% rating source important or very important minus % rating unimportant or very unimportant).

[c]Note that these figures are not strictly comparable to the *Consumer Reports* Index in the United States. All American subscribers are from *CR*, while German subscribers are divided approximately equally between *DM* and *test*.

There is little doubt that advertising is an important force in consumer decision making in both countries—perhaps the most important single force. It is reasonable to assume that the consumers' perceptions of use are understated, both because of the current social bias against advertising and because the sheer volume of messages and media have made exposure constant, expected and sometimes almost unnoticed. It would be a mistake, therefore, to place great credence in these perceptions as an *absolute* indicator of use, but they are certainly helpful and interesting when compared between samples as *indicators* of relative importance in various groups.

Table 6-9.   Information Sources–Auto Purchase[a] (National Mail Samples)

Consumer Reports Subscriber (Base = 597)		DM–test Subscriber (Base = 470)	
Rank Source	Index	Rank Source	Index
A. Ranked by Index Number[b]			
1. Personal Observation	81	1. Personal Observation	81
2. Past Experience	47	2. Past Experience	50
3. *Consumer Reports*	36	3. Other Mags. or Newsp.	18
4. Friend, Relative, etc.	16	4. Friend, Relative, etc.	13
5. Advertising	-16	5. *DM*	6
6. Salesman	-21	6. *test*	-5
7. Other Mags. or Newsp.	-24	7. Counseling Services	-30
8. Other Consumer Mags.	-33	8. Advertising	-37
		9. Salesman	-41

Consumer Reports *Subscribers compared to* DM–test *Subscribers*

	40	20	0	20	40
B. Ranked by Difference in Index Numbers[b]					
1. Advertising				(21)	Sources more
2. Salesman				(20)	important to
3. Friend, Relative, etc.				(3)	American
4. Personal Observations	Sources more		(0)	(0)	Subscribers
5. Past Experience	important to		(3)		
6. Other Mags. or Newsp.	German		(42)		
(Others not comparable)	Subscribers				

[a]Data based upon section 3 of questionnaire reproduced in appendix G.

[b]Index = (% of sample rating source important or very important minus % ranking unimportant or very unimportant).

3. *Other Magazines and Newspapers* are perceived as much more useful in Germany than in the United States. Though not among the top-rated sources even in Germany, they are regarded as relatively more important there, particularly in auto purchases. This may be in part accounted for by the fact that the German magazines place less emphasis on auto testing than *Consumer Reports*, and that several popular German magazines (e.g., *Stern, Auto-Sport*) have regular features evaluating autos.

German attitudes toward advertising were much more favorable than those of Americans (table 6-2 above). This intriguing question is covered extensively in chapters 8 and 9. It might be helpful, however, to present a preview of coming attractions at this point. There seems to be a clear distinction among consumers between advertising's economic and social dimensions, a distinction which may be involved in the inconsistent finding that American subscribers are less favorable toward advertising, but use it more.

1. In *Economic Aspects* (several questions gauging general beliefs in the utility of advertising in the marketplace) the American Information Seeker is more *favorable* toward advertising.
2. In *Social Aspects* (questions regarding the most common criticisms of current advertising practice) Americans are generally more *critical* than the Germans.
3. In some *General Attitudes* (is your attitude toward advertising favorable, or unfavorable) German subscribers are more favorable to current advertising overall.

These findings aid in an attempt to explain the inconsistencies between advertising use and attitudes. The Americans feel more strongly about the general usefulness of advertising in the marketplace and are not afraid to utilize it as a viable input for the decision process; yet they are critical of certain aspects of current advertising practice, a fact which apparently causes them to express a generally unfavorable opinion. The implication of these limited findings may be that general attitudes are based more upon social dimensions of advertising, but that actual use is more dependent upon economic attitudes. If this is true, it might have interesting practical application in the strategies of both businessmen and consumer advocates.

Satisfaction and Product Test Reports

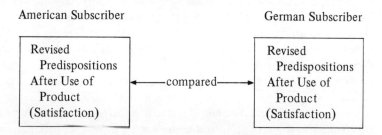

Summary of Within-Country Comparisons
  Opposites: This was the one area in the country studies where clear opposite trends appeared. German subscribers were generally more satisfied with products, information available, personal shopping activity and safety than AC, while American subscribers were less satisfied.

Our original hypothesis regarding satisfaction was that subscribers in general should be better satisfied than AC with their purchases and buying activity, because using more sources, planning better, having the benefit of product tests and other expert information, they should perceive themselves as making better purchases and being better satisfied. This hypothesis was supported strongly by the results from Germany, but was completely unsupported by the United States data which, in fact, showed an opposite trend. Further analysis of the United States data, however, revealed that subscribers who perceived themselves as having *used* the test results were better satisfied on all dimensions than those subscribers who had not. It was concluded that in the United States at least, subscribers are a harder lot to satisfy than AC, but that their satisfaction on all measured dimensions was greater when ratings were consulted. The Germans seemed to behave in accordance with the original hypothesis: simply better satisfied than non-subscribers.

The results from the mail samples shown in table 6–10 reinforce the results of the smaller metropolitan samples in the country studies reported in chapters 4 and 5. For both types of product, the German Information Seeker is better satisfied on all measured dimensions except one—safety. The Americans had more confidence in the safety of both the durable goods and autos they had purchased. There is no clue in the data as to whether this is a result of the current stress on product safety in the United States, the suspicious nature of Germans, or something else less obvious. The American Information Seeker once again seems to be a tougher customer than his German counterpart.

The new wave of consumerism was far more advanced in the United States than in Germany at the time of the study, and current consumerism has tended more to be fostered and supported by the affluent and intellectual than previous manifestations of this phenomenon. The expert consumers in the United States sample might certainly be expected to have been exposed to the product-critical, consumer-protecting tone of the movement, particularly since *Consumer Reports* is considered one of the bastions of consumerism. It seems likely, therefore, that some of the critical tone of the American subscriber implied by lower satisfaction is a function of the advanced stage of consumerism in the United States.

A single question was included in an attempt to measure *perceived risk*. Theory in this area projects that the less the experience with purchase of a product, the greater the uncertainty and perceived risk. For both durables and automobile purchases perceived risk was significantly higher among German Information Seekers, indicating again the greater sophistication and experience of the Americans in the act of consumption, and maybe also the worrying, skeptical nature of the German character.

Up to now we have discussed measures of satisfaction comparing all German and American subscribers who had made a purchase. Since it is generally assumed that use of ratings should lead to better purchases, it is revealing now to

Table 6-10. Selected Satisfaction Measures[a] (National Mail Samples) (Results in Index Numbers)[b]

	Durable Goods Purchase			Auto Purchase		
	CR Subscriber (Base = 530)	DM-test Subscriber (Base = 549)	High Group Difference	CR Subscriber (Base = 597)	DM-test Subscriber (Base = 470)	High Group Difference
Product						
Turned out to be all I expected	72	75	G +3[c]	57	71	G +14
I would recommend to a friend	77	77	Tie	72	73	G +1
Information Availability						
Little trouble finding how brands differ	25	30	G +5	32	60	G +28
Plenty of information available	42	48	G +6	58	60	G +2
Personal Shopping Activity						
Even with more information–no better brand	55	61	G +6	55	64	G +9
Shopped enough to get lowest price	37	67	G +30	36	56	G +20
Safety						
This brand is safe to use	90	63	U.S. +27	70	63	U.S. +7
Advertising						
Advertising was accurate and helpful	20	39	G +19	-15	32	G +45
Perceived Risk						
Worried–mistake upsetting	17	62	G +45	37	68	G +31

[a]Data based upon part 3 of sections 2 and 3 of questionnaire, reproduced in appendix G.
[b]Index = (% sample agree and strongly agree minus % sample disagree and strongly disagree).
[c]Read G +3, German subscribers more satisfied by 3 index points.

compare those who *used* the ratings of one of the magazines to those who *did not use* the ratings to see if there is a difference in satisfaction. Table 6–11 summarizes comparisons of satisfaction between perceived users of test reports with perceived non-users.

The pattern of results here is quite consistent with the results in the metropolitan subscribers' samples: perceived users of reports are generally better satisfied with their efforts in all measured dimensions of satisfaction, though only a portion of the results were actually statistically significant. As theory suggests, perceived risk (as measured by single question) was consistently higher for users, at highly significant levels in both instances: the higher the risk the more likely the search for more information, presumably including test reports.

In the question regarding accuracy and helpfulness of advertising the American user was more satisfied, but the German user (showing greater consistency) was usually *less* inclined to find it helpful than the non-user.

On the whole, this section strongly supports the hypothesis that use of product test reports is coupled with greater satisfaction with both products purchased and purchase procedures.

THE PECULIAR CASE OF CONSUMER ISSUES

A series of questions was devoted to respondents' opinions on the importance of current consumer issues and the government's role in particular activities. Respondents were asked to mention as many issues as they chose and to rank them in order of importance. The mail sample respondents from each country reacted strictly according to national stereotype: on the average, Americans mentioned and ranked two or three issues while the methodical Germans mostly ranked all seven issues listed, thereby thoroughly confusing the analysis. Because of this extreme cross-cultural difference, the data were not strictly comparable; the only really interesting outcomes from qualitatively examining them are:

1. Of all issues presented, consumer education was the least interesting to subscribers in both countries (even though it has often been cited as the fundamental solution to most consumer problems in the long term). Most consumers may feel that they are already well-informed.
2. There is decidedly more subscriber interest in increased government activity in product testing in the United States than in Germany, probably because there has been much less government activity in the United States.

It is disappointing that further results in this area are either inconclusive or cannot be analyzed. The within-country results in this area were discussed in chapters 4 and 5.

Table 6-11. Selected Satisfaction Measures—Perceived Users vs. Non-Users (National Mail Samples)

	Durable Good Purchase			Auto Purchase		
	CR Subscribers	test Subscribers	DM Subscribers	CR Subscribers	test Subscribers	DM Subscribers
Product						
Turned out to be all I expected	U	U	Tie	U	U*	
Would recommend to friend	U	U	N	U	N	
Information Availability						
Little trouble finding how brands differ	U	U	U**	N	U	User Sample Too Small
Plenty of information available	U**	U**	U**	U**	U**	
Personal Shopping Activity						
Even with more information— no better brand.	U**	U**	N	U*	U	
Safety						
This brand is safe to use	U	U	U	U	U	
Advertising						
Advertising was accurate and helpful	U	N	N*	U	N	

U = Perceived user more satisfied than non-user
N = Perceived non-user more satisfied than user

$* p < .05$
$** p < .01$

SUBSCRIBERS' USE OF TEST REPORTS—
PERCEPTIONS AND ATTITUDES

The study collected a great deal of information on the subscribers' perception of their use of information from product tests as well as their attitudes toward both the information and the organizations which disperse it. These are perceptual questions, and there is little doubt that subscribers tend to overstate the importance of product tests in purchase decisions. They should be accepted and used as absolute values with caution. Nonetheless, this study is one of the first attempts to evaluate the nature of influence and the effectiveness of product test reports from the viewpoint of the users themselves. As a pioneering effort, it contains a number of insights which should be of value, particularly when one searches for patterns and proportions rather than accepting absolutes. Put another way: it may be questionable whether one should accept as quantified gospel that over half of American subscribers actually used the ratings in a durable product purchase and that nearly all who did were delighted with the purchase outcome (see table 6-12); but it may be quite significant to policy-makers that all users from throughout the study (whatever sample) consistently feel that test reports are less influential in auto buying than in other durable purchase decisions.

The implication of the perceived use statistics in table 6-12 is at least an indication that test magazines have loyal subscribers, and if taken literally, that they strongly influence purchase decisions by their recommendations. For the durable purchase in both countries there is a consistent pattern of high awareness of ratings, high use in purchase, and high satisfaction with resultant purchases—a substantial vote of confidence for the ratings. For autos, the influence

Table 6-12.   Perceived Use of Product Test Recommendations[a]
(National Mail Samples) (By Percent of Actual Purchases)

	American		German	
	Durable	Auto	Durable	Auto
Aware of Recommendations	64%	47%	56%	27%
Recommendations Important in Purchase Decision	53%	38%	52%	18%
Purchased Highly Rated Brand	41%	29%	45%	18%
INDEX[b] of agreement with recommendations after experience with products among purchasers of recommended brands	92	86	89	89

[a]Data taken from questions 38–41, section 6 of questionnaire, reproduced in appendix G.
[b]Index = (% of sample strongly agree or agree minus % sample disagree or strongly disagree).

is less in the United States than for durables but still sizable; influence in autos is much less in Germany. This probably reflects the far greater emphasis given to autos by *Consumer Reports*, which dedicates one of its 11 monthly issues entirely to autos each year, and devotes considerable space throughout the year to special tests and general comments on auto purchases. Even given this heavy emphasis and the fact that the auto issue is always *CR*'s largest selling issue on the newsstands, influence is seen here as elsewhere (chapters 4 and 5) as less in autos than in durable purchases. Autos receive far less attention than this in both *DM* and *test*.[3]

Selected issues related to use of product test reports are summarized in table 6-13. It was noted in chapter 1 that one interesting facet of this investigation was the fact that the three organizations had three different types of sponsors. Since there was a possibility that the credibility of information is linked to the credibility of the sponsoring organization, it was instructive to see if subscribers could correctly identify the nature of the sponsoring organizations. As shown in table 6-13, about 80 percent of the subscribers correctly identified the nature of the sponsoring organization.

When subscribers were asked to give the source of tests in which they would place the most confidence, they tended to cite their own magazines. It is interesting to note here that virtually all answers in both countries included only consumer groups alone or consumer groups aided by the government. There was negligible support for testing sponsored by business, and (surprisingly) almost none for government alone. There was a strong mandate from all respondents to continue the recommendation of specific brands, despite the frequent criticism of this practice by business and sometimes by consumerists.

The patterns of general use of the magazines on the "how long do you keep" and "do you lend" questions were quite consistent between countries; copies remain on hand (or at least in magazine racks) for a much longer period of time than most magazines, and there is a high incidence of lending of individual issues as well.

Subscribers were questioned extensively on their attitudes toward or satisfaction with various aspects of the product test reports. The results are summarized in table 6-14 and figure 6-2. We were specifically interested in gauging several separate dimensions which were presupposed in accordance with communication theory to be relevant to the effectiveness of the reports, including: credibility of source and reliability of information offered; availability, timeliness and relevance of the information; and clarity of presentation. In addition, several questions relating to overall effectiveness were included. This is not presented as an exhaustive set of criteria nor is any true scale value imputed to the "indexes" which have been calculated from the questions. Our interest was to gain some crude measures of users' perceptions of the effectiveness of product tests. We hoped for beginning information which would lead to more sophisticated investigation and measurement in the future.

Table 6-13. Summary of Selected Opinion and Usage Questions[a] (National Mail Samples) (Percent of Total Respondents)

	United States (Base = 630)	Germany DM (Base = 498)	test (Base = 505)
What kind of organization sponsors (the publication to which you subscribe):			
Commercial Publisher	1%	85%	2%
Business Firm	1	0	1
Government Agency	0	0	6
Trade Association	0	0	0
Non-Profit Consumer Group	77	2	3
Foundation	NA	2	78
Don't Know or No Answer	21	11	10
	100%	100%	100%

(Base = 610)

	United States	Germany
I would have most confidence in tests sponsored by:		
Government Alone	1%	2%
Business Alone	1	0
Consumer Group Alone	57	33
Consumer Group and Government	30	47
Consumer Group and Business	5	5
Business and Government	1	1
Don't Know or No Answer	5	12
	100%	100%
Should product test reports recommend particular brands?		
Yes	85%	72%
No	13	20
Don't Know or No Opinion	2	8
	100%	100%
How long do you keep copies of the magazine?		
Throw away when read	1%	0
For a few weeks	7	4%
For a year or two	33	36
Indefinitely	50	50
It depends	6	8
Pass them along to someone else	3	2
	100%	100%
Do you ever lend copies to others, or pass copies along?		
Lend to others	65%	61%
Pass along	4	4
Neither	31	35
	100%	100%

[a]Data taken from questions 34–36 and 44–45 of section 6 of questionnaire, reproduced in appendix G.

Table 6-14. Satisfaction with Selected Magazines and Agency Qualities[a] (National Mail Samples) (By Index Numbers)[b]

	Consumer Reports	DM	test
General			
Recommendations highly useful	89	87	95
Generally satisfied with recommended product	87	75	83
Mean Index	(88)	(81)	(89)
Reliability and Credibility			
Test information is quite reliable	90	72	84
Believe in independence and integrity	91	54	86
Confidence in testing methods	91	82	92
No government or business influence	63	57	55
Mean Index	(84)	(66)	(79)
Relevance, Timeliness and Availability			
Is not too much stress on safety	27	7	13
Tests features of interest	66	53	62
No nuisance to get right copy	44	33	32
Information is seldom too old	38	56	55
Has tested products wish to buy	55	77	78
Mean Index	(46)	(45)	(48)
Clarity and Readability			
Style bright and stimulating	50	65	57
Not too much technical detail	56	70	62
Information clear, not hard to read	86	82	86
Mean Index	(64)	(72)	(68)
Mean Index–All Questions	(67)	(62)	(67)

[a]Data based upon section 6 of questionnaire, reproduced in appendix G.
[b]Index = (% strongly agree or agree minus % disagree or strongly disagree).

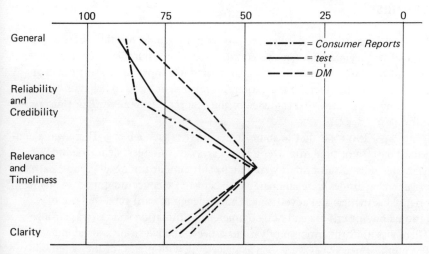

Figure 6-2. Satisfaction With Magazines and Agencies on Four Dimensions (Summary of Index Numbers from Table 6-14).

Once again, the raw results amount to a substantial vote of satisfaction with each of the three magazines. All indexes were positive for all questions for all magazines—mostly at very high levels. When patterns and proportions rather than absolute numbers are examined, however, some interesting findings are visible:

1. As gauged by both the general measures and overall index, *CR* and *test* are more satisfactory to their subscribers. The major difference is in credibility, where *DM* is substantially lower. (*DM* is the only commercial venture and the only one which accepts advertising.);
2. *DM*, with its more colorful and flamboyant style, (which has been moderated some since the survey) is given the highest mark in style and general readability, while *CR* is rated lowest;
3. *CR*, which has painstakingly avoided any contact with business over time to protect its independent reputation, is highest in credibility and reliability;
4. By far the lowest score given each of the three magazines was in the relevance –timeliness–availability area. Criticism here is only relative, since all marks are still favorable, but obviously over-emphasis of safety features, difficulty of having copies available at proper times, and senility of available ratings are regarded as the most serious weakness of the ratings.

Although these measures are far from definitive, they delineate for the agencies the "product features" of their magazines which are in greatest need of improvement.

THE UNIVERSAL INFORMATION SEEKER— A REPRISE

The purpose of this chapter has been to compare groups of subscribers to three product testing magazines in two countries on a large number of characteristics relevant to purchase behavior and information use—not only to sort out characteristics of subscribers to the various magazines, but also to help answer the question posed in the first sentence of the chapter, "Is there *really* a Universal Information Seeker?"

It is clear that to some degree there is such a being. There was a consistent pattern of similarity over a broad array of variables: demographic characteristics of subscribers were remarkably similar among all groups; patterns of general attitudes were comparable, except those concerning specific, liberal-oriented activities, and advertising. The tendency toward perceived use of rational buying criteria and non-commercial information sources was strong. There was uniform criticism of various aspects of advertising's social impact. Product test magazines were seen as successful, with praise for their credibility and reliability but less enthusiasm for the relevance of their criteria for evaluation and the timeliness of available information. Given the extent of the questioning in the survey and the geographic and cultural dispersion of respondents, the similarities in results, although not all-inclusive, are remarkable.

There were also differences between countries and between agencies. German subscribers were much more prone to support action-oriented liberal measures. American subscribers were simultaneously more *critical* of advertising's social impact, more *positive* about its economic role, but *less favorable* in overall attitude. Germans worried more about product economy and placed less reliance on brand reputation. Americans perceived themselves as using commercial sources of information more in making purchases, and as being more avid readers, listeners and viewers than the Germans. In all ways, Americans were more involved in the game of consumption. They owned more durables and had greater past experience in purchase. Germans were more worried about making mistakes when they purchased, but Americans were harder to satisfy *after* they had purchased. Although the similarity among groups was notable, it is apparent that differences are too large to be ignored.

It can thus be said that while a core of basic characteristics identifies the Information Seeker, there is no doubt that strong environmental influences from a culture, an economy, or an agency will also cause substantive differences in characteristics. In this study at least three major national characteristics seem to have cropped up with enough regularity to bear mention:

1. *The United States is a more advanced consumer economy.* It has been suggested that the United States, Sweden, Switzerland and perhaps others have entered the *post-industrial* stage of development in which there is a certain reaction to the protracted preoccupation with more and more production and consumption. After a certain accumulation of wealth, this theory holds, a stage occurs when services attain greater importance, the rights of the consumer are rediscovered, and more restrained stewardship of resources is demanded; in short, a more statesmanlike approach to economics—a seeking after a nation's economic, social and cultural self-fulfillment.

   Whatever the validity of this concept, it is clear that America is further advanced in consumption and in consumerism than is Germany. Its greater experience in buying and using goods, its lower perceived risk in purchasing; its more strident criticism of advertising's social impact as compared to its economic dimensions, and perhaps its greater respect for advertising's economic role are all part of this picture. So is the lower satisfaction with purchases, implying tougher performance criteria and/or higher aspiration level. (An alternative explanation might be that Germany simply has higher quality products overall, or that the Germans perceive it as higher.)

2. *Germans are less trustful and more worrisome individuals.* Not only is this a part of the national stereotype as outlined at the chapter's beginning, but it also has been substantiated by a number of serious studies of national cul-

tures.[4] Thus the German subscriber trusted businessmen much less than did the American. He worried more about making the right purchase, and his reluctance to trust others or even himself fully showed up in places in this and other chapters. Katona contends that this basic "worrisome" character-istic manifests itself in the German's economic activity, making it difficult for him to act as expansively as Americans even in the same type of rapidly-developing, affluent economy. "(D)efense of the status quo is valued beyond adjustment to long-term income gains."[5]

According to Katona, the American acts as though prosperity will never end, while the German acts as though he can't believe it ever began. Perusal of recent German economic data, magazines, and other indicators of buying activity and life style suggests that Katona's evaluation may be too strong, or that it was made too early. The Germans act increasingly as if they have found and enjoy the life of affluent consumers.

3. *Germany has a longer and more deeply-engrained history of government activity, particularly in business areas.* This was noted in the liberal action questions in government-business and welfare as well as in other questions that related to governmental activity throughout the survey.

There is reason to believe that there *is* a sizable contingent of affluent, intelligent, product-knowledgeable information-conscious consumers homoge-nous enough internationally to be considered a unit by business, government, and CI policy-makers. The first stage of naiveté in international marketing was to believe that all consumers were alike wherever they were found. The second stage was to believe that a given culture's consumers were different from all others. Yet a third stage may recognize that international cross-cultural segments exist, whether it be for automobiles, for product information, or for other important products. The trick is to isolate the important similarities from the important differences.

NOTES TO CHAPTER 6

1. Gabriel A. Almond and Sidney Verba, *The Civic Culture: Political Attitudes and Democracy in Five Nations* (Princeton, New Jersey: Princeton University Press, 1965).
2. George Katona, Burkhard Strumpel and Ernest Zahn, *Aspirations and Afflu-ence—Comparative Studies in the United States and Western Europe* (New York: McGraw-Hill, 1971).
3. Hans B. and Sarah V. Thorelli, *Consumer Information Handbook: Europe and North America* (New York: Praeger, 1974) includes a listing of the types and numbers of tests by individual agencies.
4. For example, see Almond and Verba, and Katona et al.: 84. In a 1965 study commissioned by *Stiftung Warentest* and comprising a representative

sample of 1,952 Germans the question was asked, "Do you think that people in general can be trusted, or should one rather be wary (*misstrauisch*)?" No less than 50 percent of respondents declared that one should rather be wary, while 29 percent felt people in general can be trusted and 20 percent were undecided. The percentages were remarkably similar for different sex, age, income and social groups. Intermarket, *Warentest—Eine Studie über Verbraucherwünsche*. (Berlin, 1965. Mimeographed). Table of answers to question 40.

5. Katona et al.: 84.

Chapter Seven

Other Studies of Consumer
Information Views

The part of the International Consumer Information Survey accounted for in this volume is probably the most broad-gauged and systematic survey of representative and separate samples of Information Seekers and Average Consumers undertaken thus far. It is also the only cross-cultural study of consumer attitudes to CI programs and of the relations of such views and attitudes to advertising. A broader perspective as well as a more detailed understanding of consumer attitudes to and use of CI programs may be obtained by bringing into account pertinent aspects of related studies by ourselves and others. This is the purpose of the present chapter.

Relatively few of these studies have been carried out with academic rigor, and surprisingly few studies have been made under the auspices of CI organizations themselves. One would assume that such bodies would have sufficiently strong interest in appraising their impact and effectiveness to allocate at least part of their resources to this type of research. As late as 1973, CI organizations sponsoring large-scale studies of this kind with any degree of stringence were to be found only in Germany, the United States, Norway, Britain, France and Sweden. Except in the United States and Britain, most of the research has been of a "one-shot" nature or, in any case, not ongoing. Only in the last few years has there been any appreciable interest in this field among academic researchers.

We will confine our attention here to studies dealing in large part with the types of questions to which the research accounted for in prior chapters was addressed. Research design and credibility will be discussed only briefly, primary attention being given to results. Types of research that have been deemed beyond the purview of this chapter include surveys of consumer buying intentions[a], studies of information processing among consumers not directed to CI

[a]Buying intentions, ownership of durable goods and consumer experience with different types of goods are recurring features in CU's broad-gauged annual subscriber surveys, each of which also includes a variety of special topics. Pioneering research on buying

programs[b] and studies directed towards such specialized topics as whether one type of informative label will be more easily recognized and digested by consumers than another[c] or whether, and to what extent, consumers make use of such special-purpose information as unit pricing data in supermarkets.[d]

The material to be reviewed will be introduced on a country-by-country basis. Because the leader of the present project was a co-sponsor of research in Norway in part directly coordinated with this project, we shall begin with that country.[e] For obvious reasons we shall then discuss related research in Germany and the United States. Other nations will follow in alphabetical order.

No claim of exhaustiveness is made; it has not been practicable to undertake a full search of all countries in the North Atlantic community. We have, however, examined all attitude surveys of consumer information known to over 50 CI organizations in these countries by 1970 (whether or not sponsored by those agencies) and made available to us. A few later studies are also included. Our comments will be confined to studies conducted with a reasonable degree of rigor from a survey research point of view.

NORWAY

Early in 1969 the Consumer Council of Norway, a government body, commissioned the Central Bureau of Statistics of Norway to undertake a survey to determine readership of the Council's magazine and its comparative product test reports. While the survey instrument was still in the design stage, these agencies

---

intentions has been done by George Katona and others at the Institute of Social Research at the University of Michigan. The Institute, as well as the Federal Reserve Board, carry out standard surveys of buying intentions at regular intervals.

Since 1970 the Belgian *Association des Consommateurs* has carried out an annual survey of consumer (subscriber) buying intentions. Similar surveys of consumer buying intentions are now becoming increasingly common in different countries as one means of macroeconomic forecasting.

[b]A great number of such studies have been made, constituting an important part of the burgeoning area of "consumer behavior" research. Again, American researchers have been in the forefront.

[c]A pioneering effort in this area was made in the 1960s by the Swedish *Varudeklarationsnämnden* (VDN).

[d]A considerable number of studies of the impact of unit pricing have been sponsored by the Consumer Research Institute in Washington, D.C. American research in this area has been summarized by James M. Carman, "A Summary of Empirical Research on Unit Pricing in Supermarkets," *Journal of Retailing* (Winter 1972–73): 63–71, and Kent B. Monroe and Peter J. LaPlaca, "What Are the Benefits of Unit Pricing?" *Journal of Marketing* (July 1972): 16–22.

[e]Attempts at achieving similar cooperation with *Association des Consommateurs* in Belgium, Consumers' Association in Britain and *Konsumentrådet* in Sweden were abortive. We are prepared to hypothesize that the difficulties in bringing about coordinated multinational research grow exponentially with the number of prospective countries involved.

graciously accepted our co-sponsorship of the study.[f] This led to the addition of a number of items to the questionnaire with these aims: to increase comparability of the Norwegian data with our research on CI program awareness, attitudes and use among consumers in Germany and the United States; to permit comparisons of impact between two different *types* of CI programs, that is, comparative testing and informative labeling; and to permit comparisons with our research on advertising image. The data on advertising image will be discussed below in chapter 8. Results in the first two categories will briefly be analyzed here and some comparisons will be made with our German and American findings.[1]

The Norwegian data base was big and of unusually high quality. First, 93 sample districts were randomly drawn from the 1541 official population districts which make up 53 geographic and economic strata. One sample district was drawn for each of the 13 strata comprised by Oslo, Bergen and Trondheim, and two sample districts were drawn from each of the other 40. Second, a total of 1817 households were interviewed out of a sample of 2061 households drawn randomly from the 93 districts. Due to the fact that the *Forbruker-rapporten*, the comparative testing journal published by the Consumer Council, has the highest subscriber rate of any such magazine in the world, no fewer than 324 households of the 1817 were subscribers.

The data in table 7-1 demonstrate the kind of differences in demographic characteristics between subscribers and consumers encountered in our German and American country studies. These income and education data are particularly striking in view of the fact that Norway is customarily regarded as one of the most homogeneous countries in the world. The Norwegian occupational scale is not directly comparable with those used elsewhere in this work, tending to mix job hierarchy with job-type categories. At least one familiar distinction seems to be present: professional, supervisory, office and sales personnel represent 41.8 percent of all subscribers and only 19.2 percent of non-subscribers. On the other hand, mining, transport and industrial employees (mostly workingmen) represent 32.8 percent of subscribers which compares impressively with the 35.7 percent among non-subscribers. Actually, there is no doubt that the Norwegian CI journal is better represented among worker households than any other such magazine. With regard to age composition, the heads of Norwegian subscriber households show a strong concentration to middle brackets, with a notably small proportion (for Norwegian conditions) in the age group 65 and over.

[f]The Project Leader expresses personal thanks to Mrs. Inger Louise Valle, Minister of Family and Consumer Affairs of Norway (then Bureau Chief of the Consumer Council) and Mr. Sverre Hove, Bureau Chief of the Central Bureau of Statistics of Norway for agreeing to let the International Consumer Information Survey co-sponsor this study.

Table 7-1.   Comparisons of Subscriber and Non-Subscriber Income and Education in Norwegian Survey

	Subscribers[b] (Base = 324)	Non-Subscribers (Base = 1493)	All Households (Base = 1817)
Income[a]			
50,000 Nkr and over	14%	4%	6%
40,000–49,999	28	10	13
30,000–39,999	20	14	15
20,000–29,999	20	25	24
10,000–19,999	9	16	15
Under 10,000	9	31	27
	100%	100%	100%
Education			
University	22%	7%	10%
Gymnasium	29	18	20
Secondary school	28	28	28
Primary school	21	47	42
	100%	100%	100%

[a]Based on income declarations in tax returns. The rate of exchange was Norwegian crowns 7.16 to U.S. $1.00.
[b]The Mann-Whitney U test was used to test the differences between subscribers and non-subscribers. For both income and education $p < .001$.

Age	Subscribers	Non-subscribers
Under 34	13.3%	12.1%
35–49	40.0	27.5
50–64	35.6	32.9
65 and over	11.1	27.5
	100.0%	100.0%

As to awareness of the sponsorship of the Consumer Council, of the existence and sponsorship of the Norwegian Informative Labeling Institute, of the fact that Institute labels verify facts about the product rather than its quality, and of the existence of special consumer complaint bodies, high-education or high-income respondents were significantly better informed than lower education or income groups. The difference in awareness of these matters between subscribers and non-subscribers tended to be even greater than between different income and educational groups. (Thorelli, 431.)

Respondents were also asked about their use of the following information sources for a specific major purchase:

Advertisements
Consumer reports (*Forbruker-rapporten*)

Other magazines and newspapers
Family
Friends or relatives
Shopping more than one store
Brochures
Demonstration of product

Again, all information sources except shopping and other magazines were used significantly more by high education or income respondents than by those with lower education or income. It may well be that people in the top education and income group value their time too highly to shop around. At the time the study was made, Norwegian popular magazines and newspapers offered relatively little material of consumer interest beyond advertising. As might be expected, subscribers made significantly greater use of most sources than non-subscribers. "Other magazines" was the only information source utilized more by non-subscribers (Thorelli, 429). All in all, the data make it unequivocally clear that the Information Seeker as we have found him in Germany and the United States also exists in Norway, and that subscribers to comparative test reports constitute the elite core of the total group of Information Seekers.

The Norwegian data also permit some reflections concerning comparative testing and informative labeling, two principal variants of CI programs. As to awareness, we may note that the percentage of respondents stating that they had heard of the Labeling Institute was practically identical, by income level and educational level, with those who said they had heard of the Consumer Council. A very similar pattern was observed with regard to knowledge of the sponsorship of the two agencies, although awareness of the sponsorship of the Labeling Institute on the average was a few percentage points lower (Thorelli, 431). This may be due to the fact that the Institute has joint sponsorship of government and business, while the Council is a government agency. In any case, these results are remarkable, in view of the fact that the Institute had labeled less than 600 brands covering about 25 different products at the time.

Usage rate of labeling information was high, considering the relatively small number of products and brands. A full 50 percent of respondents declared that they at least sometimes bought Institute-labeled products, while 25 percent said they failed to notice whether goods bought were labeled. Some 9 percent said they rarely or never bought labeled products, and the remaining 16 percent did not know.[2] As might be expected, subscribers used the labels more than non-subscribers. While usage rates were somewhat larger in high education and income groups, this relationship was much weaker than in the case of subscribership to test reports. Thus, the Norwegian data suggest that informative labeling has the ability to permeate all social groups to a greater extent than comparative testing. Apart from greater readability, labels undoubtedly benefit from the fact that they appear affixed to the product at the point of purchase.

GERMANY

Two studies from Germany are of special interest here. One was sponsored by *Stiftung Warentest* in 1965 and the other by the government of Nordrhein-Westfalen in 1972.[3]

The *Warentest* study was based on a representative nationwide quota sample of 2000 persons between 18 and 70 years of age. To the question, "Who in your opinion should carry out comparative testing?" the answers were distributed as follows:

A consumer group	36%
Business	10
A journal publisher	8
An institute independent of government and business	30
A government agency	17
Others, don't know	28
	129%

The percentage totals more than 100, as respondents were free to give more than one answer.

The study was made before publication of the first issue of *test*. It is interesting to note that no less than 20 percent of respondents at the time stated that "in the last few months" they had read *DM* "every now and then," which compared favorably even with *Der Spiegel* (19 percent). The percentage of men giving positive answers was twice as high as that of women for both journals. In the case of "regular" reading, however, *DM* with 4 percent trailed *Der Spiegel* with 8 percent. Some 28 percent of respondents had personally bought *DM* at least once. It may be noted that 1965 was the turning point in *DM*'s early success.

Respondents who had either bought or read *DM* were also asked what appealed to them and what they objected to in the journal. The 617 respondents gave these answers:

Strengths		*Weaknesses*	
The test reports	24%	Tests not always up to par	8%
Critical in tone	23	Not always objective	8
Functional, objective	21	Contents unorganized	11
Keeps consumer posted	13	Too much advertising	6
Others, don't know	32	Too expensive	5
	113%	No weaknesses	34
		Others, don't know	37
			109%

Percentages again add up to more than 100 due to multiple responses by some respondents. It is clear that at least before the arrival of *test* with its government backing, *DM* ranked quite high in the opinion of its readers. One-third of respondents specifically stated that they had no objections at all to the journal, and only 6 percent stated that there was too much advertising. At least in its earlier years, then, *DM* did not seem to have much of a credibility problem with its readers on account of accepting advertisements. Whether it was the arrival of *test* or *DM*'s later more free-wheeling style (or both) that made respondents in our own survey a bit more critical in this regard is difficult to say.

The second German study made use of two samples, one limited to the state of Nordrhein-Westfalen and a nationwide representative interview sample comprising 1878 persons (lower age limit: 14, percentage of men in sample: 47). As the former sample had limitations other than that of geography, we will confine our attention to the nationwide aspects of the study. A very interesting part of the research concerned the perceived informedness and needs for information in the households of which the respondents were a part, and the importance attached by respondents to increased government effort in various areas (including consumer information and advisory services). Some of the responses dealing with informedness and information needs follow:

	Household well informed	*Would like to be better informed*
Nutrition	71%	27%
Household products and appliances	72	27
Advantageous buying opportunities	52	47
Price movements	41	57
Savings and investment opportunities	62	36
Insurance	57	41
Complaints procedures	36	62
Consumer rights	40	58

Our notion that one of the major problems in the CI area is that so many consumers perceive themselves as well informed about consumer products seems to be supported by these findings. Almost three-fourths of respondents were satisfied with their product information, only about one-fourth felt the need for more information. These figures are striking, even though the results might well have been different if a similar question had been asked about specific product categories. On the other hand, the data also indicate two areas into which CI might well be extended further. One is the pinpointing of advantageous buying opportunities ("who sells what at a low price") and of price trends of individual commodity categories. The other is services, such as money management and insurance, the type of problems to which *DM* allocates considerable space and to which the British *Money Which?* is entirely devoted. The table strikingly illustrates the need felt by German consumers for more information about consumer rights and complaints processes.

Table 7-2 indicates the importance attached by respondents to increased governmental appropriations in various areas. It appears that consumer problems are a matter of medium concern. An obvious weakness in this type of question is that the items frequently do not lend themselves to easy comparison with each other; another shortcoming is that most respondents may be presumed not to know exactly what the government is currently spending—in which case they are really responding to a request simply to list the items in aggregate importance.

Respondents were also asked about how they would inform themselves in the postulated purchase of a washing machine. The perceived relative usefulness of various information sources was classified by type of information, as shown in table 7-3. (The striking importance of store visits was also encountered in our Norwegian data.) Test reports compare favorably with prior personal experience, with relatives and friends, and with brochures and catalogs in this imaginary purchase. The perceived relative strength of such reports with regard to performance and quality information is clear, as is their relative weakness in regard to price and availability of data.

Table 7-2. Priorities of Public Expenditures Indicated by German Respondents

Interviewer question: In this list there is a range of things for which the government is spending money. Would you please tell me for each item whether the government should spend more money, about the same, or less than in the past?

	Percentage of respondents in favor of		
	more	*same*	*less*
Air and water pollution	89	9	1
Health	78	20	1
Education	75	22	3
Highways	63	32	5
City planning and redevelopment	53	41	5
Public transport	51	42	6
Consumer Information and Advice	47	45	7
Small business	30	47	23
Agriculture	25	46	28
Space research	20	35	45
Aid to developing countries	15	36	48
Defense	9	32	58

Source: Bernd Biervert, *Wirtschaftspolitische, sozialpolitische und sozialpädagogische Aspekte einer verstärkten Verbraucheraufklärung* (Köln: Krupinski, 1972), table 4.3.30.

A majority of respondents (55 percent) were aware of product test-ing magazines. *DM* was known to 44 percent, *test* to 27 percent and auto magazines carrying tests from time to time to 22 percent of the sample. Those who were aware of one or more of the testing journals were asked about their reading habits.

	Read regularly	*Read infrequently*
DM	5%	32%
test	4	20
Auto magazines	9	11

The same group was also asked about the reliability of tests of the type reported in these journals. The answers were distributed as follows:

Table 7-3. Information Sources in Purchase of Washing Machine Indicated by German Respondents

Interviewer question: If you make a big purchase, such as that of a washing machine, a number of questions would tend to arise, and there are various means of informing oneself about individual matters. Here is a list of sources.

Where would you inform yourself about the *best place to buy*, in terms of value for money, good customer service, etc.?

How about *performance characteristics*, such as capacity, consumption of washing powder, laundry cycles, wear on fabrics?

How about *quality*, such as durability, electrical safety, degree of rustproofness? And how would you inform yourself about *price*?

	Percentage of respondents			
	Best place to buy	*Perfor-mance*	*Quality*	*Price*
Brochures, catalogs	11	7	4	10
Newspapers	9	3	1	3
Comparative Test Reports	6	10	13	4
Consumer advice centers[a]	4	4	5	2
Relatives and friends	7	11	12	4
Window displays, exhibits	12	3	2	9
Visit in store	27	35	39	49
Prior personal experience	9	11	15	4
No answer	17	13	10	14
	102[b]	97	101	99

[a]Described under Germany in *Consumer Information Handbook.*
[b]Deviations from 100 due to rounding.
Source: Biervert, table 4.2.10.

Tests are very reliable   20%
Tests are fairly reliable   72
Tests are hardly reliable   8
                            100%

Thus, no less than 92 percent of all those aware of test reports thought that the tests are fairly or very reliable.[4]

Becker Dissertation.   The most intensive study of the relationship between the German comparative testing organizations and their users is contained in Becker's "Consumer Information and the Image of Advertising in Germany." Since the most important results of this thesis are included in other chapters of this book, no attempt will be made to further summarize here. Readers interested in a more detailed examination of certain phases of the empirical data of the present project are referred to the dissertation.

THE UNITED STATES

There is no cumulative chain of research in the United States related to the nature and use of product testing agencies, even though such organizations originated here. There have, however, been a number of independent studies during the past 20 years which have generated a modest number of empirical findings.

CU Subscriber Surveys.   The only continuing research effort over this time has been the Consumers Union Annual Questionnaire. This is circulated each spring along with the ballot for officers and directors, and has consistently drawn a response rate of 10 to 20 percent of all subscribers—currently meaning responses in the hundreds of thousands. For the most part, this powerful sample has been used only for collecting demographic data, opinions on future magazine content, and use data for a variety of products. There has been little attempt to examine the manner in which subscribers use the magazine nor to attempt an in-depth critique of the magazine and organization by its users. A few more searching questions in the most recent questionnaires suggest the beginning of a trend toward using the survey more imaginatively. Demographic data from the 1969 survey are compared with our own mail subscriber sample and United States 1970 census data in table 7–4. Age and income compositions of the CU 1969 survey and our own mail subscriber sample are strikingly similar. The differences between the CU and our own survey data with regard to education are almost certainly largely accounted for by the fact that the CU survey used different categories, as explained in a note on the table.
          It is apparent that *CR* readers follow the international pattern of

Table 7-4. Consumers Union Annual Survey 1969. Demographic
Data with Comparisons

	CU 1969 Subscribers[b]	*Our Mail Subscriber Sample*	*U.S. 1970 Census*
Age of Respondent[a]			
Under 25	6%	5%	7%
25–34	33	31	21
35–44	25	23	21
45–54	19	22	21
55–64	12	14	16
65 or older	5	5	14
	100%	100%	100%
Education of Main Wage Earner[c]			
More than 16 years	58%	36%	11%
13–16 years	22	34	10
9–12 years	17	27	51
8 years or less	3	3	28
	100%	100%	100%
Household Income			
$15,000 and over	43%	45%	19%
10,000–14,999	35	31	27
5,000– 9,999	19	18	34
Under $5,000	3	2	20
	100%	100%	100%

[a]As subscribers were generally heads of households, United States census data include heads of households only. By comparison, *all* persons aged 18–24 years represented 18 percent of the *total* population.

[b]Taken from a summary entitled, "Consumers Union Annual Questionnaire–1969–5000 Sample," furnished by Consumers Union.

[c]Note that CU 1969 survey data used the categories "college graduate (16 years or more)," "some college (13–15 years)," "high school graduate" and "grade school graduate or less."

higher income and higher education for test magazine subscribers. The age comparisons here suggest that the usual "younger" designation for subscribers is oversimplified. It is true that subscribership is substantially overrepresented in the 25 to 34 category. But it is somewhat underrepresented among heads of household in the 18 to 24 group and vastly underrepresented among unmarrieds in that age group—not to speak of teenagers in general.

Subscribers in the 1969 CU survey gave the *Annual Buying Guide* a resounding vote of confidence: 96 percent of respondents declared that they used the *Guide* in making purchases, and no less than 93 percent were "satisfied with it in its present form." In addition, the questionnaire that year collected a great deal of information on: readership of various ratings and features (guitar and ski-binding ratings were least read and auto and auto tire the most); problems encountered in using the *Buying Guide* (rated models not available, in-stock models not rated, criteria of interest not reported); and extensive data on ownership of and experience with lawn mowers and auto insurance (used as the basis for 1970 articles). There were 85 individual questions in this typical annual questionnaire, with about one-third each in demographics-readership, lawn mowers and auto insurance.

Between the 1969 and 1970 annual surveys, CU commissioned a market research firm to conduct a mail survey of subscribers and lapsed subscribers.[5] Their purpose was to search for factors related to nonrenewal of subscriptions and seek means of lowering what was seen as a rather high rate of turnover in CU's rapidly growing list of subscribers. Fifteen hundred questionnaires were mailed to respondents selected at random from CU's subscriber files. These were equally divided among current subscribers, renewal expires (had renewed at least once before) and new expires (first time subscribers who did not renew). Overall response rate was 62 percent (quite comparable to the 65 percent rate in our own United States study) with highest response predictably coming from active subscribers.

The questions in this study were much more searching than those in the annual subscriber questionnaires, relating directly to perceived use of, satisfaction with, and attitudes toward the ratings and publications. Some of the most interesting findings included:

1. Between 20 and 30 percent of active and expired subscribers are "in and out," that is, they have let subscriptions expire for a time, then have renewed at some future time.
2. Many former subscribers (around 30 percent) continue to read the magazine from some other source.
3. The principal reasons given for non-renewal were:
   a. Out of the market for products tested
   b. Still in market but disappointed by lack of relevant information in *CR*
   c. Difficulty in interpreting test information.
4. Over 99 percent of respondents reported that CU recommendations are more often right than wrong, and over two-thirds of those who consulted *CR* said they bought the *top-rated* brand. (It is our opinion that this may be a very biased perception.)
5. New expires are significantly below active members in education and income and are more likely to report difficulties in interpreting test reports. This caused the market researchers to comment: "This suggests that while you have attracted a demographically elite audience among your active subscribers, the publication is less viable for some new expires. In other words, unfortunately, those who may need the publication the most are the least able to use it effectively."[6] This is but another view of a recurring message.
6. Regarding *CR*'s somewhat strident editorial and general consumer interest

content (excluding test reports), about 90 percent claim to read such material and are in general agreement with *CR*'s view. About 3 percent of expires say that such articles influenced them *against* renewal, but 20 percent of expires and 40 percent of renewals say that such articles were a *positive* influence. About 14 percent of all respondents said that their *principal* interest was in CU's involvement in consumer affairs rather than in specific product tests.

Overall, this survey probably contains some of the best available data on the differences between avid product test users and those who "got away."

CU followed up this survey with an intensive attempt to interview the non-respondents by telephone to determine if a systematic bias of some sort existed. Over half were reached and interviewed, but no important differences were noted between this new sample and original respondents.[7]

Beem Studies. One of the first in-depth looks at product testing agencies was a 1951 dissertation by Eugene Beem.[8] There are no empirical data in the study, but it is a thoughtful historical commentary on the parallels and contrasts in the growth of Consumers Union and Consumers' Research, Inc. A condensed and updated look at the development of these two organizations may be found in the *Handbook.*

Beem attempted to make an estimate of the total influence of *Consumer Reports* by patching together some results from the annual questionnaire with answers to a single question concerning perceived use of product ratings in a past Gallup Poll. He suggested that perhaps 2 percent of total United States spending units were then reached by the ratings, with about half of these using ratings on a regular basis as a guide to purchase.[9] A later estimate by Beem and Ewing placed percentage of spending units reached at 4 percent, which because of high income levels account for 5 percent of the nation's total expenditures for products.[10] In both cases, the author admits that the estimates are highly subjective projections based upon consumers' perceptions and the researcher's judgment.

Beem and Ewing surveyed the attitudes of business decision makers toward product tests and the agencies that conduct them. The authors initiated a series of personal interviews and correspondence with a large number of technical personnel and marketing officers of 127 different manufacturing firms.

The tenor of their findings was that business respects the general integrity and independence of Consumers Union and Consumers' Research but often finds fault with their specific test methods, criteria and especially small sample size. Specifically, two-thirds of executives polled thought that such agencies were a healthy influence, and half agreed that products actually were being improved because of the influence of test ratings. Respondents felt that ratings had relatively small influence on sales, but that good ratings improved sales more than bad ones harmed them. Nonetheless, the executives were anxious to obtain good ratings and to avoid or correct bad ones. Beem and Ewing attribute this as much to corporate pride as to pressure for changes in sales.

Lane Dissertation. A 1957 doctoral dissertation by Sylvia Lane goes over some of the same historical and descriptive material previously covered by Beem but adds several other quality marketing agencies such as Underwriters Laboratories and *Good Housekeeping* to the discussion.[11] Her empirical content is limited to a mail survey regarding the perceived influence of *CR* on the decision making of department store buyers (professional buyers of merchandise for stores, not customers). Two-thirds of the 85 buyers who responded perceived themselves as regular readers of *Consumer Reports*. Of those who read *CR*:[12]

67 percent found it was "useful."
75 percent said it "guided buying."
66 percent "agree with it most of the time."
29 percent "go out of way to stock rated product."
54 percent "would stock product rated as unsatisfactory."

Lane offers the general comment that, ". . . those who read Consumers Union seem to pay heed, for the most part, to their counsel, and tend to buy products that are rated 'acceptable' rather than other products."[13] She also suggests that these people are community leaders or consumption leaders who have purchasing influence in the community well beyond their own numbers. Both comments are logical, but unsupported by any actual research in the dissertation.

Sargent Dissertation. A dissertation by Hugh Sargent was apparently the first study in the United States to make a substantial effort at determining users' attitudes toward product tests and attempting to evaluate the nature and importance of ratings' use by consumers.[14]

Sargent mailed a questionnaire to two samples, one consisting of a random selection of *CR* subscribers chosen from a six state area and the other a control group chosen randomly from metropolitan phone books in the same area. There were 731 respondents in the subscriber and 563 in the control sample. The questionnaire included a listing of recent durable goods purchases, a brand preference listing for selected convenience goods, a series of questions on general usage of ratings and five demographic characteristics.

For analysis, Sargent combined the answers of subscribers with those from the control sample who perceived themselves to be users (consultors) of the ratings. He then calculated purchases of recommended brands as a percentage of total purchases for the two groups, and compared results. He found:

1. Consultors had a significant tendency to purchase recommended brands in 8 of 13 durable products listed.
2. Consultors had a significant tendency to prefer recommended brands in only 2 of 19 convenience items and there was a significant tendency to *prefer a non-recommended* brand in one case.[15]

Other findings of the study included:

1. The basic demographic characteristics of subscribers to *Consumer Reports* and *Consumer Bulletin* as well as those non-subscribers who perceived themselves as consulting the results were quite homogeneous: they are younger, have higher incomes, and are more highly educated than the mean of non-subscribers and non-consultors. This homogeneity also in general extended to attitudes and purchase behavior, though minor differences were noted in some responses.
2. Consultors and subscribers perceived themselves as consulting more information sources and engaging in more shopping activity and more deliberation than non-subscribers and non-consultors.

It is Sargent's overall conclusion that: "Apparently these publications are a 'trusted source' of product information fairly well meeting the needs of those who consult them."[16]

Sargent's work is an interesting first effort at examining the relationship between the product test agency and its users. It should be noted, however, that there are several methodological weaknesses in the study, including possible bias caused by stating the study's purpose in the cover letter; questionable sampling procedure for the "control" sample; lack of sensitivity of measures for conformance with ratings in purchases; and generalized nature of questioning on use of ratings.[17] All of these items suggest that results of this study be interpreted cautiously.

Hempel—A Laboratory Setting. Product tests in the United States have generally been conducted by independent (non-commercial) agencies, and testing by nature has been concerned basically with measurable physical properties and performance criteria (durability, price, etc.). It has frequently been theorized, therefore, that product testing commands high credibility as an information source, and that it is most useful for products where physical performance rather than psycho-social benefits are important.[18]

Donald Hempel conducted a laboratory study in 1966 in which he experimentally manipulated information inputs to a simulated buying situation and measured the effects on purchase outcomes.[19] Specifically, subjects were to purchase a white shirt after being subjected to different information inputs.

In varying combinations, the subjects were exposed to (spurious) *Consumer Reports* ratings, and a recording of a conversation between a salesman and a student, either of which might be favorable or unfavorable toward the subject's premeasured brand preference. The findings were:

1. The communications did have a significant effect on evaluation of the product.
2. The influence of *CR* was generally greater than or equal to that of the salesman, particularly when the recommendation was contrary to the subject's predispositions. (Rating says Brand X is best where subject has expressed preference for Brand Y.) Hempel equates this with the greater credibility of *CR* information.
3. Hempel sees some suggestion that the salesman is proportionately more effective when *subjective* criteria are involved (more stylish, prettier color), and *CR* ratings are more effective on *objective* criteria (quality of fabric, durability).[20]

The effect of Hempel's study overall was to support under controlled experimental conditions some truisms which had often been proposed about the use of product test reports by individual consumers.

Various Studies by Morris.   Over a period of time, Professor Ruby Turner Morris has conducted studies of Consumers Union and its test results. The data gathered have been analyzed in various ways, to monitor ratings performance of individual companies and brands, overall trends in unacceptable products, types of product flaws, price vs. quality of various brands, and other issues related to the tests. These studies have been summarized in a single booklet, *Consumers Union—Methods, Implications, Weaknesses and Strengths*, which also includes the author's subjective conclusion regarding the usefulness of the organization to the individual consumer and to the economy. Since most of the actual analysis is only tangentially related to impact on the consumer, the reader is referred to this monograph for detailed results.[21]

Engledow Dissertation.   The most recent and perhaps the most intensive study of the relationship between Consumers Union and its users is contained in Engledow's "Impact of *Consumer Reports* Ratings."[22] Since the most important results of this thesis are included in other chapters of this book, no attempt will be made to further summarize here. Readers who are interested in further details about earlier American studies, or in a more detailed examination of certain phases of the empirical data of the present project, are referred to the dissertation.

BELGIUM

In 1970, the Belgian *Association des Consommateurs* (*AC, Verbruikersunie*) initiated an annual series of surveys of subscribers to its journal, *Test Achats*. As a loose insert in the magazine there went to all subscribers—over 100,000—a questionnaire containing four basic parts: demographics, an inventory of household equipment owned, a forecast of 1970 family purchases, and attitudes toward public policy.[g]

Some results of this first survey by *AC* of its subscribers were reported in the December 1970 issue of *Test Achats*, though unfortunately no information was included—or made available on our specific enquiry—as to sampling technique and number of respondents. Only the demographic data were presented in a form meaningful here.[23] Table 7-5 presents some of these data. A study of a sample of 616 French-speaking subscribers to *Test Achats* undertaken by C. Vaneetveld about the same time, posed similar (unfortunately, not identical) questions as well as others looking to a more detailed picture of the subscriber-consumer.[24] The most startling item gleaned from the two surveys is the large number—about one-half—of subscriber households with only one or two members. The *AC* survey suggests that many of these subscribers are 51 years or older (although the proportion of respondents in this category in the Vaneetveld study was only 24 percent). However this may be, the age distribution data of both surveys imply that the average age for *Test Achats* subscribers is higher than that for any other testing journal for which comparable data are on hand.

It also appears that *Test Achats* is actually reaching the lower income groups to a fair extent, an achievement it has in common with the Norwegian *Forbruker-rapporten*. A full 16 percent of subscribers had less than $3,000 income in 1969 and no less than 47 percent had less than $5,000.[h] On the other hand, the *AC* survey had only 9 percent of subscribers in the skilled and unskilled worker groups, and the Vaneetveld study had only 4 percent in the "worker" category. The latter study also had 30 percent of the heads of subscriber households reporting as university-level engineers, architects, doctors, and various categories of teachers. In all, no less than 33 percent of the heads of household had university-level training—a proportion surely several times that in the general population. While this study confirmed that only about one-fourth of all subscribers (27 percent) lived in rural areas, it must be remembered that Belgium is a heavily urbanized country.

---

[g]The public policy questions were supplied by the leader of the present project. For reasons discussed in the *Handbook*: 85–6, the data collected in this area were unfortunately not usable.

[h]Regrettably, the Belgian Statistical Yearbook does not carry comparable income data, and the unabridged 1970 census reports are not at hand.

Table 7-5.   Demographica Data From Survey of *Test Achats/ Test Aankoop* Subscribers 1970

Residence		*Age*		
City	13%	Husband or single man		
Suburban	31	21–35	24%	
Other towns	33	36–50	33	
Rural	23	51 or older	43	
		Wife or single woman		
Profession		16–20	1%	
Industry and trade		21–35	22	
executives and high		36–50	27	
government officials	9%	51 or older	50	
Agriculture	–			
Self-employed	9	*Size of family*		
Higher staff				Belgian
(kaderbediende)	41		Subscribers	Population
Other salaried				
employees	29	1	17%	3%
Skilled workers	7	2	31	20
Unskilled workers	2	3	22	22
Pensioners and		4	14	28
occupations not		5	8	14
elsewhere classified	3	6	4	8
		7	2	3
Wives working	39%	8	1	1
full-time	29%	9 or more	1	1
half-time	10			
Income				
Less than BF 100,000[a]	8%	250,000–350,000	25%	
100,000–150,000	8	350,000–500,000	18	
150,000–200,000	15	500,000–750,000	7	
200,000–250,000	16	750,000 and more	3	

[a]The rate of exchange was Belgian francs (BF) 50 to U.S. $1.00.
Source: Compilation summarized from *Test Aankoop* (December 1970): 324–8.

Two-thirds of the Vaneetveld questionnaires were filled out by men, 23 percent by women and 8 percent jointly. In 63 percent of the cases the husband had proposed subscription (or the subscriber was a single man), in 25 percent the wife (or the subscriber was a single woman). *Test Achats* more often than other testing journals for which data are available is read by only one house-hold member—this was reported by 84 percent of respondents. On the other hand, no less than 76 percent of respondents had given or lent other persons copies of the magazine.

Concerning the perceived impact of *Test Achats*, Vaneetveld found that 72 percent of subscribers consulted the journal primarily for reports on consumer durables and 25 percent primarily for non-durables. The prime characteristic of *Test Achats* in the minds of 78 percent of respondents was its objectivity, while for 10 percent the journal primarily represented a symbol or means of a unified consumer movement. Given a choice of adjectives with which to characterize the position of the consumer, no less than 63 percent of respondents felt that consumers are poorly informed, and another 12 percent that they are misled or defrauded. That *Test Achats* subscribers are also Information Seekers is at least suggested by the fact that 11 percent of them were also subscribers to other magazines concerned with consumer information.

BRITAIN

Before 1971, at least, there appears to have been little interest among British academic circles in research into the consumer information field. Consumers' Association (CA)—the opposite number to Consumers Union—has in the last few years undertaken annual or even more frequent surveys. CA, however, has taken a surprisingly restrictive view about cooperation with outside researchers in the survey area and tends to view most of the information generated from its own surveys as proprietary. Thus, although the reports from a number of CA-sponsored studies are on hand we are not certain to what extent they are representative.

The most recent of these reports known to us indicates that the subscribers to CA's *Which?* constitute a socioeconomic and educational elite much like fellow German and American subscribers.[25] A qualitatively oriented yet rigorously executed study comparing small groups of *Which?* readers with small groups of non-readers indicated that the readers much more often were aware of the only other non-commercial CI program in the UK at the time, the Kite Mark of the British Standards Institution.[26] Yet readers also tended to consult as many or more other sources of information (stores, friends, advertising, etc.) as non-readers. We conclude that the *Which?* subscribers constitute the core of Britain's Information Seekers.

The same study reported that "among middle class women readers there were a few mild criticisms" of the CA attitude to safety, which, it was felt, from time to time ruled out consideration of brands which in the eyes of these consumers were perfectly acceptable.

Conclusions from a few other studies pertaining to the impact of *Which?* are reported in the *Handbook*.[27] In addition, we may note a survey of separate random samples of 108 non-subscribers, 112 lapsed subscribers, and 147 subscribers made in 1962.[28] Some time before the non-subscribers were interviewed they had been sent two issues of *Which?* To the question what they thought of advice given by *Which?* respondents replied as follows:

	Non-Subscribers	*Lapsed Subscribers*	*Current Subscribers*
Which? gives good advice	76%	90%	93%
Misleading and unfair advice	1	5	3
Don't know	23	5	4
	100%	100%	100%

Respondents were also asked what they thought of Best Buy recommendations:

	Non-Subscribers	*Lapsed Subscribers*	*Current Subscribers*
Best Buy is useful	67%	87%	93%
Rather work this out myself	22	9	7
Don't know	11	4	0
	100%	100%	100%

In the 1967 survey reported in the *Handbook* no less than 95 percent of current subscribers found Best Buys useful. It is interesting to note that while there is every reason to believe that subscribers in general would be more capable of working out best buys for themselves than non-subscribers a significant minority of the latter objected to Best Buy recommendations. Possible explanations include a greater premium on time placed by subscribers and greater confidence among them in their ability to retain independent judgment in the face of *Which?* Best Buys. Among the non-subscribers 55 percent said that they had heard of CA and/or *Which?*, a fairly high percentage a mere five years after CA's formation.

The CA membership survey reported in 1965 was based on the first 2748 questionnaires returned by members in a 22,000-questionnaire mailing.[29] (There may be some bias in this procedure.) As in most other surveys by comparative testing journals, subscribers were asked to name the products they would like to see tested (characteristically for Britain at that time, central heating received by far the most votes). No less than 51 percent of respondents said that they read through the entire magazine upon arrival, while 47 percent declared that they read some of the contents at once and kept the rest for later. Again, 96 percent found Best Buy recommendations useful.

This survey also gave some insight about subscriber newspaper reading habits as compared to the adult population at large. As might be expected, subscribers showed a distinct preference for what the British call the posh papers, as demonstrated by replies to the question, "Which paper do you read regularly?"

Dailies	*Subscribers*	*All adults*
Daily Telegraph	35%	9%
Guardian	14	2
The Times	11	2
Financial Times	7	1
Daily Mirror	11	38
Sunday papers		
Sunday Times	30	8

	Subscribers	All adults
Observer	28	4
Sunday Telegraph	16	5
Sunday Mirror	12	34
People	10	40
News of the World	8	42
Sunday Express	37	28

A clue to other media habits is furnished by the fact that 58 percent of subscribers read *Radio Times* (all adults: 37 percent), while only 28 percent of subscribers (all adults: 29 percent) read *TV Times*. Of the Information Seekers 8 percent supplemented their *Which?* with *Good Housekeeping*, which was read by 7 percent of all adults.

CANADA

In 1972, the Consumers' Association of Canada made a firstling, well-intended but unscientific attempt to survey its clientele. A questionnaire was included as a non-tearout sheet in an issue of the Association journal, *Canadian Consumer*.[30] Although approximately 80,000 subscribers received the issue, the tabulation of results is based on only 385 replies. (It is not known whether this was all answers received, though this would seem most unlikely.) The survey was directed to demographic data and the subscribers' relative interest in 18 products and consumer topics dealt with in previous issues.

The demographic data are summarized in table 7-6. Subscribers are clearly well represented among young marrieds in the 25-34 age group, but underrepresented both among the under-25 and over-65 groups. This is quite similar to conditions south of the Canadian border. As usual, the income distribution is clearly skewed upwards. No less than 58 percent of respondents had done graduate work and/or graduated from college. Again, the limitations of this survey leave both reliability and validity of findings in doubt.

DENMARK

In 1966, *Forbrugerrådet* (FRD), publishers of the comparative testing and consumer journal *Taenk*, commissioned a market research firm to do a major study of buying habits and life styles of recently married, young Danish couples.[31] A representative nationwide sample of 800 such families was selected, stratified by Copenhagen, provincial cities and rural areas. Of interest here are a few questions which concerned the impact of *Taenk* and the *Råd og Resultater*, the test reports published by the government *Statens Husholdningsråd*,[32] and some of the characteristics of readers and non-readers of these journals. As the project report did not contain any of the latter type of data, we commissioned the

Table 7-6.   Demographic Data on *Canadian Consumer* **Subscribers and the Population of Canada**

	Subscribers	All Canada
Age[a]		
Under 25	5%	26%
25–34	34	19
35–44	26	18
45–54	21	} 26
55–64	10	
65 or over	4	11
Income[b]		
Less than $3,000	2%	9%
3,000– 4,999	4	12
5,000– 7,499[c]	7	12
7,500– 9,999[c]	14	22
10,000–14,999	32	28
15,000–19,999	22	} 14
20,000–24,999	10	
25,000 or more	?	3

Additional data from *Canadian Consumer* subscriber survey:

Sex[b]		*Highest degree of education attained by main wage earner*[b]	
Female	55%	Postgraduate work	31%
Male	43	College graduate	27
		Some college	18
Relation to main wage earner		High school	24
Main wage earner	45%	Grade school	4
Husband or wife	52		
Son or daughter	2		
Other	1		

[a]Age distribution for subscribers as derived from the 385 questionnaires. For Canadian population, percentages refer to the total of age groups 15 and up only; the "under 25" group here is 15–24 years old.
[b]The percentages in these columns do not total 100, for reasons unknown.
[c]Statistics Canada categories are $5000–6999 and 7000–9999, respectively.
Sources: Consumers' Association of Canada 1972 survey and Statistics Canada 1972. The Association data refer to March–April 1972, Statistics Canada to the year 1971.

market research agency responsible for the study to make a number of special tabulations to be briefly reviewed here.

The positive answers to the question, "Do you ever read *Taenk* (*Råd og Resultater*)?" were distributed as follows:

	Copenhagen (Base = 254)	Provincial cities (Base = 271)	Rural areas (Base = 275)	Total (Base = 800)
Taenk	47%	31%	13%	30%
Råd og Resultater	16	12	7	11

As shown in table 7-7 the Danish data permit the tabulation of the educational background of both marriage partners in the families which responded to the question. As might be expected, there is relatively little difference between the sexes in basic education, but major differences with regard to specialized training. The proportion of readers of both sexes with higher basic or special education is manifestly higher than that of non-readers. Although there were more than twice as many readers of *Taenk* as of *Råd og Resultater*, the proportion of *R og R* readers without specialty education is greater than that in case of *Taenk*. One possible explanation is that a subscription to *Taenk* cost more than twice as much as one to *R og R*, which was heavily subsidized.

The traditional correspondence between readership and income is evidenced in table 7-8. We may add the proposition that the income bias would have been even more clear cut if the survey had sampled *all* readers (not only young marrieds) and, especially, if it had been directed towards subscribers rather than readers. *Taenk* is a kiosk item, and presumably a fair number of its readers are so only on an occasional basis. The fact that *Taenk* readership is even more linked to income than that of *R og R* again may at least be in part due to the marked difference in price. The general economic aspiration level, too, of readers of either of the two magazines appears greater than that of non-readers: 39 percent of the readers planned to move to a larger dwelling, while only 28 percent of non-readers had such plans.

The Danish study went into some details of household finance management. It was found that almost as many non-readers (24 percent) as readers (28 percent) kept formal accounts of their expenses. Nevertheless, the readers—in line with our German and American findings—appear to be more planful: no less than 70 percent of them made budgets for the near future while only 54 percent of non-readers did this. That there is a fair degree of economic democracy in young Danish households is suggested by the responses to the question, "Who manages the family income?"

	Readers	*Non-readers*
Husband	20%	23%
Wife	12	6
Jointly	68	71
	100%	100%

The only significant difference between readers and non-readers is that the proportion of reader wives managing the family income was twice as great as that among non-readers.

It is legitimate to assume that the young married couples constituting the focus of the survey had had a number of important buying experiences in setting up their households. Respondents were asked whether they went out of

Table 7-7. Man and Wife in Reader and Non-Reader Families of *Taenk* and *Råd og Resultater* by Types of Basic and Specialized Education (In Percent)

	Reader of Taenk?						Reader of Råd og Resultater?					
	Husband			Wife			Husband			Wife		
Type of Education	Yes (Base 237)	No (Base 563)	Total (Base 800)	Yes (Base 237)	No (Base 563)	Total (Base 800)	Yes (Base 91)	No (Base 709)	Total (Base 800)	Yes (Base 91)	No (Base 709)	Total (Base 800)
Basic Education												
Primary school	45	75	66	49	75	67	52	68	66	48	69	67
Secondary school	40	22	28	41	23	29	31	27	28	41	27	29
Gymnasium	15	3	6	10	2	4	17	5	6	11	4	4
Total, percent	100	100	100	100	100	100	100	100	100	100	100	100
Specialized Education												
University, etc.	21	11	14	13	4	6	23	13	14	17	5	6
Trade schools, etc.	66	52	57	58	35	42	61	56	57	48	41	42
None	13	37	29	29	61	52	16	31	29	35	54	52
Total, percent	100	100	100	100	100	100	100	100	100	100	100	100

Table 7-8. Reader and Non-Reader Families of *Taenk* and *R̊ad og Resultater* by Income (By Percent)

Income Categories Danish Crowns[a]	Reader of Taenk?		Reader of R og R?		
	Yes (Base 237)	No (Base 563)	Yes (Base 91)	No (Base 709)	Total (Base 800)
Under 15,000	3	9	4	8	7
15,000–20,000	7	16	9	13	13
20,000–25,000	24	28	29	27	27
25,000–30,000	19	21	25	20	20
30,000–35,000	12	10	10	11	11
35,000–40,000	11	5	8	6	6
Over 40,000	16	7	12	9	10
No answer	8	4	3	6	6
Total, percent	100	100	100	100	100

[a]The rate of exchange was Danish crowns 6.90 to U.S. $1.00.

their way to procure brochures or catalogues in their purchases of a) furniture and carpets, b) major appliances and c) radio, TV, phonograph, tape recorder, camping goods or other entertainment or hobby equipment. The percentages of readers and non-readers engaging in this type of information search were as follows:

	Readers	Non-readers
Furniture and carpets	39%	20%
Major appliances	42	24
Radio, TV, etc.	38	20

The difference between readers and non-readers was less striking in the affirmative replies to the question, "Did you visit more than one store?"

	Readers	Non-readers
Furniture and carpets	52%	44%
Major appliances	19	18
Radio, TV, etc.	36	19

A clear majority of both categories of respondents were satisfied with the information obtained from the stores, as evidenced by the following positive answers:

	Readers	Non-readers
Furniture and carpets	81%	81%
Major appliances	53	61
Radio, TV, etc.	66	67

The great significance of retail stores as information sources—be it for better or worse—is once again affirmed.

In reviewing the Danish data two familiar things stand out. Readers of testing journals in Denmark are significantly higher educated and enjoy significantly higher incomes than non-readers. There are also indications that readers consult other sources of information to a greater extent than non-readers. In short, these readers are members of that great cross-cultural fraternity, the Information Seekers. This conclusion is further indicated by the fact that no less than 24 percent of the respondents who were readers of at least one testing journal were also readers of the other one.

FRANCE

In 1968 the newly formed *Institut National de la Consommation* (INC) commissioned the *Institut Français d'Opinion Publique* (IFOP) to make a study with the ostensible aim of determining what type of consumer journal might be most acceptable to the general public.[33] The survey, based on a representative sample of 1779 persons aged 20 and older, also included background data concerning French consumers and their views of more direct relevance here. Perhaps the most interesting results obtained were the answers to the question, "In general, do you personally feel that you are sufficiently or insufficiently informed about the products that you buy?" No less than 63 percent of the French replied that they were indeed sufficiently informed, while only 31 percent felt insufficiently informed (and 6 percent expressed no opinion). The differences in responses among age and income groups were rather minor. Of men 59 percent thought they were sufficiently informed, of women 66 percent. More significantly, 36 percent of the men felt insufficiently informed while these feelings were shared by only 27 percent of the women. A possible explanation is the relatively slow emancipation of French women.

The farm population felt less well informed (56 percent sufficiently, 37 percent insufficiently) than did business and professional people (67 and 25 percent, respectively). Respondents who had completed primary education felt more often that they were sufficiently informed (66 percent) than those with university-level background (57 percent). While 60 percent of the rural population felt informed, Parisians were more sanguine with 67 percent. By contrast, only 52 percent of the less developed Southwestern region regarded themselves as sufficiently informed.

In another INC survey undertaken three years later, the distribution of responses had shifted markedly—presumably a reflection of the wave of French consumerism of which the creation of INC itself was one expression. This 1971 survey comprised a representative national sample of 1815 persons aged 20 and older. Respondents declaring themselves sufficiently informed were now only 53 percent, while 41 percent felt poorly informed. At this time 44 percent of the men and no less than 38 percent of the women said they were insufficiently informed. However, in all categories of the population, the number of respondents satisfied with their information exceeded those unsatisfied.[34]

Even allowing for the notion that Frenchmen like to think of themselves as an unusually self-sufficient group of people, these findings certainly should make all administrators of CI programs pause to think. It is unfortunate that few data on this basic issue of perceived informedness exist from other countries. Clearly, if the French data are indicative at all, CI programs are really faced with the challenge of *converting people to the notion that they need more information*, that is, the mission of creating a market for their programs rather than merely satisfying already existing demand.[i]

The IFOP study reported that in 1968 the television program *"Consommateurs Informations"* (see *Handbook*) was watched regularly by 30 percent of respondents, now and then by 25 percent and never by 30 percent. Only 10 percent of respondents regularly read consumer advice columns in newspapers and magazines, 21 percent read them now and then and 55 percent never read them. In stark contrast, 77 percent of respondents felt that advertising in general is a good source of information.

The 1968 respondents were also asked whether they would be interested in a journal specializing in consumer information in the form of comparative test reports. Some 13 percent declared themselves very interested and 32 percent fairly interested, while 37 percent said they had no interest at all. Among the very interested there was a heavy concentration of city dwellers with high education, managerial and professional occupations and high income. Those with no interest included large groups of poverty-stricken, old-aged, low-education respondents living in small towns or villages.

Respondents were also asked if they would be prepared to buy such a journal. Of the 29 percent who said they would surely or perhaps buy it a total of 313 respondents were given a second interview in which they were presented with mock-ups of the journal. When asked for their opinion about the exclusion of advertising from it, 84 percent of these respondents replied that this was a good thing. To the further question, "Do you think that when a journal carries advertising one can have confidence in consumer advice and information included in its non-advertising material?" 35 percent of the group said "yes," 52 percent said "no," and 13 percent gave no answer. There can be no doubt that the answers would have been different if these questions had been directed to the total sample. In view of the positive opinion among the population as a whole about advertising as an information medium, it is likely that only a minority would have voiced lack of confidence in consumer advice in journals carrying advertising. In the absence of data there is little point in carrying conjecture any further.

[i]This problem will be further discussed in *Consumer Information Systems*.

Finally, there are some French data concerning the awareness of CI organizations. According to the 1971 INC study, 57 percent of French citizens 20-years-old or older had heard about INC. The importance of TV as a medium is demonstrated by the fact that 48 percent of respondents had learned about INC through its TV programs (some of the respondents were aware of INC through other media as well). Among Frenchmen owning TV sets only 34 percent were unaware of INC, while among non-owners no less than 57 percent had never heard about INC.

One of the two major French quality certification programs is the appliance quality marking scheme administered by the national standardization organization, AFNOR. According to a 1965 survey "by a specialized organization," 100 percent of appliance distribution personnel were aware of these marks. A full 43 percent also knew about the meaning of the mark and the controls of licensee conformity. Of an undefined sample of the general public, 64 percent of respondents said they had seen the mark before; 50 percent related it to such notions as quality, tests, safety, control and standards. Forty-four percent declared that they preferred an appliance with the quality mark. While any serious student of advertising effectiveness would be cautious indeed in interpreting such data, they are suggestive of a respectable impact.[35]

THE NETHERLANDS

Consumentenbond, the big (1970 membership around 300,000) and well-managed Dutch consumer organization, is best known as publisher of the comparative testing journal, *Consumentengids,* which goes to all members. By 1973 the *Bond*, despite some good intentions, had not as yet directly sponsored any survey research of its members. It did have at its disposal, however, two interesting readership surveys of a number of papers and magazines, among them *Consumentengids*. These studies had been made by the *Nederlands Instituut voor de Publieke Opinie* (NIPO) in 1966 and in 1969–70.

Table 7–9 presents the demographic data on *Consumentengids* subscribers compared to all subscribers of selected journals from these surveys. It cannot be assumed that the "all subscribers" group in the NIPO studies are representative of the Dutch population. We would assume, for instance, that the all-subscribers group would tend to have higher income and education than average consumers. In any case, we may legitimately postulate that the all-subscribers category—being associated with a great variety of journals—is closer to average consumers than are the subscribers to *Consumentengids*. As we might expect, *Consumentengids* subscribers come out way ahead of the all-subscriber category on all conventional measures of education, income, and property ownership as well as occupational and social classes.

Among the several CI programs in the Netherlands one is the work of the *Instituut voor Huishoudtechnisch Advies* (IVHA), a quality-marking

Table 7-9. Demographic Data on *Consumentengids* (CG) Subscribers and on all Subscribers to Selected Dutch Journals, 1966 and 1969–70 (In Percent)

	1966[a]		1969–70	
	All N = 31,699[b]	CG N = 2,145	All N = 3,890,000	CG N = 295,000
Profession				
Office staff	9	16	7	12
Government	34	15	12	25
Laborer	6	2	24	7
Agriculture	16	41	4	1
Self-employed			10	10
Higher staff	19	13	10	21
Other			11	12
None/unknown			22	11
Shop and service personnel	16	13		
Education				
Elementary	67	35	61	25
High School	21	32	23	31
Gymnasium	9	19	12	27
University	3	14	4	17
Gross income (Dfl)				
Less than 6,000	15	6	5	1
6,000–10,000	37	24	27	8
10,000–15,000	11	23	30	24
15,000–21,000			16	26
21,000–24,000			3	9
Over 24,000	6	21	6	21
No information	31	26	12	10
Social class				
Lowest	11	3	8	1
Middle (lower)	42	21	38	16
Middle	39	53	46	59
Highest	8	23	8	23

	1966[a]		1969–70	
	All N = 31,699[b]	CG N = 2,145	All N = 3,890,000	CG N = 295,000
Vacations				
Left home	57	78	61	81
Foreign	24	43	27	46
Housing and services				
Telephone	35	61	43	72
Checking account	19	35	41	63
Post office checking	30	63	44	77
Bathroom	12	24	18	29
Shower	53	58		
Rented house	69	66		
Own house			34	41
Ownership data				
Automobile	38	57	51	73
Washing machine	76	76	60	73
Refrigerator	47	67	79	91
TV	73	73	86	85
Camera	6	12	9	19
Sewing machine	34	49	46	70
Piano	7	18	6	18
Central heating			20	43
Tape recorder			21	33
Dishwasher			2	7
Electric stove			6	10
Motorcycle			34	32
Tent			16	30
Trailer			3	7
Motorboat			3	5

[a] In 1966 NIPO also queried whether salary/wages were paid monthly-weekly, province of residence, church affiliation, and whether respondent belonged to a health insurance plan.

[b] Numbers for 1966 are the number of respondents. Numbers for 1969–70 are numbers of subscribers; sample size unknown.

Source: Data on the studies by *Nederlands Instituut voor de Publieke Opinie (NIPO)* in both 1966 and 1969–70 were obtained from *Consumentenbond*. Table reproduced from Hans B. Thorelli and Sarah V. Thorelli, *Consumer Information Handbook: Europe and North America* (New York: Praeger, 1974): 302–3.

organization which grew out of the Dutch housewives association. While IVHA itself has never sponsored any survey of its own impact, the Philips Company conducted a study of consumer awareness of IVHA in 1962. According to a Philips spokesman, of 500 families queried 60 percent said they were familiar with the name IVHA.[j] The IVHA quality mark was also recognized by 60 percent of respondents when displayed to them. After having been shown the mark, about 50 percent stated that they had bought articles with the mark at one time or another. Approximately 15 percent of interviewees stated that they shopped especially for articles with the IVHA mark. To the extent that these data are representative they give a respectable view of the impact of the IVHA quality marking scheme which thus far comprises a rather limited range of products.

SWEDEN

With the exception of the United States no nation can compete with Sweden when it comes to the development of the consumer policy area in general. The Swedes reign supreme in the launching of government investigations in the field; in each of the last 20 years there has been on the average at least one major investigating committee recommending new policy measures. In this light, and in view of the advanced state of social science research in the country, one might legitimately expect a flowering of studies of the impact of CI programs. Instead, there is a disappointing near void. One of the explanations for this state of affairs is that, during its 1957–72 life span, the Consumer Council, whose specific duty it was to support research of consumer policy interest, failed to support a single study of this kind. Indeed, a proposal to extend the German and American field studies of this project to Sweden was side-tracked by the executive secretary of the Council.

The comparative testing journal *Råd och Rön,* then the organ of the State Institute for Consumer Information, in 1965 carried a summary report of 1070 subscriber households of some interest here. No less than 43 percent of the heads of respondent households were university or gymnasium graduates, while the corresponding proportion in the population at large was perhaps one-third as great. The impressive list of appliances and other durables owned also showed that respondents tended to be quite well-to-do. Some 62 percent of the respondents indicated that they had made use of suggestions or data in the

[j]Data concerning the study were sent us by Mr. H.F. Heyting of Philips's Marketing Research Department in April 1970. Among those who had heard of IVHA there were over twice as many "well-to-do" as "low-income" respondents. This particular finding must be taken with caution, as these terms were not specified (at least not to us), and as we do not know the composition of the 500 families constituting the sample. Assuming that the sample was representative and that income groups were properly defined, policy makers might draw an inference from this finding: though quality marks at the point of purchase is a good example of a CI program well suited to reach underprivileged groups it must (unlike IVHA) be aggressively promoted in order to make an impact on those groups.

journal in purchasing specific products and another 41 percent in the planning of housework.[36] There may be some positive bias behind these percentages, stemming from the fact that respondents were informed about the sponsorship of the survey.

A similar, methodologically and analytically unsophisticated study was carried out by the Government Statistical Office on a sample of 2198 *Råd och Rön* subscribers in 1968 (this was approximately one out of every 40 subscribers). Some 71 percent of the subscribers were women. This may well be the highest percentage of women subscribers to any comparative testing journal in the world, which might be explained by the relatively advanced stage of women's liberation in the country and by the historical roots of the State Institute for Consumer Information in the home economics movement. Again, over 44 percent of the heads of subscriber households were university or gymnasium graduates, as were 32 percent of the subscribers themselves.[37] The inventory of consumer durables owned by subscribers was again impressive, though difficult to relate to the general population as other categories were used than in Swedish census and family budget data. Table 7-10 has been pieced together from different sources and only includes durables for which comparative data exist. Table 7-11 gives the distribution of income of average subscribers, married subscribers and average married consumers. From these data, it is obvious that *Råd och Rön* subscribers constitute an educational and economic elite.[38]

The 1968 survey also had some impact data of interest. It was found, for instance, that in 10 percent of the subscriber households consisting of three or more persons, more persons than husband and wife read the magazine. While *Råd och Rön* carried many articles on home economics, nutrition, environmental protection, health, and other matters of general consumer interest, the com-

Table 7-10. Ownership of Certain Consumer Durables Among Subscriber and Average Consumer Households in Sweden in 1968-69 (In Percent)

	Type of household	
Type of consumer durable	*Råd och Rön Subscribers*	*Average Consumers*
Automobile	84%	65%[a]
Freezer	69	45[b]
Electric mangle or ironing machine	52	38[b]
Vacation dwelling	35	16[c]
Tape recorder	40	21[c]
Dishwasher	22	4[c]

[a]Based on census data.
[b]1969 Family Expenditure Survey.
[c]*Industria*, 1969.

Table 7-11.   Income Distribution of *Råd och Rön* Subscribers and
Average Married Consumers (In Percent)

Income	Average Råd och Rön Subscribers	Married Subscribers[a]	Average Married Consumers[a b]
Less than 10,000 Sw. Crowns	3%	1%	2%
10,000–29,000	29	26	30
30,000–49,900[c]	38	40	50
50,000–69,900[d]	18	20	} 13
70,000–99,900	7	8	
100,000 and more	2	3	3
Others, don't know	3	2	2

[a]For married subscribers and average married consumers the aggregate income of the spouses is given.

[b]Data for average married consumers based on 1971 census data, when most Swedish incomes would be at least 10 percent higher than in 1968 when the subscriber survey was taken.

[c]For average married consumers 30,000–59,900 Crowns.

[d]The combined figure for average married consumers is for incomes in the range 60,000–99,900 Crowns.

parative test reports were ranked ahead of all other items by subscribers in terms of importance to them. Table 7-12 presents the proportion of respondent men, women and households in the subscriber survey stating that they had made use of advice in *Råd och Rön*. The high percentage of women making use of advice on efficient housework and food and nutrition is again a reminder of the home economics heritage of the then State Institute for Consumer Information.

Little research on the effect of ongoing informative labeling programs has been done anywhere in the world, but at least two studies have been made of the general impact of the Swedish VDN labels at the consumer level. [39] A 1959 study involving a representative sample of 1105 households indicated that 49 percent of the respondents had heard of or personally observed "informative labels marked off within a special box."[40] The percentage of positive replies was appreciably higher for the young and well-to-do. On recall, 48 percent of respondents said they recognized the VDN label. Experience from our Norwegian field study reported earlier suggests that this percentage would be much higher ten years later. A 1966 study on the impact of VDN labels among 194 customers in the bedding departments of three department stores revealed that 47 percent of all those questioned knew about the status of VDN and the significance of its labels. Some 25 percent mistakenly believed that the label constituted a quality certification. Of those respondents who had made a brand decision, 40 percent declared that the VDN label had been of significance in their choice.[41]

Table 7-12. Proportion of Male and Female Subscribers and Subscriber Households Making Use of Certain Types of Advice in *Råd och Rön* (In Percent)

Type of Advice	Male (Base = 600)	Female (Base = 1472)	Households[a] (Base = 2072)
Buying of products	56%	67%	71%
Food and nutrition	21	47	46
Efficient housework	14	46	44
Safety around the home	22	26	29

[a]Note that the males and females in the table all represented different households, and that another member of the household may also have used *Råd och Rön* advice.

SUMMARY AND CONCLUSIONS

There is a general paucity of research on the impact of consumer information programs. In particular, there is a striking lack of serious effort on the part of all but a handful of such programs to gauge their own rapport with their clientele. It thus appears, somewhat paradoxically, that most CI programs, at least up to now, have been lacking in consumer orientation in one major respect. It must further be said, in all fairness, that some of the survey research sponsored by CI agencies is of a quality that ill compares with the strictness applied in their own product testing procedures.

Even the relatively modest material at hand permits some conclusions. It is clear, for instance, that subscribers to comparative testing journals constitute a cross-cultural elite of well educated, medium-and higher-income, largely urban consumers with a heavy concentration in the 25-55 age groups. The age composition within this span differs somewhat from one country to the next, as does the mix of men and women among subscribers and readers. Incidentally, the proportion of women seems to be a function both of their general status and of the origins of the CI program. It is hardly surprising that in countries where the CI program grew out of a housewives' (or women's) movement or had its genesis in home economics circles, one tends to find greater female representation than otherwise might be expected.

There is also a fair amount of evidence suggesting that subscribers constitute the core of the cross-cultural group which we have labeled the Information Seekers. In the half-dozen studies from which data on consultation (or awareness) of different types of information sources and media are available, subscribers to testing magazines typically seem to be aware of and consult more sources than average consumers. It appears that information seeking is indeed a cumulative process. Naturally, we are not saying that *all* Information Seekers among consumers are subscribers to comparative testing journals. Nor, for that matter, are we implying that *all* subscribers are Information Seekers. In countries where such journals have gained any prominence at all, however, it clearly seems that their subscribers constitute the most readily identifiable proxy for the local set of Information Seekers.

A significant incidental finding in most studies of the relative importance of different information sources is the critical role played by store visits, especially in the search processes of average consumers. Policy makers, private or public, interested in promoting CI programs beyond the necessarily limited circle of Information Seekers may draw an obvious inference: it is crucial that such broadly aimed information programs focus on the point of purchase.

By and large, subscribers are quite pleased with their testing journals. They do indeed also think of themselves as using the information. In all studies in countries where the journals issue Best Buy or other brand recommendations, subscribers are solidly behind this practice.

NOTES TO CHAPTER 7

1. For further detail on various aspects of the Norwegian survey, see Hans B. Thorelli, "Concentration of Information Power Among Consumers," *Journal of Marketing Research* 8 (November 1971): 427–32 and (in Norwegian) Rapport fra kontoret for intervjuundersökelser Nr. 8, *Undersökelse om Forbruker-rapporten, vareundersökelser og reklamasjoner 1969* (Oslo: Statistisk Sentralbyrå, 1970) and Terje Assum, *Om utnytting av servicetiltak som tilbys forbrukerne* (Oslo, Mimeographed, 1970). Our present account draws freely on these sources. The first-named article will be cited as Thorelli in the text.

2. Assum, table III:13. There may have been some bias to overstate usage of Institute labels as a commendable activity, kin to the bias demonstrated by average consumers in Indianapolis when asked whether they subscribed to *Consumer Reports.*

3. The *Warentest* study was commissioned to INTERMARKET, a Düsseldorf survey research organization. The bound mimeographed report is entitled, *Warentest–Eine Studie über Verbraucherwünsche* (Berlin, 1965). *Stiftung Warentest* prepared a mimeographed summary report, *Zusammengefasste Ergebnisse einer Studie über Verbraucherwünsche* (Berlin, 1965).
   Title of the Nordrhein–Westfalen study: Bernd Biervert, *Wirtschaftspolitische, sozialpolitische und sozialpädagogische Aspekte einer verstärkten Verbraucheraufklärung* (Köln: Krupinski, 1972). Report and tables in separate covers.

4. Biervert, tables 4.2.15–4.2.18.

5. Survey of Present and Former Subscribers to Consumer Reports (Princeton, New Jersey: Benson and Benson, Inc., February 1970). Courtesy of Consumers Union.

6. Benson and Benson: 12.

7. Survey of Former Subscribers to Consumer Reports–Telephone Check of Non-Respondents (Princeton, New Jersey: Benson and Benson, Inc., June 1970). Courtesy of Consumers Union.

8. Eugene R. Beem, "Consumer-Financed Testing and Rating Agencies in the United States" (Ph.D. diss., University of Pennsylvania, 1951).

9. Beem: 194–6.

10. Eugene R. Beem and John Ewing, "Business Appraises Consumer Testing Agencies," *Harvard Business Review* 32 (March-April 1954): 113–26, 115.

11. Sylvia Lane, "A Study of Selected Agencies That Evaluate Consumer Goods Qualitatively in the United States," (Ph.D. diss., University of Southern California, 1957).

12. Lane: beginning 476.

13. Lane: 250.

14. Hugh W. Sargent, "The Influence of Consumer Product Testing and Reporting Services on Consumer Buying Behavior," (Ph.D. diss., University of Illinois, 1958).

15. Sargent: 158, 161.

16. Sargent: 239–40, 249.

17. For a more detailed critique see Jack Engledow, "The Impact of *Consumer Reports* Ratings on Purchase Behavior and Post-Purchase Product Satisfaction," (DBA diss., Indiana University, 1971): 17–18.

18. Donald M. Cox, *Risk Taking and Information Handling in Consumer Behavior* (Boston: Graduate School of Business Administration, Harvard University, 1967): 605–8.

19. Donald J. Hempel, "An Experimental Study of the Effects of Information on Consumer Product Evaluations," (Ph.D. diss., University of Minnesota, 1966).

20. Hempel: 182–96.

21. Ruby Turner Morris, *Consumers Union–Methods, Implications, Weaknesses and Strengths* (New London, Conn.: Litfield, 1971).

22. See note 17.

23. For a summary of the buying intentions data in the first three annual surveys see Y. Langaskens and C. Van Lierde, *Het verbruikersgedrag en de aankoopintentie voor duurzame verbruiksgoederen van de Belgische konsument in de jaren 1970-1971-1972* (Brussels: Free University, Centrum voor Ekonometrie en Management Science, 1973, Mimeographed).

24. C. Vaneetveld, "Résultats bruts de l'enquête réalisée en mai sur la population francophone abonée à Test Achats," (Louvain, 1969, Mimeographed).

25. The data are summarized in *Consumer Information Handbook*: 17. Note that missing figure for income group "Under £250" should be 4 percent.

26. Emer Rodnight, "Attitudes to Spending Money on Consumer Goods and Services: A Small-Scale Psychological Survey," (Prepared for Consumers' Association, February 1965, Mimeographed, 27 pp.).

27. *Consumer Information Handbook*: 28–9.

28. *Enquiry into Which?* (London: Social Surveys [Gallup Poll] Limited, 1962). Several mimeographed reports.

29. Jeremy Mitchell, *What Do You Want in Which?* (London: Consumers'
    Association, 1965, Mimeographed, 16pp.).
30. The questionnaire appears in *Canadian Consumer,* March-April 1972 issue:
    61-2.
31. *Unge nygiftes indkøb af langvarige goder etc. og deres varekendskab* (Hel-
    lerup: AIM Markedsanalyse, 1966, Mimeographed, unpaginated).
    All respondents had been married five years or less and none of the
    partners were over 35 years of age.
32. A 1970 impact study of the *Rad og Resultater* was briefly covered in
    Consumer Information Handbook: 150-1.
33. Institut Français d'Opinion Publique, *L'information des consommateurs.*
    Étude préalable au lancement d'une revue. Rapport de J. Labrousse.
    (Paris, December 1968).
34. "Consommateurs et commerçants," *Consommateurs Actualité* 36 (December
    1971): 3-18. It may be noted that a substudy of the 1968 IFOP
    survey was directed to 272 persons connected with consumer organi-
    zations (typically in leader or employee roles). As might be expected
    only 28 percent of this group felt sufficiently informed, while a full
    68 percent declared themselves insufficiently informed.
35. Association Française de Normalisation, *Courrier de la Normalisation* (No-
    vember-December 1969): 621-8. For a detailed discussion of the
    AFNOR consumer products certification program see *Handbook*:
    220-4.
36. *Rapport ang. en enkät bland tidskriften Råd och Röns läsare* (Stockholm:
    Statistiska Centralbyrån, Utredningsinstitutet, 1965. Mimeographed).
37. *Rapport ang. en enkät bland tidskriften Råd och Röns prenumeranter 11.12.
    68* (Stockholm: Statistiska Centralbyrån, Utredningsinstitutet, 1968.
    Mimeographed): 3. It is characteristic for the lack of coordination
    among government agencies in Sweden as elsewhere that the income
    categories used were different from the census data, and that there
    was only accidental correspondence with some of the categories used
    on consumer durable ownership in the 1969 Family Expenditure
    Survey.
38. The statement in *Råd och Rön* 1969:1 that the journal was now reaching
    "more readers within the low income groups" was a misleading half-
    truth of the type critics often associate with advertising. It was true
    only in the sense that, as the total number of subscribers had more
    than doubled between the two studies, *some* part of the increase was
    obviously represented by low-income groups. It is really more
    remarkable that the "elitist" nature of the magazine could remain
    unchanged despite this fairly dramatic increase in the stock of sub-
    scribers. Cf. discussion in *Handbook*: 371-2.
39. The VDN labeling system is presented in *Handbook*: 37-52.
40. *Varudeklarationer: en studie för VDN* (Stockholm: AB Marknadsbyrån,
    1959. Mimeographed).
41. Hans Adolfsson and Felix Folkebo, *VDN--66* (Stockholm, 1956, Mimeo-
    graphed).

Part Three

Advertising Image and Consumer Information

Chapter Eight

The Advertising Image

Consumers are exposed to a continuous flow of market information from a great variety of sources, which may broadly be classified as personal, commercial or independent. As we have seen in chapters 4 and 5 and again in chapter 6, the importance attached to various information sources differs, depending on individual respondent and specific purchase situation, as well as on the type of information itself. Because of the increasing complexity and, even more, the volatility of the modern marketplace, it is hypothesized in *Consumer Information Systems* that the relative role of personal sources in the information mix is likely to remain stable or decline slightly in the future. Independent consumer information (CI) sources, on the other hand, are expected to increase in importance. So long as their thrust remains focused on rather complex product test reports, however, their immediate effectiveness will continue to be limited to the relatively small segment of the education-and income-elite.

While we do not have any proof, it is likely that in modern society advertising represents the single most important source of product information; and we deem it likely that it will remain so in the foreseeable future. As the major commercial communications link between sellers and buyers, however, advertising is often surrounded with controversy, perhaps because it serves so many diverse purposes, some of which may not be clear to the public. Often, too, these different purposes are mixed in the design of any given advertisement.

The primary purpose of advertising may simply be to generate attention. In this respect it differs from CI in that consumers presumably look for CI on their own initiative, while advertising has to seek their attention.[1] Beyond that, advertising emits at least two types of information: an O-component, that is, "objective" information and an S-component, "subjective" or persuasive information. Persuasion per se is a legitimate activity, common to almost any field of human endeavor from love to politics. One problem with advertising is that the O-component and the S-component are often subtly intermingled, thus giving rise to this controversy. For this reason alone image research of advertising is important.

Further than this, there is an obvious interdependence between advertising and other product information sources—not least CI. Hence it is obviously of interest to study attitudes toward advertising. The trends in the image will reflect advertising's credibility and perceived usefulness and possibly point to needs for government regulation or to relevant areas of supplementation and improvement by CI organizations, including possible coordination with other types of CI. It is also clear that the image of advertising has important managerial implications for the dissemination of product information as well as for public relations.

In this part of the present volume we want to study the interrelation of CI and advertising at the consumer level. A truly meaningful discussion of advertising-CI interactions must be preceded, however, by an examination of the image of advertising itself. We attempt this in the current chapter. We have already studied the impact of CI in chapters 4 and 5 and have focused upon it in depth in chapter 6. In the next chapter we will combine these results into an extended discussion of the interdependence between advertising and CI as sources of consumer intelligence. The reader is reminded that this discussion is confined to CI in the form of comparative product testing by independent organizations as accounted for in the three test report magazines included in this study. In a separate epilog, finally, we will highlight the characteristics which pinpoint Information Seekers as distinguished from average consumers (AC) and ponder what directions can be taken to communicate product information more effectively to the public.

In this chapter we center our discussion on attitudes toward advertising in German and American metropolitan areas. Replicating in part the pioneering effort by Bauer and Greyser,[2] respondents were quizzed on a number of general, economic and social dimensions of advertising as they pertain to the environments of the two countries. Their responses were then compared and contrasted in light of pertinent cross-cultural similarities and differences. The study was focused squarely on the image of advertising as a societal institution rather than on individual advertisements. The validity of any such cross-cultural comparison, however, would largely depend on the answer to another vital question, To what extent is advertising and the role it plays in the cultural-economic life of the two countries similar, and to what extent is it different?

THE BIG PICTURE

At the outset if may be helpful to cite a few comparative advertising statistics so that the reader can gain an appreciation of its scope in the countries concerned. One well-known source estimated that the 13 top advertising nations in the world spent, in the aggregate, some $28 billion in 1968.[3] Of this total, American advertisers laid out a staggering $18 billion or 65 percent,[4] about 2.1 percent of the Gross National Product of the United States. Germany emerged as the second largest advertising country in the world with 1968-expenditures of $3.9 billion or approximately 2.9 percent of that country's GNP. In absolute dollar terms, then, United States advertising expenditures exceeded German by a margin of four and a half to one; but as a percent of GNP, advertising assumed a greater role in Germany. Per capita spending of $90 on advertising in the United States, on the other hand, exceeded the corresponding German figure of $65 per capita by nearly 40 percent.[a] Overall, one is inclined to conclude that the advertising density and intensity is greater in the United States than in Germany. Although no universal yardstick is available, it would also appear that German consumers on the average are exposed to a smaller number of daily advertisements than their American counterparts.

There is, too, some variation in the media mix. We find, for example, that newspaper advertising, while the largest single outlet in both countries, assumes a more commanding role in the United States than in Germany. (See table 8-1.) Americans spend 29 percent on newspaper advertising compared to the Germans' 18 percent. Of that amount, 90 percent goes to local or regional newspapers in Germany and 80 percent in America.

Proportionate spending on direct advertising (primarily direct mail) is almost the same in both countries. Magazine advertising is the third largest medium in Germany with 13 percent of total expenditures, but assumes a relatively less vital role in the United States where it is only 7 percent of the total. Cinema advertising, representing only a minor proportion of the advertising budget, is rather common in Germany, but is virtually unknown in the United States.

Part of the variant role of these media must be ascribed to the relative importance of broadcast advertising in the two countries. Radio and television play a much more significant part in America than in Germany and combined spending on the broadcast media devours a quarter of American advertising budgets. Compared to this, the 5 percent spent in Germany appears like a drop in the bucket, both in absolute and relative terms. The reason for this discrepancy lies, of course, in the different legal and organizational structures governing the operation of the broadcast media.

In the United States, both television and radio are predominantly supported by advertising revenues, and American broadcasting networks vie for

[a]Following the more recent rounds of US-$ devaluations and D-Mark revaluations from 1971 to 1973, the German per capita figure would have to be revised upward to over $110. This could alter the argument somewhat although not in substance in the authors opinion. See also explanatory note on table 8-1.

Table 8-1.   Total Advertising Expenditures in Germany and the United States 1964 and 1968

Advertising Media	Germany				United States			
	1964		1968		1964		1968	
	Millions	%	Millions	%	Millions	%	Millions	%
Newspapers	$ 425	16%	$ 693	18%	$ 4,069	29%	$ 5,265	29%
Magazines	348	13	525	13	1,108	8	1,351	7
Television	94	3.5	151	4	2,236	16	3,193	18
Radio	21	0.8	42	1.0	830	6	1,140	6
Cinema	16	0.6	15	0.4	–	–	–	–
Outdoor	38	1.4	63	1.6	175	1	208	1
Reference Publications	22	0.8	31	0.8	–	–	–	–
Direct Advertising	338	13	632	16	2,171	16	2,612	14
Miscellaneous	1,374	51	1,785	45	3,393	24	4,247	24
Grand Total	$2,676	100%	$3,937	100%	$13,981	100%	$18,016	100%

Note: The figures for Germany were computed on the basis of the 4:1 official exchange ratio between D-Mark and US-$ prevailing in 1968. The reader may keep in mind that the $ amounts for Germany would increase by over 70 percent under the "floating" exchange rate, hovering around D-Mark 2.30 per US-$ during the summer of 1973.

Sources: *Der Deutsche Markt in Zahlen* (Frankfurt: DIVO-INMAR Gmbh., 1970): 380. *Printers' Ink* 290 (February 12, 1965): 12 and *Advertising Age* (June 8, 1970): 101.

the advertisers' dollars in a fierce struggle for viewer ratings. In Germany, television and radio are largely supported by user fees and operated by the public sector. Commercials are much regulated and restricted: rather than a staccato flow of commercial interruptions to ongoing programs, television advertising is bunched into 30 minutes before prime viewing time on weekday evenings, interspersed with music and cartoons. There are annually only some 6–8000 television minutes for advertising made available to regional stations by each of the two national network programs, less than 5 percent of total viewing time. The restrictions on radio advertising are similar, except that up to three 30-60 minute periods are made available for commercials. Taking out the musical intermissions between advertisements in this *Werbefunk*, only about 12,000 minutes annually, or 2.5 percent of total radio time, are left on the average for commercials. There appears some variation among local stations, however, and some stations make no time at all available for advertising purposes.

There are no analogous restrictions on commercial time on the American broadcasting systems, except through voluntary compliance with the code of standards as defined by the National Association of Broadcasters.[5] For television, this code prescribes a maximum of 10 minutes of "non-program" material in any 60-minute period of prime time and no more than four commercial interruptions; 16 minutes are allowed during any other television hour with eight interruptions. The time used for radio advertising should not exceed 18 minutes per hour of program time. There are numerous exceptions to the guidelines, and enforcement is not very strict. The ultimate sanction against non-compliance is expulsion from the Association; non-member stations are not subject to the code.

Clearly, advertising through broadcast media in Germany is limited by the limited available commercial time so that German advertisers rely to a greater extent on magazine and direct advertising. It also explains the large expenditures for "miscellaneous" items, which include free samples, point-of-purchase displays, advertising gifts and exhibitions, as well as expenses for advertising design and production. Also included would be the *Litfassäulen* (kiosks), a typically continental medium: large diameter, concrete columns, strategically placed on sidewalks, and used for commercial advertising as well as for public and political announcements.

It is interesting to note in table 8–1 that the *increase* in advertising expenditures in the United States between 1964 and 1968 was equal to the *total* amount for 1968 in Germany; nevertheless, the German growth rate of 47 percent was two and a half times the American. German advertising has also been growing at a much faster pace than GNP. Using 1962 = 100 as a base, the German advertising index had risen to 185 by 1968 in terms of current prices, and the 1968 index for GNP stood at 137. The American advertising index reached 145 in 1968, only slightly higher than the GNP index of 141.

The comparative, general advertising picture in Germany and the United States is summarized as follows:

> In some respects, Americans may be credited as being the originators of modern, large-scale advertising. But there is little doubt that the role of advertising is growing rapidly in the German market system. While total and per capita spending on advertising in the United States exceed that of Germany, Germans spend a larger share of their GNP on marketing communication. German advertising is also growing at a faster pace. There are some obvious differences in the media mixes in the two countries. Thus, magazine and direct mail advertising are more important in Germany, whereas television and radio commercials are significantly more extensive and pervasive in the United States. These differences are largely the result of legal and cultural-political differences, rather than of differences in the economic and marketing objectives of advertising.

It is evident that advertising is rapidly gaining in size and significance on both sides of the ocean. If one assumes that the objectives of advertising and its relative importance as a demand-influencing tool are similar in the American and German marketing contexts, several relevant questions can be asked:

> In view of similar as well as dissimilar economic and advertising conditions of Germany and the United States, how much alike or different are the attitudes of German and American consumers toward the institution of advertising? Are Germans annoyed about the large volume of direct advertising invading their homes? Do Americans have a more critical view of advertising than Germans because of the ubiquitous commercials on American television and radio? Are consumption-oriented Americans more tolerant toward advertising in general than tradition-bound Germans?

These are some of the obvious questions to which this chapter is addressed. First it may be useful to look briefly at the overall framework for comparing and contrasting advertising attitudes in the two countries.

FRAMEWORK FOR COMPARISON

We have seen that the magnitude and execution of advertising in the two cultures diverge in several important ways. Their divergence may be ascribed to differences in the political, legal, cultural and economic constraints, which are part and parcel of each country's environmental make-up. As a result, the attitudes consumers hold toward advertising can be affected in many different ways. The comparison of attitudes between the two countries is, therefore, embedded in the context of the German and American environments which helped to shape these attitudes in the first place.

Variables for Comparison

Four sets of variables were combined to construct the basic framework for comparison: 1) advertising attitude variables; 2) perceived use of advertising as an information source; 3) consumer characteristics (demographic and socioeconomic); and 4) environmental variables. The four sets of variables are detailed in figure 8-1. Advertising as an institution could have been included as a fifth variable, but for our purpose we have assumed that its basic role as a purveyor of market intelligence and as a selling tool is similar in advanced countries based on the market economy despite observable differences in magnitude and media mix. The role and nature of advertising and its raison d'être were therefore treated as constants in the comparison.

I. Attitudes Toward Advertising
   A. *General Attitude:* On the whole, would you say that your attitude about advertising was favorable or unfavorable?
   B. *Particular Aspects of Attitude:*
       1. *Economic Impact*
           a) Advertising is essential
           b) Raises the standard of living
           c) Results in better products
           d) Helps to lower prices
       2. *Social Impact*
           a) Seldom persuades people to buy things they do not want
           b) Presents a true picture of the product
           c) Does not insult the intelligence
           d) Advertising standards are higher today than ten years ago

II. Perceived Usage of Advertising as Information Source
   A. Durable Product Purchase
   B. Automobile Purchase

III. Demographic and Socioeconomic Variables
   A. Sex of respondents
   B. Occupation of chief wage earner in household
   C. Years of formal education
   D. Family income
   E. Age of respondents
   F. Subscribership to product testing magazines

IV. Environmental Factors
   A. Educational
   B. Cultural
   C. Economic
   D. Politico-legal

Figure 8-1. Variables for Comparative Analysis of the Advertising Image in the United States and Germany (Metropolitan Population).

The Comparison Process

The initial step in the cross-cultural comparison consists of an identification of differences and similarities of the advertising image between German and American consumers. This comparison includes the general dimension of advertising attitude, as well as its various economic and social aspects. These attitudes are also examined in light of perceived use of advertising as an information source in two purchase situations (a durable product and an auto). Further on, the views of advertising are related to demographic and socioeconomic characteristics of respondents in the two countries. An important comparison in this connection involves the attitudes of average consumers and subscribers to the three product testing magazines in this study: *Consumer Reports, DM* and *test*. Finally, the environmental factors are continuously interwoven in the analysis, to help us explain and understand the similarities and differences in the image of advertising between German and American consumers.

The comparison process is illustrated in figure 8–2. The arrows between the sets of variables indicate their interaction. Of particular interest is the interaction between environmental characteristics and consumer attitudes toward advertising. This interaction works in many ways: for example, a country's environment in part helps shape consumer attitudes toward advertising; but these attitudes (formed over time) also have an impact on the structure and performance of advertising. Thus, consumer attitudes are partly responsible, via public pressure groups and politico-legal processes, for changes in the way the advertising function is carried on in a society.

Social and cultural forces, moreover, help determine the type of advertising and appeals that are most effective within a firm's communication mix. The educational level predominant in key market segments to some extent will dictate the degree of sophistication of advertising messages. Economic considerations are taken into account when selecting media and deciding on the most efficient allocation of advertising budgets. Politico-legal constraints also have an impact on message content and even the amount of permissible advertising (e.g., on broadcast media in Germany). In short, the environmental interaction is manifold and its impact on consumer advertising attitudes can be both direct and indirect.

Samples and Illustrative Propositions

The sample used in this chapter consisted of the 301 American and 295 German respondents interviewed respectively in Indianapolis and Frankfurt. As such, it encompasses both the respondents of the general metropolitan population (the so-called average consumers) and the subscribers to *DM, test* and *Consumer Reports*.

For the direct cross-cultural comparison of advertising attitudes among German and American consumers at the beginning of the analysis, these

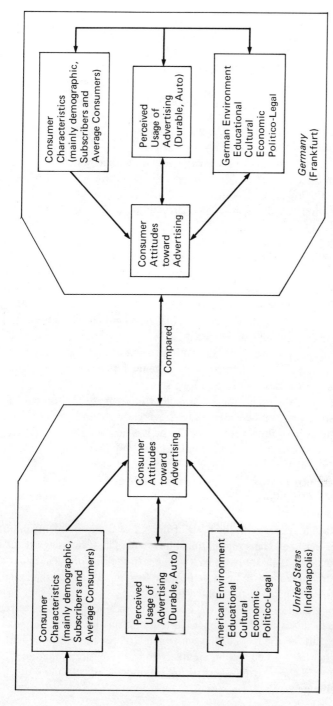

Figure 8–2. Schematic for Comparison of Advertising Attitudes Between the United States and Germany. Metropolitan Populations.

samples are *combined* to obtain a larger base of respondents. The resulting de facto oversampling of the education-income elite is somewhat analogous to that used in the Bauer and Greyser study although their methodology differed.[6] The procedure was carried out consistently and systematically in both countries and is unlikely to affect the *cross-cultural* comparability of the data. The rationale for the sample design was explained in chapter 3. Later in this chapter, the samples are separated again to permit comparisons between subscribers and average consumers. This was done also in the interest of readers possibly skeptical of the use of combined samples.

On the basis of our own research and familiarity with the German and American cultures and by drawing upon the literature and the findings of others, notably the work of George Katona et al.,[7] we anticipated certain consumer reactions to advertising. These are summarized as follows:

1. Americans on the whole are likely to be more favorably inclined toward advertising in general than Germans. Large-scale commercial advertising is a newer institution in Germany; Germans tend to be more closely tied to tradition and the past and less adaptable to innovations and social change; Germans also tend to be less trustful and more negative toward advertising.

2. With respect to economic impact variables (see figure 8-1), Americans are likely to have a more favorable attitude. It is plausible that Germans do not perceive advertising as capable of improving the economic condition of the consuming public. Americans may in general be more aware of economic and market processes, including advertising.

3. With respect to the social impact variables (see figure 8-1), Germans as well as Americans can be expected to show relatively unfavorable attitudes. Other studies have shown Americans to be less positive about advertising's social aspects than about its economic aspects.[8] For Germans, the negative attitude is likely to carry over into social aspects.

4. In both countries, respondents with a favorable attitude toward advertising in general will exhibit a more favorable attitude with respect to its economic and social impact.

5. Similarities in attitudes on the basis of the sex of the respondents in both countries may well transcend national differences in advertising attitudes. For instance, in their study on advertising attitudes in America, Bauer and Greyser found women to be more positive toward advertising than men. A similar relationship is anticipated for Germany.

6. The demographic variables of age, occupation and income are not expected to produce any startling differences in responses in either Germany or America; but, on the basis of the Bauer and Greyser study, respondents with higher levels of education are likely to be more discriminating in their views, that is, supportive of advertising's economic aspects and critical of its social impact.

7. In both countries, subscribers will tend to be less favorable toward advertising than average consumers.

8. German and American subscribers may represent the universal Information Seeker and resemble each other more than the respective AC in the two countries in their image of commercial advertising.

These propositions are representative but not exhaustive; and they suggest our expected findings from the cross-cultural comparisons in this chapter.

THE IMAGE OF ADVERTISING

Metropolitan Consumer Reactions in America and Germany

General Attitude Toward Advertising. If one views modern commercial advertising as a peculiarly American creation, the attitudes Germans hold toward it may be somewhat surprising. The Frankfurt sample suggests that a majority of Germans are favorably disposed toward advertising in general. That is, 60 percent of the respondents expressed a favorable attitude; 22 percent were unfavorably inclined, and 16 percent had mixed feelings (See table 8-2.)

As expected, American respondents viewed advertising in an even more favorable light, with 75 percent showing a positive outlook and only 15

Table 8-2.   General Attitudes toward Advertising in Germany and the United States (Frankfurt and Indianapolis Samples)

Question: On the whole, would you say that your attitude about advertising was favorable or unfavorable?[a]

Degree of Attitude	United States Sample (Base = 301)	Germany Sample (Base = 295)
Strongly favorable	5%	4%
Favorable	53	24
Slightly favorable	17	32
Neither favorable nor unfavorable (mixed)	10	16
Slightly unfavorable	6	13
Unfavorable	6	6
Strongly unfavorable	3	3
No opinion	1	1
Overall Attitude Index[b]	60	38

[a]Section 5 of questionnaire, question 6, reproduced in appendix G.

[b]Index = (% of sample favorable, in whole or in part, minus % of sample unfavorable).

percent negatively inclined. It seems that advertising is generally accepted in America in spite of its pervasiveness—or perhaps because of it. In any case, it is evident that German consumers have some way to go before catching up with their American peers in their degree of favorableness toward advertising. It is possible, however, that a survey made at the time of this writing (five years later) would reveal a deterioration of American attitudes.

Historically speaking, in both Germany and the United States large reserves of pent-up consumer demand were freed by the end of World War II. In America it was comparatively easy to fill that demand with the gradual conversion of the wartime to a peacetime economy; but in Germany top priority of business and government was given to rebuilding the country's economic and industrial base from the ravages of war. It was not until the late 1950s that Germany gradually evolved into what Riesman calls a "consumption society."[9] Industrial and business firms soon learned that consumers had to be informed about product features, brands and supplies through advertising and other marketing tools in order to keep demand stimulated and the production machinery humming at efficient levels.

It seems to the authors, however, that advertising in Germany does not reflect the same degree of cultural and economic integration as in America— despite large-scale spending. This may partly be due to the relative newness of modern advertising and its techniques in German marketing, and partly to the alleged reluctance on the part of Germans to adapt behavior patterns to changing environmental conditions.[10] German consumers—although favorably disposed toward advertising—do not appear ready to accept and support it to the same degree as Americans.

Particular Aspects of Advertising.   The somewhat less enthusiastic acceptance of advertising generally in Germany is reflected throughout the responses to particular aspects of advertising attitude. The comparative results of the German and American respondents are shown in table 8–3.

Some Germans obviously believe that advertising is essential and that advertising standards are higher today than ten years ago. While the Germans may also see a moderately positive relationship between advertising and better quality products, negative feelings of various degrees were expressed by the respondents on the remaining dimensions. According to their perceptions, advertising fails to contribute to a higher standard of living for all consumers and does not result in lower prices. Advertising insults the intelligence, fails to present a true picture of products, and persuades people to buy things they do not really want. The impression gained from the data is that the indictment of advertising, particularly in the area of social impact, is relatively strong in Germany. Despite this criticism, advertising is largely seen as an essential part of economic life.

The data from our survey suggest that Americans are much more

Table 8-4.   Relationship between General Attitude toward
Advertising and Particular Aspects of Advertising[a] (Frankfurt
and Indianapolis Samples)

	United States		Germany	
General Advertising Attitude:	*Favorable*	*Unfavorable*	*Favorable*	*Unfavorable*
Base:	*(224)*	*(45)*	*(179)*	*(65)*
Statement	*Index[b]*	*Index[c]*	*Index[b]*	*Index[c]*
Ranked by "Favorable" Index[b]				
Economic Aspects				
Advertising				
is essential	89	80	59	-17
results in better products	66	16	31	-32
helps raise standard of living	49	45	-7	-34
results in lower prices	-16	-27	-14	-51
Social Aspects				
Advertising				
standards are higher	49	9	39	-1
does not insult intelligence	26	-38	-16	-67
presents a true picture	11	-45	-2	-62
does not persuade people	-38	-66	-51	-43

[a]Data based on section 5 of questionnaire, questions 6-14, reproduced in appendix G.
[b]Index = (% of sample *favorable* toward advertising in general, strongly or slightly agreeing
with statements minus % strongly or slightly disagreeing).
[c]Index = (% of sample *unfavorable* toward advertising in general, strongly or slightly
agreeing with statements minus % strongly or slightly disagreeing).

improve product quality or raise the standard of living, or even that it is
essential. On the contrary, in their view advertising increases prices and merely
persuades people to buy things they do not really want. Advertising is not to
be trusted and can only be regarded as an insult to the intelligence of consumers. Such a broadside indictment of advertising, while not typical of all
Germans, nevertheless reflects in a sense German thoroughness and consistency
so often cited as a national stereotype.

Americans seem to be more flexible. In line with the partial cross-
cultural similarity noted above, Americans with a poor general view on the
merits of advertising also expressed less positive (or more negative) opinions
about particular advertising aspects. But the American respondents showed a
greater independence of judgment. They seemed to make up their minds
separately on each issue independently of the overall image. Thus, American
respondents, even those with an unfavorable view of advertising in general,
largely acknowledged that it is essential, raises the standard of living, and (by
promoting competition) fosters the creation of better quality products. Agreeing, on the other hand, with the Germans on the social issues, they admit that
advertising is not always truthful, sometimes persuades people to buy the
unnecessary and insults the consumer's intelligence.

The data were also tested for relationships between advertising attitudes and various demographic and socioeconomic variables. No clear-cut or consistent response patterns emerged from these tests. However, several interesting observations can be made which document cross-cultural similarities as well as differences.[11]

1. *Sex of Respondents.* German women exhibited a more favorable attitude than men, and to a smaller degree, so did American women. Women in both countries agreed more often than men that advertising persuades people to buy things they should not. Women also were more convinced that advertising results in better products for the public. It is interesting to note that German women agreed, at least partially, more with American women than with German men; and German men were in some respects more similar to American men.

2. *Education.* The highly educated are less favorably disposed to advertising than the general public. Although this was true for both countries, Germany's educational elite think even less of advertising than America's. But the Americans exhibited a remarkable degree of discrimination between the various aspects of advertising. From the economic viewpoint, they accepted it as an essential element of the market system, and agreed more often that it helps raise the standard of living and results in better products. They did not believe very strongly in its power to lower consumer prices, and they decried its social impact to a considerable degree. The Germans made no such distinction between advertising's economic and social impact. The recognition of the essentiality of advertising in the market economy merely seems to reflect a narrow tolerance of advertising as an institution. This tolerance is tested by what is perceived as untruthful commercialism, an insult to one's intelligence. On the whole, the German responses were much more diffused than the American, and no pronounced patterns were discernible.

3. *Occupation.* A flexible class structure in America may be reflected in the relative absence of large attitudinal differences between occupational groups. For example, American managers and officials were only slightly less favorably inclined toward advertising than blue collar workers. In line with their more extended education and training, however, managers consistently followed the typical American pattern to greater extremes than the worker respondents, and thus discriminated more sharply among advertising attributes. In other words, they lauded advertising's economic functions but disfavored its social impact to a greater extent than the blue collar worker.

In a 1970 survey of *Harvard Business Review* subscribers, Greyser and Reece found a similar pattern, perhaps even more extreme.[12] Their respondents, 82 percent of whom were businessmen from top to lower management, agreed strongly that advertising is essential and that the public has greater confidence in advertised products than in unadvertised ones. They also thought that advertising results in better products and, in general, helps raise our standard of living. The businessmen believed that advertising standards were higher today than ten years ago, even though, at the same time, they complained about a greater proportion of irritating, annoying or even offensive advertisements, particularly on television and in direct mail advertising. They criticized most severely advertising's power to persuade people and its "unhealthy influence" on children. Perhaps Greyser and Reece's most interesting, though not surprising, finding was that the image of advertising had slipped from a similar 1962 survey, even in the economic area.[13]

Attitudinal differences between occupations were more pronounced in Germany. Not only did officials and managers view advertising generally in a more favorable light, but their degree of favor toward particular aspects of advertising consistently exceeded that of workers. They were, for example, more convinced that advertising is essential and results in better products and they perceived it as fairly truthful with standards superior to those of ten years earlier, whereas German workers felt strongly over-persuaded and their intelligence insulted by advertising.

In some respects one concludes from the data that American and German businessmen resembled each other in their favorable outlook, but that German workers differed from their American counterparts. Whereas the German workers seemed to reject advertising on most fronts, the Americans appeared to have accepted several aspects of it. There is no obvious reason for this discrepancy, but one might cite lack of interest, familiarity and awareness of the functions and diverse purposes of advertising as possible explanations for these lower attitudes. In some way this attitudinal divergence may reflect the more rigid social class differences of Germany. It remains to be seen what effect the current push for greater worker participation in management in Germany will have on the local social structure and on the image of advertising among workers. At present, however, in the environment in which the German worker's child typically grows up, there is little or no teaching about the functioning of the free market system. In America, the emphasis on market processes generally is readily apparent and economic news, good and bad, is widely publicized. As a result, American workers may be more aware of the positive as well as the negative features of advertising.

Other demographics. None of the other conventional characteristics commonly used to describe population segments were related to any kind of a differential attitude pattern about advertising. In both Germany and the United States, pockets of support and criticism of advertising were randomly distributed and no consistent patterns could be discerned. For instance, the positive correlation between education, income and certain types of occupation was generally unrelated to advertising attitudes. Thus the views of high income respondents did not substantially differ from those of low income. The intermittent but distinct response patterns reflected by various educational and occupational groups were not repeated at the corresponding income levels. A couple of examples may serve to illustrate deviations from this pattern.

An intriguing note was struck by the German high income respondents. They more often agreed significantly with the notion that advertising leads to better quality products. Although this attitude was not shared by other respondent groups in either Frankfurt or Indianapolis, a possible explanation of this may be linked to the perceived association between national brands, higher prices and product quality. Nationally advertised brands tend to be higher priced than private labels in both countries, and they often enjoy an image of superior quality. High income consumers are presumed to represent a vital target for these brands.

A large proportion of American low income respondents, as another example, thought that advertising standards today are higher than ten years ago. The higher income groups did not do so to the same extent. High income, of course, is often associated with higher levels of education and with the upper social strata generally. It is plausible that these people discriminate to a greater degree, are more conservative, and do not unquestioningly conclude that today's world is better than yesterday's or that advertising standards are higher than ten years ago. That prerogative belongs to the younger, particularly in the United States, who thrive on novelty and who expressed a strong preference for today's advertising over yesterday's.

One important part of the sample remains to be looked at separately: The Information Seekers. In the following section, product test subscribers are compared to average consumers in their outlook toward advertising.

Subscribers and Average Consumers

The Information Seeker was previously characterized as a partly conservative, partly liberal, somewhat intellectual member of the educational and income elite. As a subscriber to product testing magazines, he should not be too favorably inclined toward advertising. He is less likely to perceive a great need for the type of information usually supplied by advertising which, intended as a selling tool, would not mention actual or potential product flaws. The results are shown in table 8-5.

Average American consumers, as expected, showed a more favorable attitude toward advertising than subscribers, but, surprisingly, German sub-

Table 8-5. General Attitude toward Advertising[a] Subscribers Compared to Average Consumers. Germany and the United States (Frankfurt and Indianapolis Samples)

Question: On the whole, would you say your attitude about advertising was favorable or unfavorable?

Degree of Attitude	United States		Germany	
	Subscribers (Base = 101)	Average Consumers (Base = 200)	Subscribers (Base = 97)	Average Consumers (Base = 198)
Strongly favorable	5%	5%	6%	4%
Favorable	41	59	25	24
Slightly favorable	23	14	34	31
Mixed	11	9	9	20
Slightly unfavorable	9	4	14	13
Unfavorable	8	5	6	6
Strongly unfavorable	4	3	4	2
No opinion	0	1	1	1
Overall Attitude Index[b]	48	66	41	38

[a]Data based on section 5 of questionnaire, question 6, reproduced in appendix G.
[b]Index = (% of sample favorable in whole or in part, minus % of sample unfavorable).

scribers gave it slightly more positive overall ratings. In neither country did the data suggest a statistically significant difference, but it is interesting to note that the attitude held by Information Seekers in both countries moved against the general population trend—in reverse directions. The net result can be summarized as follows:

> Americans on the whole are more positive about advertising than Germans as was expected. But a certain similarity in general attitude toward advertising between German and American Information Seekers seems to transcend, in part, the national differences between the two countries.

The explanation for the cross-cultural similarity among Information Seekers with respect to their advertising attitudes, must be sought on different grounds, however. For the United States one could argue, for example, that the educational elite, heavily represented among Information Seekers, tend to be quite critical of advertising. The favorable stance of German Information Seekers vis-à-vis average consumers is anchored more probably in the fact that a major proportion of their occupations is of a managerial professional nature. In Germany these occupations were associated with a more positive image of advertising which outweighed the slightly adverse effect injected by the education factor.

The suggested similarity between German and American Information Seekers must be viewed in its proper perspective, however. The similarity is *relative* in comparison to the reaction by the general public in America and Germany. Thus, in dissecting advertising into its related attributes, we find that American Information Seekers rather consistently tend toward the more positive side in comparison to the German ones, particularly with respect to the economic aspects of advertising. *CR* subscribers are a bit more convinced than *DM* and *test* subscribers that advertising is essential and also that it results in better products and helps raise our standard of living. German subscribers recognize the necessity for advertising in the established marketing system, but they do not otherwise support it on these dimensions. In neither country did subscribers or average consumers feel that advertising contributes to a lower price level. (See table 8-6.)

On the social dimensions, *CR* subscribers are rather cautious, even critical, as is typical for the educated elite in America. For instance, advertising was strongly faulted by these respondents for its persuasive power. Indeed, their criticism of advertising on the issue of persuasion was even more pronounced than that of the German subscribers, who otherwise ranked below the Americans in their judgment of advertising. The German subscribers were more likely to perceive advertising as an insult to the intelligence. Further, they did not believe in the efficacy of advertising as a means to raise the standard of living, though they admitted that advertising as an institution is essential.

As the data in table 8-6 suggest, the reversal pattern noted above is partially carried on for several advertising aspects: German subscribers exhibit a more favorable and Americans a less favorable attitude toward advertising than the general population. While the subscribers in the two countries reflect similar as well as divergent images of advertising, however, German and American average consumers are consistently further apart on nearly all issues surrounding advertising.

In summary, the data suggest that American and German subscribers to product test reports are closer together than the general public in their intermittent, cross-cultural resemblance as far as advertising attitudes are concerned. Their identification with what might be called the "universal information seeker" is not complete, however, as respondents in each country retain part of their national idiosyncracies. Lacking the element of subscribership and other commonalities associated with it, average consumers in the two countries reflect in their attitudes the full range of cross-cultural differences: Americans appear to favor wholeheartedly advertising in general, selectively accepting and criticizing distinct attributes of advertising. Germans seem to favor advertising to a more moderate degree, but consistently express a less positive (or more negative) view on various advertising issues.

Table 8-6. Attitudes toward Particular Aspects of Advertising[a] Subscribers and Average Consumers Compared. Germany and the United States (Frankfurt and Indianapolis Samples)

Statements	United States		Germany	
	Subscribers (Base = 101)	Average Consumers (Base = 200)	Subscribers (Base = 97)	Average Consumers (Base = 198)
Ranked by U.S. Index Numbers[b]				
Economic Aspects				
Advertising				
is essential	86	86	51	37
results in better products	45	60	8	14
helps raise standar1 of				
living	44	48	-19	-14
results in lower prices	-22	-22	-21	-30
Social Aspects				
Advertising				
standards are higher	27	49	15	30
does not insult intelligence	12	10	-25	-33
presents a true picture	-4	-6	2	-31
does not persuade people	-54	-35	-38	-56

[a]Data based on section 5 of questionnaire, questions 7–14, reproduced in appendix G.
[b]Index = (% of sample strongly or slightly agreeing with statement minus % strongly or slightly disagreeing).

The reader should be reminded here that the German sample of Information Seekers consisted of subscribers to two product testing magazines. Actually, because of the nature of the two magazines, one might expect *DM* subscribers to indicate a more positive attitude toward advertising than *test* subscribers. Besides the fact that *DM* carries advertisements and *test* does not, the editorial philosophy of the two magazines also differs. *Test* tends to lean toward the consumer protectionist side of many issues, including truth in advertising. *DM* is a bit more "muckracking" in its criticism of business and marketing practices, yet seems to present a freewheeling image toward the world.

DM subscribers supported the expectation to a small degree and assumed a slightly more favorable stance toward advertising than *test* subscribers. The difference is statistically insignificant, however, and is mentioned only inasmuch as it is quite consistent across nearly all aspects of advertising. In reading their magazines, *DM* subscribers are looking at product test reports along with product advertisements in every issue. As a result of this, they should, for example, be more atuned to advertising (it is essential) and less pessimistic about it (generally presents a true picture) in comparison to *test* subscribers.

THE IMAGE OF ADVERTISING AND
PERCEIVED USAGE

Television, radio, newspapers and magazines are the chief vehicles for trans-
mitting commercial messages to the public in the United States as well as
in Germany. An individual making extensive use of these media is exposed to a
great number of advertisements. Compared to others who do not read so
much or watch television or listen to radio so frequently, it is reasonable to
assume that this individual is more aware of advertising in general; that he pays
greater attention to many ads; that he is more likely to recognize advertising as
an important information source in important purchase decisions; that post-
purchase, he will be more satisfied with the informational input in these
decisions; and ultimately, that he expresses a more favorable attitude toward
advertising and its various attributes. These are the kinds of relationships
examined in this section.

Media Usage and Advertisements

We have already seen in chapters 4 and 5 that in both Germany and
the United States, AC tend to watch more television and listen to more radio
than subscribers; subscribers to read more. In chapter 6, on the other hand,
it was revealed that Americans read more newspapers and magazines and also
attend more often to the broadcast media than Germans. The reader may be
reminded that chapter 6 dealt primarily with the national subscriber samples in
the two countries. Statistical tests showed the same to be true for all the metropolitan samples used in the present chapter; that is, the Indianapolis respondents
(both subscribers and average consumers) professed to a more extensive media
usage than the Frankfurt ones. Table 8-7 indicates to what extent respondents
perceived themselves as "paying attention" to commercials and advertisements.

For the most part, the attention given to advertising follows the
media usage patterns rather closely. Chi square analysis showed significant
relationships between "paying attention to ads" and the frequency of usage of
all media for both German subscribers and AC. Thus, German AC, attending
to a greater extent to the broadcast media, also perceive themselves as paying
attention more often to commercials on them. Since radio and television commercials are broadcast in Germany only during specifically designated periods,
they require specific time and effort on the part of the individual who observes
them. In a parallel fashion, though the evidence is somewhat weak, German
subscribers, who read more than average consumers, look at a greater number of
newspaper and magazine advertisements.

The patterns are similar in Indianapolis, although not as pronounced
and consistent as in Frankfurt. As an exception, American AC, despite their
lower reading frequency, still say they pay greater attention to newspaper ads
than subscribers. The relationships between media usage and frequency of

Table 8-7. Perceived Extent of Paying Attention to Commercials and Advertisements[a] Subscribers and Average Consumers Compared United States and Germany (Indianapolis and Frankfurt Samples) (In Percent)

	United States		Germany	
	Subscribers (Base = 101)	Average Consumers (Base = 200)	Subscribers (Base = 97)	Average Consumers (Base = 198)
Television Commercials				
None or almost none	27%	19%	36%	23%
A few	44	38	51	54
Many	19	16	10	20
All or almost all	11	27	3	3
Radio Commercials				
None or almost none	50%	47%	44%	35%
A few	37	25	43	47
Many	9	10	9	14
All or almost all	4	17	4	4
Newspaper Ads				
None or almost none	14%	11%	17%	24%
A few	40	35	55	53
Many	37	23	18	14
All or almost all	10	31	10	9
Magazine Ads				
None or almost none	10%	16%	15%	19%
A few	46	37	57	54
Many	37	27	22	19
All or almost all	8	20	5	8

[a]Data from section 5 of questionnaire, reproduced in appendix G.

paying attention to ads was significant in the United States only for AC. American subscribers apparently read, watch television, or listen to the radio independently of the number of ads they consciously observe.

Cross-culturally we again find that Americans, both AC and subscribers, pay attention to a larger number of commercials than do the Germans in at least three media—television, newspapers and magazines. The exception here is the radio. The popular, entertaining, musical nature of the German *Werbefunk* seems to attract a comparatively larger audience than the slam-bang commercialism of many American radio stations.

Contrary to expectations, there does not seem to be a relationship between the amount of advertising noticed and its perceived importance as an information source. This was true for all samples in both countries. It appears that consumers on each side of the Atlantic are routinely exposed to large doses of commercial information without actually becoming aware of a direct association between them and the particular products or brands involved in a purchase decision. Many individuals perhaps do not recognize advertising as an important informational input precisely because of this routine, everyday exposure to commercial messages. Others refuse to attribute importance to advertising in the decision-making process because they distrust its content, feel insulted by it, or dislike to be persuaded. In any case, the consumer who notices many ads on the media does not necessarily hold advertising more important than one who observes few or none.

Advertising Usage and Image

Are persons who pay much attention to ads and commercials more favorably inclined toward advertising than those who pay little or no attention? On the whole, the answer is yes. There is consistent evidence throughout the data to suggest that people who observe many advertisements reflect a more favorable attitude toward advertising generally as well as toward its economic and social aspects. There are some exceptions to this pattern, however. For example, American subscribers find advertising as insulting to one's intelligence and not truthful, no matter how many television commercials they watch. American AC do not perceive advertising as a tool for lowering price, even if they see a great number of newspaper and magazine ads. German subscribers seem to be negative toward and suspicious of advertising on several dimensions, even those who take the trouble to listen to the *Werbefunk* quite regularly. This category is represented by an admittedly small number of respondents, but it does suggest an independence of behavior and attitude by no means unique in the behavioral sciences. Bower, in his study on television viewing habits in the United States found, for example, that people today watch more television than ten years ago, even though their attitudes toward that medium have declined. And those who claimed they would prefer a greater amount of informational programs and "food for thought" still watched about the same number of entertainment programs as other respondents.[14]

Are individuals who recognize advertising as an important information source in a purchase more likely to reflect a favorable attitude toward it? The data strongly support this proposition for the Frankfurt respondents, but the results are somewhat mixed for Indianapolis. Table 8–8 displays the combined attitude data in the customary index form for the durable product and automobile purchases.

Clearly, the Germans were consistent in their view of advertising across both purchase situations. Subscribers as well as AC in Frankfurt who said that advertising was important to them in their purchase decisions, still did not agree that it lowers prices; and they were neutral or slightly negative on the question whether advertising raises their standard of living. They also faulted advertising for its potential or actual persuasion of people and sometimes feel insulted by it. But even so, this category of respondents was much *less negative* about advertising on these dimensions than those who did *not* consider advertis-

Table 8-8. Relationship Between Importance of Advertising and Attitudes toward Advertising in the Durable Products and Automobile Purchases[a] (Indianapolis and Frankfurt Samples) (In Index Numbers)[b]

| | United States | | | | | | | | | | Germany | | | | | | | | | | |
| | Subscribers | | | | | Average Consumers | | | | | Subscribers | | | | | Average Consumers | | | | | |
Advertising Attitude Statements Base	R	I Index (31)	R	NI Index (148)	Index I-NI	R	Index (41)	R	NI Index (274)	Index I-NI	R	I Index (39)	R	NI Index (70)	Index I-NI	R	Index (68)	R	NI Index (117)	Index I-NI
General Attitude																				
On the whole, attitude toward advertising is favorable		26		50	-24		80		64	+16		69		28	+41		76		18	+58
Economic Aspects																				
Advertising																				
is essential	1	87	1	86	+1	1	92	1	84	+8	1	74	1	40	+34	1	57	1	23	+34
helps raise standard of living	2	52	3	41	+11	2	78	3	44	+34	3	-3	4	-29	+26	3	-4	3	-20	+16
results in better products	3	42	2	46	-4	3	73	2	58	+15	2	36	2	-2	+38	2	39	2	-1	+40
results in lower prices	4	-3	4	-25	+22	4	-27	4	-22	-5	4	-28	3	-14	-14	4	-12	4	-29	+17
Average Index		44.5		37.0	+7.5		54.0		41.0	+13.0		19.8		-1.2	+21.2		20.0		-6.8	+26.8
Social Aspects																				
Advertising																				
standards are higher	1	19	1	27	-8	1	46	1	50	-4	2	33	1	18	+15	1	45	1	15	+30
does not insult intelligence	2	13	2	12	+1	2	27	2	7	+20	3	5	3	-28	+33	3	-16	2	-33	+17
presents a true picture	3	0	3	-7	+7	3	17	3	-3	+20	1	40	2	-6	+46	2	18	3	-50	+68
does not persuade people	4	-48	4	-58	+10	4	-53	4	-33	-20	4	-13	4	-50	+37	4	-47	4	-69	+22
Average Index		-4.0		-6.5	+2.5		9.3		5.3	+4.0		16.3		-16.5	+32.8		0.0		-34.3	+34.3

Legend: R = Rank of attitude index number.
I = Advertising perceived as very important or rather important information source in purchase decision.
NI = Advertising *not* perceived as important information source in purchase decision.
I-NI = Difference between I and NI indexes. Positive difference is in direction predicted.

[a]Data from sections 2, 3 and 5 of questionnaire, reproduced in appendix G.

[b]Index = (% of sample agreeing with advertising attitude statements minus % of sample disagreeing). Positive Index means a favorable attitude; negative Index implies an unfavorable attitude.

ing to be an important information source in their decision making. On the remaining economic and social aspects of advertising as well as on the general attitude question, respondents with high perceived importance of advertising were distinctly more favorable than those with low importance.

The results for the Indianapolis samples are much more diffused and irregular. Table 8-8 indicates that average consumers reacted in a manner more consistent with expectations than did subscribers. That is, if AC perceived advertising as an important information source in the durable product purchase decision, they also responded more positively to the advertising attitude questions, at least in the economic dimensions. The statement on whether or not "advertising persuades people" provided a notable exception. Apparently, persuasion is felt to be a negative factor, no matter how useful commercial information may be perceived to be. American subscribers did not perceive any significant relationship between the importance of advertising as an information source and attitudes toward it. It seems that this group does not necessarily let its actions be dictated by their attitudes. In any case, American subscribers appeared to make up their mind about advertising independently from its use as an information input.

When making cross-cultural comparisons on the use and image of advertising, a note of caution must be sounded. The methodology in this instance was not strictly comparable in the two countries. The Indianapolis respondents were asked by *unaided* recall which information sources they used in making their purchases. Of those mentioned, the respondents were then asked to indicate the importance of each source on a five-point scale from very important to very unimportant. As a rule, all sources mentioned were also checked as being very important or rather important. Seventeen Indianapolis subscribers and 20 average consumers mentioned advertising as an important information source in the durable product purchase; and 14 and 21 listed it in the automobile buying situation respectively. The remaining proportion of the buyers in the sample were assumed to hold advertising as not important. This may be a small overstatement of the latter category, since some of them may feel that advertising is *neither* important *nor* unimportant. In Frankfurt, *aided* recall was used on the information usage questions and respondents were simply asked to check the degree of importance of each source in the purchase decision process on the five-point scale. The "important" groups in the German samples are therefore somewhat larger than the corresponding categories in the United States samples, and the "unimportant" groups in Germany are smaller than the American counterparts, because there was no way to exclude the "neutrals" from the United States respondents.

Advertising Satisfaction and Image

All respondents who had purchased a product or a car during the specified period were also queried whether or not, post-purchase, they agreed with the statement that "advertising for this product/auto was accurate and helpful" in arriving at their buying decision. This question was intended to measure "satisfaction" with advertising in a particular purchase situation. Several important interrelationships of this satisfaction question with other advertising variables in the questionnaire became evident, but not all were consistent with expectations.

Table 8-9 shows the relationship between the identification of advertising as an important source of information and post-purchase satisfaction with it in the two major purchase decisions. The American samples were

Table 8-9. Relationship Between Importance of Advertising and Satisfaction with Advertising[a] (Indianapolis and Frankfurt Samples) (In Index Numbers)[b]

| | United States | | | | | |
| | Subscribers | | | Average Consumers | | |
Purchase Situation	I	NI	Index I-NI	I	NI	Index I-NI
Durable Product						
Base	(17)	(66)		(20)	(129)	
Index	70	32	+38	55	39	+16
Automobile						
Base	(14)	(82)		(21)	(145)	
Index	0	−13	+13	48	0	+48

| | Germany | | | | | |
| | Subscribers | | | Average Consumers | | |
Purchase Situation	I	NI	Index I-NI	I	NI	Index I-NI
Durable Product						
Base	(20)	(39)		(43)	(62)	
Index	90	31	+59	77	31	+44
Automobile						
Base	(19)	(31)		(25)	(55)	
Index	37	55	−18	80	31	+49

Legend: I = Advertising perceived as important information source in purchase decision.
NI = Advertising perceived as *not* important information source in purchase decision.
I-NI = Difference between I and NI indexes. Positive difference is in direction predicted.

[a]Data based on attitude statement: "Advertising for the product/auto was accurate and helpful." Sections 2 and 3 of questionnaire, reproduced in appendix G.

[b]Index = (% of sample agreeing with statement minus % of sample disagreeing). Positive index reflects agreement with statement that advertising was "accurate and helpful."

rather consistent in this case; respondents who perceived advertising as an important information source were also more likely to express agreement with the statement that it was "accurate and helpful." This was interpreted as relative satisfaction with advertising in the particular purchase situations.

Among German respondents, a similar tendency was apparent with one exception: German subscribers who did *not* perceive advertising as important in the automobile purchase scored higher on the advertising satisfaction question than those who perceived it as *important*. It is quite possible that this group, having used advertising to some extent in their decision making, were more aware of advertising's little (or big) exaggerations and persuasion and hence were, post-purchase, somewhat less enthusiastic about its accuracy and helpfulness. Actually, similar comments can be made about the American subscriber sample in the auto purchase situation, where those high on perceived advertising importance had a neutral index on the satisfaction questions; those who did not perceive advertising as important scored negatively. These results indicate mild dissatisfaction or at least indifference with the accuracy and helpfulness of auto advertising among American subscribers.

Relating the combined results on the advertising satisfaction question in the two purchases to the image variables (see table 8-10), the results are somewhat mixed. On the general dimension, all samples reacted in the anticipated direction, indicating a positive relationship between satisfaction with advertising and overall attitude toward it. This was not always true for the particular attributes. For example, no pattern could be found among the American average consumers who seemed to react to the image questions independently, whether or not advertising was perceived as "accurate and helpful" in the durable product or automobile purchase decisions. American subscribers, on the other hand, were a bit more consistent.

Conclusions about the Germans seem in some respects not too dissimilar from those drawn about the Americans, but they go to greater extremes both on the positive and negative sides. Part of the reason for this is the small cell size of those who *disagreed* with the statement, leaving the German results somewhat inconclusive. It should be pointed out, however, that the cell size problem stems precisely from the fact that the German sample contained a much larger proportion of respondents satisfied with advertising and a far smaller percentage of dissatisfied customers than the American. Given the stereotypical distrust of the German in general this may come as a surprise. On the related issue of persuasion of advertising, the German respondents were as adamantly negative as the Americans. It could be that product quality expectations on the part of Germans and the corresponding quality image projected by advertising were perceived to be sufficiently congruent. Hence, advertising is given higher marks for being accurate and helpful in the purchase decision than might be the case in America.

Table 8-10. Relationship Between Satisfaction with Advertising Accuracy and Helpfulness and Attitudes toward Advertising in the Durable Products and Automobile Purchases[a] (Indianapolis and Frankfurt Samples) (In Index Numbers)[b]

Advertising Attitude Statements Base	United States										Germany									
	Subscribers					Average Consumers					Subscribers					Average Consumers				
	R	A Index (73)	R	NA Index (50)	Index A-NA	R	A Index (139)	R	NA Index (65)	Index A-NA	R	A Index (83)	R	NA Index (11)	Index A-NA	R	A Index (140)	R	NA Index (22)	Index A-NA
General Attitude																				
On the whole, attitude toward advertising is favorable		51		30	+21		73		60	+13		60		9	+51		58		10	+48
Economic Aspects																				
Advertising																				
is essential	1	84	1	80	+4	1	89	1	90	-1	1	64	1	37	+27	1	42	1	28	+14
results in better products	2	60	3	39	+21	2	60	2	69	-9	3	23	3	-18	+41	2	21	2	-5	+26
helps raise standard of living	3	46	2	42	+4	3	55	3	39	+16	2	-20	2	0	-20	4	-12	4	-42	+30
results in lower prices	4	-10	4	-11	+1	4	-28	4	-16	-12	4	-11	4	-82	+71	3	-14	3	-33	+19
Average Index		45.0		37.5	+7.5		44.0		45.5	-1.5		14.0		-15.8	+29.8		9.3		-13.0	+22.3
Social Aspects																				
Advertising																				
standards are higher	1	29	2	10	+19	1	45	1	55	-10	2	30	1	-18	+48	1	38	1	6	+32
does not insult	2	19	1	22	-3	2	12	2	8	+4	3	-19	2	-18	-1	3	-24	3	-55	+31
presents a true picture	3	14	3	-24	+38	3	6	3	2	+4	1	44	4	-72	+116	4	-3	4	-73	+70
does not persuade	4	-49	4	-58	+9	4	-23	4	-30	+7	4	-21	3	-27	+6	2	-38	2	-51	+13
Average Index		3.3		-12.5	+15.8		10.0		8.8	+1.2		8.5		-33.8	+42.3		-6.8		-43.3	+36.5

Legend: R = Rank of attitude index number.
A = Advertising for product perceived as accurate and helpful (in whole or in part).
NA = Advertising for product not perceived as accurate and helpful (in whole or in part).
A-NA = Difference between A and NA indexes. Positive difference is in direction predicted.

[a]Data from sections 2, 3 and 5 of questionnaire, reproduced in appendix G.
[b]Index = (% of sample agreeing with advertising attitude statement minus % of sample disagreeing.) Positive index means a favorable attitude; negative index implies an unfavorable attitude.

SUMMARY OF GERMAN-AMERICAN COMPARISONS

Advertising on the whole is accepted, or tolerated, by broad metropolitan population segments in the United States and to a lesser degree and extent in Germany. As a well-established institution in both countries, it is largely seen as an essential ingredient of the free market system. Beyond that, few similarities between American and German respondents remain in what appear to be distinct, culture-bound, attitudinal patterns.

Americans are more likely to distinguish between economic and social impact in expressing their attitudes about advertising than Germans. Americans supported advertising from an economic view but criticized its social image. This dichotomous tendency was particularly evident in the educated segment in the United States. Germans, on the other hand, while not denying the necessity for advertising per se, did not greatly support advertising on either economic or social grounds. In broad terms, then, Americans appear farthest from Germans in their view of advertising's economic impact; they are closest in their much less favorable appraisal of advertising's social image.

In Germany as well as the United States, those respondents who reacted favorably to advertising in general were also more positive about its economic and social aspects.

Those in the American sample with college education showed a greater degree of discrimination and differentiation in their evaluation of separate advertising issues than German respondents with a comparable education.

Greater response differences between occupational groups were found in Germany than in the United States. For example, consumers with professional–managerial occupations expressed their favorable view of advertising more distinctly than blue collar workers. As a result, professional–managerial respondents in Germany resembled their American counterparts more closely than other occupational groups.

Young and old share similar attitudes in each country, although the attitude distributions were less favorable in Germany than in the United States.

In America as well as Germany, women showed a greater apprehension about the persuasive power of advertising than men. It appears that this attitude, related to sex, transcends other cross-cultural differences.

German subscribers were somewhat *more* favorable toward advertising than average consumers; American subscribers, to a lesser degree, were *less* favorable. As a result, American and German Information Seekers resembled each other more closely in their views of advertising than average consumers.

Media usage patterns tend to be linked to "paying attention to advertisements" in both countries. Thus, average consumers are more likely to notice broadcast commercials and subscribers printed ads. With the exception of radio commercials, Americans on the whole pay greater attention to advertising messages than Germans.

Individuals who pay much attention are not necessarily the ones making greatest use of advertising information or most satisfied with its accuracy and helpfulness for decision making.

Persons who perceive advertising as an important information source and who are generally satisfied with it tend to have a more favorable overall attitude toward it. With respect to particular economic and social attributes of advertising, this relationship becomes less clear cut. It is more consistent, however, among German respondents than among American. This suggests a degree of independence between behavior and attitudes in the American sample not found in the German.

The reader will bear in mind that all comparisons of attitudes toward advertising in this chapter are based on metropolitan samples of Indianapolis and Frankfurt and not on the whole of the United States and Germany. It is possible that national and metropolitan attitudes in a country are not identical. Indeed, one might argue that metropolitan similarities and contrasts in part obliterate national differences and resemblances between the two countries.

A check on this possibility revealed that the Indianapolis respondents exhibited attitude patterns substantially similar to those of the national American sample used by Bauer and Greyser in their 1964 study.[15] (See table 8-11.) A 1969 Gallup survey, however, suggests a slight but consistent worsening of American attitudes toward advertising on the national level not reflected in our 1970 Indianapolis sample.[16] Thus, the data appear to indicate that the metropolitan response to advertising questions is somewhat more favorable than the national response in America. It could also be that the proverbial conservatism of Indianapolis Hoosiers is a contributing factor to the more favorable attitude on the metropolitan level.

The reverse occurred in Germany. The Frankfurt sample was slightly less positive toward advertising than the 1969 national sample included in a multinational *Reader's Digest* survey.[17] In comparison to our metropolitan respondents, the national survey in Germany showed a more positive perception of advertising's contribution to improving product quality, a more neutral view toward truthfulness in advertising, and a less pessimistic image of advertising's persuasive power.

Aside from obvious demographic differences in occupation, income and education, one reason for the attitudinal differences could be the different

Table 8-11. Attitudes toward Particular Aspects of Advertising[a] in Germany and the United States (Metropolitan and National Data Compared) (In Index Numbers)[b]

	United States			Germany	
Statements	*India-napolis 1970[c]*	*National*		*Frank-furt 1970[c]*	*National 1969[f]*
		1964[d]	*1969[e]*		
Advertising					
1. is essential	86	60	57	40	37
2. results in better products	55	60	40	12	41
3. results in lower prices	-22	-5	-29	-28	-25
4. presents a true picture	-3	-12	-24	-20	3
5. does not persuade people	-42	-34	-45	-50	-24

[a]Data based on section 5 of questionnaire, selected questions from 7 to 14, reproduced in G.
[b]Index = (% of sample agreeing slightly or strongly with statement minus % of sample disagreeing slightly or strongly).
[c]Our own surveys in Indianapolis and Frankfurt.
[d]Raymond A. Bauer and Stephen A. Greyser, *Advertising in America: The Consumer View* (1968): 102.
[e]Gallup Organization Survey of December 1969.
[f]The Reader's Digest Association, *A Survey of Europe Today* (1970): 186-7.

levels of exposure to advertising which is thought to be more concentrated in the metropolitan environment. Why the heavier doses of advertising would affect American and German city dwellers in opposite ways is a matter of conjecture and would be an interesting subject for future, cross-cultural investigations. In sum, while national differences in advertising attitudes between the United States and Germany are unmistakably in the direction indicated by this study, the discrepancy between the metropolitan samples appears more pronounced than in surveys based on national samples.

OTHER COUNTRIES—OTHER STUDIES

The Reader's Digest Study

A universal parallelism seems to be evident in the pattern of distinction between some economic and social aspects of advertising which the respondents, metropolitan and national, German and American alike, tend to follow. This pattern is apparent among virtually all the countries included in the international *Reader's Digest* survey conducted in 16 European countries.[18] A selection of countries and a condensed version of data from that survey are shown in table 8-12.

The data for the United States and Germany, repeated in table 8-12, have been discussed in the previous section, including their relationship

Table 8-12. Attitudes toward Particular Aspects of Advertising Selected Countries Compared (In Index Numbers)[a]

Statement	United States	Germany	Britain	Belgium	Denmark	France	Ireland	Italy	Netherlands	Spain	Sweden	Switzerland
Advertising												
1. is essential	57	37	42	32	42	28	51	17	14	40	36	36
2. results in better products	40	41	25	9	22	26	22	15	11	19	14	40
3. results in lower prices	-29	-25	-28	-10	-25	-12	-12	-37	-15	-34	-52	-24
4. presents a true picture	-24	3	-18	-19	-28	-15	-24	-9	-33	-14	0	6
5. does not persuade people	-45	-24	-41	-41	-45	-36	-32	22	-45	-42	-46	-29

[a]Index = (% of sample agreeing slightly or strongly with statement minus % of sample disagreeing slightly or strongly.

Sources: For the United States, Gallup Organization Survey of December 1969. For all other countries, The Reader's Digest Association, *A Survey of Europe Today* (1970): 186-7. Reproduced from "A Survey of Europe Today" (Price $60.00) by kind permission of the Reader's Digest Association, 25 Berkeley Square, London W1X 6AB.

to the results from our own study. The cross-cultural response patterns apparently common to all countries in the table are summarized as follows:

> Consumers in the developed countries universally (from mildly to strongly) consider advertising to be an essential ingredient for the proper functioning of the economy and, presumably, an impetus for economic growth. Advertising is recognized as an important communications link between buyers and sellers in the market place. In its role as a communicator it is often perceived as leading to higher quality products, presumably by acting as a stimulant to competition.
>
> Beyond these economic justifications, advertising acquires a somewhat dubious image. Consumers seem to be aware of its cost which acts as a barrier against lower prices. They apparently do not consider potentially lower prices resulting from larger sales volume stimulated by advertising. In addition, advertising is seen as inflicted with social ills, for which consumers pay, at least indirectly. As a competitive weapon, advertising would not always be truthful, and people would be persuaded to buy things they neither need nor perhaps even want.
>
> The cross-cultural response pattern which has crystallized suggests that, to the extent that consumers accept advertising, it is in the economic sphere and in the specific role assigned to it within the market system. The major criticism of advertising is derived from the actual or potential social impact of advertising, perceived as adverse to consumer welfare.

Within this general, cross-cultural pattern, there are, of course, variations and exceptions. Outside the United States, advertising is most readily accepted on economic grounds in Ireland. The overall response pattern of the Irish seems to resemble that of the Americans more than that of other nationalities. The Germans are most similar to the Swiss, and the Britons to the Danes. The Swedes seem to criticize advertising's persuasive capacity most, and also distrust its efficacy as a price reducing agent. The Dutch appear to have the least favorable attitude toward advertising, all dimensions considered. The Italians have the distinction of being the only national group surveyed who substantially agreed with the statement that advertising does not persuade people. Perhaps Italians perceive themselves as being persuasive but not persuasible.

We may note that the highly negative finding with regard to the truthfulness of advertising in Denmark was not corroborated in a 1972 survey by the Gallup Institute, according to which 59 percent of respondents believed that advertising was fairly (or very) reliable, while only 32 percent thought it was "not so" (or not at all) reliable (index +27). Again, this may be just a reminder that we are still at a stage of technique development where all results of survey research should be taken with a large grain of salt!

In addition to these gross comparisons between many countries, a few country studies may be singled out to illustrate further cross-cultural patterns.

Britain

Thanks largely to the efforts of Dr. John Treasure, Britain offers the best data concerning public attitudes to advertising over time.[19] During the period 1961-72 on five separate occasions large, representative national samples, ranging in size from 1257 to over 2300, each time a different sample, were asked their feelings about advertising. Table 8-13 summarizes the results grossly, and while they have fluctuated quite a bit, two things seem clear. During the decade there was an overall decline in the rate of approval of advertising from four-fifths in 1961 to two-thirds in 1972. On the other hand, Britons still are fairly positive—certainly more so than Americans.

Of those who approved of advertising, either a lot or a little, in 1972, some 55 percent did so because of its informative value, that is, advertising "tells about products (prices)," "tells about new products" or "helps people choose products." Other reasons given for a positive attitude were largely economic or commercial. Awareness of advertising's positive impact on the economy and marketplace thus seemed to be high among British respondents. Of those disapproving of advertising, 35 percent objected on economic grounds, namely, that advertising is a waste of money and raises prices. It appears that Britons, in common with the Americans and (particularly) the Germans in our study, perceive the effect of advertising on price as a negative one. Another 35 percent of the "disapproving" respondents did so because there is simply too much advertising, too much repetition; advertising spoils TV, gets at your nerves, insults your intelligence. Most of the remaining third of

Table 8-13. Public Attitude to Advertising in Britain 1961-72

Question: In general, do you approve or disapprove of advertising? A lot or just a little?

	September 1961	May 1963	August 1966	May 1969	April 1972
Percentage who:					
Approve a lot	33%	}74%	22%	35%	25%
Approve a little	51		46	44	42
Disapprove a little	5	}20	14	10	14
Disapprove a lot	8		11	6	10
No opinion/don't know	3	6	7	4	9

Source: *Public Attitudes to Advertising—A Survey April 1972* (London: The Advertising Association, 1972): 7.

negative respondents had "moral" objections: no less than 23 percent felt that it is misleading and another 10 percent based their objections primarily on advertising's influencing people to "buy what they don't want to." Thus, all in all, some two-thirds of the negative attitudes in Britain were rooted in the area of what we have called the social aspects of advertising. Between 1966 and 1972 there was a dramatic increase in those thinking advertising is misleading, from 10 percent to 23 percent.

Again, we may note some discrepancies between the 1972 study and the British data reported in the *Reader's Digest* survey. In terms of our index numbers, the 1972 survey revealed the Britons as more skeptical of advertising's ability to lower prices than the *Digest* data (-56 vs. -28) as well as of advertising presenting a true picture of products advertised (-28 vs. -18). On the other hand, the 1972 survey found people less convinced than indicated by the *Digest* data about advertising making people buy things they don't want (-9 vs. -41).

Norway

At the request of the leader of this project, several advertising attitude questions were included in a 1969 survey of over 1800 households sponsored by the Norwegian Consumer Council.[20] We are grateful to the Council and to the Central Statistical Office of Norway for this cooperation. It was found that the overwhelming majority of respondents (83 percent) agreed that advertising is "necessary in the modern society;" only 12 percent disagreed. It appears that Norwegians endorse advertising in this respect almost as much as the American and far more than the German respondents in our study. Despite this enthusiastic support on the economic front, an almost equally large number of Norwegians (71 percent) thought that advertising "persuades people to buy things they do not need," while only 25 percent disagreed. The persuasive quality of advertising is perceived as particularly objectionable in Norway. Persuasion, on the other hand, is not necessarily linked to truth in advertising, as 52 percent of the sample felt that it "generally gives a true picture of the product advertised," whereas 41 percent disagreed with that statement.

No fewer than 18 percent of the sample households were subscribers to *Forbruker-rapporten*, the Norwegian equivalent to *Consumer Reports* or *DM* and *test*. This rate of subscription is higher than that of any other country in the world. Although Thorelli found that subscribers did indeed constitute an elite group of Information Seekers among Norwegian consumers,[21] it is interesting to note that the subscribers actually differed little from other respondents in their view of advertising. They agreed a bit more that advertising is necessary and they were a little less impressed by its persuasive powers, but they also said somewhat more often than did average consumers that advertising does not generally give a true picture of the product. The differences were small and were not statistically significant. Although the Norweigian subscriber represents an income-education elite similar to that of other countries, it appears that the *average consumer* in Norway is rather sophisticated when asked to express his views on advertising. He is perfectly capable of discriminating between positive and negative aspects of advertising. In looking for explanatory factors one is tempted to refer to the relative homogeneity of Norwegian society in general.

A smaller 1970 Norwegian study based on a stratified sample of 656 persons in the Oslo metropolitan area confirmed our own observations in the realm of truthfulness, in that 51 percent of respondents thought advertisements "by and large give correct information concerning the product," while 42 percent disagreed.[22] Some other results of interest are summarized in table 8-14.

Table 8-14.   Certain Aspects of Advertising Image, Oslo Metropolitan Area, 1969-70

Question	Positive to advertising	Neutral to advertising	Negative to advertising	No opinion, Don't know
Do you think advertising raises or lowers standard of living?	58	34	3	5
Do you think advertising results in better or poorer products?	55	37	3	5
Do you think advertising results in higher or lower prices on products advertised?	24	23	48	5
Some people feel that the information in advertisements generally is sufficient, others that it is deficient. What is your own view?	44		46	10
There is a movement toward equality between the sexes these days. Do you feel advertisements implement this by presenting women correctly, or is it your view that they present women incorrectly?	39		46	15

Percent of responses which were[a]

[a]The table does not give the exact formulation of response alternatives. It is believed, however, that the significance of "positive," "neutral" and "negative" to advertising would be fairly clear for all questions.

Source: *Undersökelse om forbrukernes instilling till reklame* (Oslo: Forenede Annonsebyråer A/S, 1970. Mimeographed).

Sweden

We have previously emphasized the critical attitudes toward advertising in contemporary Sweden. While standards of advertising (truthfulness, taste, etc.) are difficult to compare from one country to the next, we definitely do not have the impression that such standards are lower in Sweden than in most other industrialized countries. If anything, we would think the reverse was true even before the new regulatory measures of the 1970s. The critical views are probably due more to the intense consumerist public debate in that country and to the fact that the tone-setting, radical elite have vented their venom on advertising for a good many years. (The persuasive techniques employed in this campaign have been every bit as refined as those used by any commercial advertiser.) It is unfortunate indeed that none of the half dozen studies of advertising attitudes in Sweden in the last ten years has been very sophisticated. This state of affairs is also strange, in view of the heated debate on the subject and of the advanced development of social science research in general in the country.

Of greater interest here is a pioneering study carried out as early as 1950.[23] The main sample comprised 1635 randomly selected persons from the entire nation. After using the somewhat questionable device of counting all interviews from rural areas twice (resulting in 2234 "observations"), the sample faithfully reproduced the distribution by sex, age, occupation, marital status, social class and geographical dispersion of the total population. Some of the more pertinent results follow: Question: If all advertising for products would cease, do you think that this would leave the public better off or worse off, or would it have no effect on the public? The percentage distribution of responses was

Better off	4%
No effect	13
Worse off	63
Don't know	20
	100%

The majority of respondents who felt that the public would be worse off were asked the open-ended question, "What reason do you particularly have in mind?" The responses were classified in this way:

No overview of the market without advertising	38%
Public knowledge of products would deteriorate	25
Would not find out about new products	11
Sales would decrease	12
Advertising promotes competition	4
Other replies, don't know	10
	100%

In one part of the study respondents were asked (in separate questions) about the credibility of advertising and political propaganda. The percentage distribution of responses to the two questions was the following:

	Advertising	Political Propaganda
Almost all advertisng (political propaganda) is unreliable (*ovederhäftig*)	3%	9%
A major part of it is unreliable	16	25
About fifty-fifty	32	37
A major part is reliable	36	16
Almost all of it is reliable	9	3
Other replies, don't know	4	10
	100%	100%

These findings reenforce the oft-made observation that most social institutions in the Western world have had credibility problems in the last quarter of a century. This, in turn, does not mean all is well with advertising.

This 1950 study was fairly unique also in classifying the replies to the advertising credibility questions by party loyalties among respondents:

	Conservatives and Liberals	Social Democrats	Communists
Almost all advertising is unreliable	2%	3%	5%
A major part of it is unreliable	16	13	10
About fifty-fifty	26	34	54
A major part is reliable	47	36	26
Almost all of it is reliable	7	11	3
Other replies, don't know	2	3	2
	100%	100%	100%

There are clear traces of underlying philosophies concerning the free market system here. We should assume that corresponding data at least for the Socialist parties in Sweden would be a good deal more negative today, reflecting the fanfare with which their intellectuals have been attacking advertising in recent years. By contrast, there was very little difference between Labour voters and respondents in general in the 1972 UK study on the "approval of advertising" question. (See also table 8-13.)

	All Respondents	Male	Female	Labour Voters
Approve a lot	25%	28%	24%	23%
Approve a little	42	39	44	42
Disapprove a little	14	13	14	13
Disapprove a lot	10	12	8	11
Don't know	9	8	10	11
	100%	100%	100%	100%

We have included data on male and female responses from this question to illustrate the general observation that there are few significant differences between the sexes with regard to advertising attitudes in either Britain or Sweden.

United States

As might be expected in the country most closely associated with the development of modern mass media advertising, a fair number of studies of public attitudes toward advertising in the United States have been made. Most of this research, beginning in the late 1930s under the leadership of Neil H. Borden, has been adequately summarized by Bauer and Greyser, to whose work, in turn, our own research has been related.[24] As the Bauer–Greyser volume is obligatory reading for any student of advertising image, there would be little point in recapitulating the history of American advertising image research here.

In this context, we wish only to comment briefly on the more recent study by Robert T. Bower, *Television and the Public*. Pertaining to 1970 conditions, this research is of special interest in that it permits direct comparison with the massive pioneer work in this area done exactly ten years earlier by Gary A. Steiner.[25] Both studies were based on personal interviews with large representative samples; the basic Bower sample contained 1900 persons and the Steiner sample over 2000. Table 8-15 reproduces some of the principal findings concerning the public's attitude to TV advertising in 1970 as well as in 1960. It appears that in general the public became just a shade more critical of TV advertising during the ten year period. It may be added that in 1970 some 70 percent of respondents said that "there are just too many commercials." (This statement did not appear in the 1960 study.) To us, it is not quite clear whether the public was really reacting to the number of commercials or to the number of program interruptions. According to Bower, in both the 1960 and the 1970 surveys "the reactions to commercials did not vary much among segments of the audience. The two sexes and people of different ages felt similarly; even the critical socioeconomic variables, such as education, produced only modest differences (the better educated were more critical of commercials)."[26] Certainly, the split in table 8-15 between white-collar and blue-collar respondents displays remarkable similarities. That the blue-collar group found commercials a more helpful means of product information than the white-collar group is in line with our own findings about media habits.

One final reflection. Some 30 percent of the 1970 respondents said they would rather pay a "small" (undefined) amount yearly in order to have TV without commercials. In contrast, in a 1972 survey in Germany by the well-known *Allensbach Institut für Demoskopie* in which respondents were posed with the alternatives "more advertising in TV or higher subscription fees,"

Table 8-15. Public Attitude to TV Advertising in the United States 1960 and 1970

Interviewer: Here are some statements about commercials. I'd like you to read each statement and mark whether you generally agree or disagree with each statement.

	1960 Total	1970 Total	1970 Occupation of Head of Household	
			White Collar	Blue Collar
Percentage Who Agree That:				
Commercials are a fair price to pay for the entertainment you get.	75%	70%	69%	71%
Most commercials are too long.	63	65	67	65
I find some commercials very helpful in keeping me informed.	58	54	50	57
Some commercials are so good that they are more entertaining than the program.	43	54	56	52
I would prefer TV without commercials.	43	48	49	47
Commercials are generally in poor taste and very annoying.	40	43	42	43
I frequently find myself welcoming a commercial break.	36	35	31	38
I'd rather pay a small amount yearly to have TV without commercials.	24	30	30	29

Source: Robert T. Bower, *Television and the Public* (New York: Holt, Rinehart and Winston, 1973): 84.

58 percent were for more advertising and only 22 percent for higher subscriptions. Perhaps this is an expression of the oft-noted human credo that the grass is always greener on the other side.

Conclusion

We have seen that there are many commonalities in attitudes toward advertising in the United States and Germany, as well as in other developed countries. In addition to a great number of similarities, we find subtle differences in degree as well as opposing views on advertising which tend to be culture-bound and related to national idiosyncracies of the countries involved in the comparisons.

How effective, persuasive or trustworthy advertising is, whatever other characteristics it possesses as an information source, can in the final analysis be evaluated more meaningfully in comparison with other information sources available in the marketplace. In the next chapter, the image of advertising is directly compared with consumer reactions to another important source of consumer information: comparative product test reports.

NOTES TO CHAPTER 8

1. It may be interesting to note at this point that Consumers Union (CU) itself engages in a considerable amount of promotional activity. Advertising and promotion for *Consumer Reports* accounts for over 30 percent of CU's annual budget. For further detail see the relevant section on CU in *Consumer Information Handbook.*

2. Raymond A. Bauer and Stephen A. Greyser, *Advertising in America: The Consumer View* (Boston: Harvard University, Division of Research, Graduate School of Business, 1968).

3. International Advertising Assn., "Levels of 1968 Advertising Expenditures in Various Media in 46 Countries," *Advertising Age* (June 8, 1970): 101–2.

4. The reader may also be interested to know that CU of the United States accounts for about one-half of the global expenditures for CI programs.

5. For additional detail of the time standard code, see *1971 Broadcasting Yearbook* (Washington, D.C.: Broadcasting Publications Inc., 1971): D-5 and D-8.

6. Bauer and Greyser: 57–8 and appendix C.

7. George Katona, Burkhard Strumpel and Ernest Zahn, *Aspirations and Affluence–Comparative Studies in the United States and Western Europe* (New York: McGraw-Hill, 1971).

8. Bauer and Greyser.

9. David Riesman, Nathan Glazer and Revel Denny, *The Lonely Crowd: A Study of the Changing American Character* (New Haven: Yale University Press, 1950).

10. This theme appears repeatedly in Katona et al.

11. Supporting data for these results are in Helmut Becker, "Consumer Information and the Image of Advertising in Germany with Significant Comparisons to America," (DBA diss., Indiana University, 1971), chapter 11.

12. Stephen A. Greyser and Bonnie B. Reece, "Businessmen Look Hard at Advertising," *Harvard Business Review* 29 (May–June 1971): 18–26, 157–65.

13. See Stephen A. Greyser, "Businessmen Re Advertising: 'Yes, But . . . ,' " *Harvard Business Review* 40 (May–June 1962): 22–30, 34ff.

14. See Robert T. Bower, *Television and the Public* (New York: Holt, Rinehart and Winston, 1973), particularly chapters 1–3 and 6.

15. Same reference as note 2.

16. Gallup Organization Survey, December 1969.

17. The Reader's Digest Association, *A Survey of Europe Today* (London: The Reader's Digest Association, 1970).
18. Reader's Digest Association, *A Survey*.
19. See John Treasure, "What They Think About Us" (London. Mimoegraphed. 1962), John Treasure and Timothy Joyce, *As Others See Us: A Study of Attitudes to Advertising and to Television Advertisements* (London: Institute of Practitioners in Advertising, 1967), and *Public Attitudes to Advertising—A Survey April 1972* (London: The Advertising Association, 1972).
20. *Rapport fra kontoret for intervjuundersökelser Nr. 8. Undersökelse om Forbruker-rapporten, vareundersökelser og reklamasjoner 1969* (Oslo: Statistisk Sentralbyrå, 1970).
21. Hans B. Thorelli, "Concentration of Information Power among Consumers," *Journal of Marketing Research* 8 (November 1971): 427–32.
22. *Undersökelse om forbrukernes instilling till reklame* (Oslo: Forenede Annonsebyråer A/S, 1970. Mimeographed).
23. Ralph Rilton, *Opinioner om reklam* (Borås: Svenska Försäljnings- och Reklamförbundet, 1953).
24. Bauer and Greyser, especially appendix A.
25. Gary A. Steiner, *The People Look at Television* (New York: Alfred A. Knopf, 1963).
26. Bower: 83–5. Parentheses in original.

Chapter Nine

Consumer Information and Advertising Image

Product test reports published by organizations independent of any single business or industry are sometimes hailed as the only objective type of consumer information available in the market place.[1] As such, they are also contrasted with commercial advertising, perceived by its opponents as the epitome of subjective communication, designed to sell products and services at the expense of the gullible consumer.[2] From the standpoint of the social scientist, neither product test reports nor commercial advertising need be viewed as polar extremes on the objective–subjective continuum of consumer information. As stated here and elsewhere,[3] advertising and product tests are not regarded as necessarily conflicting sources of consumer information. On the contrary, much advertising, besides being persuasive, also performs a vital informative role in the market environment; and some product test reports certainly reflect the subjective criteria of the tester rather than the more common standards of consumer use—if, indeed, such objective use standards could be defined.[4] Product testing and advertising are thus considered information sources which partly compete with each other and partly complement and supplement each other. Indeed, it could be argued that without the abundant availability of advertised brands, comparative test reports would be of little market value to consumers.

In the last chapter, the image of advertising was highlighted separately. Impact of product test reports was discussed in chapters 4 and 5 and again emphasized in chapter 6. In this chapter, the perceptions consumers express about product testing and advertising are combined to give a view of the interaction within and between these two information sources. That is, subscribers to product testing publications (our Information Seekers) and average consumers in the United States and Germany are compared and contrasted in regard to their common and differential attitudes toward product testing and advertising as market information sources. The emphasis is on interaction between the two at the consumer level.

INFORMATION SOURCE ATTRIBUTES AND
METHOD OF INQUIRY

Attitude toward an object tends to be multidimensional rather than unidimensional in nature, and it is likely to vary to a large extent across several, distinct attributes of the object. For the purpose of the present study, eight information source attributes were isolated with respect to product testing and advertising.

1. Trustworthiness of the information source
2. Informative value of the source content
3. Cost of information relative to its worth to the consumer
4. Helpfulness of information for product and brand comparisons
5. Timeliness of information source and content
6. New product information content
7. Degree of difficulty in understanding information content
8. Time and effort required for reading and/or comprehending message content.

Each of these attributes was represented identically in the American and German versions of the questionnaire by a separate statement requiring a direct comparison between product testing and advertising as alternate information sources. A few examples will serve to illustrate the methodological procedure followed in the questioning.

Take the statement for the first attribute. In the questionnaire it read, "Compared to advertising, product testing is more trustworthy." The responses were recorded on a five-point Likert scale, whereby strong agreement reflected a highly favorable attitude toward product testing compared to advertising with respect to the criterion of trustworthiness; strong disagreement with the statement implied the opposite. A response at the neutral midpoint indicated indifference between product testing and advertising on this dimension.

Now consider the seventh attribute listed above as another example. It was expressed as, "Compared to advertising, product testing is more difficult to understand." This question referred to the readability and comprehensibility of the two information sources relative to each other. Strong agreement with the statement indicated in this case a highly favorable attitude toward advertising in comparison to product testing with regard to the degree of difficulty of understanding the message content; strong disagreement with the statement reflected the reverse.

In addition, the statements themselves were reversed for half the respondents, to read, "Compared to product testing, advertising is . . . (e.g., more trustworthy)." For coding purposes, the numerical response was then also reversed in the analysis, so as to render the two statement formulations equivalent.

In general, we attempted through this somewhat complex methodology to minimize, to the greatest extent possible, response biases, particularly in favor of product testing. We assumed this to be the case, because comparative test reports are often perceived as a socially acceptable means of gathering product information. This phenomenon has been repeatedly inferred in this study from exaggerated claims of knowledge and use of and even subscription to the test magazines. Perhaps it seems socially acceptable or even desirable to downgrade advertising as something societally bad. Indeed, there may well be a consistent perceptual bias against advertising along the mainstream of current social thinking, especially in contrast to product testing. Beside the split sample technique, we tried to reduce bias by including positive as well as negative aspects about both product testing and advertising in the questionnaire. Thus, agreement with some of the statements would indicate a favorable view of product testing compared to advertising. Agreement with other statements would reflect a more positive attitude of advertising. We made no attempt to assign weights to the individual attributes.

FRAMEWORK OF COMPARISON AND ILLUSTRATIVE PROPOSITIONS

The framework for comparison is essentially similar to that of the last chapter. The analysis moves on three levels. The first one is the cross-cultural. Its aim is to identify transatlantic commonalities as well as national idiosyncracies with regard to the attitudes toward advertising/product testing among American and German respondents. The second level might be called "sectoral," and it concerns the similarities and differences between subscribers and average consumers within each country. The third level of comparison, finally, combines the first two and reflects upon the attitudinal characteristics of American versus German subscribers and American versus German average consumers.

The objects of the comparison are the two information sources (advertising and product testing), including the attributes which describe their varied impact and image. The subjects of the comparison encompass, as in the previous chapter, the American and German subscriber and average consumer respondents interviewed in the metropolitan areas of Indianapolis and Frankfurt, as described in chapter 3.

This comparison is diagrammed in figure 9-1. Its logic suggests that, at some level, intercultural discrepancies in response patterns will appear as a result of national–environmental–cultural factors, which tend to make reactions on the part of Germans in general different from those of Americans. The history of the two countries, their ways of doing business, their peculiar media mix, the awareness level and availability of comparative testing and advertising are examples of these factors. Given our ecological perspective, we assume that

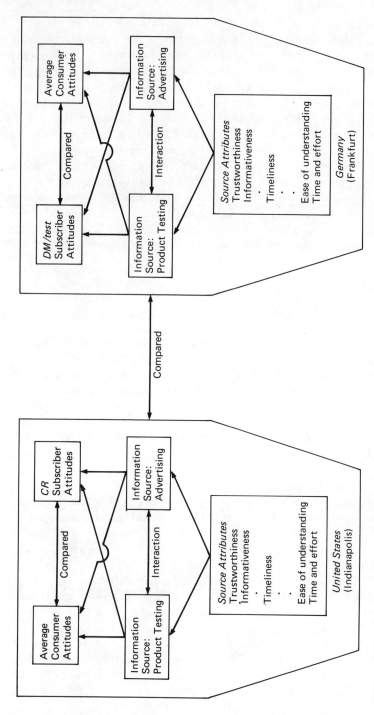

Figure 9–1. Schema for Comparing Product Testing/Advertising Interaction Between the United States and Germany (Metropolitan Populations).

such environmental influences account for the differences between the two countries. On the basis of these factors and the results from previous chapters we would anticipate, for example, that:

1. American and German consumers in general will evaluate product testing favorably over advertising; but due to the more extensive history of comparative testing in the United States, Americans may exhibit a higher degree of relative enthusiasm for that medium than Germans;
2. Product testing is likely to fare better on such dimensions as trustworthiness and informativeness, and worse on timeliness, cost and effort, and difficulty of understanding. Given our cross-cultural assumptions, we might expect Americans to be more trustful than Germans, and Germans to be less concerned with cost and effort than Americans;
3. Compared to average consumers, subscribers most probably will rate product testing in general much higher. Subscribers in both countries are more knowledgeable about product testing than average consumers, and therefore will mention the positive sides of testing more often. They will also be more likely to recognize its weaknesses vis-à-vis advertising at least in a relative sense. In other words, subscribers are expected to be more discriminating between individual attributes in their evaluation of the two information sources;
4. As "universal" Information Seekers, subscribers in the two countries may exhibit certain common, attitudinal characteristics, not present among German and American average consumers.

One could easily expand the list of propositions by including a greater number of details. These are sufficient, however, to illustrate our thinking and the direction of our analysis.

CONSUMER REACTIONS IN AMERICA AND GERMANY

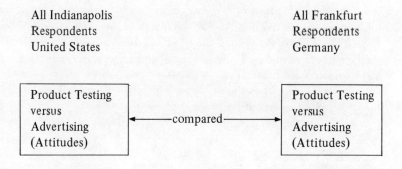

For the most part, both American and German consumers are more favorably inclined toward product testing than toward advertising when comparing them as information sources. This is particularly true with such dimensions as trustworthiness of both the source itself and its informative content, suggesting that advertising lacks these characteristics in the eyes of consumers. When it comes to time involved in reading and ease of understanding, the perceptual distinction between the two information media becomes much less pronounced. In fact, the comparison can change direction in favor of an actual preference for advertising over product testing.

Table 9-1 shows, side by side, the reactions of all American and German respondents. A positive index in this and the following tables means that in the comparative evaluation of the two information sources, product testing received a more favorable rating than advertising. A negative index implies a more favorable rating of advertising. Reactions to the various source attributes are discussed in the following paragraphs.

Trustworthiness

Trustworthiness appeared universally as *the* attribute where product testing was favored *most* over advertising by German and American respondents alike. Apparently, product testing over the years has acquired a reputation for objectivity which is mirrored in the image of trust held universally, whatever else might be the shortcomings of product testing.

The data suggest that the Americans' faith in comparative testing is even greater than the Germans'. The difference is only one of degree, but it is noteworthy for its consistency with other findings. On the surface it might appear that the difference in the character of the magazines themselves might explain a difference in attitudes. As previously mentioned, every issue of *DM* comprises about one third advertising; and consequently, the relative status of advertising may be enhanced in the eyes of the reader. However, even though *test* does not publish any advertisements and is in character very similar to *CR*, *test* subscribers responded nearly identically to *DM* subscribers on this point, as a separate analysis clearly showed.

Beneath the surface, the perceptual difference between Americans and Germans on the issue of trust may be caused by an underlying cultural difference between the two peoples. Compared to the more easy-going outlook toward the world of Americans, the relative distrust of Germans toward both their environment and each other has been noted previously in this volume and by Katona and others. For instance, Germans will always, as a matter of custom, lock their houses and car doors—a practice often routinely neglected in the United States, particularly in the small town setting.

On the whole, however, it seems that product testers in America and

Table 9-1.   Attitudes toward Product Testing as Compared to Advertising[a] (All Indianapolis Respondents Compared to all Frankfurt Respondents)

All Indianapolis Respondents (Base = 299)			All Frankfurt Respondents (Base = 295)		
Rank	Source Attribute	Index	Rank	Source Attribute	Index
A. Ranked by Index Numbers[b]					
1.	Trustworthy	66	1.	Trustworthy	59
2.	Helpful to compare	51	2.	Helpful to compare	46
3.	Informative	41	3.	Tells about new products	40
4.	Inexpensive (Cost)	31	4.	Informative	37
5.	Tells about new products	30	5.	Inexpensive (Cost)	34
6.	Up-to-date	22	6.	Little time and effort	20
7.	Little time and effort	2	7.	Easy to understand	16
8.	Easy to understand	-1	8.	Up-to-date	12

Indianapolis Respondents compared to Frankfurt Respondents

	15	10	5	0	5	10	15	20
B. Ranked by Differences in Index Numbers[b]								
Up-to-date				(10)	Americans			
Trustworthy				(7)	are higher			
Helpful to compare				(5)	than Germans			
Informative				(4)				
Inexpensive (Cost)			(3)					
Tells about new products		Germans are	(10)					
Easy to understand		higher than	(17)					
Little time and effort		Americans	(18)					

[a]Data based on question 4, section 5 of questionnaire, reproduced in appendix G.

[b]Index = (% of sample strongly or slightly agreeing with statement minus % of sample strongly or slightly disagreeing). Positive index means more favorable attitude toward product testing than advertising.

Germany have succeeded in creating an aura of integrity and independence. The notion of trust was already clearly evident in chapter 6 where it was shown that subscribers at least exhibit great confidence in the reliability and credibility of the testing publications' testing methods. They believe that test information is reliable, and they have faith in the independence and integrity of the organizations themselves which they trust are free from government or commercial influences. A mild exception was *DM* which suffered to a slight degree on the "influence" question relative to *CR* and *test*. But overall, all three magazines had high, positive index marks. As a result, the absolute level of consumer trust in the impartiality of information contained in them far exceeds that of advertising in both countries, despite the relative index difference between countries. Yet it has been noted in chapters 4 and 5 that only a moderate minority say they actually make use of comparative test reports and an even smaller one subscribe to such reports.

Helpfulness for Product Comparisons

To the extent that the tests published in *CR* as well as in *DM* and *test* are in fact "comparative" product tests, the attribute of product comparability appears to be one of the stronger features of this type of consumer information. This was definitely borne out by the data in this study. Both American and German respondents were convinced that product testing excels advertising in its usefulness for comparing products.

It is interesting to note that again Americans exceeded Germans by *degree* in this belief. The reason for this difference could be the relative lack of historical perspective on comparative testing in Germany and the consequently lagging awareness level and perceived usefulness of this medium.

Informative Value and Cost

Informative value is an integral element of the communications source providing the message recipient with the quality and quantity of data perceived by him as both necessary and helpful in making the purchase decision. Hence, this attribute refers to the degree of usefulness of content to satisfy previously unfulfilled information needs. Informative value complements trustworthiness in the sense that the content is useful only to the extent it is also believable.

On the attribute of perceived informative value, ranked third by American respondents and fourth by the Germans, comparative testing still received a broad-based vote of confidence over advertising by consumers of both countries. Although the difference in rank could lead one to conclude otherwise, the indexes of 41 and 37 (see table 9-1) respectively suggest that the discrepancy in the actual rating between the two groups was almost negligible.

A similar conclusion can be drawn about the cost of information relative to its value. Ranked fourth by the Indianapolis respondents and fifth by the Frankfurt ones, perceived relative cost of information hardly differed between the two samples. Actually, the Germans favored product testing slightly more than the Americans on this point, despite the reverse order of their ranking.

The purchase of a testing magazine requires, of course, an out-of-pocket expenditure on the part of the consumer while advertising is supposedly "free." Cost might therefore be a potential shortcoming of product testing, particularly for lower income segments. Hence it may come as a surprise that a good proportion of consumers in both countries generally felt that "product testing is less expensive than advertising for what it is worth." Germans found the cost aspect even less objectionable than Americans, even though *DM* cost more and *test* cost about the same as *CR*. To consumers in both countries, the cost of comparative test reports might not appear out of line with their high perceived information value. Hence product testing is favored despite the seemingly cost-free nature of advertising, although there is quite a distance between favorable attitude and the actuality of subscriptions. It may be that the positive image of the magazines leads consumers to disregard what they might otherwise consider some weaknesses at the level of particulars.

Timeliness and New Product Information

Timeliness with regard to consumer information here refers to its availability at the moment when it is of greatest benefit to the decision maker, obviously a function of the ability of a communications source to make current and up-to-date information available as early as possible for maximum usefulness. Timeliness can indeed be crucial to the consumer, particularly in a world of accelerating technological change.

Because of the long lead times required for testing, timeliness is considered a relative disadvantage of product tests. It may take as many as twelve months from the time a specific product test is decided upon, the products purchased, the actual tests prepared, carried out and evaluated, until publication of the test results can take place. By then, some of the tested products may have been changed, replaced by new models, or even withdrawn from the market.

These kinds of shortcomings apparently were recognized by the respondents in this study, particularly the Germans, who rated product testing vis-à-vis advertising less favorable on the timeliness factor than on any other of the eight attributes. Even so, the Frankfurt respondents felt that advertising was only close to par with comparative testing in being timely. The Indianapolis sample also gave advertising more credit on the timeliness question than on the previously discussed attributes.

One may ponder the question of why product testing still fared so well in juxtaposition to advertising in the eyes of the respondents. On the one hand, these perceptions could reflect the generally high esteem surrounding testing journals coupled with indifference toward advertising and a low social opinion of it. On the other hand, this finding may lead one to suspect that the non-subscriber portion of the sample at least may not actually be too well informed. Subscriber-average consumer differences are discussed in the next section, but the interested reader may wish to refer to chapter 6 where a variety of measures of satisfaction with the testing magazines among subscribers were discussed. It was found there that the lowest scores were given to the relevance-timeliness-availability factors. While these indexes were still positive, they clearly stood out as the weakest points of testing reports in relationship to other, more favorable aspects, pointing to an area of possible improvement of the publications.

Related to the timeliness factor is the information about new products contained in test magazines and in advertising respectively. It is perhaps surprising that all respondents rated comparative testing higher on this score than on timeliness. In fact, the Germans' index for the new product information criterion was in third place, markedly higher than the Americans' fifth place. This may be so because *DM* features a unique section on new product information. Although *test* did not carry an equivalent new products column, there was no statistically significant difference between the subscribers to the two magazines.

Time and Effort and Ease of Understanding

The time and effort required in reading test reports and the degree of difficulty in understanding them can be two major shortcomings. This would be particularly true where the reports are written in a technically complex language. American respondents clearly recognized that drawback, rating product testing lowest on these two attributes. Overall, they seemed unable to decide whether test reports or advertising would take more time and effort and would be more difficult to comprehend.

The German respondents were more favorably impressed by product test reports on these two points. They perceived considerably less effort—requirement to read the reports than the Americans, and seemed to find their data understandable.

These outcomes can again be related to the satisfaction measures of the testing magazines presented in chapter 6. On the questions of readability and clarity, *DM* was given the highest rating by the national subscriber samples, followed by *test* and *CR* in that order. This is likely to result from the different styles of these journals. While *test* and *CR* are perhaps more academic and technical in style, *DM* has adopted a popular stance. Americans tend to be spoiled by popularization of almost everything from economics to sex education, and it is possible that this demand is not being met by *CR*. We would place *CR* and *test* on par in this respect, while *DM* probably makes easier reading than the other two.

We may summarize the overall German-American comparisons to this point as follows.

1. In general, both American and German respondents evaluated comparative testing more favorably than advertising as a consumer information source. Of the eight attributes included in the study, respondents of both countries universally rated product testing higher as being more trustworthy, more helpful for product comparisons, and more informative than advertising.
2. The American sample perceived the time and effort required for reading and the difficulty in understanding as the greatest shortcomings of testing relative to advertising. The Germans judged product testing lowest for its lack of timeliness.
3. On the whole, neither the American nor the German respondents can be said to be the more ardent supporters of product testing compared to advertising on the measures included in the study. That is, each of the two groups scored higher, i.e., more in favor of comparative testing, on four of the eight source attributes. In other words, the differences between American and German respondents were *relative* rather than absolute.
4. In comparing product testing and advertising on individual attributes, the differences between the American and German respondents were greatest on timeliness, and trustworthiness which Americans scored higher than Germans. German respondents rated testing more positively on the time and effort dimension and on the difficulty of understanding the content.

Beyond the differences and similarities between the countries, one also expects differential responses between segments within each country. This kind of sectoral comparison between information seekers and average consumers in their product testing–advertising perceptions is presented in some detail in the following section.

INFORMATION SEEKERS AND AVERAGE CONSUMERS

The Information Seeker identified in chapters 4–6 should be expected to rate product testing as an information source superior to advertising. This logically follows from the nature of the characteristics ascribed to him, from his reading and subscribing to testing magazines which have often adopted an anti-advertising editorial position. Our expectation in this respect should hold, no matter where the Information Seeker lives or which country he would call his own.

To the extent that subscribers are identical with Information Seekers in both Germany and America, they convincingly met our expectations. Subscriber respondents in the two countries overwhelmingly favored comparative testing over advertising while average consumers did so to a much more moderate extent. Although this finding may not be too surprising in and of itself, it is noteworthy for its cross-cultural validity. Before going further in discussing these cross-cultural universals, it is useful to look for a moment at more detailed discrepancies between Information Seekers and average consumers in each country separately.

United States

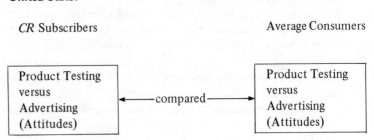

CR Subscribers   Average Consumers

| Product Testing versus Advertising (Attitudes) | ←——compared——→ | Product Testing versus Advertising (Attitudes) |

As measured by all eight source attributes, *CR* subscribers from the Indianapolis sample are convinced that product testing is superior to advertising in providing consumer information. Average consumers in many respects also favor product testing over advertising, but at markedly lower levels. The differences in attitudes between the two groups, although very large in most instances, are, therefore, primarily a matter of *degree*.

Individually, the differences as well as some similarities between American Information Seekers and average consumers are made plainly evident by table 9-2. Information Seekers and AC share common attitudes in that both perceive product testing as more trustworthy than advertising and also more helpful for product comparisons. They agree, furthermore, that the weakest characteristics of product testing are difficulty of understanding and the time and effort required in reading. These findings corroborate the discussion in the last section.

In spite of this commonality, great perceptual differences occur in the *relative* evaluation of the information sources. It can be noted, for example, that AC assigned a negative index to the last two criteria, implying that, in their eyes, advertising requires less time and effort and is easier to understand. Subscribers are much less likely to see these as absolute disadvantages of product testing.

By far the biggest perceived difference in attitudes is over the cost of test reports. Subscribers strongly disagreed that testing is too expensive compared to advertising; average consumers were more likely to be neutral on this point. The smallest difference in attitude between the groups occurred with respect to timeliness. Neither subscribers nor average consumers felt

Table 9-2.   Attitudes toward Product Testing as Compared to Advertising[a] (Indianapolis Samples)

Subscribers (Base = 101)			Average Consumers (Base = 198)		
Rank	Source Attribute	Index	Rank	Source Attribute	Index
A. Ranked by Index Numbers[b]					
1.	Trustworthy	79	1.	Trustworthy	60
2.	Helpful to compare	62	2.	Helpful to compare	45
3.	Inexpensive	57	3.	Informative	34
4.	Informative	54	4.	Tells about new products	22
5.	Tells about new products	46	5.	Up-to-date	17
6.	Up-to-date	30	6.	Inexpensive	17
7.	Little time and effort	21	7.	Little time and effort	-7
8.	Easy to understand	13	8.	Easy to understand	-8

Subscribers compared to Average Consumers, Indianapolis

	40	25	20	15	10	5	0	
B. Ranked by Differences in Index Numbers[b]								
Inexpensive								(40) Subscribers
Little time and effort								(28) are higher
Tells about new products								(24) than AC
Easy to understand								(21) on all
Informative								(20) attributes
Trustworthy								(19)
Helpful to compare								(17)
Up-to-date								(13)

[a]Data based on question 4, section 5 of questionnaire, reproduced in appendix G.
[b]Index = (% of sample strongly or slightly agreeing with statement minus % of sample strongly or slightly disagreeing). Positive index means more favorable attitude toward product testing than advertising.

too strongly that product testing is more up-to-date than advertising, although both groups are really more positive than we had anticipated.

Germany

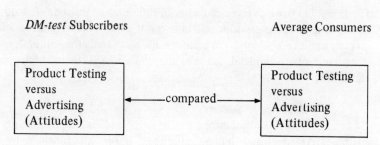

The Frankfurt subscriber respondents followed a path similar to the Indianapolis ones in that they also were much more likely than average consumers to agree that product testing is superior to advertising. One lone exception, the attribute of timeliness, received identical scores from both groups. Although both their indexes are positive, subscribers as well as average consumers put their collective finger on product testing's most vulnerable characteristic, and advertising fares better, being perceived as almost on a par with product testing in its up-to-dateness. The overall results are presented in table 9-3.

Both the Frankfurt subscribers and AC ranked product testing highest on the same three criteria: product testing was perceived as more trustworthy, more informative, and more helpful in comparing products. Similarly, all agreed (though not in the same order) on the three lowest attributes: timeliness, understandability, and effort required in reading. These perceptions of attribute rankings parallel closely the discussion of the all-Frankfurt respondents earlier in the chapter.

Despite the similarity in *ranking* product testing on the highest and lowest attributes, significant attitudinal differences persist between subscribers and average consumers. The greatest differences were noted with regard to the ease of understanding and trustworthiness of product tests over advertising. Trustworthiness, ranked highest by both sets of respondents, was much more strongly endorsed by subscribers than by average consumers. One may ponder the possibility that its relatively high ranking by average consumers is due to lack of experience and knowledge of comparative test reports. That those who are not used to reading product test reports may have difficulty in understanding their content is underscored by the fact that average consumers gave the lowest index to that criterion.

Neither subscribers nor average consumers thought that product testing is overly expensive for what it is worth. But the two groups agreed only slightly that product testing does not take too much time and effort compared to advertising.

A CROSS-CULTURAL SYNTHESIS

The foregoing findings revealed universal and opposite attitudes toward product testing and advertising, within and between the Indianapolis and Frankfurt survey samples. Combining the main results, an overall cross-cultural, comparative picture of attitudinal differences and similarities is created in this summary section.[5]

Information Seekers
Despite several differences in rating and ranking the various source attributes, American and German subscribers, our proxies for the universal

Table 9-3. Attitudes toward Product Testing as Compared to
Advertising[a] Subscribers Compared to Average Consumers
(Frankfurt Samples)

Subscribers (Base = 97)			Average Consumers (Base = 198)		
Rank	Source Attribute	Index	Rank	Source Attribute	Index
A. Ranked by Index Numbers[b]					
1.	Trustworthy	73	1.	Trustworthy	52
2.	Helpful to compare	55	2.	Helpful to compare	42
3.	Informative	47	3.	Informative	32
4.	Tells about new products	42	4.	Inexpensive	32
5.	Inexpensive	40	5.	Tells about new products	25
6.	Easy to understand	33	6.	Little time and effort	16
7.	Little time and effort	28	7.	Up-to-date	12
8.	Up-to-date	12	8.	Easy to understand	9

Subscribers compared to
Average Consumers, Frankfurt

	25	20	15	10	5	0	5	10
B. Ranked by Differences in Index Numbers[b]								
Easy to understand							(24)	Subscribers
Trustworthy							(21)	are higher
Tells about new products							(17)	on all
Informative							(15)	attributes
Helpful to compare							(13)	except one
Little time and effort							(12)	
Inexpensive							(8)	
Up-to-date						(0)	(0)	

[a]Data based on question 4, section 5 of questionnaire, reproduced in appendix G.
[b]Index = (% of sample strongly or slightly agreeing with statement minus % of sample strongly or slightly disagreeing). Positive index means more favorable attitude toward product testing than advertising.

Information Seekers, showed some measure of agreement in their evaluation of the relative merits of testing and advertising on five of the eight criteria. The data are illustrated in table 9-4 and may be divided into categories of common or similar attitudes and opposite or dissimilar attitudes. *Common attitudes*, where only minor differences in the indexes between American and German subscribers emerged, are summarized as follows:

1. Without question, comparative testing scored highest relative to advertising on the dimension of *trustworthiness* on both sides of the Atlantic. The difference between the two samples was small, but its direction was again

consistent with numerous other findings of this study: German respondents expressed a slightly lower level of trust than the American. Product testers in both the United States and Germany, however, can take pride in the fact that they have been able to instill such a high degree of confidence in the integrity and independence of their publications among their readership.

2. At a somewhat lower level, respondents still gave relatively high marks to product testing on the attributes of *helpfulness for product comparisons, general informativeness,* and *specifically new product information.* The data suggest that subscribers in both countries were quite satisfied with product testing on these dimensions, at least when compared to commercial advertising.

3. Product testing was appraised lower, albeit still positively, on the criterion of *time and effort.* On both sides of the ocean, subscribers rated advertising less unfavorably, the Americans somewhat less so than the Germans. It may be that either Americans value their own time more than Germans, or *CR* indeed requires more effort to read than *DM* and *test*. An indication to this effect was given in chapter 6.

Opposite attitudes, where substantial index differences between American and German subscribers could be identified, were:

1. *Americans higher:* Indianapolis subscribers indicated that lack of *timeliness* might be a potential shortcoming of product tests. They still rated it higher than the Germans who placed it at the bottom of the list of the eight characteristics. It may well be that the relative paucity of product tests in Germany compared to the United States in 1970 unfavorably affected the evaluation of timeliness of test reports among German subscribers. The Americans also regarded the relatively low *cost of product testing relative to its worth* as a more significant advantage than the Germans.

2. *Germans higher:* Indianapolis subscribers considered the *difficulty of understanding* the content of product tests as the least favorable element. The Frankfurt sample, in contrast, did not fault tests too severely on this point. This comparative degree of ease in understanding could well be due to the more thorough and conscientious reading habits of Germans in general, or due to the influence of *DM* subscribers, whose magazine was rated highest in readability.

Considering the eight source attributes *in toto*, American subscribers can be said to be slightly more favorable to product testing in comparison to

Table 9–4.   Attitudes toward Product Testing as Compared to Advertising[a] (Indianapolis and Frankfurt Subscribers)

Indianapolis Subscribers (Base = 101)		*Index*	*Frankfurt Subscribers (Base = 97)*		*Index*
Rank	*Source Attribute*	*Index*	*Rank*	*Source Attribute*	*Index*
A. Ranked by Index Numbers[b]					
1.	Trustworthy	79	1.	Trustworthy	73
2.	Helpful to compare	62	2.	Helpful to compare	55
3.	Inexpensive	57	3.	Informative	47
4.	Informative	54	4.	Tells about new products	42
5.	Tells about new products	46	5.	Inexpensive	40
6.	Up-to-date	30	6.	Easy to understand	33
7.	Little time and effort	21	7.	Little time and effort	28
8.	Easy to understand	13	8.	Up-to-date	12

Indianapolis Subscribers compared to Frankfurt Subscribers

B. Ranked by Differences in Index Numbers[b]		
Up-to-date	(18)	American Subscribers
Inexpensive	(17)	are higher than
Helpful to compare	(7)	German Subscribers
Informative	(7)	
Trustworthy	(6)	
Tells about new products	(4)	
Little time and effort	(7)	German Subscribers
Easy to understand	(20)	are higher than American Subscribers

[a]Data based on question 4, section 5 of questionnaire, reproduced in appendix G.

[b]Index = (% of sample strongly or slightly agreeing with statement minus % of sample strongly or slightly disagreeing). Positive index means more favorable attitude toward product testing than advertising.

advertising than German. On six of the eight attributes. the indexes of the American exceeded those of the German. The American sample had an average index of 45.3 to the German 41.3. The American respondents were also somewhat more discriminating than the Germans in differentiating between individual attribute ratings.

Average Consumers

The average consumers in the two countries reflected a divergence of attitudes as well. Table 9–5 presents the data, which give a slightly different cross-cultural picture than expected. *Common attitudes*, where Indianapolis and Frankfurt average consumers showed quite small differences in their responses, were identified and divided into three groups:

1. As was the case in the subscriber samples, average consumers in Germany and the United States valued product testing most for its quality of *trustworthiness*, at least when comparing it to commercial advertising. The indexes for both countries were much lower for average consumers than for subscribers as was expected. German average consumers were again somewhat lower than American in their confidence in tests.
2. Continuing to follow the subscriber pattern, average consumers rated test reports at a lower, but still positive, level on three attributes: *helpfulness for product comparisons, general informativeness,* and *specifically new product information.* Responses by Americans and Germans were virtually identical for these criteria, but substantially less favorable than those of Information Seekers.
3. Both average consumer samples considered the lack of *timeliness* on the part of comparative tests, although barely positive, a relative disadvantage opposed to advertising. This was recognized, as in the subscriber samples, as a somewhat greater shortcoming by the Germans than by the Americans.

   Opposite attitudes, where German and American respondents differed most in their attitudes, revealed themselves to be rather one-sided: contrary to expectations, the *Indianapolis* sample did not exceed the Frankfurt sample by a large amount on any of the criteria. With a difference of eight in the index, *trustworthiness* showed the largest cross-cultural difference in favor of the Americans.

   German average consumers were higher than American by a large margin on three attributes: *Cost relative to the worth* of product testing, *time and effort* required for reading, and *degree of difficulty of understanding.* Germans were still positive on understanding tests and on the time and effort dimension, while Americans scored negatively, reflecting an absolutely more favorable perception of advertising on these two points.

   Overall, it appears that the Frankfurt sample of average consumers reacted more favorably to product testing than the Indianapolis one. The average index for the Germans was 27.5 as against the American 22.5. The cross-cultural response direction was thus reversed from that of subscribers, albeit at a substantially lower level of relative favorableness toward product testing. Again, American respondents differentiated their answers on various attributes more than Germans. In both countries average consumers rated product testing highest on trustworthiness and lowest on understandability.

Table 9–5. Attitudes toward Product Testing as Compared to Advertising[a] (Indianapolis and Frankfurt Average Consumers)

	Indianapolis Average Consumers (Base = 198)			*Frankfurt Average Consumers (Base = 198)*	
Rank	*Source Attribute*	*Index*	*Rank*	*Source Attribute*	*Index*
A. Ranked by Index Numbers[b]					
1.	Trustworthy	60	1.	Trustworthy	52
2.	Helpful to compare	45	2.	Helpful to compare	42
3.	Informative	34	3.	Informative	32
4.	Tells about new products	22	4.	Inexpensive	32
5.	Up-to-date	17	5.	Tells about new products	25
6.	Inexpensive	17	6.	Little time and effort	16
7.	Little time and effort	−7	7.	Up-to-date	12
8.	Easy to understand	−8	8.	Easy to understand	9

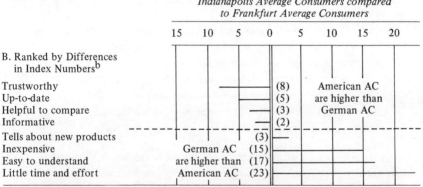

Indianapolis Average Consumers compared to Frankfurt Average Consumers

B. Ranked by Differences in Index Numbers[b]

Trustworthy	(8) American AC
Up-to-date	(5) are higher than
Helpful to compare	(3) German AC
Informative	(2)
Tells about new products	(3)
Inexpensive	German AC (15)
Easy to understand	are higher than (17)
Little time and effort	American AC (23)

[a]Data based on question 4, section 5 of questionnaire, reproduced in appendix G.
[b]Index = (% of sample strongly or slightly agreeing with statement minus % of sample strongly or slightly disagreeing). Positive index means more favorable attitude toward product testing than advertising.

In conclusion, it may be noted that the differences in attitude between subscribers and average consumers within the Frankfurt sample, while for the most part significant, were somewhat less pronounced than those of the Indianapolis sample. The American subscribers were a bit more favorable in their product testing–advertising evaluation than the German, but the German average consumers were somewhat more positive than the American. As a result, the overall comparison of the two surveys revealed some interesting universal attitudes on both continents in addition to some expected, culture-bound opposites.

INTERACTION OF ATTITUDES: PRODUCT
TESTING AND ADVERTISING

The data on the product testing-advertising evaluation were also tested in relation to the respondents' attitude toward advertising itself.[6] The image of advertising was treated in the last chapter. In this section we wanted to test whether any interaction existed between a positive or negative image of advertising and its separate comparison with product testing. In general, we anticipated:

1. *Universals:* Respondents with a generally favorable attitude toward advertising itself, would also rate advertising more favorably in comparison with product testing. Conversely, respondents with a generally unfavorable attitude toward advertising, would rate product testing higher in comparison with advertising.
2. *Culture specifics:* Along with some previous findings, Americans overall would be somewhat more positive about product testing than Germans, regardless of their attitude toward advertising.
3. *Sectoral comparison:* In both Germany and the United States, Information Seekers would be more favorable toward product testing than average consumers, regardless of their attitude toward advertising.

The results of this analysis are shown in table 9-6. With respect to individual attributes, rankings are quite similar to previous results. Thus all respondent groups, whether favorably or unfavorably inclined toward advertising, whether subscribers or average consumers, Americans or Germans, scored the highest positive indexes on the criterion of *trustworthiness*. This result underlines previous discussions in this chapter concerning the universal perception of product testing as an independent, objective information source in which consumers have a high degree of confidence, irrespective of attitudes toward advertising.

Similarly, respondents in both countries, no matter what their attitude toward advertising otherwise might be, clearly recognized that *timeliness, time and effort* requirements, and *difficulty of understanding* are product testing's greatest shortcomings. These attributes received the lowest rating indexes generally by all groups, although not in identical rank order. This outcome suggests that the relative evaluation of product testing, as measured by the eight dimensions included in this study, is at least somewhat independent of the general image of advertising as an information source.

Table 9-6. Evaluation of Product Testing as Compared to Advertising on Eight Attributes in Relationship to Attitude toward Advertising in General[a] (Indianapolis and Frankfurt Samples) (In Index Numbers)[b]

| | United States | | | | | | | | Germany | | | | | | | |
| | Subscribers | | | | Average Consumers | | | | Subscribers | | | | Average Consumers | | | |
Source Attributes	R	F Index	U Index	Index U-F	R	F Index	U Index	Index U-F	R	F Index	U Index	Index U-F	R	F Index	U Index	Index U-F
Trustworthy	1	72	95	+23	1	57	75	+18	1	72	71	-1	1	54	66	+12
Inexpensive	3	55	76	+21	5	16	29	+13	5	31	53	+22	3	36	50	+14
Helpful to compare	2	51	81	+30	2	39	75	+36	2	47	70	+23	4	36	57	+21
Informative	4	49	52	+3	3	32	42	+10	3	46	39	-7	2	39	36	-3
Tells about new products	5	43	38	-5	4	15	42	+27	4	38	42	+4	5	21	42	+21
Up-to-date	6	30	33	+3	6	18	8	-10	8	12	-4	-16	8	15	3	-12
Little time and effort	7	17	29	+12	8	-8	-12	-4	7	21	39	+18	6	15	19	+4
Easy to understand	8	3	24	+21	7	-8	-8	0	6	31	29	-2	7	7	10	+3
Average Index		40.0	53.5	+13.5		20.1	31.4	+11.3		37.3	42.4	+5.1		27.9	35.4	+7.5

Legend: R = Rank of Source Attribute by Index Number
F = Favorable Attitude toward Advertising in general
U = Unfavorable Attitude toward Advertising in general

[a]Data from sections 5 and 6 of questionnaire, reproduced in appendix G.

[b]Index = (% of sample agreeing with statement minus % of sample agreeing). Positive Index means a more favorable attitude toward product testing in its direct evaluative comparison with advertising.

Apart from the attribute rankings, however, there is solid evidence of the existence of varying degrees of interaction between the product testing attribute *ratings* and attitudes toward advertising. From table 9-6 it may be noted that, as a group, those respondents who reacted *unfavorably* toward advertising in general showed significantly higher indexes on several dimensions of product testing than respondents with a *favorable* advertising image. For the sake of convenience, this will be referred to as the "U-F difference." A positive U-F difference indicates an advertising-testing interaction in the predicted direction. Several observations can be made from table 9-6.

1. The greatest absolute U-F differences in the indexes among all sample groups, American and German subscribers and average consumers alike, were found for these attributes: *helpfulness to compare products, cost relative to the worth* of information, and (excepting German subscribers) *trustworthiness*. It appears that in these categories a universal interaction pattern between advertising perceptions and product testing exists. That is, consumers unfavorable toward advertising view product testing in a substantially brighter light than those favorable toward advertising.
2. In addition, subscribers in both countries reflected a great U-F difference on the *time and effort* dimension, while average consumers remained relatively neutral. It is plausible that AC, having little knowledge of product tests per se, have little basis on which to judge the relative amounts of time and effort required to read reports, entirely independent of their advertising image.
3. Average consumers on both sides of the Atlantic scored a large U-F difference on the criterion of *new product information*, while subscribers varied little. This finding can perhaps again be traced to the lack of familiarity with product testing on the part of average consumers. Subscribers on the other hand, more knowledgeable about comparative testing, judged test reports on the merits of new product information as an issue separate from their advertising attitudes.

Overall it should be noted that the *average* U-F difference is positive for all samples. That is, respondents unfavorable toward advertising on the whole valued product testing more highly than those favorable toward advertising. The average U-F difference was higher among the American respondents than among the German. It was highest among American and lowest among German subscribers, although it is to be noted that intra-country variations between subscribers and average consumers were much smaller in Germany than in the United States.

USAGE OF AND ATTITUDES TO ADVERTISING
AND TESTING

It was also thought that the importance respondents perceived in the use of one of the two information sources in a purchase situation would interact with their attitudes toward these sources. Thus persons claiming that *CR, DM* or *test* was an important information source would compare product testing more favorably to advertising than others who did not attach importance to it. Conversely, those regarding advertising as an important source would rate it higher, at least relatively, than those *not* thinking it important. From this it follows that respondents who mentioned a testing journal as an important source would show higher product test/advertising indexes than those who mentioned advertising. The combined results are tabulated in table 9-7. In interpreting the table, the reader is reminded that Frankfurt average consumers deeming *DM* or *test* an important information source had the benefit of "aided recall" in the interview, while Indianapolis average consumers did not.

American Respondents

Comparing respondents mentioning *Consumer Reports* as an important information source (CRI) in their durable product and/or automobile purchases with respondents indicating advertising as important (AI), the results are somewhat mixed. In general, one would expect the CRI-AI difference to be positive. For American subscribers, this was the case only for such dimensions as helpfulness for product comparisons, general informativeness, and (perhaps surprisingly) ease of understanding.

For the timeliness dimension (up-to-dateness) and the time and effort requirements for reading, the CRI-AI difference was decidedly negative. Apparently, the subscriber respondents who thought *CR* to be an important information source and presumably used it to a greater extent, perceived these criteria to be disadvantageous in comparison to advertising.

The results for the average consumer sample are inconclusive because of the low awareness level of *CR* as information source. It is noteworthy, however, that even the AI group among AC favored product testing over advertising on most attributes.

German Respondents

The results for the German respondents were much more consistent with expectations, particularly for the subscriber sample. The DM/TEI subscriber group (those who thought *DM* and/or *test* was an important information source) scored higher indexes on all eight product testing-advertising attributes

Table 9-7. Relationships Between Importance of CR, DM and test and Advertising as Information Sources in Durable Product and Automobile Purchases and the Comparative Evaluation of Product Testing and Advertising[a] (Indianapolis and Frankfurt Samples) (In Index Numbers)[b]

| | United States | | | | | | | | | | Germany | | | | | | | | | |
| | Subscribers | | | | | Average Consumers | | | | | Subscribers | | | | | Average Consumers | | | | |
Source Attributes Base	R	CRI Index (41)	R	AI Index (31)	Index CRI-AI	R	CRI Index (7)	R	AI Index (41)	Index CRI-AI	R	DM/TEI Index (144)	R	AI Index (39)	Index DM/TEI-AI	R	DM/TEI Index (53)	R	AI Index (68)	Index DM/TEI-AI
Helpful to compare	1	91	2	71	+20	6	29	2	27	+2	2	58	2	36	+22	2	44	1	31	+13
Trustworthy	2	83	1	87	−4	1	57	1	51	+6	1	84	1	75	+9	1	61	2	29	+32
Informative	3	81	5	55	+26	2	57	3	20	+37	3	51	3	28	+23	3	42	4	21	+21
Inexpensive	4	71	4	62	+9	7	0	4	12	−12	6	34	6	15	+19	6	9	3	29	−20
Tells about new products	5	68	3	68	0	3	43	5	7	+36	4	43	7	15	+28	4	29	6	11	+18
Easy to understand	6	18	8	−3	+21	8	−14	6	5	−19	5	36	4	21	+15	7	8	7	10	−2
Up-to-date	7	−2	6	32	−34	4	43	7	−5	+48	8	13	8	6	+7	8	1	5	19	−18
Little time and effort	8	−10	7	20	−30	5	43	8	−5	+48	7	26	5	18	+8	5	15	8	4	+11
Average Index		50.0		49.0	+1.0		32.3		14.0	+18.3		43.1		26.8	+16.3		26.1		19.3	+6.8

Legend: CRI = *Consumer Reports* (CR) mentioned as important information source Durable Product and/or Automobile Purchase
DM/TEI = DM or test or both mentioned as important information source in Durable Product and/or Automobile Purchase
AI = Advertising mentioned as important information source in Durable Product and/or Automobile Purchase
R = Rank

[a] Data based on sections 2, 3, and 6 of questionnaire, reproduced in appendix G.
[b] Index = (% of sample agreeing with attribute statement minus % of sample disagreeing). Positive Index means a more favorable attitude toward product testing compared to advertising. Negative Index means a more favorable attitude toward advertising compared to product testing.

than the AI group. Thus the German subscriber sample showed substantial interaction between the perceived usage (importance) of testing and advertising and relative attitudes toward them.

German AC were not so consistent and scored negative DM/TEI–AI differences at least on the timeliness dimension and the cost relative to information worth. This may partly reflect a lack of knowledge of or familiarity with the two magazines. It may also indicate a more detached, objective judgement on the part of those respondents who used *DM* and/or *test* at least to some degree in their purchase decisions.

It may be concluded from this section that there is at least intermittent interaction between the *use* of comparative test reports and advertising as information sources in a purchase situation and relative attitudes toward them. Incidentally, it appears that the relationship is more direct and pronounced in the area of durable goods, which has traditionally received much greater emphasis in comparative test reporting than automobiles. Respondents who cited one of the testing journals as an important information source, generally gave very high marks to comparative testing vis-à-vis advertising on such attributes as helpfulness for product comparisons and informativeness, and sometimes also for the criterion of "cost for what it is worth." The lowest indexes, frequently negative, were scored on dimensions such as timeliness and time and effort required for reading. The latter two attributes often had higher indexes among the AI groups, reflecting perhaps a lack of intimate knowledge on their part compared to those who actually used comparative test reports in their decision making.

Beyond these general conclusions we have noted several cross-cultural differences between American and German respondents. The most outstanding of these is the fact that Germans tended to react in a more predictable, consistent manner. The American responses, on the other hand, seemed to be more diffused and individualistic. This may reflect an ability among American consumers more readily to see two sides of an issue rather than only one.

SUMMARY AND CONCLUSIONS

It is clear from this research that consumers on both sides of the ocean have definite opinions about product testing and advertising, two major sources in the market information mix. One outstanding feature of product testing, universally recognized by consumers in both Germany and the United States, is its trustworthiness. Since consumers often feel threatened by the persuasive power of advertising (see chapter 8), the contrasting perception of test reports as a reliable and independent information source, in which consumers apparently have great confidence, is sharply crystallized by the universal response patterns in this study.

In public debate, product testing is often rated low in comparison to advertising on such criteria as time and effort requirements, difficulty of understanding, and timeliness. Nevertheless, our research shows that people often rate product testing as superior to advertising even on these criteria. Only when related to perceived usage in a purchase situation, did the indexes of these attributes occasionally turn negative, implying an absolute favoring of advertising over comparative testing. The fact that many respondents feel that test reports supply information *more* up-to-date than advertising is perhaps explained by the fact that consumers are not always aware of the information problem for a given product until they are ready to buy—at which time they look up the test report. In this way they may gain the impression that the test report is really up-to-date and timely, since they have not consciously been taking in advertisements which have been talking about the product for a long time.

Similarly, at the time the consumer is actively looking for information for a specific, planned purchase, he may not perceive the cost, time and effort he invests in the search as great disadvantages, especially not in comparison with the perceived value of information contained in test reports vis-à-vis advertising. Eager to enrich his knowledge and to prepare satisfactorily for his purchase, this consumer also may not find it too difficult to understand test reports.

In addition, a screen of criticism about advertising and a halo of good will about test reports may well be carried from one question to another in the questionnaire itself. Although we have valiantly attempted to minimize this possibility through careful design of the measuring instrument and methodology, these combined effects may reflect an unconscious bias in favor of product testing as the preferred information source when contrasted directly with advertising. This seems to be true, even where a specific attribute may be objectively viewed as a shortcoming of one information source and an advantage of the other. Only when related to perceived and specific usage, as the data indicate, does product testing occasionally suffer in comparison with advertising, in not just a relative, but an absolute sense.

There is also a substantial degree of interaction between the perception of product testing and the image of advertising per se which reflects upon their complementary nature in the field of consumer information. Obviously, a change in attitudes toward one may have an impact on the status of the other. But rather than viewing advertisers as antagonists, product testers could strive toward a concept of coordination, if not cooperation, which would provide important supplementary information to increase market transparency for average consumers as well as subscribers.

In the next and final chapter, we will try to pull the strings together and return to the original question: Is there an individual consumer who could be typified as an Information Seeker? In attempting to answer that question, we will also touch on public and private policy issues regarding the dissemination of product information to the consuming public.[7]

NOTES TO CHAPTER 9

1. See, for example, Eugene R. Beem and John J. Ewing, "Business Appraises the Consumer Testing Agencies," *Harvard Business Review* 32 (March-April 1954): 113–26. In an earlier article, Beem discusses in detail advantages as well as disadvantages of comparative product tests. See Eugene R. Beem, "Consumer Financed Testing and Rating Agencies," *Journal of Marketing* (January 1952): 272ff.
2. The prime example of this type of criticism is Vance Packard, *The Hidden Persuaders* (New York: David McKay, 1958).
3. The reader may refer to the relevant discussion in chapter 3. See also Helmut Becker, "Consumer Information and the Image of Advertising in Germany with Significant Comparisons to America," (DBA diss., Indiana University, 1971).
4. For a related discussion, see Hans B. Thorelli, "Testing, Labelling and Certifying: A Perspective on Consumer Information," *British Journal of Marketing* (Autumn 1970): 126–32.
5. This section is based on the subscribers interviewed in metropolitan Indianapolis and Frankfurt. It does not include the respondents from the national mail surveys of subscribers who were treated separately in chapter 6.
6. The differential reactions of *DM* and *test* subscribers to the two questions concerning advertising in testing journals are noted in appendix C.
7. For a deeper view and a more detailed discussion of policy implications, the reader is referred to the companion volume, *Consumer Information Systems* (in process).

Chapter Ten

Epilog

The specific findings of this international and comparative research project on consumer information and advertising image have been presented in condensed form in the Executive Summary. There would therefore be little point in our final chapter's following in the classic summary-and-conclusions tradition. We have deliberately opted for a different approach. Having been somewhat rigidly disciplined by the canons of scientific procedure in earlier chapters, we feel that the reader still with us—as well as we the authors—are now entitled to some easy-chair philosophizing. We will discuss a few issues and themes which have been raised by our work (without any ambition to say the last word about them) in a broad-ranging and freely interpretive way. On occasion we will even draw a consumer policy conclusion—although we do wish to emphasize that the planned volume on *Consumer Information Systems* will be more specifically focused on policy problems.

The fact that the authors are letting their guards down does not necessarily mean the reader may enjoy complete relaxation. It behooves him to watch for unwarranted conclusions and personal biases so difficult to suppress in any impressionist discussion.

The themes we have chosen for this broad-brush treatment are the following:

1. The Information Seekers and Their Significance;
2. Attitudes versus Behaviors;
3. Dos and Don'ts in Comparative Testing;
4. Advertising's Image Problem;
5. Future Research Needs.

THE INFORMATION SEEKERS AND
THEIR SIGNIFICANCE

The Information Seekers are here. It seems to us that chapters 4 and 5 demonstrate this and that chapter 7 and the references cited there reenforce this overall conclusion and throw added light on many corners left obscure in our German and American field studies. The Information Seekers (IS) represent a consumer elite, composed of people of middle or upper-middle class income who are highly educated, typically in professional or managerial jobs and living in city or suburb.[a] IS are more sophisticated consumers than are average citizens, first in that they possess a significantly larger assortment of durables and take greater care in their acquisition and second because they are generally far more knowledgeable about the institutions of the marketplace and about the nature of consumer rights and responsibilities therein.

Our study—like most of those cited in chapter 7—focused on subscribers to comparative testing journals simply because they are the most easily definable and reachable proxy for the total group of IS. Clearly, however, not *all* subscribers are IS. Doubtlessly some of them are subscribers because subscribing is "in" among the circles in which they move rather than because they are information-minded consumers; some may habitually renew subscriptions without really making any use of the magazines, and so on. Conversely, one need not necessarily be a subscriber to qualify as an IS. After all, nonsubscribers have access to test magazines in libraries, on newsstands or through subscriber friends. In Germany, *Warentest*'s reports are frequently reprinted in summary form by newspapers and other magazines, and not infrequently broadcast on radio and TV. Dissemination beyond subscribers is becoming increasingly widespread in several countries.

More important, the definition of IS cannot reasonably be limited to those consumers who come in active contact with comparative test reports. It is true that such reports presently constitute by far the most sophisticated and systematic means of obtaining comparative product information–a point that must not be forgotten in this discussion. On the other hand, a sensible view of the IS concept would include any consumers to whom information availability tends to be an important buying criterion in any significant purchase and/or who consult a broad range of different information sources before making such a purchase. (Presumably there is also a qualitative element pertaining to the manner in which the individual processes and uses the information, although this is considerably more difficult to research and demonstrate.) Comparative test reports are not available in all industrialized nations, and the journals are

---

[a]It is in some ways particularly striking that the demographic background of *DM* and *test* subscribers was well-nigh identical, even though the two journals (apart from their concern with comparative testing) are quite different in character.

often poorly promoted. In some countries informative labeling and/or quality marking take the place of comparative testing and in others there are no CI programs to speak of. Even in such locales—Italy and Spain come to mind—one must assume the existence of at least a sprinkling of IS.

    While information availability certainly ranked significantly lower as a buying criterion for average consumers (AC) as a group than for IS as a group (see tables 4–7 and 5–7), there were naturally some members of the former group to whom information was very important and who might thus more properly have been labeled IS. In our German and American studies IS (in the sense of subscribers) did consult a greater number of information sources than AC, although the difference was not statistically significant.[b] The difference was stark, however, between IS (subscribers) and non-subscribers in our Norwegian data and was also clear cut in some of the other studies cited in chapter 7. No doubt a modest minority among the non-subscribers would have qualified as IS. It would be our hypothesis that highly educated, middle-income groups would be heavily over-represented among the members of this minority.

    What we have said must not be taken to mean that all highly educated middle class people are Information Seekers—any more than they are, say, golf players. This was clearly demonstrated in our American field study, in which Engledow also included a special "matched" sample of non-subscribers with the same demographic characteristics as the subscribers. By and large, the information sources listed and ranked by the "matched" sample of non-subscribers were much more similar to those named by AC than by IS (subscribers). In the case of consumer durables, too, information availability figured as modestly among the "matched" as among the AC, while it was a rather important criterion to subscribers.[1] Even in Norway, with the world's greatest subscription rate, a highly developed consumerist climate, and a population unusually homogeneous on almost any criterion you might care to name, it appears that a majority of highly educated middle income people are not IS in the sense defined here. A minority of this group of citizens, then, will constitute the core of the IS set in any given country and will presumably vary with such factors as culture, economic development, degree of consumer consciousness, and information media infrastructure—in line with our general ecologic view of social institutions.[2]

    The Information Seekers constitute a cosmopolitan group in the sense that they represent a cross-cultural set. This international set of consumer sophisticates is fairly homogeneous in demographic characteristics. Chapter 6 demonstrates that beyond the similarities in demographics and information-mindedness there are a goodly number of attitudinal as well as behavioral differences among national IS groups. To us, these differences appear clearly rooted in general cultural variations. What is much more significant, it would

[b]Our list of sources may well have been too small.

seem to us, is that these cross-cultural differences between IS groups are much smaller than the cross-cultural differences between AC groups. In other words, the average consumer is a great deal more culture-specific or local (not to say parochial) in outlook than the information seeker. We may also note that the IS set is growing in the industrialized nations with the concommitant rise in standards of living and education, information aspiration levels, consumer consciousness and, of course, the spread of comparative testing and other consumer information (CI) programs.

What is the significance of the Information Seekers? Their importance is dual. In what may be called their private role, the members of this group represent a fairly well definable market segment. To satisfy the needs of these consumer sophisticates may well be worth a special effort by many businesses, notably in the consumer durables, hobby, recreations and "modest luxury" goods markets. At the level of marketing strategy, businesses interested in IS patronage could do worse than increasing the information content of advertising. The special needs of IS may also support marketing organizations of other types, as witnessed by the success of *Consumer Reports*. IS constitute a cosmopolitan clientele of natural interest to the multinational corporation, which is able to seek out the IS group in any industrially advanced country around the North Atlantic with a relative minimum of adjustments in strategy to take into account local variations in taste and lifestyle.

The importance of the Information Seekers to the viability of the open market system as a whole—what may be called their public role—may be less obvious and yet even greater. Our findings suggest that the IS is an opinion leader whose advice in matters of consumer concern is sought by others. More crucially, we believe that the IS group contains within itself most of the vigilantes of the modern marketplace. In a very real sense this corps serve as spokesmen and proxy purchasing agents for other consumers. Fortunately, these sophisticates have sufficiently individualized tastes to assure a range of alternatives. It is especially worthy of note that they have no other power in a free market than their own taste and their ability to set examples for others. We are indeed talking about a phenomenon in the best democratic tradition. Finally, when manufacturers make shoddy or unsafe goods, when advertisers mislead, and when merchants are irresponsible, these are generally the consumers who will carry the banner of complaint and protest on behalf of consumer rights.

In some Swedish socialist circles it is a fashionable thesis that public moneys should not be spent on CI programs, since these programs will merely benefit a privileged few. What we have just said indicates why we consider this point of view antediluvian. Indeed, by the same logic Sweden might as well abolish her universities, still attended by less than 15 percent of the population!

ATTITUDES VERSUS BEHAVIORS

We have alerted the reader that, for the purpose of stimulating discussion and further research in an important area of consumer policy, we are taking some liberties in this chapter in elaborating on the findings of our research. It must also be emphasized that there is a need for caution in accepting the validity of some of these findings as they stand. There are a number of real (and imagined) weaknesses afflicting attitude and opinion research in general. Equally important, the entire set of relationships between attitude and behavior is still very imperfectly understood. Methodologically, we are aware that our research is part of a pioneering effort of international comparative research, of which little yet exists in *any* area of social science. But we make no claim to any methodological breakthrough, eliminating inherent weaknesses in survey research or shedding new light on the general nature of the attitude-behavior complex, nor do we see much point in trying to inventory the problems in these areas. We do, however, want to reflect upon some of our experiences in the course of the project.

As a large part of our research was focused on perceptions and attitudes without any necessary or direct link to behavior, we will first confine our observations to attitude research as such. Like others before us, we have noted problems of bias, intensity and stability of attitudes. To try to minimize bias, three important steps were taken in the research design itself. Respondents were told that this was a university study of consumer information problems; but consumer information was never given the technical definition used in this book, and questions about comparative testing in general and *CR, DM* and *test* in particular were deferred until after general opinions, data concerning specific purchases and media habits had already been collected. In an effort to prevent what might otherwise have been "stream-of-consciousness" answers about hypothetical situations of little tangible interest to respondents, our questions concerning buying habits, criteria, and associated information sources and uses were linked to specific, recent purchases. Finally, we inverted the direction of the questions, whenever this was feasible, in every other questionnaire.

There is no doubt we still encountered some biased answers. A fair number of people (we are not in a position to say how many) who are not really Information Seekers are still aware that to be a "rational" consumer is "in," and this awareness occasionally colors their answers to questions about their attitudes (and behavior) as consumers. In only one case were we able to test the validity of this type of assertion: average consumers in Indianapolis who said they were subscribers to *CR* were checked against the subscriber files of Consumers Union, showing that the number of alleged subscribers exceeded that of the real number by a substantial margin. We do not see how one can entirely eliminate this type of bias. Some answers by non-discriminating respondents also seem to have been influenced by "halo effect." If such a respondent had a high (low) opinion about comparative testing in general, or a low (high) opinion about advertising in general, this opinion frequently seemed to carry over without further reflection to questions about highly specific aspects of testing or advertising. Again, this is a problem as old as survey research itself.

We made no effort at measuring the strength (intensity) with which respondents held their opinions. (A person might express a highly favorable opinion about comparative testing but still not care very much one way or the other about the subject.) Past efforts in this direction seem only moderately successful, and it was more important to us to obtain data on a broad range of pertinent topics. It is likely that we got our share of weakly felt, unstable opinions as well. This seems especially plausible with respect to some of the average consumers—who could hardly be expected to be members of the "issue public" of consumer information. It is difficult to assign degrees of credence when many such respondents say that *Consumer Reports* is easy to understand, does not cost very much, is more up to date than advertising, etc.—even though respondents who had never heard of *CR* or "just heard the name, nothing more" were deliberately exempted from this type of question.[3] At least one scientist interested in cross-cultural attitude research has found that one may raise questions about the stability of opinion even in the "advanced sections of the most advanced societies."[4]

A special problem is that people may be of short memory or lack the diagnostic skills to reconstruct their own experience adequately. While our respondents did not say so, we still have a hunch that advertising is the *single* most important source of product information for most consumers, especially when it comes to pointing out new products and new alternatives. Nevertheless, respondents did not rank advertising remarkably high among their information sources, and in a surprising number of instances even felt that comparative testing journals gave more up-to-date information. We think these responses in a fair number of instances reflect lack of awareness on the part of respondents of the fact that they are in *continuous* contact with advertising and the effects thereof, while they refer to a test report (or go back to it) only at the time when a purchase is to be made.

The first question encountered in considering the interaction between attitudes and behaviors is whether indeed there is any. The common man, as well as psychologists and marketing people, is inclined to think there is. However, the relationship seems to range all the way from direct causality to a linkage of a highly complex and tenuous nature. There is a marked discrepancy between our findings of striking enthusiasm about comparative test reports as a source of consumer information and the rates of subscription to such reports, to take only the most glaring example of a tenuous linkage between attitudes and behavior in our data. Like other researchers we encountered the old "chicken-or-egg" question: "Do attitudes come before behaviors, or does behavior change come before attitude change?" Many IS gave an example of attitudes apparently governing behavior, in stating that information availability was important to them in their purchases and also consulting more sources than others.

That behavior may precede attitude formation was illustrated by our data on IS satisfaction with purchases. True, those IS who consulted testing journals in advance of purchases but did not act on the recommendations of the journals tended to be less satisfied than average consumers with their purchases. This is in line with the hypothesis that aspiration levels grow even faster than affluence and education. But those IS who *used* the comparative testing recommendations tended to be highly satisfied with their purchases. The relationship between information and satisfaction is a fascinating one, in need of a great deal more research.

DOS AND DON'TS IN COMPARATIVE TESTING

Our research focused on the impact of CI on consumers and on their views and relative use of various information sources. It was not directly concerned with the CI organizations themselves. Nonetheless, an incidental finding—of crucial significance, it seems to us, to such organizations—is the wealth of data of direct relevance to policy-making and program planning by CI bodies obtainable through survey research. In this connection, other CI organizations around the world have a lot to learn from Consumers Union. It is indeed a paradox that the consumer orientation of many CI organizations should remain subject to doubt.

Most of our findings (in this project and elsewhere) relevant to operating aspects of CI programs will be discussed in detail in *Consumer Information Systems*. We will limit ourselves here to some results pertaining to consumer impact of comparative test reports.

Our results emphasize indeed the singular importance of integrity and credibility in CI programs. There can be no doubt that this is the prime requirement for long-term viability of CI organizations. It is also clear that being a non-profit organization and refusing to accept advertising are powerful means of establishing integrity. However, they are not the only means. While *DM*—a for-profit organization freely accepting ads—has somewhat less credibility among consumers than either *test* or *CR*, the striking fact is rather that it enjoys such a high rate of consumer confidence. This is especially remarkable considering its free-wheeling and sometimes flamboyant style. One might add that *Good Housekeeping* and *Parents'* enjoy enormous goodwill as quality certifying organizations, even though they carry considerable advertising and their modes of operation and test procedures are shrouded in mist. Whether this confidence is justified we are not able to say, due to the relative secrecy of their operations; but they exemplify the observation that an image of credibility may be built by other means than refusing advertising or being non-profit. In a similar vein, we seem to have found that sponsorship of CI organizations, as long as it is not confined to producer interests alone, or to producer-government combinations, is less critical to public confidence than one might perhaps assume. (This statement may be more valid in Europe than in the United States.) Interestingly, in the case of governmentally sponsored organizations, an important criterion seems to be that the public perceive the everyday operations of the program as effectively isolated from political influence.

So long as the comparative testing bodies' means of disseminating information is confined to journals of the type of *Consumer Reports*, their direct reach will be limited to a relatively limited sector of the consuming public (although this sector is both quantitatively and qualitatively important in the United States). From this point of view there is reason to welcome experimentation with ancillary forms of reporting, such as the pocket-size KOMPASS summaries on perforated carton paper which *test* adopted about the time of the study, and the large-scale dissemination of condensed test reports through the press, TV and radio to which *Warentest* devotes much effort. Struggling to remain economically viable next to its government-financed competitor, *DM* has experimented with various ways to present test reports as only one element of a general consumer affairs journals.

Whatever outside observers may think about Best Buy and other types of recommendations in comparative test reports, it is abundantly clear that subscribers to these reports, in every country where such advice is given, want such recommendations. This observation will hold true at least as long as such advice constitutes only a modest part of a full-length test report which allows the consumer to form an independent judgment on the basis of his own needs and buying criteria, should he so desire. It is clear, too, that anything that can be done to make reports more understandable and easier to read will be warmly welcomed.

Consumers turn to test reports primarily for information on appliances and other durables. Contrary to popular impression, all our American and German samples indicated that such reports are less influential on automobile than on home appliance purchases. It may be that buying an automobile is such a highly "personal" decision (even when made on a "family" basis), that it is greatly affected by taste and psycho-social variables. Certainly, much car promotion appears based on this idea. In any case, our findings seem to caution against over-investment by testers in the auto areas. (Many auto reports, however, may be read for the pure fun of it.) Although it is frequently suggested that testers should forget about low-priced, high turnover items such as toothpaste, canned foods and other convenience goods, our data suggest that a sizeable proportion of readers are interested in reports on these products. In the

German-American field study we did not inquire about attitudes towards the testing of services, such as insurance, charter travel and resort hotels. While *DM* had done some experimentation in this area for several years, comparative test reports on services were still far from common at the time. Subsequent developments, and the great success of *Money Which?* published by Consumers' Association in England, indicate that this is indeed an area of the future, although it often presents rather formidable testing problems.

To our frank surprise we found a great number of consumers— average consumers as well as subscribers—in both Germany and the United States who felt that comparative testing journals do a better job than advertising of informing the public about new products (tables 9-3 and 9-4). Whatever the objective merits of this belief may be, it provides the testmakers with a differential advantage which could be used to much greater effect and consumer benefit, by giving a great deal more emphasis to the testing and reporting of new product developments.

Any truly comparative international study raises the issue of the cross-cultural transferability of findings. We have already seen that the Information Seekers constitute a significant minority of great significance to the market system in all industrialized countries of the North Atlantic Community. The similarity in IS values wherever they are found indicates that the technology of comparative testing (including types of products and testing methods, reporting formats, Best Buy and similar recommendations, emphasis on integrity, and so on) is indeed freely transferable from one of these societies to the next. As always, some adjustments have to be made to local environments, such as with respect to degree of cooperation with producers, the selection of specific products and brands to be tested (sometimes even with respect to the mix of characteristics to be tested). But by and large these problems are not insuperable. As one might expect under the circumstances, a fair amount of international cooperation and experimentation in testing has taken place, as discussed in the *Handbook*. In our view a great deal more could be accomplished in this area. On the other hand, we would warn against uncritical attempts at transferring comparative testing as practised in Germany and the United States to less developed countries with a narrow sector of Information Seekers and a huge gap in consumer sophistication between them and average local residents. The priorities of consumer policy relative to underprivileged consumers are markedly different from those of industrial and postindustrial societies, a matter further developed in *Consumer Information Systems.*

ADVERTISING'S IMAGE PROBLEM

Our own findings, in common with those of several of the other studies sum- marized in chapter 8, indeed indicate that advertising has an image problem. The fact that government, churches, the educational system, the military establishment, political parties, as well as business in general and most other major social institutions have had more or less serious image crises in the last three decades, places advertising's problem in perspective. So does the fact that when people in Western countries are asked to mention or rank what they consider the most serious public problems of the day advertising is seldom spontaneously mentioned or highly ranked. But these observations are hardly reassuring and certainly do not justify complacence on the part of advertisers, agencies or private and public consumer policy makers. This is especially so considering that some studies suggest that the public's views of advertising are gradually deteriorating further rather than improving.

It is not that advertising's right to exist is being questioned. Most people around the North Atlantic still have at least a mildly positive view about advertising in general, and an even greater majority realize that it fills a necessary function in our economic system. A fair number also believe that advertising leads to better products. But unlike the Procter & Gamble Company,[5] (the largest manufacturer-advertiser in any single country) the man in the street tends not to believe that advertising lowers cost to consumers. And as we move from economic to social aspects of advertising, the picture becomes more dismal.

Most North Atlantic consumers believe that advertising often persuades people to "buy things they shouldn't buy." While in free societies one consumer can hardly be the judge of what another consumer "should" or "shouldn't" buy (just as we would deny that role to J.K. Galbraith), it does seem that a majority of people feel that advertising persuades consumers to buy things *they themselves* would not have bought on more sober reflection. Especially in cases when this opinion in actuality represents a restatement of what respondents perceive as their own experience, it is a serious indictment. Even if the indictment is invalid (as it well may be in a world of countervailing pluralist forces) the view clearly points up an image problem. Less serious perhaps is the fact that many people feel that advertising insults the intelligence. After all, advertising *is* a mass medium.

The principal most important aspect of advertising, it seems to us, is not its capacity for persuasion but its quality as a product information medium. Here advertising's image is bleak; there is ample reason to believe that consumers are not consciously aware of the great role advertising does play as an information source. Aggregating the impact of our data with those of the Reader's Digest Association, we conclude that most consumers, in the North Atlantic Community at least, do not subscribe to the view that advertising presents a true picture of the products it promotes. Finally, in both Germany and the United States the prevention of misleading advertising clearly emerges as a key consumerist concern.

We are aware that in most Western countries efforts are being made through both self-regulation and public policy to keep misleading advertising under control. It was not the object of our research to study the effectiveness of these measures. Whatever their effect may be, the public is still concerned about this matter, and we predict that the pressure for tighter standards and for further experimentation with various forms of policing and control is likely to continue in many of these nations.

This is not the place to attempt the presentation of a detailed program to improve the image of advertising. We would like to suggest, however, that the image is likely to improve as advertising itself improves. The most obvious step in a positive direction is simply to make advertising more obviously and incontestably informative. In the end, advertising has an important positive mission, one not attained by mere suppression of misleading elements—essentially a negative policy, however necessary it may be. The logic is clear: the interests of consumers and of progressive producers and distributors alike would be a great deal better served by cooperative effort between advertising and independent consumer information programs. Meeting the consumer's manifold needs for information in a complex society calls for a systems approach. The use of United States Department of Agriculture grade symbols and the Swedish VDN labels in advertising point the way. These and other avenues of joint effort will be further explored in *Consumer Information Systems*.

FUTURE RESEARCH NEEDS

Without encylopedic ambition, we would still like to bring up some needs for future research in areas touched by our investigations.

Cross-Cultural Baselines

In planning our research we took it for granted that there would be a wealth of easily accessible comparative literature and data about the German and American cultural and economic environments in which CI programs operate and consumers work and live. It was indeed a major disappointment to find that this was not the case. Not even in these data-oriented cultures are census data always collected or reported on a comparable basis. There appear to be no standard reference works comparing styles of life, cultural values, standards of living, social classes and other local characteristics in terms readily employable in research on specific cross-cultural institutions and phenomena.

The relative lack of such readily available broad-gauged, cross-cultural baseline data made it unexpectedly difficult to relate similarities and differences in our German and American research results to the broader environment of the two countries of which IS and AC as well as the local comparative testing organizations are parts. This was especially distressing as we are quite impressed with the potential value of ecologic (situational) analysis in cross-cultural research. We are well aware that most of our observations in the environmental interaction area are of the nature of ad hoc speculations.

There is, in short, a critical need for cross-cultural reference works providing the kind of broad baseline data which might be used by a great variety of researchers interested in relating specific social phenomena to their local settings.

In Quest of the Information Seekers

Being an Information Seeker, like being a golf player or an opinion leader, is a matter of degree. It may not be possible—nor indeed needed—to give the IS concept any other than a purely operational definition. Our own definition focused on subscribership to comparative testing journals. For reasons discussed in this epilog this definition has some obvious limitations. Other definitions, presumably based on media habits and/or quantitative and qualitative gauges of information-seeking and (perhaps) information-using behavior, should be applied in further research comparing IS and other consumers. Implications to consumer as well as managerial policy of the existence of IS should be examined. For this purpose it would be of special interest to see research exploring to what extent IS really do serve as the vigilantes of the marketplace and as proxy purchasing agents for average consumers.

Much research is needed to detail further the characteristics of IS, individually and as a group. How large a proportion of highly educated, middle-class consumers do they comprise in different cultures? Is there anything to the hypothesis that the very rich do not care about CI—presumably because they do not need to? How knowledgeable about the open market system in general and individual product markets in particular are IS in comparison with AC? Are IS more information-minded than AC in other areas of decision-making or human knowledge than product and market characteristics? What is the growth rate of IS as a group, and what are the determinants of this growth? What is the effect of consumer education in the public school system on the size of the IS group? In the United States, possibilities exist for comparative research in this regard inasmuch as only a handful of states as yet have such programs.

Research on CI Program Operations

We have criticized most CI organizations (CU is a major exception) for their lack of interest in behavioral science research aimed at measuring the impact and improving the nature of their operations. For the types of applied research typically involved in such efforts, a battery of fairly sophisticated marketing research techniques have been developed in the schools of business administration in North America and Scandinavia and by marketing research and public opinion survey agencies all over the Western world.

But there is also need for research of a more basic nature. We need to develop more advanced methods of gauging the effectiveness of information programs. We need to know more about the determinants of effectiveness and of satisfaction with information. More research is needed on the relative demand for information on automobiles, other durables, convenience goods and

services. To what extent are subscribers interested in seeing CI organizations
engage in debate—or even lobbying—concerning consumer policy, business
practices and other matters of consumerist concern? How interested are they in
environmental protection, in the conservation of energy? What is the elasticity
of demand with respect to price of comparative testing journals? What is the
effect on subscriber volume of broadcast dissemination of test reports via the
daily press, hobby magazines, radio, TV—or even as integral parts of advertising?

Beyond the Information Seekers

We have no doubt that in the highly complex markets of the
industrially advanced nations product information is insufficient—or at least
not typically easily available at the right place and time. Thus, in *Consumer
Information Systems* we speak of "consumer information gap" and about
the desirability for increased transparency of the marketplace (what the Germans
call *Markttransparenz*). Given these beliefs, it was natural in the present context
that we never thought of exploring in any depth the question of how informed
consumers actually perceive themselves. This was a deplorable oversight. As
suggested in chapter 7, there is a clear need for research in this area.

Paradoxically, preliminary evidence suggests that average—and,
especially, underprivileged—consumers tend to think of themselves as well-
informed consumers much more often than Information Seekers. To play on a
currently fashionable term, many of these people are likely to face "unperceived
risk" in the marketplace. To reach underprivileged consumers represents a
special challenge to CI organizations. Simplified programs in the form of
informative labeling and quality certification are almost bound to play a role.
The way these programs—and the information about individual products which
they are intended to give—should be presented to consumers needs a good
deal more research than the subject has been given in the past. Research is also
needed on new types of CI programs, such as computerized CI data banks with
built-in dialog facilities for custom-tailored information.

The Dynamics of Satisfaction

Consumer satisfaction is emerging as a key concept in the marketing
world as business is becoming, or trying to become, increasingly customer
oriented under the double impact of market forces and consumerist pressures.
Although satisfaction measurement is already a hot topic in doctoral thesis
research in schools of business and home economics, a great deal more needs to
be done. CI organizations have, or should have, a dual interest in this area.
Being spokesmen for consumer interests, they are presumably eager to structure
their information services in such a way that the satisfaction of consumers with
the purchases they make is enhanced. More than that, a principal means of
gauging the effectiveness of CI agencies themselves, one would assume, is the
degree of satisfaction of consumers with the quality, quantity, timeliness,

relevance and readability of the product information disseminated by these organizations.

Much work needs to be done relative to the concept of satisfaction itself. We need better answers to such basic questions as, What is it? What are its determinants? How do you measure it? What is the relationship between satisfaction with a product as a whole and varying degrees of satisfaction or dissatisfaction with its specific attributes? Are satisfaction and dissatisfaction "poles apart" on a single scale of measurement, or should satisfaction and dissatisfaction rather be viewed, at least in part, as separate dimensions?

The dynamics and ecology of satisfaction also need to be more fully researched. A key question here is the relationship between satisfaction and aspiration levels. The latter seem to play a vital role as satisfaction criteria. Aspiration levels often seem to change as the consumer moves through the process of contemplating a purchase, buying the product and using it. If this is the case, a key concern must be to research the determinants of aspiration (expectation) levels, and to undertake longitudinal studies. It also becomes quite important to an organization interested in measuring its ability to satisfy consumers to determine at what point (or points) in the process it wishes to measure satisfaction.

Somewhat analogous challenges appear at the macro level. Do IS and AC differ as regards consumer satisfaction? Our American data suggest that IS have higher aspiration levels and are harder to satisfy. In Germany IS seemed more satisfied. A reasonable hypothesis, it would seem, is that expectations grow with education, experience, an increasingly cosmopolitan view and general sophistication. On the other hand, a counterbalancing influence may be the relativism and realism that sometimes go with greater sophistication. Another hypothesis for which there is a good deal of common-sense evidence is that the demands which will have to be met for a certain degree of consumer satisfaction increase dramatically with degrees of economic development and the intensity of consumerist consciousness.

Advertising and Consumer Information Systems

Considerable progress is being made in developing valid and reliable methods of measuring the effectiveness of advertising. CI organizations would do well in following this work closer than in the past, adapting the technology to measuring the impact of their own programs. Our studies point to two major areas of research pertinent to advertising and advertisers: research providing the basis for further attempts to improve the image—and the reality—of advertising, and research aimed at the possibilities of improving advertising as a product information medium. In the first area we need answers to such questions as, What do consumers perceive as misleading advertisements? What ads do people find overly persuasive, or insulting to the intelligence? Is advertising's image affected by the length, number and spacing of commercials on radio and

TV? What are the effects of advertising on competition, prices and on product innovation and quality?

There are many ways in which advertising could be made more informative. Admen frequently claim that if advertisements were injected with more information consumers would not bother to read them. This claim needs research. It is also fashionable to speak of the dangers of "information overload" among consumers—a subject in itself worthy of a great deal more serious research than it has so far been given. Even if it were demonstrated that information overload is a very real problem, we need not necessarily conclude that the present degree of information content in advertising is the right one. If there were less "static," for example, there might be more room for information. Perhaps, too, more specialty media could be designed for those really concerned with information.

We also assume that the willingness and ability of consumers to absorb information must be related to how it is presented. Advertisements that compare key characteristics of models and brands may have a potential as yet largely unrealized. Comparative advertisements including any important characteristics where the advertiser's brand does not outrank all other brands might add not only information but also goodwill to the advertiser as well as advertising. Research also needs to be made on ways of combining the impact of advertising and the objectivity of CI programs. This might, without endangering the independence and credibility of the latter, take forms ranging all the way from a simple reference to a test report in an advertisement to the incorporation into advertising material of a complete informative label issued by a CI organization.

This brings us to our final point: a major research challenge is to provide the baseline data needed for the design of comprehensive consumer information systems. At the present time no effort has been made to study how the three principal types of independent consumer information programs— comparative testing, informative labeling and quality certification—can be made to reenforce each other as information media. Yet their potential here is obvious.[6] We also need to research in much greater detail the inherent strengths and weaknesses of commercial, personal and independent information sources in relation to different groups of consumers and products. A broader data base of this kind would be of great value in contemplating alternate approaches to general market information systems of the future, serving the interests of buyers and sellers alike.

NOTES TO CHAPTER 10

1. Jack Engledow, "The Impact of *Consumer Reports* Ratings on Product Purchase and Post-Purchase Product Satisfaction," (DBA diss., Indiana University, 1971), tables 7–4, 7–5 and 7–1.

2. See chapter 3, note 5. The ecologic approach to consumer information programs and policy will be developed further in *Consumer Information Systems.*
3. See questionnaire, section 5, questions 5 and 12, in appendix G.
4. Philip E. Converse, "New Dimensions of Meaning for Cross-Section Sample Surveys in Politics," *International Social Science Journal* 16 (1964): 19–34.
5. "The New World of Advertising," special issue of *Advertising Age* 44 (November 21, 1973): 26.
6. Hans B. Thorelli, "Testing, Labelling, Certifying: A Perspective on Consumer Information," *British Journal of Marketing* (Autumn 1970): 126–32.

Appendixes

Appendix A

National and Metropolitan Subscribers Compared

In this survey, two subscriber samples were used from each country: a random sample from a selected metropolitan area was surveyed by personal interviews and a random sample drawn from each agency's complete subscriber list received a mail questionnaire. The rationale for this multi-sample method is explained in chapter 3. The ideal methodology would have been a large national sample of subscribers from each country and a nation-wide control group of average consumers (AC), each receiving a personal interview, a difficult and extremely expensive procedure. The sampling plan actually used was selected because it captured many of the valuable features of the ideal solution within the budget restrictions of the project. It also has some obvious disadvantages. If the subscribers in the metropolitan areas are significantly different from "average" subscribers on important characteristics or if the mail questionnaire systematically elicits different responses than personal interviews, the inferential power of the study is considerably weakened. Accordingly, the national subscriber samples in each country were tested against the corresponding metropolitan sample on each question to determine what differences in response actually existed. The Chi Square two sample test was used to identify significant differences.

Relatively few significant differences were found between national and metropolitan samples in either country. The results of the tests can be summarized as follows:

United States

1. Of the 18 basic demographic dimensions measured in the study, only one—sex of respondent—shows a significant difference. Probably because of the fact that less control over reaching the subscriber of record was possible in the mail sample, 17 percent of the national questionnaires were answered by women, but only 9 percent of the Indianapolis were. No significant

differences were found in the important areas of income, education, and occupation, or in any other of the demographic characteristics.

2. The national subscribers consistently showed differences from the metropolitan sample in two areas:

   a. They are more critical of advertising on most dimensions measured.

   b. They are more favorable toward government involvement in most business-related matters.

   Both of these results represent slightly more extreme views in the same direction in which metropolitan subscribers differ from average consumers, and may result from the well-established conservatism of the Indianapolis area.

3. Though a few other scattered individual variables showed significant differences, the only variable clearly at odds between samples was attitude toward business, where national subscribers were significantly less convinced than their Indianapolis counterparts that business "performs the job of providing good products at reasonable prices rather well." This suggests that the pro-business bias of subscribers found in chapter 4 may be more of a local subscriber phenomenon than a national trend.

Germany

1. As in the United States, there was little discrepency between national and metropolitan samples in demographic characteristics. There was a significant difference in income, perhaps reflecting the fact that Frankfurt's per-capita income is substantively above that of West Germany as a whole. As in the United States, more females responded to the national mail questionnaire than to the metropolitan personal interview (25 percent vs. 17 percent). Again, this can be attributed to less control over reaching the subscriber of record.

   An interesting cultural difference was noted in the Germans' notable reluctance to discuss income with an interviewer. In the personal interview, 27 percent refused to answer income questions, as contrasted to only 9 percent in the mail survey. No such difference was found in the United States. It might also be speculated that the refusals to answer came from lower income families thereby injecting a bias with regard to this particular variable, reflected in the higher income distribution of Frankfurt subscribers noted above.

2. There was a slightly greater incidence of ownership of durables and particularly automobiles in the national sample. Given the rather heavy congestion of Frankfurt streets and the satisfactory public transportation, this is to be expected. There were no noteworthy differences otherwise in shopping behavior, information usage, and other purchase behavior and attitude variables.

3. In all, the national subscribers differed little from the metropolitan. The few apparent differences in individual variables seemed not to be concentrated in any specific area nor to constitute any perceivable pattern.

Considering the results in both countries, the significant differences between national and metropolitan samples were few, scattered, and were generally predictable and acceptable consequences of the differences in sampling and methodology, and not likely to influence greatly the overall conclusions made by the study. The assumption that national and metropolitan samples were drawn from a homogeneous population is reasonably well supported.

Appendix B

Sampling Procedures

The survey populations in both the United States and Germany were divided into three sample groups:

1. Metropolitan general population sample of "average consumers;"
2. Metropolitan subscriber sample; and
3. National subscriber sample.

As explained in some detail in chapter 3, the major reasons for this three-layer sampling design were:

1. Low concentration of product test report subscribers in the general population necessitated a separate sampling of subscribers in addition to average consumers;
2. Interviewing was initially decided upon as the preferred mode of data collection. Cost considerations pre-empted two national interview surveys. Hence, the compromise solution of two metropolitan samples was devised to permit direct subscriber-average consumer comparisons; and
3. To generate data for international comparisons of subscribers whom we labeled "Information Seekers," the national mail surveys in the two countries augmented our data from the metropolitan interviews.

The sampling procedures in the two countries were designed to duplicate each other as much as was possible within local constraints. Under the direct supervision of two team members and the project director, the services of two reputable research firms, Walker Research Inc. of Indianapolis and the *DIVO–Institut* of Frankfurt, were utilized for the execution of the surveys. Their assistance in designing, preparing and executing the surveys is gratefully acknowledged. The design, rationale and selection procedures for the three sample layers are described in the following paragraphs.

297

Metropolitan General Population Samples of "Average Consumers"

Indianapolis. Like most American cities, Indianapolis sprawls far beyond its city limits and into surrounding areas and suburbs. Therefore, Marion County which includes Indianapolis and has more natural population boundaries, was selected as the more appropriate survey area. This move became even more logical when Indianapolis officially extended its city limits to the Marion County boundaries (the Uni-Gov System) beginning in January of 1970, exactly coincident with the beginning of our interviewing. One problem which this area choice posed, however, is the fact that the population of Marion County is fairly diffuse, so that the potential geographical dispersion of interviews became a significant cost factor. To minimize travelling and interview costs, a stratified cluster sampling technique was adopted.

Post zip codes proved to be a practical means for stratifying the area comprised by Marion County. Zip code boundaries are clearly marked, and they correspond closely to the County borders at the extremes. By combining contiguous, less populated zip code areas, it was possible to attain a reasonable, proportionate balance in population size, maintaining at the same time the desirable characteristic of demographic homogeneity within the individual strata. In the final sampling plan, 16 strata were formed by varying combinations of contiguous zip code areas. The strata ranged in size from one to six zip code areas and from 8409 to 20,142 residential addresses.

Cluster size was determined by examining the implications of various sized clusters on the polar considerations of increased sampling costs as clusters grow smaller, versus less accurate proportional representation of individual strata as clusters grow larger. Based on these dual criteria, a cluster size of four respondents was chosen. With a predetermined sample size of $n = 200$, the 50 resulting clusters were proportionately assigned to the 16 strata, based on the number of addresses in each.

The sampling frame (population list) consisted of the 1969 edition of the *Haines Criss-Cross Directory*, a reference book containing the listing of all Marion County addresses with telephone service. This listing seemed to furnish an adequate as well as convenient source for selecting respondents to fill the 50 clusters, since it is updated annually from telephone company records, has a good reputation for accuracy, and groups addresses by zip codes, our chosen units for stratification. The obvious disadvantage of this sampling frame is the omission of non-phone addresses, and this bias must be admitted. It is generally not believed to be an important bias, however. In one recent study it was estimated that 92 percent of Indianapolis residences have telephone connections. According to figures supplied by the local post office and the telephone company, the official number of residences listed in Marion County was 244,194 in 1969 with 264,251 main residential phone lines. If these lines in fact reached only 92 percent of the residential addresses in the County, the discrepancy is accounted for by households with two or more phone numbers.

The actual selection of addresses from the directory proceeded in the following manner:

1. A set of three random numbers was selected: the first random number (from 1 to 665) to select the page in the directory; the second random number (from 1 to 3) to select the column on that page; and the third random number (from 1 to 154) to select a line in that column of the page.
2. The first address established in this way from the directory was designated to be a "qualified address" if it appeared to be a genuine residential address. If qualified, it became the starting point for building a cluster of four; if not qualified, it was rejected and a new address was drawn in the prescribed manner.
3. Beginning with the first "qualified address" a cluster of four was built by counting each eighth further qualified address. This counting proceeded up in the column, if the third random number (i.e. the address line) was odd; if this number was even, the counting proceeded down in the column.
4. The three residential addresses following each qualified address in a cluster were used as second, third and fourth choice alternates in case of nonresponse on the part of the primary respondents. Before going on to an alternate, a total of three calls (the original plus two call-backs) to the primary respondent was made.
5. This address selection procedure was continued until all 50 clusters in the 16 strata were filled with 200 primary respondents and their alternates.
6. If a randomly selected cluster-starting address was qualified but fell into a stratum which already contained the proportionately allotted number of clusters, it was rejected, and a new address was chosen by the same method as described above. If the stratum changed before the cluster could be completed, the selection procedure continued on a closely adjacent street within the stratum according to a pre-determined systematic random selection rule.

The 50 address clusters chosen in this manner served the purpose of determining the households from which the respondents were to be selected for interviewing. Due to budget constraints, the time-consuming and costly procedure of listing all the sample household members and their alternatives was avoided by using instead a simple quota system, in which the final sample composition would consist 40 percent of male heads of household, 40 percent of housewives or female heads of household, and the remaining 20 percent of any and all categories of persons over 18 years of age. The purpose of this system was to approximate in the sample the actual demographic composition of the population over 18, which proved to be the case in the final result. To achieve these quotas the interviewers were instructed to proceed as follows:

1. Initially, the person opening the door was to be interviewed if he or she appeared to be over the age of 18.
2. If a child opened the door, the interviewer was alternately to ask for either the mother or the father.
3. If neither could be interviewed at that time, the interviewer was to attempt to make an appointment if possible or obtain information when one of the parents could be reached, or else treat the respondent address as a not-at-home.
4. If no one answered the door or if the interview could not be completed on the first call for other reasons, two more call-backs were to be made to that primary address before continuing with one of the alternates.
5. The interview supervisor had the responsibility to check the proportion of respondents after the first 100-plus interviews were completed, and arrange the final interviews so as to achieve the demographic balance described above.

The 200 interviews among the "average consumers" in the metropolitan area of Indianapolis in Marion County were completed during the months of January and February 1970.

Frankfurt. The sampling procedure in Frankfurt paralleled the one in Indianapolis very closely. To minimize redundancy, only the differences will be pointed out here.

No demarcation similar to Marion County existed in Frankfurt, hence the official city limits of Frankfurt were chosen to provide the geographic and demographic border lines. Also, no partitioning method equivalent to zip code was available in Frankfurt. Instead, the city area, with the exception of a large park and forest area (the *Stadtwald*), was divided into ten strata on the basis of Frankfurt's 36 *Stadtteile* or city parts. These are politically and geographically well defined areas or boroughs of Frankfurt, former enclaves and exclaves of the city until their annexation over the centuries. The last such incorporation occured in 1933. Each of the strata contained two or more contiguous *Stadtteile* and from three to eight clusters of four respondents which were proportionately assigned on the basis of the total number of residents in each stratum.

Respondent households were selected from the 1969 edition of the *Frankfurt City Criss-Cross Address Directory*, a listing of all Frankfurt addresses by *Stadtteil* and by street, but completely independent of telephone numbers. The directory is regularly up-dated, contains an accurate and complete listing of all residential addresses within the city limits, and represents an excellent sampling frame for the general population of Frankfurt. The determination of a "qualified address" as a starting point for building sample clusters proceeded in similar fashion to that of Indianapolis by initially drawing three random numbers: the first random number (from 1 to 749) to select the page number in the directory; the second random number (from 1 to 7) to select the column on that page; and the third random number (from 1 to 160) to select the line in that column of the page.

The remaining procedures for building the 50 clusters, filling the ten strata with the proportionate number of clusters, and selecting individual respondents from the sample households in Frankfurt were identical to those in Indianapolis. In total, 198 metropolitan "average consumers" were interviewed in Frankfurt during the months of January and February 1970.

Metropolitan "Subscriber" Samples

There was no practical way of using a stratified clustering technique for chosing the subscriber respondents analogous to that used for the metropolitan average consumer samples. Instead, a systematic random sampling method was applied which is both economical and convenient when name or address listings serve as the sampling frame. In this technique, the survey population (N) is divided by the desired sample size (n) to establish the appropriate sampling interval (k). A randomly chosen number between 1 and k then determines the starting point in the name or address list, beginning the count from the top. After that, every k^{th} name or address is counted for inclusion in the sample. As in the average consumer samples previously described, government, professional or commercial subscriber addresses were weeded out.

Indianapolis. The Indianapolis subscriber sample was generated through the cooperation of Consumers Union, with the card file of *Consumer Reports* (*CR*) serving as a sampling frame. These subscriber address cards are arranged by zip code in file drawers, wherein individual names are sorted in alphabetical order according to CU's own system. The same zip code numbers from which the "average consumer" respondents were selected, were used for the subscriber sample. The actual sampling proceeded in two stages as follows:

1. The Indianapolis (Marion County) survey population at the time of the study consisted of N = 5532 *CR* subscribers. With a sampling interval of k = 19, 284 subscriber addresses were originally counted out. Of these, 24 were determined to be ineligible "commercial" addresses and rejected, leaving 260 "private" subscriber addresses, from which 100 primary respondents would eventually be selected and interviewed.

   Since the response rate was unknown, the initial oversampling provided the interviewers with additional panels of respondents to make up for possible non-response. It also served as a sequential control mechanism to assure proper sample size without further imposition on CU.
2. In the second stage, the acceptable subscriber addresses were numbered

sequentially from 1 through 260. From a pool containing these numbers, 260 random numbers were drawn, one at a time. The first subscriber whose previously assigned number was drawn was given a priority number of 1, the second a priority number of 2, and so forth until each subscriber had a priority number. The actual interviewing started with priority number 1 and continued with 2 and so forth until the subscriber sample was completed.

In contrast to the average consumer sample where only the household addresses were given without identifying a specific person in that household, the subscriber sample required that *the individual under whose name the CR subscription was listed was to be interviewed*. If that person was not available and could not be reached after two more call-backs, the interviewers were instructed to proceed to the next address priority card. This process was continued until the desired sample size was reached. In the end, a total of 101 *CR* subscribers had been interviewed in Indianapolis.

Frankfurt.   The Frankfurt subscriber samples were selected in a fashion much like that used in Indianapolis: the same systematic randomized selection process was applied to the address listings of the two German product testing magazines, naming subscribers within the Frankfurt city limits.

1. *DM.* Out of a total monthly circulation of about 180,000 throughout Germany at the time of the survey (early 1970), *DM* had approximately 24,000 subscribers, 708 of whom resided within Frankfurt. Of these, a primary sample of $n = 50$ and 100 reserve addresses was randomly selected. The 50 primary respondents were sought out and interviewed first, followed by the alternates in the sequential order in which they were drawn. A total of 63 *DM* subscriber interviews were completed.
2. *test.* There were 34,000 *test* subscribers in all of Germany and 545 in Frankfurt. At the time of the field work, *test* was not being sold on newsstands. The randomly selected primary sample of $n = 50$ plus another 50 back-up addresses was available for interviewing. Of these, 34 usable interviews were completed.

The combined interviews in Frankfurt yielded, then, 97 completed and usable subscriber questionnaires.

National Mail Subscriber Sample
The national subscriber surveys were conducted via a mail questionnaire nearly identical to that used in the interview surveys. Since respondents were to be selected from the subscriber address files of the three agencies

publishing the product test reports, we used the same systematic random selection method previously described for the metropolitan interview surveys.

The questionnaires along with a cover letter and free return envelope were mailed to all respondents in the samples during the month of January 1970. The questionnaire forms themselves were marked with an identification number to keep track of the returns. Beyond that, the confidentiality of all information provided by respondents was assured in the letter. Two follow-up letters and questionnaires were sent to non-responding sample members at two-week intervals.

United States. The sampling frame for the United States national mail subscriber survey was comprised by the entire *CR* address card files for the United States which, as mentioned above, are arranged in alphabetical order by zip code areas. Dividing the *CR* subscribership of approximately $N = $ 1,600,000 by the desired sample size of $n = 1000$, a sampling interval of $k = 1600$ was determined. Starting in the first file drawer with a randomly drawn address between numbers 1 and 1600, every 1600th address card was included in the sample. Where the selection fell on a card containing: an Indianapolis subscriber address previously included in the metropolitan sample for interviewing (an admittedly small chance), or an apparent government, commercial, professional or similarly ineligible address, it was rejected and replaced by the address card immediately following. Of the 1030 subscribers finally selected, 630 completed questionnaires were returned for an overall response rate of 61 percent.

Germany. The sampling frame for the German national subscriber survey consisted of *DM* and *test* address files for all of Germany including West Berlin. These are arranged by regional and local postal zones which are somewhat analogous to the zip code areas in the United States. The previously described systematic random selection procedure again was used, excluding: Frankfurt address already selected for interviewing, and apparent business, organizational and professional addresses which were not of interest to this study. When an address was ineligible for this reason, the card immediately following was taken.

DM subscriber sample. The national *DM* subscriber population of 24,000 was divided by the intended sample size of $n = 515$ to determine the sampling interval of $k = 46$. Starting with a randomly selected number between 1 and 46, every 46th address was chosen for inclusion in the sample. After mailing the 515 questionnaires and two follow-up letters spaced at two-week intervals, a total of 285 usable questionnaires were received from *DM* subscribers for a response rate of 55 percent.

test subscriber sample. The predetermined sample size for *test* subscribers was also n = 515. With a survey population of N = 34,000, this approximated a sampling interval of k = 66. The 515 mailings resulted in a total of 325 completed questionnaires for a response rate of 63 percent.

Thus the national subscriber survey in Germany consisted of a combined mailing of 1030 questionnaires of which 610 usable ones were returned after the two follow-up waves.

A Comparative Note on DM and Test and Their Subscribers

DM and *test* are the two most prominent consumer information magazines in Germany. In part they supplement each other; in part they compete with each other as well as with commercial advertising for the consumer's attention. However, as was mentioned in chapter 3, they differ dramatically as to sponsorship. While *test* is published by the government-sponsored *Stiftung Warentest* (officially a foundation in "private law"), *DM* is the product of a commercial publishing company. A detailed description and analysis of the two organizations, their precise sponsorship and the nature of their publications is contained in the companion volume, *Consumer Information Handbook*; and a synopsis of *DM*'s and *test*'s major characteristics was presented in chapter 5 of this volume. Suffice it to say at this point that observable differences between *DM* and *test*, the publications, exist as might be expected on account of differences in the sponsoring organizations.

Of the two, *test* resembles most closely *Consumer Reports* with its emphasis on comparative product test reports as all-dominant concern. Like *CR*, *test*, in accord with its charter provisions, does not contain any commercial advertisements. *DM*, on the other hand, seems more consumer-education oriented, whereby greater weight is given to general consumer-interest articles and relatively less to product tests per se. Although three to five test reports are a regular *DM* feature, many of them are (and have been since as early as 1969) adapted from *test*. As an added twist—and important source of revenue—*DM* includes commercial advertisements (in sharp contrast to both *test* and *CR*), comprising about 30–35 percent of the content of each issue. All in all, *DM* appears much more popular in style, occasionally even frivolous or flamboyant, at least when compared to *test*.

Despite these noted and notable differences in the nature of the two publications, the results of this study make it consistently clear that *DM* and *test* are catering to the same clientele—a fact which in retrospect lends credence

to our original contention that both journals are competing for essentially
the same market segment, a segment characterized by distinctly higher income,
education, and occupational status than the average population. However, as
displayed below, each subscriber group is predictably more loyal to its own
journal and, as might also be anticipated, the two groups differ in their views on
the dangers of advertising in testing magazines. Beyond that, the overall differences between *DM* and *test* subscribers are minimal, particularly as regards
demographic and socioeconomic characteristics. The relative homogeneity of
the two subscriber groups thus confirmed the "no difference" hypothesis which
had led us to treat them for the most part as *one* Information Seeker sample
throughout this volume.

A "No Difference" Test between *DM* and *test* Subscribers

Since the bulk of our analysis has been based on the metropolitan
samples, the Frankfurt subscriber samples are used here for testing the "no
difference" hypothesis between *DM* and *test* subscribers. But our conclusions
would not change in substance even if such a test were based on our German
national samples.

Based on results from the Frankfurt respondents, then, *DM* and
test subscribers not only reflected substantial similarity in their income distribution, education, and occupation, but also in age and marital status. *DM* subscribers did include a somewhat (not significantly) greater percentage of large
households (five or more persons) than the *test* subscribers. This was mirrored in
such factors as number of children in the family and the type and size of living
quarters (see tables C-1–C-3). Other than that, the data leave no doubt that
both *DM* and *test* subscribers are at home in the same upper socioeconomic
strata.

DM and *test* subscribers did not differ in their media habits. They
varied little from each other in the amount of TV watching and radio listening
and in the number of magazines and newspapers read. They pay attention to
a similar number of commercials, and their attitudes to advertising and various
aspects of advertising show no significant differences—although *DM* subscribers
reflected a slightly more favorable tendency, as might be expected. This may
be illustrated by two exceptions to the "no difference" rule in subscriber
attitudes: in the area of advertising *DM* subscribers were more likely than *test*
subscribers to agree that "advertising is essential," and that it "presents a true
picture." The fact that *DM* subscribers see advertisements side by side with
product test reports and other consumer-interest materials in every issue of their
magazine may be reflected in their more favorable attitude concerning essentiality and truthfulness of advertising.

With respect to more general attitudes of interest *DM* and *test*
subscribers again did not exhibit any systematic or significant differences. *Test*

Table C-1. Comparison of Three Socioeconomic Factors—*DM* vs. *test* Subscribers[a] (Frankfurt Samples)

	Subscribers		
	DM *(Base = 63)*	test *(Base = 34)*	*Significance Test[b]*
1. *Family Net Income Per Month*			
2500 D-Mark and more	21%	12%	
2000–2499 D-Mark	14	15	*MWU*
1500–1999 D-Mark	18	18	*DM* Subscribers higher
1000–1499 D-Mark	23	18	*p* = .75
Under 1000 D-Mark	2	3	not significant
No answer	23	35	
2. *Education of Household Head*			
16 years and more	30%	26%	
13–15 years	19	18	*MWU*
12 years	8	6	*DM* Subscribers higher
9–11 years	43	41	*p* = .87
Under 9 years	0	0	not significant
No answer	0	9	
3. *Occupation of Household Head*			
Professional, technical	30%	24%	
Proprietor, manager, official	25	21	
Clerical, sales	24	18	*Chi Square*
Craftsman, foreman, service	5	3	*p* > .10
Operative, laborer	10	12	not significant
Retired, others	2	9	
Not classified	5	14	

[a]Data based on questions in section 7 of questionnaire, reproduced in appendix G.
[b]Where applicable, the Mann-Whitney U test (MWU) for determining the higher group is used. Otherwise, the Chi Square test (χ^2) for any difference in distribution is used.

subscribers were more likely to agree that "government has too much control over business" than *DM* subscribers. Except for this preliminary impression however, neither *DM* nor *test* subscribers can be said to be more pro-business or government, or more conservative or liberal on the basis of our survey results. Subscribers as a group and average consumers as a group were compared and contrasted in some detail in chapters 5, 8, and 9.

Respondents were also asked to express their feelings and attitudes toward the two magazines themselves. As could be anticipated, *DM* subscribers overall rated *DM* more favorably than did the *test* subscribers; and vice versa (see table C-4). The same predictable responses were obtained for other criteria, such as reliability and credibility of the information contained in the two publications. It is interesting to note here that *DM* subscriber ratings of *DM* were consistently higher on all dimensions (except the overall) than the corresponding ratings of *test* by *test* subscribers. At the same time, a larger percentage of *DM* subscribers appeared more favorably inclined toward *test* than were *test*

Table C-2. Relationship Between Five Demographic Variables and
DM vs. *test* Subscribers

	Subscribers		
	DM *(Base = 63)*	test *(Base = 34)*	*Significance Test*
1. *Sex of Respondent*			
Male	81%	65%	*Chi Square*
Female	19	35	$p > .05$
			not significant
2. *Marital Status*			
Married	90%	82%	*Chi Square*
Single	7	15	$p > .40$
Widowed, divorced	3	3	not significant
3. *Age of Respondent*			
Under 25 years of age	3%	6%	
25–34	27	29	
35–44	35	26	*MWU*
45–54	19	12	*DM* Subscribers higher
55–64	13	18	$p = .86$
65 years and over	3	9	not significant
4. *Persons in Household*			
One person household	5%	12%	*MWU*
Two person household	33	39	*DM* Subscribers higher
Three person household	21	30	$p = .03$
Four person household	22	15	significant
Five or more persons	19	3	
5. *Children Under 18*			
None	46%	71%	*MWU*
One child	25	15	*DM* Subscribers higher
Two children	18	12	$p = .02$
Three or more children	11	3	significant

subscribers toward *DM*. It may be that *DM* subscribers reflect greater enthusiasm about the usefulness of consumer information in general, regardless of its source; it may also be that the advertising in *DM* raises a mental barrier among *test* subscribers.

In the specific purchase situations for durables, autos and convenience goods, *DM* subscribers significantly more often rated *DM* as an important information source than *test*; and *test* subscribers perceived *test* to be more important than *DM*. But for the rest of the purchase sequence questions, *DM* and *test* subscribers again did not differ in their perceptions of shopping concerns, important information sources, and post-purchase satisfaction. Not even the statement about advertising helpfulness and accuracy in post-purchase retrospect elicited significant differential responses from the two groups.

Table C-3. Relationship Between Three Housing Variables and *DM* vs. *test* Subscribers

	Subscribers		
	DM *(Base = 63)*	test *(Base = 34)*	*Significance Test*
1. *House Type*			
Single Family House	25%	10%	*Chi Square*
Apartment	75	90	$p > .05$
			not significant
2. *House Ownership*			
Own house or apartment	24%	6%	*Chi Square*
Rent house or apartment	76	85	$p < .05$
Other arrangements	0	9	significant
3. *Number of Rooms*			
Less than 2 rooms	5%	12%	
2 rooms	13	21	*Chi Square*
3 rooms	43	29	$p > .40$
4 or 5 rooms	21	38	not significant
6 or more rooms	19	0	

Table C-4. *DM* and *test* Subscriber Evaluation of Magazines[a] (Frankfurt Samples) (By Index Numbers)[b]

		Magazines			
	Subscribers	DM		test	
Evaluation Criteria	DM *(Base = 63)* test *(Base = 34)*	*Index*	*Higher Group Significance[c]*	*Index*	*Higher Group Significance[c]*
1. Reliability	*DM*	89	*DM**	49	
	test	32		79	test*
2. Clarity	*DM*	37	*DM**	14	
	test	6		32	test*
3. Credibility	*DM*	92	*DM**	40	
	test	29		64	test*
4. Relevance	*DM*	69	*DM**	32	
	test	26		79	test*
5. Timeliness	*DM*	63	*DM**	34	
	test	12		38	test*
6. Overall Evaluation	*DM*	86	*DM**	51	
	test	38		97	test*

[a]Data based on questions from section 6 of questionnaire.

[b]Index = (% sample agree or strongly agree minus % sample disagree or strongly disagree). The higher the index number, the more favorable is the rating of the magazine on each evaluation criterium.

[c]Statistical significance based on Mann-Whitney U test. *$p < .01$.

Table C-5. *DM* and *test* Subscriber Evaluation of Magazines with Advertising Content Considered[a] (Frankfurt Samples) (By Index Numbers)[b]

	DM			test		
	Subscriber		*Differ-ence*	*Subscriber*		*Differ-ence*
Base	DM *(63)*	test *(34)*	TE-DM[c]	DM *(63)*	test *(34)*	TE-DM[c]
DM/test carries too much advertising[d]	-2	6	+8	-3	-6	-3
If *DM/test* carried more ads, I would believe it less	0	18	+18	-3	35	+38

[a]Data based on questions from section 6 of questionnaire.

[b]Index = (% of sample agreeing with statement minus % of sample disagreeing). Positive Index means objection to advertising content in *DM/test*. Negative Index implies no objection to advertising content in *DM/test*.

[c]Difference between *test* and *DM* subscriber index. Positive difference is in the direction predicted.

[d]As *test* carries no advertising, this question must be interpreted with caution as regards that journal.

Considering, however, the inclusion of advertising in their respective magazines, it is evident that *DM* subscribers are significantly more tolerant than *test* subscribers of the dangers which this might entail. While both groups are more or less neutral about the amount of advertising content, *test* subscribers apparently would "believe" product testing magazines much less "if they carried more ads," and in any case would believe them much less than *DM* subscribers. Interestingly, the image of *DM* would suffer considerably less than the image of *test* on the believability score. Since *DM* carries ads anyway, the inclusion of additional advertising would not hurt its credibility so much as that of *test*. At least this is the way *test* subscribers perceived it; *DM* subscribers remained quite unaffected by the prospect of "more" ads in either product testing magazines. (See table C-5.)

From the foregoing we have concluded that *DM* and *test* subscribers belong to a fairly homogeneous population group. Certainly, they differ in some respects as might be anticipated on the basis of obvious differences between the two magazines. But, by and large, we have found them to share many demographic, socioeconomic and attitudinal characteristics, which appear to be common to Information Seekers.

Appendix D

Sample Tests from Consumer
Reports, DM and test

Instant-
load
Autoexposure Cameras

There's no doubt that Americans are a picture-taking lot. But it's also true that many picture-takers lack the interest in photography needed to master a camera that can be adjusted for a variety of conditions and photographic effects. A good many such snapshooters content themselves with a simple, inexpensive camera, such as the ones CU reported on in November 1967. There's no way to focus most of those and no way to change the lens aperture or shutter speed. Thus you can take pictures with cameras of that type only under very limited light conditions—on a fairly bright day or with flash at relatively close distances. Several of the cameras in that project listed at under $10, although most of the top-rated models were priced at around $30.

If you're willing to spend more money, but still want a camera that's extremely easy to use, you can extend your picture-taking range considerably with one of the quick-loading, autoexposure cameras CU tested for this report. Our 21 models ranged in list price from $21.95 to $119.50, with most falling in an intermediate range of about $40 to $70. Instant-load autoexposure cameras of the type tested for this report have been very popular for a number of years, no doubt because they're nearly as simple to use as the cheap cameras reported on two years ago and often offer the possibility of getting good pictures in light less favorable than bright sunlight.

But the tested cameras are far from simple in themselves, since they take over or simplify many of the judgments and adjustments the photographer would otherwise have to make himself. Two models—the *Kodak 714* and the *Capromatic* —let you select the shutter speed. Mechanisms on all the others automatically set the shutter speed or lens aperture or both, according to the light conditions measured by an electric eye. It's possible to focus 15 of the tested models sharply on your principal subject. But the remaining six (the *Revere Automatic 1064*, the *Kodak S20*, the *Viceroy 126EE*, the *Kodak 134*, the *Anscomatic 326* and the *Ricoh 126CEE*) have fixed-focus lenses.

Easy loading: a plus

All the tested models have the quick-loading feature, which uses the type 126 film in a cartridge developed by Kodak for its *Instamatic* cameras and now made by a number of other companies as well. There's no threading or rewinding of film. You just insert the cartridge assembly, which includes a take-up spool, and pull it out when the film has been exposed. On some models the film is advanced electrically or by a spring-driven motor; on most of the others you advance the film by a simple push of the thumb

CU'S KEY FINDINGS

These cameras offer slip-in-slip-out film loading but, in most cases, no manual adjustment of aperture or shutter speed. Most provide only one exposure combination for any given kind of light conditions. Too, they seem particularly vulnerable to assembly-line gremlins. In a product that allows no adjustment by the user, such defects may well mean you'd have a piece of worthless equipment. The accompanying report tells what you can reasonably expect from these models and how to protect yourself if you decide to buy one. But CU urges you to consider another camera option, which is described in the box on page 431.

313

on either a lever or a wheel. A notch in the film cartridge enables the camera's autoexposure system to adjust to the light needs of the particular film you're using.

The best of the tested models should more than satisfy the casual snapshooter—but even the best of them will likely frustrate anyone with grander photographic ambitions. For all the cameras are limited by the fact that they have no manual override on the autoexposure systems. That means you can't, even if you wish, make your own settings. (There are autoexposure cameras in the same price range as the ones we tested that provide greater versatility; for a brief general description of that type of camera, see page 431.)

Some minuses

On most of the tested models, you can't adjust shutter speed (to stop action, for example) or choose the lens aperture (perhaps to throw backgrounds slightly out of focus and therefore concentrate attention on the main subject). Only the *Kodak 714* and the *Capromatic* offer even a limited choice of shutter speeds; the camera then gives you the right aperture for the light conditions and the speed selected.

The fixed-focus Revere is automated to a fare-thee-well. It even has a lens cover that retracts when you snap the picture

Well, let's say that you decide to accept those limitations in return for automaticity. Certainly, then, you at least want the camera to be automatically right, not automatically wrong. More than one-quarter of those tested consistently produced overexposed or underexposed pictures—probably a result of individual sample defects rather than of poor design. Such defects are particularly frustrating in a fully automatic camera, since there's nothing you can do to compensate for the mechanism's incorrect settings. We found other defects, too; in fact, more than half of our original test models were defective enough so that they would have been all but useless to a buyer. Given the unusually large proportion of defective cameras among our samples, we strongly advise that you buy one of these cameras only if the dealer makes a firm agreement for exchange or refund on a camera that doesn't expose correctly or is otherwise defective. Don't settle for the usual repair agreement; it may well take weeks or months to fix the camera and return it.

Soon after you buy the camera, take a cartridge or two of color transparencies under the widest possible variety of light conditions, from brightest sunlight to the dimmest light that will still keep the unsuitable-light warning from showing. Check, too, the flash performance throughout the range of distances given in the manufacturer's instructions. If the transparencies you get are too dark or too light, go back to the dealer for an exchange or a refund. And be sure to get the same agreement on a replacement camera and to check it out in the same way as you did the original.

Unlike most models, the Kodak 714 has a shutter-speed dial, which allows you to vary the exposure for the effect you want

Electric eyes and batteries

Each camera uses either a selenium or a cadmium sulfide (CdS) photocell or electric eye. We found no clear technical advantage for either type with the tested models. Although CdS cells are inherently capable of much greater sensitivity than selenium cells, great sensitivity in responding to dim light would be wasted in cameras of this sort; the cameras lack the aperture/shutter-speed combinations needed for dim-light photography without flash. If anything, the selenium cell might offer the buyer of one of these cameras a

For flash, you must set subject distance on two scales with Argus. Several others give right exposure with proper focusing

INSTANT-LOAD CAMERAS
continued

slight advantage in convenience. Selenium cells don't need a battery; CdS cells do. The battery you use with a CdS cell should last a good year in typical use, and unless your camera has a battery tester (as do the *Anscomatic 626*, the *Kodak 714* and the *Argus*) we suggest that you change the battery automatically every year. Otherwise, it may go dead on you at an inopportune time. You may find in a picture-taking situation that you simply can't click the shutter on some models, or, perhaps worse, learn later that the camera has improperly exposed the film. In any event, do save the battery by shielding the camera's eye with the case or a lens cap when you're not taking pictures.

Individual capabilities

In general, the larger the maximum aperture and the wider the range of shutter speeds, the greater the range of conditions of light and motion you can expect a camera to handle. As noted in the Ratings, the nine highest-ranked cameras have a maximum aperture of f/2.8. Those with fairly slow shutter speeds (1/50th or slower; see Ratings table) could expose the popular color films under light conditions ranging from sunny bright outside to well-lighted interiors. (With interior shots though, the subject had best stay still if you expect to see an unblurred picture.)

As noted, some models have a relatively small maximum aperture. As shown in the Ratings table, those models have fixed shutter speeds that, combined with their small apertures, would limit your use of popular color film outdoors to light no dimmer than cloudy-bright; on a dull day, you would need a flash to get a passable picture. Four models—the *Argus*, the *Kodak 714*, the *Capromatic* and the *Keystone*—have "bulb" settings, which allow you to keep the shutter open as long as you want to for a "time exposure." To make such time exposures, however, you need a tripod and a cable release (the tripod to hold the camera steady during a relatively long exposure; the cable release to prevent even the tiny vibration so likely when you click

The 35mm film, top, gives you only slightly more area than the 28mm instant-load cartridge film (bottom). But assuming similar lenses on the cameras, the 35mm camera covers a wider angle—and you may prefer a rectangular picture to a square picture

a shot by hand). All four models have standard tripod sockets, but, of the four, only the *Argus* has a cable-release socket. A camera that has a tripod socket but no cable-release socket is something like a wedding that has a bride but no groom. If you set the *Kodak 714*, the *Capromatic* or the *Keystone* on a tripod and then took a picture with the shutter speed set to bulb, the resulting photograph would probably show at least some blur because of camera shake—it's hard to keep your shutter finger perfectly steady during a long exposure.

The 126 cartridge film comes in several black-and-white and color versions and its format is about 28mm square. That's only slightly smaller in area than the 24x36mm of standard 35mm film, but quite different in format. All else being equal, the 35mm format gives a wider view of the scene; and many photographers find the rectangular 35mm format more pleasing than a square format. (The photos below at left show how the two formats compare with an identical scene.) Other disadvantages of the 126 cartridge setup: Its cartridge is considerably bulkier than a 35mm cassette; and the 126 cartridge gives you fewer exposures (12 or 20) than the 36 available in 35mm cassettes. Cost per shot, though, needn't be a factor to consider—it's roughly the same as with comparable 35mm film.

How good are the pictures?

Under "optical performance," the Ratings note the sharpness of the pictures each camera could take. We judged lens sharpness at maximum aperture (except with the *Vitessa*, which we tested at each of its two fixed apertures) by taking black-and-white pictures of a finely detailed subject in bright sunlight and examining the negatives under 10-times magnification at center, edge and corner. Those cameras judged good should give you negatives that could be enlarged without serious loss of sharpness up to about eight inches across, or slides that could be satisfactorily projected up to about three feet across. Descending judgments indicate decreasing capability for making enlargeable pictures. On the focusing cameras with a distance scale, the closest-marked focus (usually three or four feet) was judged accurate enough for a camera of this type.

While we were taking a considerable number of shots with each camera, we also judged mechanical performance. The Ratings judgments reflect the smoothness, ease and quietness of the various parts and operations: focusing, shutter release, film advance, back latch. As with the autoexposure systems, we found a number of serious defects in mechanical operation. So it's doubly important to have a clear understanding with your dealer about exchange or refund.

Flash operation

All these cameras take the popular four-shot flashcubes. The flashcubes on all rotated properly and went off when we clicked the shutter. On most of the focusing models, the camera adjusts itself to flash operation when you plug in the flashcube; the shutter speed is then set at about 1/40th of a second, and the lens aperture is coupled to the focusing mechanism. When you focus, then, you automatically set the aperture for the right flash exposure with the subject at focused distance. On the *Yashica*, the electric eye compensates for flash automatically by measuring the

An alternative to consider

A primary reason CU tested this month's instant-load autoexposure cameras is their popularity. But, as outlined in the accompanying report, they have inherent disadvantages that, when combined with the apparently substantial chance of your buying a defective sample, can be serious. A manual override on the autoexposure system would help matters a great deal, and there's actually no technical reason why these cameras couldn't be manufactured with an override. However, they're not. Perhaps the manufacturers have decided not to change a product that combines features and price so effectively from a sales standpoint.

But if you're willing to give up instant-load, you can buy 35mm autoexposure cameras that might give you worthwhile advantages. We haven't tested those cameras, so we cannot evaluate their quality. However, a study of manufacturers' specifications leads us to believe that, at prices similar to those for the instant-loads, they would be more versatile and, one could hope, more reliable.

Some of those 35mm cameras—the *Konica Auto-S2*, the

Petri Color 35 and the *Fujica Compact Deluxe*, for example—allow you to select your own combination of aperture and shutter speed when you want to. Note that the override won't force you to learn about camera settings; on some models you can leave the camera on automatic all the time.

Other 35mm autoexposure cameras lack the override but still, we think, offer substantial advantages over the instant-load models. For one thing, the 35mm film format gives, with these models, a wider scene than does the 126 cartridge, as the two comparison photos on page 430 show. And roll-film cameras have a film-speed dial, which you could manipulate to compensate for any tendency the camera might have to underexpose or overexpose consistently. Two 35mm models that lack the override but that do incorporate the advantages of format and film-speed dial are the *Konica C35* and the *Konica EE-Matic Deluxe F*. Prices for the five cameras mentioned, and for some others of the same general type, run from about $70 to $110, well within the price range of this month's tested models.

flash intensity reflected from the subject and making the proper exposure adjustment.

Somewhat less convenient is the flash system on the *Argus* and the *Keystone*. Those cameras have a separate distance scale just for flash. To make a flash shot you have to focus the lens *and* set the flash distance scale—two adjustments instead of one. The *Argus*, by the way, has an accessory shoe and synchronization for electronic flash. But we think the user of this type of camera is likely to prefer using the more-compact flashcube. There's no flash adjustment on the *Dacora* or *Wards* or most of the nonfocusing models. Thus those cameras would satisfactorily expose flash pictures within only a very limited range of distances.

The *Minolta* and the *Revere* carry automaticity to a ridiculous length with respect to flash operation. With those, supposedly, the user needn't even decide whether or not to use a flash. Instead, say the instructions, he may leave a flashcube plugged in all the time; the camera then activates the flash when the electric eye finds the available light too dim for a proper exposure. But that arrangement could be useless and expensive. The flash may well go off when, for example, you took a picture of a sunset or mountain—and each such shot would just waste one-quarter of a flashcube. We suggest that you keep flashcubes out of the *Minolta* and the *Revere*, as with any camera, except when you intend to take flash pictures within flash range.

Film advance

On most models you advance the film with an easy stroke or two of a thumb-operated lever or wheel or, a bit less conveniently, a couple of turns of a knob. Three of the cameras, however, make the whole job superconvenient, if somewhat noisy. They automatically advance the film to the first frame when you close the camera on the film cartridge, move it to the next frame each time you shoot a picture, and complete the winding to the take-up spool after you've exposed the last frame. The *Olympus* does the job with an electric motor.

On the *Ricoh 126C* and the similar *Sears Easi-Load* there's a spring-driven motor. You're supposed to wind the motor (about 20 half turns of a large knob) about every 10 or 12 shots. But in our tests, the motor began to sound tired after about six shots, and we usually rewound at that point.

The choices

The first decision you need to make, of course, is whether you prefer one of these minimum-fuss cameras to a comparably priced model that gives you more control over the settings. If you do, and if you don't want to make any preshooting adjustments at all, you might choose one of the nonfocusing models. As we've noted, they're more limited than the cameras that do focus, being pretty much restricted to nearly ideal outdoor shooting conditions and to short distances with flash. But such conditions do embrace a good deal of casual photography.

The two top-rated fixed-focus cameras, the *Revere Automatic 1064* and the *Kodak S20*, were judged somewhat better in mechanical operation than the other fixed-focus models. But the *Kodak S20*, although the most compact of all the models, seems very high-priced: Its $58.50 tag is only about $10 less than the list prices of the top-rated focusing cameras, which can take pictures under conditions that would render the *Kodak S20* useless. The *Revere* is nearly as compact as the *Kodak S20*, and at $19 less than the *Kodak*, seems to us a better buy.

The nine top-ranked focusing models were judged close enough in overall quality so that you might reasonably choose any one for particular features you like. The *Yashica's* wide range of shutter speeds, for example, makes for greater dim-light capability than you'd get with any of the other models. The *Kodak 714* and the *Capromatic* have a manual shutter adjustment, so that you can stop moderately fast action with them in a range of light conditions, not just at the bright light that triggers fairly fast shutter speeds in some of the others.

RATINGS OF INSTANT-LOAD AUTOEXPOSURE CAMERAS

Listed by type; within types, listed except as noted in order of estimated overall quality. Except as noted, closely ranked models differed little in overall quality. Prices are list; discounts are generally available.

KEY: VG, Very Good; G, Good; F, Fair; P, Poor

ACCEPTABLE
FOCUSING MODELS

Except as noted, each has a warning in viewfinder to indicate unsuitable light, a cable-release socket, and a distance scale in feet, with closest marked focus about 3 to 4 ft. And unless otherwise indicated, none has indication of aperture or shutter speed, manual selection of aperture or shutter speed or bulb setting.

Note: An additional 11 models analyzed in similar detail in original report.

Model	Price	Case	Weight	Optical perfor-mance	Mechanical perfor-mance	Maximum aperture	Focal length	Shutter speed on autoexposure	Electric eye type	Flash operation	Comments
KONICA AUTO S261 (Konica Camera Corp., Woodside, N.Y.)	$69.95	$10.00	21 oz.	VG	VG	f/2.8	42mm	1/30 to 1/250 sec.	CdS	Distance-coupled aperture	Coupled rangefinder. No zone-focus marks. Shutter lock to prevent underexposure; judged less desirable than warning alone.
ANSCOMATIC 626 (GAF Corp., NYC)	69.95	Ⓐ	16	VG	VG	2.8	34	Ⓑ	CdS	Distance-coupled aperture	Aperture indicator. Battery tester. According to the manufacturer, this model has been discontinued but may still be available in some stores.
ARGUS 264 (Argus, Inc., West Columbia, S.C.)	89.95	9.95	23	G-to-VG	VG	2.8	40	1/30 to 1/600	CdS	Separate distance scale sets aperture	Aperture and shutter-speed indicators. Battery tester. Accessory shoe. Bulb setting.
YASHICA EZ-MATIC ELECTRONIC (Yashica, Inc., Woodside, N.Y.)	59.50	None	14	VG	G	2.8	37	2 to 1/300	CdS	Exposure electronically adjusted to flash intensity	Aperture and shutter-speed indicators.
OLYMPUS QUICKMATIC EEM (Ponder and Best, Los Angeles)	61.50	Ⓐ	17	G	VG	2.8	36	1/40 or 1/200	Selenium	Distance-coupled aperture	Electric film advance, judged convenient but noisy. Shutter lock to prevent wrong exposure; judged less desirable than warning alone.
RICOH 126C (Lenco Photo Prod., Inc., NYC)	69.95	Ⓐ	18	G	G-to-VG	2.8	40	1/125	Selenium	Distance-coupled aperture	Spring-motor film advance, judged convenient but noisy. Aperture indicator.
SEARS EASI-LOAD FC600 Cat. No. 78E9 (Sears, Roebuck)	49.50 Ⓒ	Ⓐ	18	G	G-to-VG	2.8	40	1/125	Selenium	Distance-coupled aperture	Essentially similar to Ricoh 126C, preceding.
KODAK 714 (Eastman Kodak Co., Rochester, N.Y.)	119.50	9.95	26	G	G-to-VG	2.8	38	1/30 to 1/250 Ⓓ	CdS	Distance-coupled aperture	No cable-release socket. Battery tester. Bulb setting.
CAPPOMATIC 250 (Ehrenreich Photo-Optical Industries, Inc., Garden City, N.Y.)	59.95	6.95	17	G	G-to-VG	2.8	35	1/50 or 1/250 Ⓔ	Selenium	Distance-coupled aperture	No cable-release socket. Aperture indicator. Bulb setting.

The following models were judged about equal in overall quality. Listed alphabetically.

Model	Price	Case	Weight	Optical perfor-mance	Mechanical perfor-mance	Maximum aperture	Focal length	Shutter speed on autoexposure	Electric eye type	Flash operation	Comments
BELL & HOWELL AUTOLOAD 340 (Bell & Howell, Chicago)	37.50	5.95	11	G	G	3.5	40	1/30 to 1/250	CdS	Distance-coupled aperture	Unsuitable-light indicator on top, judged inconvenient. No parallax-correction marks, distance scale or cable-release socket.

Test Zweikreis- bremsen

Test reproduced from DM, 1969: 9, with the kind permission of the publisher

Die Bremsversuche wurden von einem routinierten Autotester gefahren. Weniger geübte Autofahrer, die überraschend in eine kritische Situation geraten, werden bei Ausfall eines Bremskreises vermutlich nicht so reaktionsschnell und besonnen handeln

Audi 100 LS
Ausrüstung: vorn Scheiben-, hinten Trommelbremsen. Bremskraftverstärker, Warnlampe für ausfallende Bremskreise auf Wunsch (108 Mark). **Testergebnis:** 1. Kreis: kaum Richtungskorrekturen erforderlich. Pedalkraft wächst etwas an.

2. Kreis: Geringe Lenkradkorrekturen erforderlich. Pedalkraft wächst sehr stark an.

Citroen DS 21
Ausrüstung: vorn Scheiben-, hinten Trommelbremsen. Bremskraftverstärker. Warnlampe für ausgefallene Bremsen. Regler für Verteilung der Bremskraft. **Testergebnis:** 1. Kreis: kaum Lenkkorrekturen erforderlich. Pedalkraft wächst nur wenig an. 2. Kreis: kaum Lenkkorrekturen erforderlich. Pedalkraft wächst nur wenig an.

Ford 20 M
Ausrüstung: vorn Scheiben-, hinten Trommelbremsen. Bremskraftverstärker. **Testergebnis:** 1. Kreis: Vorderräder blockieren schnell, Wagen bleibt jedoch in der Spur. Pedalkraft wächst unwesentlich an. 2. Kreis: geringe Lenkradkorrektur erforderlich. Pedalkraft wächst merklich an.

Mercedes Benz 230
Ausrüstung: vorn und hinten Scheibenbremsen. Bremskraftverstärker. Warnlampe für ausgefallene Bremsen. **Testergebnis:** 1. Kreis: schwache Richtungskorrekturen erforderlich. Pedalkraft wächst merklich an. 2. Kreis: leichte Lenkradkorrektur erforderlich. Pedalkraft wächst sehr stark an.

BMW 2000
Ausrüstung: vorn Scheiben-, hinten Trommelbremsen. Bremskraftverstärker.

Testergebnis: 1. Kreis: Hinterräder blockieren zuerst. Lenkkorrektur erforderlich. Pedalkraft wächst merklich an. 2. Kreis: keine Richtungskorrektur erforderlich. Pedalkraft wächst sehr stark an.

NSU Ro 80
Ausrüstung: vorn und hinten Scheibenbremsen. Bremskraftverstärker und Regler für die Hinterachse. Warnlampe für ausgefallene Bremsen. **Testergebnis:** 1. Kreis: Die Hinterräder blockieren zuerst. Lenkkorrekturen erforderlich. Pedalkraft wächst deutlich an. 2. Kreis: keine Korrektur erforderlich. Pedalkraft wächst sehr stark an.

Opel Commodore
Ausrüstung: vorn Scheiben-, hinten Trommelbremsen. Bremskraftverstärker. **Testergebnis:** 1. Kreis: schwache Richtungskorrekturen erforderlich. Pedalkraft wächst merklich an. 2. Kreis: keine Korrektur erforderlich. Pedalkraft wächst sehr stark an.

Porsche 911 S
Ausrüstung: vorn und hinten Scheibenbremsen. **Testergebnis:** 1. Kreis: Hinterachse überbremst bei intakten Bremskreisen. 1. Kreis: gute Spurhaltung. Pedalkraft wächst merklich an. 2. Kreis: Hinterräder blockieren sehr schnell. Wagen will ausbrechen, ist aber leicht abzufangen. Pedalkraft wächst merklich an.

Saab 99
Ausrüstung: vorn und hinten Scheibenbremsen. Bremskraftverstärker. Warnlampe für ausgefallene Bremskreise. **Testergebnis:** 1. Kreis: Wagen zieht gleichmäßig nach links. Pedalkraft wächst merklich an. 2. Kreis: Wagen zieht gleichmäßig nach rechts. Pedalkraft wächst merklich an.

Simca 1200 S
Ausrüstung: vorn und hinten Scheibenbremsen. Bremskraftverstärker. **Testergebnis:** 1. Kreis: keine Korrektur erforderlich. Pedalkraft wird etwas größer. 2. Kreis: keine Korrektur erforderlich. Pedalkraft wächst merklich an.

Volkswagen 1300
Ausrüstung: vorn auf Wunsch Scheibenbremsen (137 Mark), hinten Trommelbremsen. **Testergebnis:** 1. Kreis: gute Spurhaltung. Pedalkraft wächst etwas an. 2. Kreis: keine Korrektur erforderlich. Pedalkraft wächst sehr stark an.

Volvo 142
Ausrüstung: vorn und hinten Scheibenbremsen. Bremskraftverstärker. Zwei Bremskraftregler. Schnellwarnlampe für ausgefallene Bremskreise. **Testergebnis:** 1. Kreis: gute Spurhaltung. Pedalkraft wächst deutlich an. 2. Kreis: keine Korrektur erforderlich. Pedalkraft wächst deutlich an.

Die zwölf Automobile im DM-Bremsentest waren mit vier verschiedenen Zweikreis-Bremsanlagen ausgerüstet

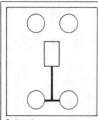

System 1
1. Kreis: Es bremsen nur die Vorderräder.
2. Kreis: Es bremsen nur die Hinterräder. (Audi 100 LS/Citroen DS 21/Ford 20 M/Mercedes Benz 230/Opel Commodore/Porsche 911 S/Simca 1200 S/Volkswagen 1300)

System 2
1. Kreis: Es bremst das linke Vorderrad und das rechte Hinterrad.
2. Kreis: Es bremst das rechte Vorderrad und das linke Hinterrad. (Saab 99)

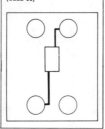

System 3
1. Kreis: Es bremsen die beiden Vorderrad- und die beiden Hinterradbremsen.
2. Kreis: Es bremsen nur die beiden Vorderradbremsen. (BMW 2000/NSU Ro 80)

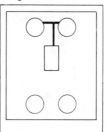

System 4
1. Kreis: Es bremsen die beiden Vorderradbremsen und das rechte Hinterrad.
2. Kreis: Es bremsen die beiden Vorderradbremsen und das linke Hinterrad. (Volvo 142)

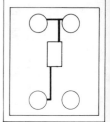

So haben wir getestet

Die Bremsversuche erfolgten aus einer Geschwindigkeit von 100 km/h auf trockener, gerader Fahrbahn im Motodrom Hockenheim.

Vor Beginn der Versuche wurde bei jedem Testfahrzeug die Tachometerabweichung mit Hilfe eines elektronischen Zählwerks und zwei Lichtschranken ermittelt. Die Geschwindigkeit wurde bei jedem Fahrversuch erneut registriert und gegebenenfalls der gemessene Bremsweg korrigiert.

Jeder Versuchsreihe ging eine Bremsung voraus, bei der die zunächst niedrig angesetzte Pedalkraft, langsam, bis zum Blockieren der Räder, zunahm. Der genaue Verlauf der Bremsverzögerung und der Pedalkraft wurden von einem Schreiber (Motometer) auf ein Diagramm aufgezeichnet.

Um die optimale Haftreibung zwischen Reifen und Fahrbahn zu erreichen, die sich bei einem Radschlupf von etwa 20 Prozent ergibt, wurden Blockierungsbremsungen nach Möglichkeit vermieden und so die kürzest möglichen Bremswege erreicht.

Der Beginn der Bremsung wurde durch eine Farbschuß-Patrone markiert. Die Patrone zündete beim Aufleuchten des Bremslichtes. Der Bremsweg konnte auf 0,1 Meter genau ermittelt werden.

Mit jedem Wagen — besetzt mit Fahrer und Beifahrer — wurden drei Versuchsreihen mit jeweils fünf optimalen Bremsungen aus 100 km/h gefahren. Aus den fünf Ergebnissen wurde ein Mittelwert errechnet. Insgesamt wurden 192 Bremsungen vorgenommen.

Bei der ersten Versuchsreihe befanden sich die Bremsen der Testwagen im Originalzustand.

Bei der zweiten Versuchsreihe wurde der zweite Kreis geöffnet und nur mit dem ersten Kreis gebremst.

Bei der dritten Versuchsreihe wurde der erste Kreis geöffnet und nur mit dem zweiten Kreis gebremst.

Wenn nötig, wurden die Bremsen von einem Spezialisten entlüftet.

Zwischen jedem Versuch wurden Pausen zum Abkühlen der Bremsen eingelegt, um Fading (Nachlassen der Bremswirkung durch Reibungshitze) zu vermeiden.

Der NSU Ro 80 war der Star des DM-Zweikreisbremsen-Tests auf dem Hockenheimer Motodrom

Zweikreisbremsen

Alle Räder bremsen

Nur die Vorderräder bremsen

Nur die Hinterräder bremsen

Linkes Vorderrad und rechtes Hinterrad bremsen

Rechtes Vorderrad und linkes Hinterrad bremsen

Vorderräder bremsen nur mit zwei der vier Radbremszylinder. Hinterräder bremsen voll

Nur die Vorderräder bremsen mit zwei der vier Radbremszylinder

Vorderräder bremsen nur mit zwei der vier Radbremszylinder. Rechtes Hinterrad bremst voll

Vorderräder bemsen nur mit zwei der vier Radbremszylinder. Linkes Hinterrad bremst voll

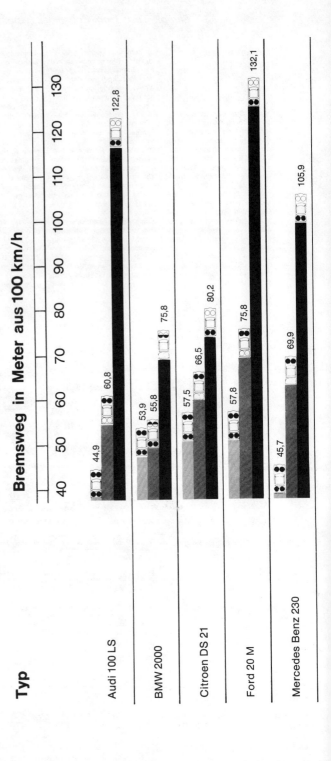

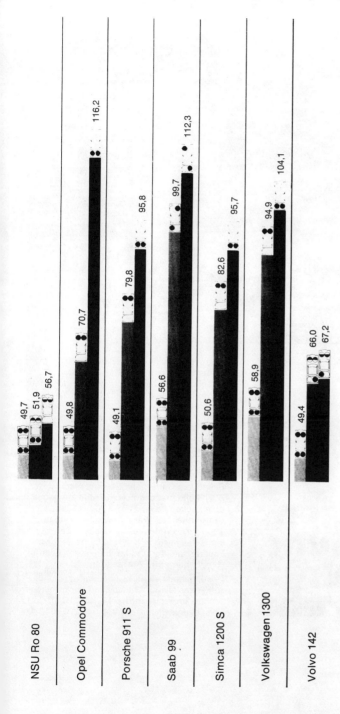

NSU Ro 80

49,7 51,9 56,7

Opel Commodore

49,8 70,7 116,2

Porsche 911 S

49,1 79,8 95,8

Saab 99

56,6 99,7 112,3

Simca 1200 S

50,6 82,6 95,7

Volkswagen 1300

58,9 94,9 104,1

Volvo 142

49,4 66,0 67,2

TEST: GEFRIERSCHRÄNKE

Partial reproduction of test from *test*, 1969:10, with the kind permission of the publisher.

Überlegen Sie in Ruhe: Schrank oder Truhe?

Eine wohlgefüllte Speisekammer war früher die Visitenkarte der perfekten Hausfrau. Gepökeltes und Geräuchertes, Eingemachtes und Gedörrtes füllte die Regale für den Winter. Viel Frisches war nicht darunter. Es hätte sich auch nicht lange gehalten. Ein Vielfaches an Nährwert bringen wir heute auf einem Bruchteil an Raum unter. Gezwungenermaßen und dank moderner Konservierungsmethoden.

Zum Beispiel in Gefriermöbeln. Sie setzen sich jetzt auch in Stadthaushalten immer stärker durch. Besonders Gefrierschränke, die wenig Stellfläche brauchen. Acht Fabrikate haben wir untersuchen lassen. Von 190 bis 320 Liter Bruttoinhalt, zu Preisen zwischen 540 und 790 Mark. Wir legten besonderes Gewicht auf die Gefrierleistung und das Einhalten der Lagertemperatur und kontrollierten außerdem Handhabung und Ausstattung.

Das Ergebnis war in keinem Fall schlechter als zufriedenstellend. Mit Abstand der beste Gefrierschrank im Test: **Liebherr GKS 210** für 550 Mark. Er ist baugleich mit **Zanker GS 210** (640 Mark).

ote: An additional six models illustrated and analyzed in similar
detail in original report.

o haben wir bewertet

acht Haushaltsgefrierschränke
den hauptsächlich nach DIN
3 und den wichtigsten Para-
hen der VDE-Bestimmung 0730
üft. Von 100 erreichbaren Be-
ungspunkten entfielen auf die
ktionsprüfung maximal 60, auf
dhabung/Ausstattung und
nische Prüfung je 20 Punkte.

ktionsprüfung: Das wich-
e Kriterium war die Gefrier-
ung. Um sie zu ermitteln, wur-
die heruntergekühlten Gefrier-
anke bei einer Raumtemperatur
+ 32 °C zu einem Viertel ihres
inhalts mit 25 °C warmen Test-
ungen (ähnlich magerem Rind-
h) gefüllt und auf Gefrier-
ung so lange betrieben, bis die
ste Meßstelle – 18 °C erreicht
. Aus der dazu benötigten Zeit
der Menge der eingelegten
ungen errechneten wir die
erleistung je 100 Liter Nutz-
t in 24 Stunden. Erfreuliches
ltat: Alle Gefrierschränke la-
über der Norm-Anforderung
7 Kilogramm. Ergebnisse bis
ilogramm beurteilten wir mit
, die darüber lagen, mit »sehr

die Wärmeisolierung gab eine
eraturanstiegsprüfung Auf-
ß: Das Institut untersuchte,
chnell bei herausgezogenem
er die Schranktemperatur von
C auf – 15 °C anstieg. Dauerte
änger als 8,5 Stunden, nann-
vir die Isolierung »sehr gut«,
hen 8,5 und 6,5 Stunden
zwischen 6,5 und 5 Stunden
edenstellend«, unter 5 Stun-
weniger zufriedenstellend«.

inhalten der Lagertemperatur
18 °C bei maximal gefülltem
nk wurde jeweils bei Raum-
raturen von + 25 °C und
 an der wärmsten Meßstelle
t.

lessung des Norm-Energie-
uchs wurden die Gefrier-

schränke mit einer Reglerstellung
betrieben, bei der die Temperatur
an der wärmsten Testpackung
– 18 °C betrug. Vorgeschriebene
Temperatur im Prüfraum: + 25 °C.
Aus dem so gemessenen Verbrauch je 24 Stunden errechneten
wir den jeweiligen Verbrauch je
100 Liter Nutzinhalt, um zu einer
vergleichenden Bewertung zu kom-
men: »Extrem gering« nannten wir
den Verbrauch von nur 0,65 kWh
je 100 Liter Nutzraum in 24 Stunden. »Gering« heißt: Zwischen 0,9
und 1,2 kWh, »mittel« zwischen 1,2
und 1,5 kWh, »hoch« über 1,5
kWh.

Handhabung/Ausstattung:
Welche Kontrolleuchten besitzt der
Gefrierschrank? Und sind sie gut
zu erkennen? Lassen sich die Tempe-
raturregler und Schnellgefrierschal-
ter gut betätigen und ablesen?
Sind die Ablagen in der Höhe zu
verstellen und bei einer Türöffnung
von 90° herauszunehmen? Die
Antwort auf diese und andere Fra-
gen finden Sie in der nebenstehen-
den Tabelle. Dort ist in der Spalte
Technische Merkmale auch an-
gegeben, wieviel Liter gemessenen
Gesamtinhalt die Schränke haben
und wieviel in die einzelnen Fächer
oder Körbe hineingeht.

Technische Prüfung: Am stärk-
sten wurde die elektrische Sicher-
heit bewertet. Ebenfalls wichtig:
die Stabilität, das heißt Tragfähig-
keit der Ablagen, ermittelt durch
eine Belastungsprüfung. Um die
Güte der Lackierung festzustellen,
wurde eine Gitterschnittprüfung
durchgeführt. Auf dieser Grundlage
entstanden unsere Bewertungs-
gruppen. Unserem Urteil über die
Geräuschentwicklung lagen dB(A)-
Messungen zugrunde. An Hand der
Zahlenwerte über Einschalt-, Lauf-
und Ausschaltgeräusch konnten
wir die Gefrierschränke verglei-
chend bewerten.

TEST 157: GEFRIERSCHRANKE

		Bauknecht GK 250 250 l	BBC GS 270 270 l
ANGEBOT		Preis: 790 DM G. Bauknecht GmbH 7 Stuttgart	Preis: 750 DM Brown, Boveri & Cie. 68 Mannheim
	baugleich mit		AEG Arctis 271 GS Preis: 700 DM
TECHNISCHE MERKMALE	Prüf- und Schutzzeichen	ausländische	keine
	Gemessen. Gesamtinhalt (netto)	224 l	218 l
	Nutzbarer Inhalt der Fächer	202 l	211 l
	Nutzbare Abstellfläche	1,17 m²	0,95 m²
	Höhe × Breite × Tiefe	140 × 60 × 61 cm	138,5 × 60 × 61,5 cm
	Gewicht	64,5 kg	62,5 kg
	Länge der Zuleitung	170 cm	230 cm
	Zubehör	5 Einschubkorbe, 1 Thermometer, 2 Schlüssel	1 Einschubkorb, 1 Thermometer
TECHNISCHE PRÜFUNG	Elektr. Sicherheitsprüfungen	geringer Mangel¹)	bestanden
	Lackierung (Gitterschnittprüf.)	gut	zufriedenstellend
	Abdichtung der Tür	dicht	dicht
	Stabilität der Ablagen	gut	sehr gut
	Geräusch	etwas laut	weniger leise
	Mängel	–	Riß in der Tür des Vorgefrier- fachs bei Gefrierprüfung
HANDHABUNG/AUSSTATTUNG	Temperaturregler: Lage	Oberseite, hinten rechts	Vorderseite unten
	Betätigung	schwergängig, nicht griffig	gut (nur bei offener Tür)
	Ablesbarkeit	zufriedenstellend	gut (nur bei offener Tür)
	Schnellgefrierschalter: Lage	Vorderseite oben rechts	kombiniert mit Regler
	Betätigung	sehr gut	–
	Ablesbarkeit	gut	–
	Kontrolleuchten: Netz (N), Ge- frieren (G), Temperaturanstieg (T)	N, G, T	N, G, T
	Erkennbarkeit	sehr gut	gut
	Ablagen: Zahl/höhenverstellbar	6/0	5/0
	Herausnehmen b. 90° Türöffnung	möglich	möglich
	Fächer in der Tür	keine	keine
	Besondere Ausstattung	Vorgefrierfach	Vorgefrierfach, Anschluß Fernkontrolle
FUNKTIONSPRÜFUNG	Gefrierleistung in 24 Std.	24,2 kg	28,6 kg
	pro 100 l in 24 Std.	gut (10,8 kg)	sehr gut (13,1 kg)
	Wärmeisolierung	weniger zufriedenstellend	gut
	Temperaturanstieg von -18 auf -15 °C	4 Std., 33 Min.	6 Std., 30 Min.
	Verbrauch pro 100 l in 24 Std.	mittel (1,39 kWh)	gering (1,1 kWh)
	Gesamtverbrauch in 24 Std.	3,12 kWh	2,37 kWh
	Wärmste Meßstelle	am Boden	am Boden
	-18° C Lagertemperatur	eingehalten	nicht völlig eingehalten
GESAMT- EINDRUCK	Technische Prüfung	zufriedenstellend	zufriedenstellend
	Handhabung/Ausstattung	gut	gut
	Funktionsprüfung	zufriedenstellend	zufriedenstellend
	test-Qualitätsurteil:	ZUFRIEDENSTELLEND	ZUFRIEDENSTELLEND

¹) Berührungsschutz am Motor-
anschluß nicht ausreichend.

Appendix E

Frankfurt and Indianapolis Compared: A Statistical Compendium

The reasons for chosing Frankfurt and Indianapolis as metropolitan areas for our interview surveys in Germany and the United States, respectively, were explained in some detail in chapter 3. The purpose of this appendix is to provide some statistical background data of the two cities.

Except as indicated, the data for Indianapolis (see table E-1) are for 1970, the year in which the survey was made. The Frankfurt data are for the most part for the years 1968 and 1969 (see table E-2). It should be noted that the Frankfurt population, while increasing slightly over the decade 1959-1968, declined somewhat from its peak of 693,000 to the 1968 figure of 666,000. Frankfurt is still the seventh largest city in Germany, including West Berlin. Indianapolis is the eleventh largest city in the United States; it should be borne in mind that the United States has a greater number of large cities than Germany. Because of the decrease in Frankfurt's population, it is likely that the size of the labor force in table E-2 for 1961 (the latest year for which this figure was available), has also declined since then. For example, manufacturing employment in Frankfurt peaked at nearly 135,000 in 1965 and decreased to under 128,000 by 1968. The data sources are listed below.

Although politically Indianapolis has traditionally been somewhat more conservative than the average large American city, marketing research men have tended to look upon the city as representing Mid-America from a consumer behavior viewpoint.

References and Data Sources

Der Westdeutsche Markt in Zahlen (Frankfurt: DIVO-INMAR, GmbH., 1969).
Market Guide 1974 (New York: Editor and Publisher, 1974).
Statistisches Amt und Wahlamt, *Statistisches Jahrbach: Frankfurt am Main, 1969* (Frankfurt: Erich Imbescheidt KG., 1969).
United States Bureau of the Census, *Statistical Abstract of the United States: 1972* (Washington, D.C., 1972).

Table E-1.   Indianapolis: Selected Statistics

1. *Total Population (1970)*	792,000
population per square mile	11,302
percent population change 1960–1970	+13.6%
White population	655,000
as percent of total population	82.7%
Black population and other minorities	137,000
as percent of total population	17.3%
2. *Age Distribution (in percent of total population)*	
under 5 years of age	9%
5–17 years	30
18–64 years	52
65 years and over	9
Median age of population	27.3 years
3. *School Enrollment*	
Below high school (number of students)	146,700
High school	22,300
4. *Vital Statistics (per 1000)*	
Birth rate	18.6
Death rate	9.0
Marriage rate	10.7
5. *Health Statistics*	
Number of physicians	1,845
per 10,000 of population	16.6
Number of hospital beds	4,581
per 10,000 of population	41.3
Number of dentists	699
per 10,000 of population	6.3
6. *Family Income (Indianapolis SMSA)*	
Under $5,000	14%
$5,000–$9,999	30
$10,000–$14,999	32
$15,000 or more	24
Base: Total number of families	282,000
7. *Total Work Force (1970)*	478,000
Employment in non-agricultural payrolls (1971)	414,000
Of this: Manufacturing	29%
Wholesale and retail trades	23%
Government	17%
Average weekly earnings in manufacturing industries	$151
Unemployed as percent of total work force (1970)	4%
8. *Housing Statistics*	
Total number of housing units	252,000
Household occupied housing units	236,000
Of this: percent owner occupied	61%
percent lacking plumbing	3%
percent with more than one person per room	8%
Median value per single family unit	$14,800
Median monthly rent per housing unit	$96

Table E-1 continued

9. *Voting Patterns in 1968 General Elections*		*% majority party*
For President—number of votes	433,000	Republican 54.1
For Senator	352,000	Republican 55.3
For Governor	418,000	Republican 57.4
10. *Rates of Reported Crime per 10,000 Population (1971)*		
Total number of serious crimes	2,884	
Violent crimes:		
Murder and manslaughter	6.1	
Forcible rape	29.7	
Robbery	208.0	
Aggravated assault	109.0	
Property crimes:		
Burglary	1,248	
Auto Theft	518	
Larceny, $50 and over	765	

Table E-2. Frankfurt: Selected Statistics

1. *Total Population (1968)*	666,000
population per square mile	8,889
percent population change 1959–1968	+2%
German nationals	609,000
as percent of total population	91%
Foreign nationals	57,000
as percent of total population	9%

2. *Age Distribution (in percent of total population)*	
under 15 years of age	16%
15–24 years	13
25–44 years	30
45–64 years	27
65 years and over	14

3. *School Enrollment*		
Grund- and Hauptschulen	(grades 1 through 8)	38,038
Realschulen	(grades 4 through 10)	7,989
Gymnasien	(grades 4 through 13)	14,636

4. *Vital Statistics (per 1000)*	*Total*	*German Nationals*	*Foreign Nationals*
Birth Rate	12.2	11.4	21.6
Death rate	12.7	13.7	2.3
Marriage rate	9.0	8.7	12.6

5. *Health Statistics*	
Number of physicians	2,149
per 10,000 of population	32.1
Number of hospital beds	8,765
per 10,000 of population	130.8
Number of dentists	637
per 10,000 of population	9.5

(continued)

Table E-2 continued

---

6. *Family Income (Annual)**
   under 7,200 D-Mark   19%
   7,200–11,999 D-Mark   38
   12,000–17,999 D-Mark   24
   18,000 D-Mark or more   19

   *Average percentages for 4.18 million households
      in German cities with 500,000 or more population.
      Computed from monthly figures.

7. *Total Work Force (1961)*   486,500
   Employment in non-agricultural payrolls   484,600
   Of this: Manufacturing   34%
             Wholesale and retail trades   20%
             Government   7%
   Average weekly earnings in manufacturing
      industries (1968)   DM 243
   Total number of unemployed persons
      (December 1968)   1,696

8. *Housing Statistics*
   Total number of housing units   268,548
      number of rooms per unit (including kitchens)   3.52
      number of persons per unit   2.48
      number of persons per room   0.70
   Average new construction cost per housing unit
      (excluding cost of land)   DM 33,998

9. *Voting Patterns in 1969 General Elections*
   Number of eligible voters   462,580
   Number of actual voters   387,137
      percent voting for party:
         SPD (Social Democrats)   51%
         CDU (Christian Democrats)   35
         FDP (Free Democrats)   8
         others   6

10. *Rates of Reported Crimes per 100,000 Population*
    Number of serious crimes and minor offenses   8,065
    Violent crimes:
      Murder and manslaughter   1.5
      Attempted murder and manslaughter   2.5
      Forcible rape   9.2
      Robbery   59.7
      Aggravated assault   148.8
    Property crimes:
      Burglary   664
      Auto theft   719
      Grand larceny   874
      Petty larceny   3,142

Germany and the United States: Some Comparative Data

The purpose of this appendix is to provide the reader with some background material comparing Germany and the United States. Included here are only data which might serve to enrich the reader's understanding of the survey results by providing some environmental perspectives. These data are compiled from readily available sources—as pointed out in the Epilog, the going gets very slow when one tries to delve deeply into various aspects of the settings of social institutions on a comparative basis. Most of the statistical data cited here are for 1970, the year in which the surveys were made.

General Background

The United States, one of the largest land masses in the world (only the Soviet Union, Canada and China are larger), comprises a gross area of more than 3,165 million square miles; and its 1970 population of over 203 million ranked fourth in the world. By most standards, the United States is considered to be the wealthiest country in the world, the most technologically advanced, with the highest standard of living for the vast majority of its people.

With an area of nearly 96,000 square miles, the Federal Republic of Germany is slightly smaller than the state of Oregon and substantially smaller than half the state of Texas. On the other hand, it is two and one half times larger than the state of Indiana. With a total population of just under 61 million (1969), the population density of Germany is 635 people per square mile, making Germany one of the most densely populated countries in the world. This compares with a population density of 57 persons per square mile for all of the United States, a country with great regional variations in population density.

One of the consequences of the great population density in Germany is the fact that a large proportion of the German people live in large cities. Excluding their suburbs, 33 percent of the German population (38 percent of the households) reside in cities of 100,000 or more; and only 19 percent live in communities of under 2000. In a random national survey in Germany, then, one of three respondents would be residing in a large city.

Actually, due to massive waves of migration to the major population centers, the urban population of the United States is also very large, although it is proportionately much less than in Germany. About 28 percent of the American people live in cities of 100,000 or more; and over 34 percent reside in small communities of under 2,500 and in rural areas. It appears that, in a sense, the United States is less urbanized than Germany. Yet there are so many similarities between the two countries as well as subtle and not-so-subtle differences and contrasts that comparisons between them are both feasible and challenging. Here are a few highlights.

Economic and Political Conditions

On the economic front, Germany has made great strides in catching up with the United States. Starting from a much lower post-World War II base, economic growth in Germany has persistently been well above American. As a result, in 1970 the German Gross National Product per capita of $3,034 lagged relatively little behind the American per capita GNP of $4,734. It is still true that at the time of this study American consumers had had a richer experience of what may be called the durable-goods civilization than German. On the other hand, widespread poverty which seems to persist in ghettos across the United States is largely unknown in Germany. The relative absence of utter poverty in Germany is mostly due to cultural differences and the fact that the welfare state, compared to the United States, has a much longer history in Germany, going back at least to Bismarck's times.

Another consequence of the rapidly rising productivity and economic growth in Germany has been the consistently high employment level—at least compared to American standards. Only once since 1950, during the recession year of 1968, did unemployment slightly exceed 1 percent. In 1969–70 there was little concern with inflation in either country (next to "Ostpolitik" inflation was a modest issue in the German 1969 elections). The tightness in the German labor market has induced the German Federal Government to institute large-scale programs to stimulate the entry of foreign labor into the German economy during much of the 1960s and early 1970s. These injections of large numbers of foreign workers into the German society has inadvertently led to minority problems not entirely unlike those experienced by the United States during most of the 1950s and 1960s.

Constitutionally, the German system of federalism and government by representation is not unlike the American. But politically, the German people appear to be less active than the American, and more neutral if not docile. On the other hand, while extremists rocked American universities during the late '60s, the radical left made itself felt in similarly disruptive ways in Germany.

Most Western democracies have a mixed economy with what is at least in principle an open market system at the base. A basic similarity between Germany and the United States is that these countries—with Canada—stand out as placing greater emphasis on the maintenance of the open market system than do any of the other nations in this group. Indeed, there can hardly be any doubt that the German "economic miracle" of the last 25 years is due in large part to the postwar reorganization of the economy along open market lines. Erhard's liberal economic policies and the institution and vigorous enforcement of strong antitrust legislation laid the groundwork in this regard. It is characteristic that the coming into power of the Brandt government in the Fall of 1969 did not herald any shift in this basic outlook on the merits of competition and consumer choice.

Education and Attitudes toward Education

The German educational system differs from the American in terms of duration, entry and transfer points, and distinct lines of progression. And actually, the history of compulsory education is older in Germany than in the United States, again going back to the times of Bismarck and the Prussian domination of Germany. Despite these historical antecedents, Katona and others concluded from their studies that compared to Germans, Americans are more progressive and more favorably inclined in their attitude toward education for the masses of people.

Measured in number of official school years, Americans appear to be better educated on the average than Germans. The number of years of formal education is more than 9 years for the average German, but it is nearly 12 years for the average American. However, looking only at the number of years of formal education, one ignores intensity and quality. Often, for example, the German "Gymnasium" is erroneously equated with the American high school. In fact, the *Abitur* which is the capstone degree of the Gymnasium after 13 years of schooling is equivalent to one or two years in an American college. But the fact remains that in 1960 only 7 percent of German youth attained the *Abitur* and in 1968 only 5 percent of a representative sample of the German adult population had at least reached that degree. In the United States, in contrast, one-third of all youths in 1970 went to colleges or universities; in Germany about 8 percent.

Pressures for change are under way in Germany, particularly from the younger generation, who are turned away from the universities in large numbers because of the limited capacity of the system to accommodate them. The pressures for change are directed toward wide ranging reforms and modernization of higher education in which the German federal government would play a greater role. These reforms would entail, among other things, an increased number of universities, improved coordination between them, intermediate three-year degrees equivalent to the American bachelors degree, and a more streamlined hierarchical professional structure to increase the number of faculty. Given the leveling off or even long-term decline in enrollment in American colleges and universities with an opposite trend continuing in Germany, it is possible that the long-run outlook for education, attitudes toward education, and the average educational levels in the two countries will become increasingly similar.

Consumption Behavior

In the area of consumption behavior, particularly as it relates to expenditures for consumer durables and automobiles, we find differences between Germany and the United States which are not so much based on the ability to spend, but rather on cultural idiosyncracies. This is perhaps most evident in the attitudes toward consumer credit, best exemplified in the concepts of *Ansparen* and *Absparen* which reflect a deep-seated abhorrence of credit among Germans in general.

Ansparen, which represents a strong German trait, means to save funds well in advance of major durable purchases or other large expenditures. This national characteristic can be observed in the rate of savings, which averaged over 13 percent in Germany during 1955-1965 and which was 12 percent in the pre-recession year of 1967. The United States savings rate averaged 6 percent for the same period and was 7 percent in 1967.

Absparen, on the other hand, means to "save" after the purchase or expenditure has taken place by paying off the credit. Only 14 percent of German households have any kind of installment debt, excluding housing, but including the 6 percent of automobiles which are purchased on credit. In contrast, over 50 percent of all automobiles including used vehicles and 66 percent of new cars represent credit purchases in the United States.

Partly, at least, as a consequence of the different attitudes toward credit, the incidence of ownership of major durables and automobiles is substantially greater in the United States than in Germany. While most German households own the more common appliances (e.g., 88 percent own refrigerators and 80 percent television sets), the market penetration was very small for such "new" household goods as automatic dishwashers and clothes dryers (2 percent and 3 percent respectively of all German households). Similarly only 48 percent of German families owned at least one automobile in 1970, compared to 82 percent of American families. In addition, 28 percent of United States households owned two or more cars, while second car ownership in Germany was negligible.

As a consumer, then, the typical German is likely to be more conservative than his American counterpart, despite the fact that he earns not much less. This conservatism may reflect a degree of uncertainty, if not pessimism, concerning the future outlook for the "good" life, attained through hard work and personal sacrifice, and whether or not it will last. On the whole, the typical American would tend to be more optimistic than the German, and in general would not seem to share the latter's great anxiety about such dismal prospects as unemployment and inflation.

This brief summary is merely suggestive of national-cultural differences between Germany and the United States. Obviously, the depth with which such a country-by-country comparison could be continued is virtually limitless. The statistical tables which follow are intended to give further comparative insights into German and American characteristics. For the most part they are based on the 1972 editions of the statistical yearbooks, containing data for 1970, the year of our surveys. Additional references are given at the end of the appendix.

Table F-1. Comparative Statistics: United States and Germany— Area and Population

	United States	Germany
Gross area (land and water) in square miles	3,615,191	95,742
Total population (in 1000)	204,800	60,600
Average number of persons/square mile	57	635
Number and size of cities over 100,000 inhabitants:		
1,000,000 or more	6	3
500,000 to 1,000,000	20	8
250,000 to 500,000	30	10
100,000 to 250,000	100	37
Total number of occupied dwellings (in 1000)	63,417	19,347
Percent with piped water	94.0%	99.0%
Percent with electric lighting	NA	99.0%
Number of households (in 1000)	62,874	21,980
Persons per household	3.23	2.77

Table F-2. Comparative Statistics: United States and Germany— Economic Data

	United States	Germany
Gross National Product (GNP) (in million $)	974.1	186.4
Per Capita GNP	$4734	$3034
Average annual growth rate of GNP (1965-1970)	3.3%	4.7%
Per Capita growth rate of GNP (1965-1970)	2.3%	4.0%
Labor force (in 1000)	82,715	26,630
Percent unemployed	4.9%	0.5%
Index of average hourly earnings of manufacturing workers (1967 = 100)	118.7	130.2
Index of real hourly earnings (1967 = 100)	102.1	116.7
Consumer price index (1967 = 100)	116.3	108.2
Industrial production index (1963 = 100) for 1971	139	156
Number of motor vehicles in use (in 1000)	106,819	14,516
Railway passenger miles (in millions)	10,770	23,692
Radio receiving sets (in 1000)	290,000	19,622
Television receiving sets (in 1000)	84,600	16,750

Table F-3. Comparative Statistics: United States and Germany— Health and Education

	United States	*Germany*
Birth rate (number of live births per 1000)	18.2	13.3
Death rate (number of deaths per 1000)	9.4	11.7
Infant mortality (deaths of infants under 1 year per 1000 live births)	19.8	23.6
Number of hospitals	7,144	3,601
Number of hospital beds (in 1000)	1,649.7	677.7
Number of physicians	302,966	103,410
Persons per physician	700	600
Number of dentists	101,874	31,177
Persons per dentist	2,000	2,000
Education–primary level (excludes kindergarten)		
Number of teachers (in 1000)	1,269	232
Number of students (in 1000)	31,955	6,098
Number of teachers per 10,000 population	62	39
Students enrolled as percent of estimated population aged 5–13	96.8[a]	87.1[b]
Education–secondary level		
Number of teachers (in 1000)	994	254
Number of students (in 1000)	19,674	4,281
Number of teachers per 10,000 population	49	42
Students enrolled as percent of estimated population aged 14–17	94.1	90.6[c]
Education–third level (college and university)		
Number of faculty (in 1000)	559	NA
Number of students enrolled for degree credit (in 1000)	7,484	288
Number of faculty per 10,000 population	27	NA
Students enrolled as percent of estimated population aged 18–24	33.3%	7.9%
Public expenditure for education (in million)	$59,500	$5,472
as percent of GNP	6.3%	3.6%
Book production (first editions, reissues, and translations)	79,530	45,369
Daily Newspapers		
Number	1,773	1,093
Total circulation (in 1000)	62,108	19,701
Copies per 1000 population	302	319

[a]includes kindergarten

[b]estimated population aged 6–13

[c]estimated population aged 14–19

Table F-4.   Comparative Statistics: United States and Germany Demographic Data (In percent)

Family Income (Annual)

United States		Germany[a]	
under $5,000	19%	under 7,200 D-Mark	21%
$5,000–9,999	32	7,200–11,999 D-Mark	38
$10,000–14,999	27	12,000–17,999 D-Mark	25
$15,000 and over	22	18,000 D-Mark and over	15

Education (years)

United States		Germany	
16 years or more	11%	13 years or more[b]	5%
13–15 years	10	11–12 years[c]	17
12 years	34	9–10 years[d]	43
9–11 years	17	Less than 9 years[e]	32
Less than 9 years	28		

Occupation (in percent of working population)

United States		Germany	
Professional and Technical	15%	Professional and Technical	NA[f]
Managers, Officials, Pro-		Managers, Officials, Pro-	
prietors	11	prietors	24%
Clerical	18	Minor Officials and Salaried	
Sales	7	Employees	21
Craftsmen and Foremen	13	Craftsmen and Foremen	26
Operators, Service Workers		Operators, Service Workers	
Laborers, Farm Workers	36	Laborers, Farm Workers	20
Retired, not classified	NA	Retired, not classified	9

Age Distribution

	United States	Germany
under 25 years of age	46%	36%
25–34 years	12	15
35–44 years	11	13
45–54 years	12	11
55–64 years	9	12
65 years and over	10	13

Family Status, Sex (population over 14 years of age)

	Male	Female	Male	Female
Married	75%	69%	75%	63%
Single	19	14	20	14
Widowed/Divorced	6	17	5	22

[a]Incomes for Germany computed from monthly figures. The exchange rate at the time of the study was DM 3.65 to U.S. $1.

[b]*Abitur* degree/University

[c]*Mittel-* or *Realschule*

[d]Primary school (*Grund-* and *Hauptschule*) with formal apprenticeship/vocational school

[e]Primary school without apprenticeship

[f]Category included in "Managers, Officials, Proprietors."

References and Data Sources

Ralf Dahrendorf, *Gesellschaft und Demokratie in Deutschland* (Munich: R. Piper, 1968).

Der Deutsche Markt in Zahlen (Frankfurt: DIVO-INMAR GmbH., 1969).

Frederick Harbison and Charles A. Myers, *Education, Manpower and Economic Growth: Strategies of Human Resource Development* (New York: McGraw-Hill, 1964).

George Katona, Burkhard Strumpel, and Ernest Zahn, *Aspirations and Affluence— Comparative Studies in the United States and Western Europe* (New York: McGraw-Hill, 1971).

Statistisches Bundesamt, *Statistisches Taschenbuch fuer die Bundesrepublik Deutschland, 1970* (Stuttgart: W. Kohlhammer Verlag GmbH., 1970).

United States Bureau of the Census, *Statistical Abstract of the United States: 1972* (Washington, D.C., 1972).

Appendix G

United States Questionnaire and List of Durable and Convenience Goods in German Questionnaire

INTRODUCTORY REMARKS

Thank you for agreeing to help us. This interview is part of what we think is an important study being carried out in several different countries by Indiana University. We will ask for your opinions on a variety of different subjects, as well as some information about how you buy things. Since we are interviewing only a limited number of people in each country, your answers are important to us, so please answer carefully and don't hesitate to ask questions if the questions or procedures are not clear. Now . . .

<u>Section 1</u>

HERE IS A GROUP OF STATEMENTS ABOUT SOME DIFFERENT THINGS OF INTEREST.
WE WOULD LIKE TO KNOW IF YOU AGREE OR DISAGREE WITH EACH STATEMENT, AND HOW
STRONGLY.

PLEASE PUT A CIRCLE AROUND THE NUMBER WHICH COMES CLOSEST TO GIVING YOUR
OPINION. THIS METHOD WILL BE USED TO MARK MOST OF YOUR ANSWERS AS YOU GO
THROUGH THIS QUESTIONNAIRE.

```
1 = Strongly agree
2 = Agree
3 = Neither agree nor disagree
4 = Disagree
5 = Strongly disagree
```

card #1
cc

1. I enjoy planning work carefully before carrying it out. 1 2 3 4 5 (14)

2. The government has too much control over business. 1 2 3 4 5 (15)

3. I don't usually like to see how other people like new brands before I try them. 1 2 3 4 5 (16)

4. When I am in a group that is discussing a problem, I seldom influence the solution or action that is adopted. 1 2 3 4 5 (17)

5. Students should have more power in university affairs than they do now. 1 2 3 4 5 (18)

6. Business has too much influence on government decisions. 1 2 3 4 5 (19)

7. I find it hard to judge quality differences between many brands of the same product. 1 2 3 4 5 (20)

8. Businessmen in general are as honest as other people. 1 2 3 4 5 (21)

9. I am better than the average shopper in getting value for money. 1 2 3 4 5 (22)

10. You can't change human nature. 1 2 3 4 5 (23)

11. I am less likely to be asked advice about product purchases than most of my friends. 1 2 3 4 5 (24)

12. Business does not perform the job of providing good products at reasonable prices very well. 1 2 3 4 5 (25)

13. Public welfare programs do not tend to make people work less hard than they should. 1 2 3 4 5 (26)

14. When a new product is adopted among my circle of friends, I am not usually one of the first persons to buy it. 1 2 3 4 5 (27)

Section 2

1. **HERE** IS A LIST OF MAJOR PRODUCTS. WE WOULD LIKE TO KNOW WHICH ONES YOU OWN, WHAT BRANDS, AND FOR SOME, WHAT TYPE. JUST GO THROUGH THE TABLE, CIRCLING 1 OR 2 FOR OWN OR NOT. IF OWNED, FILL IN BRAND, CIRCLE TYPE (IF ASKED), AND PUT DOWN YEAR. ADD MONTH (1-12) IF IN '68 OR '69. (ONLY LATEST PURCHASE OF EACH ITEM.)

card #21

	Own Yes No	Brand	Type	When Purchased Year	Mo. (if 68-69
Refrigerator	1　2 (10)	(11-12)	Top-freeze 1 Bot-freeze 2 Side-Side 3 (13)	(14-15)	(16-17)
Automatic Clothes Washer	1　2 (19)	(20-21)		(22-23)	(24-25)
Television-Color	1　2 (27)	(28-29)	Portable 1 Console 2 (30)	(31-32)	(33-34)
Television-Black-White	1　2 (36)	(37-38)	Portable 1 Console 2 (39)	(40-41)	(42-43)
Clothes Dryer	1　2 (45)	(46-47)	Gas 1 Electric 2 (48)	(49-50)	(51-52)
Kitchen Range	1　2 (54)	(55-56)	Gas 1 Electric 2 (57)	(58-59)	(60-61)
Dishwasher	1　2 (63)	(64-65)	(66)	(67-68)	(69-70)
Sewing Machine	1　2 (71)	(72-73)	Zig-Zag 1 Straight 2 (74)	(75-76)	(77-78) Begin Cd.
Typewriter	1　2 (11)	(12-13)	Manual 1 Electric 2 (14)	(15-16)	(17-18)
Rotary Power Mower	1　2 (20)	(21-22)		(23-24)	(25-26)
Room Air Conditioner	1　2 (28)	(29-30)	7000BTU&less 1 Morethan7000 2 (31)	(32-33)	(34-35)
Movie Camera	1　2 (37)	(38-39)		(40-41)	(42-43)
Home Freezer	1　2 (46)	(47-48)	Upright 1 Chest 2 (49)	(50-51)	(52-53)
Outboard Motor	1　2 (55)	(56-57)	40-50 H.P. 1 28-35 H.P. 2 Other 3 (58)	(59-60)	(61-62)
Stereo Receiver	1　2 (64)	(65-66)		(67-68)	(69-70)

If you have purchased <u>none</u> of the above in the last 2 years, is there some other **new item** costing between $100 and $1000 which you have bought in that time?

Other	1　2 (72)	(73-74)		(76-77)	(78-79)

LOOKING BACK TO THE TABLE WHICH YOU JUST COMPLETED -- IF YOU HAVE LISTED
NO NEW PRODUCTS IN THE LAST 2 YEARS, YOU MAY SKIP TO SECTION 3.

OTHERWISE, PLEASE PRINT IN THE BLANK TO THE RIGHT YOUR MOST RECENT PURCHASE
AMONG THOSE MADE IN THE LAST 2 YEARS.

LATEST PURCHASE_____   (10)

WE WOULD LIKE TO FIND OUT A BIT ABOUT HOW YOU BOUGHT THIS NEW _____
(LATEST PRODUCT PURCHASED), SO ALL OF THE REST OF THE QUESTIONS IN THIS
SECTION ASK YOU TO RECALL THINGS ABOUT THIS PARTICULAR PURCHASE.

2. How much planning did you or your family do for this purchase?

Planned very carefully for a long time.	1
Planned quite a bit.	2 (11)
Some planning.	3
Not much planning.	4
No planning at all--just saw it and bought it.	5
Don't know or can't remember	6

3. How many times would you say you have purchased a new _____?

First time we have owned or purchased one.	1
First time we have owned new one; but have owned one before.	2 (12)
This is the second time we have purchased a new one.	3
This was at least the third new one which we have purchased.	4
Don't know or can't remember.	5

4. Thinking back specifically to your experience in shopping for your
    _____, please tell us how important you considered the
    following items as you shopped:

                      1 = Very important - critical
                      2 = Rather important
                      3 = Neither important nor unimportant
                      4 = Rather unimportant
                      5 = Unimportant - not considered

a.	Styling of Product (make)	1	2	3	4	5	(14)
b.	Brand's General Reputation	1	2	3	4	5	(15)
c.	Price and/or Trade-in Allowance	1	2	3	4	5	(16)
d.	Performance of Product (make)	1	2	3	4	5	(17)
e.	Availability of Information about product (make)	1	2	3	4	5	(18)
f.	Durability	1	2	3	4	5	(19)
g.	Location of Dealer	1	2	3	4	5	(20)
h.	Availability (in stock for immediate inspection or delivery)	1	2	3	4	5	(21)
i.	Service after Purchase	1	2	3	4	5	(22)
j.	Warranty	1	2	3	4	5	(23)
k.	Credit Terms Available	1	2	3	4	5	(24)
l.	Reputation of Dealer	1	2	3	4	5	(25)
m.	Economy of Operation of Product	1	2	3	4	5	(26)

5. What sources of information did you use as you considered buying your
    _____? How did you find out the things you wanted to know?

                    1 = Very important - critical
                    2 = Rather important
                    3 = Neither important nor unimportant
                    4 = Rather unimportant
                    5 = Very unimportant - not considered

a.	Past Experience (use)	1	2	3	4	5	(28)
b.	Salesman	1	2	3	4	5	(29)
c.	Advertising	1	2	3	4	5	(30)
d.	Friend, Relative or Acquaintance	1	2	3	4	5	(31)
e.	Consumer Reports	1	2	3	4	5	(32)
f.	Other Consumer Magazine (specify)						
	_____	1	2	3	4	5	(33)
g.	Other Magazine or Newspaper Article	1	2	3	4	5	(34)
h.	Personal Observation and Examination	1	2	3	4	5	(35)
i.	Other information source (specify)						
	_____	1	2	3	4	5	(36)

6. How many stores did you visit specifically shopping for your _____?

        None (Purchased by mail, phone, or other).   1
        Only the store where purchased.   2
        The store where purchased and one other.   3   (38)
        The store where purchased and several others.   4
        Visited other stores, but purchased by mail or phone.   5
        Don't know or can't remember   6

7. How would you rate your part in the family's decision to make
    this purchase?

        Made the decision entirely by myself.   1
        I was most important, but someone else helped.   2
        I shared the decision about equally with someone else.   3   (39)
        Others were important, but I helped.   4
        Someone else made the decision entirely.   5
        No opinion or can't remember.   6

HERE IS A GROUP OF STATEMENTS WHICH HAVE TO DO WITH THE BUYING AND USE OF
YOUR _____. PLEASE CIRCLE THE NUMBER WHICH COMES CLOSEST TO
GIVING YOUR OPINION ON EACH STATEMENT.

1 = Strongly agree
2 = Agree
3 = Neither agree nor disagree
4 = Disagree
5 = Strongly disagree

card #2
cc

8.	Compared to most purchases I make, I spent more time and effort on this one.	1 2 3 4 5	(42)
9.	This brand is not safe to use.	1 2 3 4 5	(43)
10.	I had little trouble finding out how one brand differed from another while shopping.	1 2 3 4 5	(44)
11.	Advertising for this product was not very accurate or helpful.	1 2 3 4 5	(45)
12.	The brand which I purchased has turned out to be all I expected when I bought it.	1 2 3 4 5	(46)
13.	I had plenty of information available to help me pick the brand which suited my needs.	1 2 3 4 5	(47)
14.	I worried a great deal about making this purchase just right, since a mistake would have been quite upsetting.	1 2 3 4 5	(48)
15.	I would certainly not recommend this brand to a friend with needs similar to mine.	1 2 3 4 5	(49)
16.	Even if I had taken the time to get more information, I probably could not have found a more suitable brand.	1 2 3 4 5	(50)
17.	I probably did not shop enough to get the lowest price on this purchase.	1 2 3 4 5	(51)

Section 3

NOW WE WOULD LIKE TO FIND OUT ABOUT ANY AUTOS WHICH YOUR FAMILY OWNS AND
HOW YOU WENT ABOUT BUYING THE LATEST ONE. PLEASE COMPLETE THE TABLE FOR ALL
AUTOS OWNED, CIRCLE THE RIGHT RESPONSE UNDER BODY AND ENGINE, AND PRINT THE
OTHER INFORMATION. (DO NOT INCLUDE LEASED OR BORROWED CARS, COMPANY CARS, ETC.)
IF NO AUTOS OWNED NOW, PUT "NONE" IN 1a BELOW AND SKIP TO SECTION 4.

card #31

1. MAKE	MODEL	MOD YR.	BODY WAGON	OTHER	ENGINE 4	6	8	PURCHASED MO.	YR.
a (10-11)	(12-13)	(14-15)	1 (16)	2	1	2 (17)	3	(18-19)	(20-2
b (23-24)	(25-26)	(27-28)	1 (29)	2	1	2 (30)	3	(31-32)	(33-3
c (36-37)	(38-39)	(40-41)	1 (42)	2	1	2 (43)	3	(44-45)	(46-4
d (49-50)	(51-52)	(53-54)	1 (55)	2	1	2 (56)	3	(57-58)	(59-6

card #3
cc

PLEASE PRINT IN THE BLANK TO THE RIGHT THE
MAKE OF THE MOST RECENT CAR BOUGHT _____ (10)

2. How much planning did you or your family do for this purchase?

Planned very carefully for a long time.	1	
Planned quite a bit.	2	
Some planning.	3	(11)
Not much planning.	4	
No planning at all - just saw it and bought it.	5	
Don't know or can't remember.	6	

3. Including any listed above, about how many autos has your household
owned altogether?

None	1	
1	2	(12)
2-3	3	
4-6	4	
7 or more	5	

4. Thinking back specifically to your experience in shopping for your
   _____, please tell us how important you considered the
   following items as you shopped:

   1 = Very important - critical
   2 = Rather important
   3 = Neither important nor unimportant
   4 = Rather unimportant
   5 = Very unimportant - not considered

   <u>card #3</u>
   cc

a.	Styling of Product (make)	1	2	3	4	5	(14)
b.	Brand's General Reputation	1	2	3	4	5	(15)
c.	Price and/or Trade-in Allowance	1	2	3	4	5	(16)
d.	Performance of Product (make)	1	2	3	4	5	(17)
e.	Availability of Information about Product (make)	1	2	3	4	5	(18)
f.	Durability	1	2	3	4	5	(19)
g.	Location of Dealer	1	2	3	4	5	(20)
h.	Availability (in stock for immediate inspection or delivery)	1	2	3	4	5	(21)
i.	Service after Purchase	1	2	3	4	5	(22)
j.	Warranty	1	2	3	4	5	(23)
k.	Credit Terms Available	1	2	3	4	5	(24)
l.	Reputation of Dealer	1	2	3	4	5	(25)
m.	Economy of Operation of Product	1	2	3	4	5	(26)

5. What sources in information did you use as you considered buying your
   _____? How did you find out the things you wanted to know?

   1 = Very important - critical
   2 = Rather important
   3 = Neither important nor unimportant
   4 = Rather unimportant
   5 = Very unimportant - not considered

a.	Past Experience (use)	1	2	3	4	5	(28)
b.	Salesman	1	2	3	4	5	(29)
c.	Advertising	1	2	3	4	5	(30)
d.	Friend, Relative or Aquaintance	1	2	3	4	5	(31)
e.	Consumer Reports	1	2	3	4	5	(32)
f.	Other Consumer Magazine (specify)						
	_____	1	2	3	4	5	(33)
g.	Other Magazine or Newspaper Article	1	2	3	4	5	(34)
h.	Personal Observation & Examination	1	2	3	4	5	(35)
i.	Other Information Source (specify)						
	_____	1	2	3	4	5	(36)

6. How many dealers did you visit before buying this car?

None--purchased from private owner	1	
One dealer--where purchased	2	
Two dealers	3	(38)
Several dealers	4	
Purchased from individual but visited dealers	5	
Don't know or Can't remember	6	

7. How would you rate your part in the family's decision to buy this car?

Made the decision entirely by myself.	1
I was most important, but someone else helped.	2
I shared the decision about equally with someone else.	3 (39)
Others were important, but I helped.	4
Someone else made the decision entirely.	5
No opinion or can't remember.	6

HERE IS A GROUP OF STATEMENTS WHICH HAVE TO DO WITH THE BUYING AND USE OF THIS PARTICULAR AUTO. PLEASE CIRCLE THE NUMBER WHICH COMES CLOSEST TO GIVING YOUR OPINION ON EACH STATEMENT.

```
1 = Strongly agree
2 = Agree
3 = Neither agree nor disagree
4 = Disagree
5 = Strongly disagree
```

8. Compared to most purchases I make, I spent more time and effort on this one.　1　2　3　4　5　(42)

9. This auto is not safe.　1　2　3　4　5　(43)

10. I had little trouble finding out how one make differed from another while shopping.　1　2　3　4　5　(44)

11. Advertising for autos was not very accurate or helpful.　1　2　3　4　5　(45)

12. The car which I purchased has turned out to be all I expected when I bought it.　1　2　3　4　5　(46)

13. I had plenty of information available to help me pick the make and model which suited my needs.　1　2　3　4　5　(47)

14. I worried a great deal about making this purchase just right, since a mistake would have been quite upsetting.　1　2　3　4　5　(48)

15. I would certainly not recommend this car to a friend with needs similar to mine.　1　2　3　4　5　(49)

16. Even if I had taken the time to get more information, I probably could not have found a more suitable make and model.　1　2　3　4　5　(50)

17. I probably did not shop enough to get the lowest price on this purchase.　1　2　3　4　5　(51)

Section 4

1. HERE IS A LIST OF COMMON PRODUCTS. WE WOULD LIKE TO KNOW WHICH ONES YOU
    BUY FAIRLY REGULARLY AND WHAT BRAND YOU WOULD PURCHASE IF YOU WERE TO GO
    SHOPPING RIGHT NOW FOR THOSE FREQUENTLY PURCHASED ITEMS. PLEASE CIRCLE
    1 FOR YES, IF YOU - PERSONALLY - BUY THE ITEM AT LEAST EVERY SIX MONTHS,
    AND PRINT THE BRAND YOU WOULD BUY IF YOU WERE TO GO SHOPPING RIGHT NOW.
    LEAVE "LAST PRODUCT PURCHASED" BLANK FOR NOW.

card #41

PRODUCT	FREQUENT PURCHASE YES NO	BRAND WOULD PURCHASE	LAST PRODUCT PURCHASED
a. Dish Detergent	1 2 (10)	(11-12)	1 (13)
b. Hand Lotion	1 2 (14)	(15-16)	1 (17)
c. Hair Shampoo	1 2 (18)	(19-20)	1 (21)
d. Floor Wax	1 2 (22)	(23-24)	1 (25)
e. Beer	1 2 (26)	(27-28)	1 (29)
f. Frozen Fruit Pie	1 2 (30)	(31-32)	1 (33)
g. Tennis Balls	1 2 (34)	(35-36)	1 (37)
h. Auto Cleaner--Polish	1 2 (38)	(39-40)	1 (41)
i. Paper Towels	1 2 (42)	(43-44)	1 (45)
j. Insect Repellent	1 2 (46)	(47-48)	1 (49)
k. Bourbon	1 2 (50)	(51-52)	1 (53)
l. Suntan Preparation	1 2 (54)	(55-56)	1 (57)
m. Furniture Polish	1 2 (58)	(59-60)	1 (61)
n. Hair Spray	1 2 (62)	(63-64)	1 (65)
o. Fabric Softener	1 2 (66)	(67-68)	1 (69)

2. LOOKING BACK OVER THE LIST, WHICH PRODUCT DID YOU BUY THE MOST RECENTLY?
    PLEASE CIRCLE THE 1 UNDER "LAST PRODUCT PURCHASED" FOR THAT PRODUCT ONLY.
    IF SEVERAL ITEMS "PURCHASED LAST," CIRCLE THE 1 FOR THE PRODUCT CLOSEST
    TO THE TOP OF THE PAGE.

AS BEFORE, ALL THE REST OF THIS SECTION WILL ASK ABOUT THE LATEST PURCHASE OF
THE PRODUCT FOR WHICH YOU CIRCLED "1" IN THE TABLE ON THE LAST PAGE.

card #4

cc

3. What brand of _____ did you buy? _____ (10-11)

4. Had you bought this brand before?

Yes--frequently	1	
Yes--occasionally	2	(12)
No	3	
Can't remember	4	

HERE ARE SOME STATEMENTS ABOUT YOUR PURCHASE OF A _____ .
PLEASE CIRCLE THE ANSWER WHICH COMES CLOSEST TO GIVING YOUR OPINION ON
EACH STATEMENT.

1 = Strongly agree
2 = Agree
3 = Neither agree nor disagree
4 = Disagree
5 = Strongly disagree

5. Compared to most small purchases I make, I spent
    more time and effort on this one.   1 2 3 4 5   (42)

6. This brand is not safe to use.   1 2 3 4 5   (43)

7. I had little trouble finding out how one brand
    differed from another while shopping.   1 2 3 4 5   (44)

8. Advertising for this product was not very
    accurate or helpful.   1 2 3 4 5   (45)

9. The brand which I purchased has turned out to be
    all I expected when I bought it.   1 2 3 4 5   (46)

10. I had plenty of information available to help
    me pick the brand which suited my needs.   1 2 3 4 5   (47)

11. I worried a great deal about making this purchase
    just right, since a mistake would have been quite
    upsetting.   1 2 3 4 5   (48)

12. I would certainly not recommend this brand to a
    friend with needs similar to mine.   1 2 3 4 5   (49)

13. Even if I had taken the time to get more infor-
    mation, I could probably not have found a more
    suitable brand.   1 2 3 4 5   (50)

14. I probably did not shop enough to get the lowest
    price on this purchase.   1 2 3 4 5   (51)

Section 5

THANK YOU FOR STICKING WITH US. WE ARE MOVING DOWNHILL.
NOW WE WOULD LIKE YOU TO ANSWER SOME QUESTIONS ABOUT MAGAZINES, TV AND RADIO.

1. a.   How much would you say you watch TV?
    b.   "   "   "   "   "   "   listen to the radio?   card #5

	TV		Radio	
Never	1		1	
Less than 2 hrs/week	2		2	
2 - 6 hrs/week	3		3	
6 - 12 hrs/week	4	(10)	4	(11)
12 - 18 hrs/week	5		5	
18 - 24 hrs/week	6		6	
More than 24 hrs/week	7		7	

2. a.   When you watch TV, do you pay attention to the commercials?
    b.   "   "   listen to radio, do you pay attention to the commercials?

CIRCLE THE NUMBER WHICH COMES CLOSEST TO YOUR AVERAGE:

	TV		Radio	
Almost none of them	1		1	
A few of them	2		2	
Many of them	3	(12)	3	(13)
Almost all of them	4		4	

THE TABLE BELOW LISTS SEVERAL MAGAZINES. PLEASE CIRCLE THE NUMBER THAT BEST
DESCRIBES HOW MUCH YOU READ EACH ONE, THEN INDICATE IF YOU ARE A SUBSCRIBER OR
NOT BY CIRCLING 1 FOR YES AND 2 FOR NO.

3.   card #5

MAGAZINE	NEVER	OCCASIONALLY	REGULARLY--ALMOST EVERY ISSUE	YES	NO
		HOW OFTEN READ?		SUBSCRIBE?	
a. Reader's Digest	1	2	3 (15)	1	2 (16)
b. Atlantic Monthly	1	2 (18)	3	1	2 (19)
c. TV Guide	1	2 (21)	3	1	2 (22)
d. Woman's Day	1	2 (24)	3	1	2 (25)
e. Playboy	1	2 (27)	3	1	2 (28)
f. Consumer Reports	1	2 (30)	3	1	2 (31)
g. Family Circle	1	2 (33)	3	1	2 (34)
h. Life	1	2 (36)	3	1	2 (37)
i. Good Housekeeping	1	2 (39)	3	1	2 (40)
j. New Yorker	1	2 (42)	3	1	2 (43)
k. Modern Romance	1	2 (45)	3	1	2 (46)
l. Mechanics Illust.	1	2 (48)	3	1	2 (49)

4. How many newspapers do you read each day? _____   (51)

5. a. In reading the newspaper, do you also read the advertisements?
    b. What about in reading magazines, do you also read the ads?

     CIRCLE THE NUMBER THAT COMES CLOSEST TO YOUR AVERAGE:

	Newspaper		Magazines	
Almost none of them	1		1	
A few of them	2		2	
Many of them	3	(52)	3	(53)
Almost all of them	4		4	

6. On the whole, would you say that your attitude about advertising was favorable or unfavorable?

Strongly favorable	1
Favorable	2
Slightly favorable	3
Neither favorable nor unfavorable	4
Slightly unfavorable	5
Unfavorable	6
Strongly unfavorable	7
No opinion	8

(54)

HERE IS ANOTHER SERIES OF STATEMENTS -- THIS TIME ABOUT ADVERTISING. AGAIN -- PLEASE CIRCLE THE ANSWER THAT COMES CLOSEST TO YOUR OPINION.

1 = Strongly agree
2 = Agree
3 = Neither agree nor disagree
4 = Disagree
5 = Strongly disagree

7. Advertising is essential   1   2   3   4   5   (56)
8. Most advertising insults the intelligence of the average consumer   1   2   3   4   5   (57)
9. In general, advertising results in lower prices   1   2   3   4   5   (58)
10. Advertising often persuades people to buy things they shouldn't buy   1   2   3   4   5   (59)
11. In general, advertisements present a true picture of products advertised   1   2   3   4   5   (60)
12. Advertising helps raise our standard of living   1   2   3   4   5   (61)
13. Advertising results in better products for the public   1   2   3   4   5   (62)
14. Considering advertisements themselves, in your own experience would you say that today's standards of advertising are higher, lower, or about the same, compared with ten years ago?

Higher	1
Lower	2
About the same	3
No opinion	4

(63)

Section 6

WE ARE NEARING THE END. BE CAREFUL IN THIS SECTION--WE KEEP TELLING YOU TO SKIP HERE OR SKIP THERE, BUT IT'S EASY IF YOU READ THE BIG PRINT.

1. HERE ARE SOME THINGS THAT HAVE BEEN SUGGESTED AS WAYS OF HELPING THE CONSUMER. WE WOULD LIKE FOR YOU TO TELL US WHICH OF THESE YOU WOULD LIKE TO SEE MORE OF. PLEASE RANK AS MANY AS YOU WISH. "1" IS THE ACTIVITY YOU ARE MOST ANXIOUS TO SEE MORE OF, "2" NEXT, ETC. IF YOU HAVE NO WISH TO INCREASE ANY OF THESE ACTIVITIES, GIVE "NO INCREASE IN ANY" AS YOUR FIRST AND ONLY CHOICE.

card #6

Rank

a. Consumer education in our schools _____ (10)

b. Product information labeling (as on new cars, some textiles, drugs) _____ (11)

c. Product testing and reporting to the public _____ (12)

d. Preventing misleading advertising _____ (13)

e. Consumer protection (auto safety, health warnings on cigarette packages, etc.) _____ (14)

f. Helping consumers who have complaints about products or services _____ (15)

g. Establishing minimum quality standards for products _____ (16)

h. No increase in any of the above _____ (17)

2. LOOKING AGAIN AT THE LIST, WE WOULD LIKE TO KNOW HOW STRONG A PART GOVERNMENT SHOULD PLAY IN EACH OF THESE AREAS. PLEASE CIRCLE THE NUMBER THAT COMES CLOSEST TO YOUR OPINION ON EACH ACTIVITY LISTED.

1 = Government doing too little now
2 = Government doing right amount now
3 = Government doing too much now
4 = Don't know--no strong opinion

a. Consumer education in our schools   1   2   3   4   (19)

b. Product information labeling (as on new cars, some textiles, drugs)   1   2   3   4   (20)

c. Product testing and reporting to the public   1   2   3   4   (21)

d. Preventing misleading advertising   1   2   3   4   (22)

e. Consumer protection (auto safety, health warnings on cigarette packages, etc.)   1   2   3   4   (23)

f. Helping consumers who have complaints about products or services   1   2   3   4   (24)

g. Establishing minimum quality standards for products   1   2   3   4   (25)

Have you ever heard of comparative product testing?

Yes__1__   No__2__   Don't Know__3__   (26)

COMPARATIVE PRODUCT TESTING IS WHEN SOMEONE TESTS SEVERAL BRANDS OF THE SAME PRODUCT AND COMPARES THE DIFFERENT BRANDS, USUALLY ON OVERALL PERFORMANCE AND QUALITY, AS WELL AS ON SPECIFIC FEATURES.

3.   Can you name any magazines or other places where you can read about such tests?

Consumer Reports	(27)
Consumer Research Bulletin	(28)
Other (specify)	(29)
No, cannot name any	(30)

4.   Suppose that you had the results of some comparative product tests available. How would you compare them with advertising as a way of deciding which products to buy? Circle the response closest to your opinions.

        1 = Strongly agree
        2 = Agree
        3 = Neither agree nor disagree
        4 = Disagree
        5 = Strongly disagree
        6 = Don't know or No Opinion

Compared to advertising, product testing:

a. . . is more trustworthy	1	2	3	4	5	6	(32)
b. . . is less informative	1	2	3	4	5	6	(33)
c. . . is more expensive for what it is worth	1	2	3	4	5	6	(34)
d. . . is sometimes based on old information	1	2	3	4	5	6	(35)
e. . . is more helpful to compare products	1	2	3	4	5	6	(36)
f. . . tells you more about new products	1	2	3	4	5	6	(37)
g. . . is more difficult to understand	1	2	3	4	5	6	(38)
h. . . takes too much time & effort to read	1	2	3	4	5	6	(39)

5.   Have you ever heard about Consumer Reports (CR)?

                              Yes__1__   No__2__   (40)
     IF YOUR ANSWER THERE IS NO, YOU MAY SKIP TO QUESTION 42.

6.   Are you or any in your household currently a subscriber to CR?
                              Yes__1__   No__2__   (42)
     a. If "Yes," for approximately how many years?   ____Years   (43-44)

     IF YOUR ANSWER HERE WAS YES, PLEASE SKIP TO QUESTION 13; IF NO - TO 7

7.   If not now, were you or anyone in your household ever a subscriber in the past?   Yes__1__   No__2__   (48)

     a. If "Yes," for approximately how many years?   ____Years   (49-50)

FOR THE NEXT FEW STATEMENTS, CIRCLE THE ANSWER WHICH BEST DESCRIBES YOUR
FAMILY'S USE OF CR.

                    1 = Almost never
                    2 = Once per year or less
                    3 = More than once per year, but
                        not each month
                    4 = Almost every month   card #6
                                                        cc

8. Do you or does anyone in your household ever buy
    CR at the newsstand?   1   2   3   4   (54)

9. Do you or does anyone in your household ever look
    at CR in the library or borrow it from the library? 1   2   3   4   (56)

10. Do you or does anyone in your household ever borrow
    CR from friends or relatives?   1   2   3   4   (58)

11. In all, how often would you say that CR is read in
    your household, either by yourself or someone else? 1   2   3   4   (60)

12. Which statement best tells how much you know about CR?

               Just heard the name - nothing more   1

               Know just a bit about it - have glanced
                  through it or talked about it with friends   2   (62)

               Know a good deal about it   3

IF YOUR LAST ANSWER WAS <u>1</u>, YOU MAY SKIP TO <u>QUESTION 42</u>. IF YOU ANSWERED <u>2 OR 3</u>,
PLEASE CONTINUE TO <u>QUESTION 13</u>.

    A WORD OF CAUTION HERE. MOST OF THE REST OF THIS SECTION IS ABOUT <u>CONSUMER</u>
    <u>REPORTS</u>. YOUR "TOP OF THE HEAD" KNOWLEDGE AND OPINIONS ARE IMPORTANT TO US
    HERE, SO PLEASE DO NOT LOOK AT ANY MAGAZINES OR OTHER MATERIALS WHILE
    ANSWERING. THANK <u>YOU</u>!

13. Who in your household is likely to read CR?
                       Yourself?   Yes 1 No 2 (64)
                       How many others besides yourself? (number)___ (65)

14. As your household makes purchases, how often would you say that someone
    checks CR or the Consumer Reports Buying Guide to see what they have to
    say about products which they rate?
                                        Never   1
                        Less than ½ the time   2
                        More than ½ the time   3   (68)
                   Don't know or can't remember   4

15. In the cases where you have checked Consumer Reports or their annual
    Buying Guide, how often have you bought a brand which was highly
    recommended by them?
                               Rarely   1
                               Less than half the time   2
                               About half the time   3   (70)
                               More than half the time   4
                               Almost always   5
                               Don't know or can't remember 6

HERE ARE SOME STATEMENTS ABOUT <u>CONSUMER REPORTS</u>. PLEASE CIRCLE THE ANSWER
WHICH BEST GIVES YOUR OPINION ON THE STATEMENT.

1 = Strongly agree
2 = Agree
3 = Neither agree nor disagree
4 = Disagree
5 = Strongly disagree
6 = Don't know or No opinion

card #61

							cc
16.	The test information in CR is highly reliable.	1	2	3	4	5	6	(10)
17.	The style of CR is rather dull and uninteresting.	1	2	3	4	5	6	(12)
18.	CR does not contain too much technical detail.	1	2	3	4	5	6	(14)
19.	I don't find the CR recommendations very useful.	1	2	3	4	5	6	(16)
20.	CR carries too much advertising.	1	2	3	4	5	6	(18)
21.	I am generally satisfied with products I have bought which were strongly recommended by CR.	1	2	3	4	5	6	(20)
22.	I strongly believe in the independence and integrity of CR.	1	2	3	4	5	6	(22)
23.	CR is putting too much stress on the safety of product.	1	2	3	4	5	6	(24)
24.	CR generally tests all the features of a particular product that are of interest to me.	1	2	3	4	5	6	(26)
25.	It is not much of a nuisance to get hold of the right copy of CR when I want to buy something.	1	2	3	4	5	6	(28)
26.	Negative comments in CR have at least occasionally kept me from buying a particular brand.	1	2	3	4	5	6	(30)
27.	I have confidence in the technical testing methods used by the CR people.	1	2	3	4	5	6	(32)
28.	Government and business have some influence on what CR reports about various tests.	1	2	3	4	5	6	(34)
29.	The information in CR is often too old.	1	2	3	4	5	6	(36)
30.	The information in CR is not clear enough; it is hard to read or digest.	1	2	3	4	5	6	(38)
31.	I find that CR has generally tested the products I want to buy.	1	2	3	4	5	6	(40)
32.	If CR carried more ads, I would believe it less.	1	2	3	4	5	6	(42)

33. Does CR give results for brands tested without recommending special brands, or do they name what they think are the best brands?

		card #
Gives results without recommendation	1	
Recommends what they think are best brands	2	(10)
Don't know	3	

34. Do you think that CR <u>should</u> recommend particular brands, or should they just give results without recommendations?

Yes - should recommend brands	1	
No - should not recommend brands	2	(12)
Don't know or don't care	3	

35. Do you know what kind of organization publishes CR?

A Commercial Publisher	1	
A Business Firm	2	
A Government Agency	3	(14)
A Trade Association	4	
A Non-Profit Consumer Group	5	
Don't Know	6	

36. I think I would place the most confidence in product tests which were done by:

The government alone	1	
Business alone	2	
A consumer group alone	3	
A consumer group helped by the government	4	
A consumer group helped by business	5	(16)
A business group helped by the government	6	
Don't know or No opinion	7	

37. Do you think that in addition to their testing activity, CR should lobby in Washington for more rules about advertising, more control of packages and other types of consumer protection?

Yes	1	
No	2	(17)
Don't know	3	

YOU WILL RECALL THAT YOU ANSWERED A NUMBER OF QUESTIONS IN SECTIONS 2, 3, and 4, ABOUT HOW YOU BOUGHT A SPECIFIC _____, (SOME MAJOR PRODUCT), A SPECIFIC AUTO _____, AND A SPECIFIC _____, (SOME SMALL PRODUCT). WE WANT YOU TO RECORD THESE THREE PURCHASES IN THE BLANKS ABOVE. (GLANCE BACK TO SECTIONS 2, 3, & 4 IF YOU DON'T RECALL WHICH PURCHASES YOU TOLD US ABOUT). NOW, KEEP IN MIND THESE SAME THREE PRODUCTS TO ANSWER THE QUESTIONS BELOW. TAKE THE SECTION 2 PRODUCT FIRST.

card #62

	MAJOR PRODUCT Sec 2		AUTO Sec 3		SMALL PRODUCT Sec 4	
38. Were you aware of the recommendation of Consumer Reports when you finally bought your _____?						
Yes	1		1		1	
No	2	(19)	2	(20)	2	(21)
Don't know	3		3		3	
IF YES TO 38, ANSWER 39; OTHERWISE, TO NEXT PRODUCT						
39. How important was this information in helping you to make this decision?						
Very important--critical	1		1		1	
Important	2		2		2	
Neither important or unimportant	3	(25)	3	(26)	3	(27)
Unimportant	4		4		4	
Very unimportant--not considered	5		5		5	
40. Did you buy a brand highly recommended by Consumer Reports?						
Yes	1		1		1	
No	2	(31)	2	(32)	2	(33)
Don't Know	3		3		3	
IF YES TO 40, ANSWER 41; OTHERWISE TO NEXT PRODUCT.						
41. Now that you have had some experience with your purchase, do you agree with the Consumer Reports recommendation?						
Strongly agree	1		1		1	
Agree	2		2		2	
Neither agree or disagree	3	(37)	3	(38)	3	(39)
Disagree	4		4		4	
Strongly disagree	5		5		5	

ON THIS PAGE, WE SPLIT INTO 3 GROUPS:

1) IF YOU HAD <u>NEVER HEARD OF CONSUMER REPORTS</u> BEFORE THIS QUESTIONNAIRE, ANSWER <u>JUST QUESTIONS 42 & 43</u>, THEN PROCEED TO SECTION 7 (WHICH IS GUARANTEED TO BE SHORT AND THE END).

2) IF YOU ARE A <u>SUBSCRIBER</u> TO CR, PLEASE ANSWER <u>JUST QUESTIONS 44-47</u>, THEN GO TO SECTION 7.

3) IF YOU <u>HAD HEARD OF CR</u>, BUT ARE <u>NOT A SUBSCRIBER</u>, YOU MAY GO <u>DIRECTLY TO SECTION 7</u>.

THE NEXT 2 QUESTIONS ARE ONLY FOR THOSE WHO HAD <u>NEVER HEARD OF CR</u>.

42. Let us assume that a government bureau would be set up to test various products, comparing the different brands on the market in quality and typical prices. Do you think that you or your family would make any use of the products of such comparitive tests, if the reports were fully available?

card #62

Yes	1
No	2
Don't know	3

(44)

43. Suppose the reports would cost $5 a year, would you still want to get them?

Yes	1
No	2
It depends	3
Don't know	4

(45)

THESE LAST 4 QUESTIONS ARE FOR <u>CR SUBSCRIBERS ONLY</u>

44. How long do you keep your copies of CR?

Throw them away when I have read them	1
For a few weeks or a month	2
For a year or two	3
Indefinitely	4
It depends	5
Passed on to somebody else	6

(46)

45. Do you ever lend copies of CR to others, or pass copies on altogether?

Yes, lend it to others (more than once)	1
Yes, pass it on altogether	2
No, neither	3

(47)

46. What were the main reasons for your becoming a subscriber to CR? (Please rank 1, 2, 3 the reasons which apply to you.)

Expected to save money on purchases	1	(48)
Wanted to know what features to look for in buying products	2	(49)
Wanted to know CU's recommendation	3	(50)
I was in the market for certain products at that time	4	(51)
For people like me subscribing to CR is a proper thing to do	5	(52)
You can't rely on what advertising or salesmen tell you	6	(53)
Other reasons not mentioned	7	(54)

47. Which do you find most useful - monthly issues of Consumer Reports, or the annual Buying Guide issue?

Monthly issues more helpful	1
Annual Buying Guide more helpful	2
Equally helpful	3
Don't know--no opinion	4

(55)

Section 7

THAT JUST ABOUT CONCLUDES OUR INTERVIEW. WE WOULD LIKE FOR YOU TO ANSWER
A FEW FINAL QUESTIONS FOR STATISTICAL PURPOSES ONLY, TO HELP US ANALYZE
THE RESULTS OF OUR SURVEY: Card #7
                                                               cc
1. Sex: Male ___1___
                                           Female_ 2__   (10)

2. What is your marital status?   Married __1___
                                           Single __2___
                                           Widowed __3___   (11)
                                           Divorced_ 4__

3. Are you employed outside of your home for pay?
   Yes, full time (about 40 hours per week or more)   __1___
   Half-time (more than 15 hours per week but not full time) __2___
   Part time (less than 15 hours per week   __3___   (12)
   Not employed outside the home   __4___

4. If yes, what kind of work are you doing or what is your occupation?
   _____(13-15)
   (Please include job title or briefly describe the nature of the work.)

5. Are you the main wage earner in your household?
                                           Yes__1___
                                           No__ 2__   (16)

   If yes, go to question 6
   If no—What kind of work does the chief wage earner in your
   household do or what is his occupation?
   _____
   (Please include job title or briefly describe the nature or type of
   work.)
   If no to 5, go to question 7

6. (If the respondent is main wage earner) How far approximately did you
   go in school?
                       Years of grammar school_____
                       Years of high school   _____
                       Years of college   _____
                       Years of graduate school_____
                       TOTAL   _____   (17-18)

7. How far approximately did the main wage earner in your household go in
   school?
                       Years of grammar school_____
                       Years of high school   _____
                       Years of college   _____
                       Years of graduate school_____   (19-20)
                       TOTAL   _____

8. What is your age?

Under 25	1	45-54	4
25-34	2	55-64	5	(21)
35-44	3	65 and over	6

9. How many persons are living in your household?

1		5
2		6	(22)
3		7 or more
4		

10. Of the persons living in your household, how many are children under 18 years of age?

0		3
1		4	(23)
2		5 or more

11. Do you own or rent this house (or apartment)?

House	1
Apartment	2	(24)

Own	1
Rent	2	(25)
Other	3

12. Excluding bathroom and kitchen, how many rooms does your house (or apartment) have? _____ (26-27)

13. Would you please indicate your approximately annual family income before taxes below? Please include your own income and the income of all members of your family who are living with you.

Under $3,000	1	$10,000 to $14,999	6
$3,000 to $3,999	2	$15,000 to $19,999	7	(28-29)
$4,000 to $4,999	3	$20,000 to $24,999	8
$5,000 to $7,499	4	$25,000 and over	9
$7,500 to $9,999	5	Don't know, no answer	10

(These categories used by CU 1969)

14. Do you belong to a labor union?

Yes	1
No	2	(30)
Don't know	3

15. What political party generally comes closest to your own view?

_____ (31)

16. Are you now, or have you at any time in tne last three years, been an officer of:

A labor union
Political party or club
PTA
Local consumer group
Other community betterment organization or
An elected official in local, state, or federal government?

Yes 1   No 2   (32)

LIST OF DURABLES AND CONVENIENCE GOODS IN GERMAN QUESTIONNAIRE

Durables (Section 2, Question 1)

Refrigerator

Washing Machine

Color TV

Black and White TV

Ironing Machine

Kitchen Range, gas or electric

Dishwasher

Freezer

Sewing Machine

Typewriter

Power Lawn Mower

Tape Recorder, mono or stereo

Movie Camera

Vacuum Cleaner

High Fidelity Equipment

Convenience Goods (Section 4, Question 1)

Dish Detergent

Hand Lotion

Hair Shampoo

Floor Wax

Cigarettes

Frozen Foods

Stockings and Panty Hose

Auto Cleaner and Polish

Make-up

Deodorant

Whisky

Shaving Lotion

Furniture Polish

Hair Spray

Washing Powders and Laundry Detergents

Selected Bibliography

A. PUBLICATIONS FROM THE INTERNATIONAL CONSUMER INFORMATION SURVEY

Becker, Helmut, "Consumer Information and the Image of Advertising in Germany with Significant Comparisons to America," DBA dissertation, Indiana University, 1971.

Engledow, Jack., "The *Consumer Reports* Subscriber: Portrait of an Intense Consumer," *Indiana Business Review* (August-September 1972): 32–40.

——. "The Impact of *Consumer Reports* Ratings on Product Purchase and Post-Purchase Product Satisfaction," DBA dissertation, Indiana University, 1971.

Thorelli, Hans B., "Concentration of Information Power Among Consumers," *Journal of Marketing Research* 8 (November 1971): 427–32.

——. "Consumer Information Policy in Sweden—What Can Be Learned?" *Journal of Marketing* (January 1971): 50–5.

——. "Consumer Information Programmes," *International Consumer* (Autumn 1972): 15–21.

——. "Testing, Labelling, and Certifying: A Perspective on Consumer Information," *British Journal of Marketing* (Autumn 1970): 126–32.

Thorelli, Hans B., and Sarah V. Thorelli, *Consumer Information Handbook: Europe and North America*, New York: Praeger, 1974.

——. *Consumer Information Systems*, in process.

B. RELATED AND BACKGROUND WORKS[a]

Adolfsson, H., and F. Folkebo, *VDN66—en undersökning av konsumenters användning av VDN varufakta vid ett butiksbesök*, Stockholm: State Consumer Council, 1966.

[a]A more extensive bibliography of the CI field may be found in Thorelli and Thorelli, *Consumer Information Systems.*

Almond, Gabriel, and Sidney Verba, *The Civic Culture: Political Attitudes and Democracy in Five Nations*, Princeton: Princeton University Press, 1965.

Bauer, Raymond A., and Stephen A. Greyser, *Advertising in America: The Consumer View*, Boston: Harvard University, Division of Research, Graduate School of Business Administration, 1968.

Beem, Eugene V., "Consumer-Financed Testing and Rating Agencies in the United States," Ph.D. dissertation, University of Pennsylvania, 1951.

Beem, Eugene, and John Ewing, "Business Appraises Consumer Testing Agencies," *Harvard Business Review* 32 (March-April 1954): 113–27.

Biervert, Bernd. *Wirtschaftspolitische, Sozialpolitische und Sozial-pädagogische Aspekte einer Verstärkten Verbraucheraufklärung*. Köln: Krupinski, 1972.

Bower, Robert T., *Television and the Public*, New York: Holt, Rinehart and Winston, 1973.

Cox, Donald M., ed., *Risk Taking and Information Handling in Consumer Behavior*, Boston: Harvard University, Division of Research, Graduate School of Business Administration, 1967.

Downs, Anthony, "A Theory of Consumer Efficiency," *Journal of Retailing* (Spring 1961): 6–12.

European Association of Advertising Agencies, *Public Attitudes Toward Advertising*, Brussels: European Association of Advertising Agencies, Document 677, March 3, 1973.

Institut National de la Consommation. "Consommateurs et commerçants—un sondage de l'INC," *Consommateurs Actualité* 36 (December 1971): 3–18.

Katona, George; Burkhard Strumpel, and Ernest Zahn. *Aspirations and Affluence—Comparative Studies in the United States and Western Europe*, New York: McGraw-Hill, 1971.

Labrousse, J., *L'information des consommateurs*, Paris: Institut Français d'Opinion Publique, 1968.

Lane, Sylvia, "A Study of Selected Agencies that Evaluate Consumer Goods Qualitatively in the United States," Ph.D. dissertation, University of Southern California, 1957.

Linder, Steffan B., *The Harried Leisure Class*, New York: Columbia University Press, 1970.

Meyer-Dohm, Peter, *Sozialökonomische Aspekte der Konsumfreiheit*. Freiberg: Verlag Rombach, 1965.

Mitchell, Jeremy, *What Do You Want in* Which? London: Consumers' Association, 1965.

(Norway. Central Statistical Bureau) *Rapport fra kontoret for intervjuundersökelser Nr. 8, Undersökelse om Forbruker-rapporten, Vareundersökelser og reklamasjoner 1969*. Oslo: Statistisk Sentralbyrå, 1970.

Reader's Digest Association. *A Survey of Europe Today*, London: The Reader's Digest Association, 1970.

Rokkan, Stein, ed., *Comparative Research across Cultures and Nations*, Paris: Mouton, 1968.

Sargent, Hugh, "The Influence of Consumer Product-Testing and Reporting Services on Consumer Buying Behavior," Ph.D. dissertation, University of Illinois, 1958.

Stigler, George, "The Economics of Information," *Journal of Political Economy* 69 (June 1961): 213–25.

University of Missouri, *Freedom of Information in the Marketplace*, Columbia: Freedom of Information Center, 1967.

Subject Index

About the Authors

Hans B. Thorelli is the E.W. Kelley Professor of Business Administration at Indiana University. He is Project Leader of the International Consumer Information Survey sponsored by that University. A previous product of the Survey if the Consumer Information Handbook: Europe and North America, coauthored with his wife, Dr. Sarah V. Thorelli.

His prior books include The Federal Antitrust Policy: Origination of an American Tradition, International Operations Simulation, and International Marketing Strategy. He is a member of the Consumer Advisory Committee of the Federal Energy Administration and former Vice President—Public Policy of the American Marketing Association. Dr. Thorelli holds a Ph.D. and an LL.B. degree from the University of Stockholm.

Helmut Becker is Assistant Professor of Business Administration at the University of Portland, Oregon. On the team of the International Consumer Information Survey he had responsibility for the German survey research. He is teaching in the marketing, international business, and business and society areas. He is the co-editor of the 1972 Combined Proceedings of the American Marketing Association.

Dr. Becker received his basic education in Germany. He is a graduate magna cum laude of the University of Portland, has an MBA from the University of Oregon and a DBA from Indiana University. He is active in the Academy of International Business.

Jack Engledow is Associate Professor of Business Administration at Indiana University-Purdue University at Indianapolis. On the team of the International Consumer Information Survey, he has researched, written, and spoken extensively on the subject of consumer information and information agencies. His teaching and research interests focus on consumer behavior, advertising and marketing management.

Dr. Engledow is a summa cum laude graduate of Wabash College, holds an MBA from Butler University and a DBA from Indiana University. He has been a Fellow of the American Marketing Association Doctoral Consortium.